Humanities Research Centre

A history of the first 30 years of the HRC at
The Australian National University

Glen St John Barclay and Caroline Turner

Humanities Research Centre

A history of the first 30 years of the HRC at
The Australian National University

E PRESS

E PRESS

Published by ANU E Press
The Australian National University
Canberra ACT 0200, Australia
Email: anuepress@anu.edu.au
Web: http://epress.anu.edu.au

National Library of Australia Cataloguing-in-Publication entry

Barclay, Glen St J. (Glen St John), 1930- .
    Humanities Research Centre: a history of the first 30
    years of the HRC at The Australian National University.

         ISBN 0 9751229 7 5
         ISBN 0 9751229 8 3 (online document)

      1. Australian National University. Humanities Research
      Centre. 2. Humanities - Research - Australian Capital
      Territory - Canberra - History. 3. Humanities - Study and
      teaching (Higher) - Australian Capital Territory - Canberra
      - History. I. Turner, Caroline, 1947- . II. Australian
      National University. Humanities Research Centre. III.
      Title.

         001.307119471

All rights reserved. No part of this publication may be reproduced,
stored in a retrieval system or transmitted in any form or by any means,
electronic, mechanical, photocopying or otherwise, without the
prior permission of the publisher.

Text design and setting by UIN, Melbourne

© 2004 The Humanities Research Centre

To the HRC Fellows and Friends,
Past and Present

Contents

Foreword by Anthony Low	ix
Introduction	xiii
Chapter 1 To Bring to Australia Whatever Other Nations Enjoy (1969–1972)	1
Chapter 2 The Centre's Work is Gathering Momentum (1972–1975)	23
Chapter 3 A Source of New Energy and New Ideas (1975–1981)	47
Chapter 4 A Unique Institution in the World of the Humanities (1981–1991)	87
Chapter 5 In Australia there is *Only* the HRC (1991–1995)	131
Chapter 6 Endings and Beginnings (1995–2000)	161
Chapter 7 Greeting the Future (2000–2004)	199
Appendix A Humanities Research Centre Annual Themes	253
Appendix B Humanities Research Centre Visitors	255
Appendix C Humanities Research Centre Conferences	325
Appendix D Humanities Research Centre Governance	337
Appendix E Humanities Research Centre Staff, 1974–2004	343
Appendix F Humanities Research Centre Publications	347
Acknowledgements	399

Foreword
Anthony Low

The foundation and growth of The Australian National University's Humanities Research Centre has been a huge success. This book tells a remarkable story with much panache and close attention. It recounts the numerous vicissitudes particularly early on of a novel and sometimes vulnerable institution. It follows the unending tide of its seminar conferences. It picks from the great and the new in its elongated catalogue of Visiting Fellows to illustrate their calibre, and provides extracts from some of their euphoric tributes on their departures. It traverses the leadership of its successive Directors, and their stand-ins, and the vital contribution made by its administrative staff.

What more can be said? Only some few underlinings.

When the Research Schools for ANU were first mooted in the 1940s the Australian Howard Florey had lately achieved fame for his development of penicillin. If he and others like him were to be attracted back to Australia there would necessarily be a medical research school. Physics was then still the queen of the sciences, and in Mark Oliphant an Australian right at its forefront who was ready to return home. There would, therefore, be a Physics school as well. Among ANU's local architects there were a number of influential people who, with the ending of the Pacific War, believed it to be of first importance for Australia to be far better informed about its Pacific neighbours than before. They and others also believed that with the end of that war there should be both a raft of new developments in, and much greater knowledge of, Australia and its society than ever before, and in Keith Hancock they saw one more Australian with all the distinction necessary to forward this. No such case was made at that time for the Humanities. Nor did any obvious flag carrier spring to mind.

Two further science Research Schools were founded in 1967 – Chemistry and Biological Sciences. That began to suggest that a Research School of Humanities was overdue. Yet there were two problems. A push had already begun for a Research School of Earth Sciences. The Universities Commission opposed this on financial grounds and declined to make further provision for it. The Vice-Chancellor, Sir John Crawford, nevertheless pressed ahead and RSES was founded. That, however, made the chance of creating yet one more Research School all the more difficult.

There was a further issue too. As constructed by that boundary-traverser, Keith Hancock, his Research School of Social Sciences not only already had departments/units of History and Law but of the History of Ideas and Philosophy as well. Hancock indeed had even proposed to add 'Humanities' to its title. The principal lacunae here were studies in the arts, languages, literatures, and their cultural contexts, of ancient and modern Britain and Europe. There was no push, however, for these to be added to RSSS; let alone any suggestion to excise its humanities departments to join them in a separate school. So the only hope was a trimmed down version: a Humanities Research Centre, to which in 1973 the Universities Commission was ready to give its blessing.

Its founding in the following year proved, however, to be at a most unpropitious time. For it occurred just as government funding for universities first levelled off and then started on its unending decline. That meant the HRC never secured the funding which it warranted, as this book so often details. My own experience suggests, however, that this needs to be put in context. Upon becoming Director of RSPacS in 1973 I was expecting to have two more departments (Sociology and Politics). There were, however, funds for only one (Political and Social Change as we called it). I had an understanding, moreover, that I would not only have a junior but a senior colleague in my field of Indian history to revive its study at ANU. I never had the senior one, and despite a later occupant of the other appointment becoming in the 1980s the most notable world figure in the subject, it disappeared as well. The times were out of joint for so many new academic enterprises however great their significance might be.

The HRC faced another problem. Because of the differences between ANU's Research Schools and its Faculties, a Centre which was most closely associated with the Faculty of Arts but like the Research Schools was wholly committed to research frequently found itself in danger of falling between their two stools. Long awkwardly placed upon one, it was then transferred to the other, only to be transferred back again. Those leading the HRC somehow managed to learn not merely to live with these disabilities but how majestically to overcome them.

There were four elements to their triumph. First, not only was the scholarly calibre of each of its successive Directors, Ian Donaldson, Graeme Clarke, Iain McCalman, and their various stand-ins, particularly Ralph Elliott and for a memorable year Deryck Schreuder, of undoubted world standing. In each instance their wide range of interests and their gifts for friendship proved to be of quite vital importance to so small an enterprise. That was conjoined with, as it inspired, the exemplary administrative staff which with some comings and goings over the years made up the close knit, mutually trusting, team that so endeared them to its visitors. The pattern here was set from the outset by that memorable scholar/administrator, Bob Horan.

Beyond this, despite its limited budget, the HRC placed more emphasis upon its Visiting Fellowship programme than any other part of the University. I am quoted as saying early on that 'we haven't yet got the Isaiah Berlins to the HRC.' But they came: Richard Rorty, Quentin Skinner, Marilyn Butler and so many others. Together with a good many of the up and coming they not only adorned its programme. Numbers of them did more to cultivate ANU's outreach than any other part of the University, by visiting and lecturing in other universities, and then by putting it about that at the HRC a scholar could not only secure a quite invaluable stretch of peace and quiet to do some major writing (punctuated only by some agreeable talk over coffee), but once drawn into its conferences to find these ordinarily to be of the highest standard.

That in my judgment ultimately related to the crucial element in achieving the spectacular success of the HRC. Given that it never had more than two or three ongoing academic staff, and that it was expected to cover a very wide front, it decisively abjured the general pattern in the Research Schools of small groups like this focussing upon some particular field or issue; it never strove, that is, to become the world centre for (whatever?) studies. Instead, it moved to making the seminal decision to announce some important, preferably new, issue as its 'theme' for two years hence upon which it would centre its major conferences for that year while biasing its choice of Visiting Fellows towards a range of scholars relevant to it. Such a lead time not only allowed for very careful work to be done on the structure of the conferences beforehand. It meant the HRC could secure the readiness of outstanding visitors to attend before they became otherwise overly committed. Over the years it was thus able to cover a huge amount of ground. All this, moreover, without prejudice to some other visitors and some other conferences also figuring in its year's programme.

Upon this base the HRC has in subsequent years been able to expand its activities upon a prodigious scale. No wonder it has become the cynosure for comparable institutions elsewhere, and a pre-eminent leader in its field.

Introduction

This is the record of the first thirty years of an institution which was conceived in a particular economic and political environment, inspired by a particular traditional model and launched with a particular expectation of expanding financial support. The environment changed totally; the model was effectively abandoned almost before the institution commenced operations; and the expectations of expanding support became almost immediately realisations of just the opposite. But the response has been more than equal to the challenge. It is not just that the Humanities Research Centre is still here: the real measure of its achievement is that an institution which was intended to be patterned on the most traditional classical model of 'a centre within a library' has succeeded in ceaselessly reinventing itself, advancing from the classical age of academe to the electronic age, engaging with on-line teaching, electronic publishing and all the educational possibilities of the new media. It is in every sense still a work in progress. But the bottom line is that all this quite astounding adaptation, enterprise and vision shown over the past thirty years has been through the devoted efforts of what a Vice-Chancellor called a staff of 'absolute minimum size'. It is not surprising that the Humanities Research Centre has continued to receive quite unreserved, not to say rapturous accolades from many of the most distinguished academics in the world. It is certainly a story worth telling.

1 To Bring to Australia Whatever Other Nations Enjoy (1969–1972)

Professor Richard Rorty, one of the most acclaimed and influential philosophers of the present age, told the committee reviewing the Humanities Research Centre (HRC) in 1995 that in his view the Centre had 'been the principal means of communication and collaboration between Australian scholars in the humanities and their colleagues throughout the world. It has an absolutely impeccable reputation in the international scholarly community, and is thought to be one of the most successful think-tanks in the world.' The Centre had come a long way in a remarkably short time. Nobody could have imagined at the outset where the road would lead, what obstacles would have to be surmounted and what new directions would have to be explored. It was a journey without maps.

In the beginning were the words. And the words which gave origin to the concept of the Humanities Research Centre appeared in a most elegantly composed *Report on the Future Development of the Humanities and the Social Sciences in the Australian Universities* by Professor Raymond Maxwell ('Max') Crawford, one-time First Secretary in the Australian Embassy in Moscow and long-time Professor of History at the University of Melbourne, and brother of Sir John Crawford, Director of the Research School of Pacific Studies at The Australian National University from 1960 to 1967 and from 1968 to be the Vice-Chancellor of ANU who would found the Humanities Research Centre. Max Crawford forwarded his report on 4 December 1963 to Sir Leslie Martin, Chairman of the Australian Universities Commission. We can speculate that he also shared it with his brother Sir John.

Professor Raymond
Maxwell Crawford, c. 1965
*Photo courtesy Melbourne
University Archives.*

Max Crawford's theme was the perennial one of the parlous, not to say terminal, state of the humanities in academe and society in general. Some sections of the humanities, 'particularly the languages,' he argued, 'are bedevilled by a sense of being on the defensive in a world unfavourable to their values.' However, he believed that 'the cause of the traditional humanities subjects is less well served by defensive protests or last ditch stands against barbarism, than by a constructive re-thinking of the role of the humanities in a modern Australian university.' Nor did he have any doubt as to what should be the primary focus of such rethinking. The fact was, Crawford explained in the gender-exclusive language of the times, that it was 'now possible for an Australian academic in these fields, as in the sciences, to hope to play an honourable part in the world-wide debate of his subject.' The problem was that it was precisely at this point that:

> He finds most frustrating the inadequacies of our resources and the decline of leisure for study ... For the humanities and social sciences, the most important condition of scholarship is an adequate library ... If, however, we solve

Sir John Crawford, Vice-Chancellor, 1967.

> the deficiencies of our libraries and give our best men the opportunity to establish graduate seminars famous enough to attract students from more than one university ... [the] stimulus of such men and such seminars would spread through their pupils into undergraduate teaching.

He quoted Professor A.D. Hope's characteristically vivid declaration that 'because it has always been the case, the humanities have come to accept a position that the sciences would not tolerate for a moment ... for a cost equivalent to that of a single cyclotron they could have what they need.' He accordingly proposed 'a "crash programme" for the development of university libraries parallel to but on a larger scale than the computer programme of the 1964-6 Triennium.'[1]

These laments would be reiterated over the ensuing decades, in spades redoubled, and with ever-increasing urgency and pertinence. But this was the early 1960s, and it was possible to believe that some appropriate action might actually be taken. The Australian economy had expanded by 39% in the first half of the decade, while unemployment varied between 1.0% and 2.3%, which was to say from nothing at all to nothing of social significance. Posters distributed by the Australian High Commission in British underground stations depicted young, handsome and optimistic intending migrants declaring that 'In Australia I *will!*' Ten years later such persons might well have reflected that in Australia they probably wouldn't. But the most compelling cause for optimism on the part of protagonists of the humanities was that there was reason to believe that their cause would find support at the very highest level of Government. Crawford observed in his covering letter to Martin that 'the personal interest' of Prime Minister Robert Gordon Menzies 'in strong development in these fields of scholarship has greatly encouraged those of us who work in them.'[2] It was a presumption probably never entertained to anything like the same degree in respect of any other Australian Head of Government, before or since Menzies' time.

There were sufficient grounds for believing such a presumption to be justified in this case. Liberal Party historian P.G. Tiver explained that 'Menzies thought that education in the humanities made people conscious of their social responsibilities and prevented them from acquiring wholly materialistic outlooks;' and that this was a good thing in terms of a philosophy of Liberalism that had any claim to be called Conservative.[3] Menzies had indeed given remarkably convincing and consistent indications that he genuinely held such convictions: he had declared in his Commencement Address to the Canberra University College back in April 1939 that it was 'one of the proper functions of a university to be a home of pure culture and learning in a commercial world full of "practical" men with utilitarian philosophies of life.' Mere money-making was one of the lowest of arts. He elaborated on this theme as Opposition Leader in 1945, arguing that 'the greatest failure in the world', in his lifetime, had not been the failure in technical capacity 'half as much as the failure of the human spirit.' War after war had been the result of 'the fatal inability of man to adjust himself to other men in a social world.' Menzies attributed this decline to two main factors: the 'increasingly pagan and materialistic' quality of education; and the contempt that had fallen upon '"useless education,"' meaning the humanities, the study of which in schools and universities 'could at least develop a sense of proportion.'[4]

These were not just admirable sentiments. Menzies was actually prepared to put the taxpayer's money where his mouth had been: the Murray Committee was set up in 1956 to enquire into the needs of universities; the Government accepted the following year the recommendation of the Committee for a massive increase in financial aid to universities; and the Morton Committee was appointed in 1959 to examine tertiary education in Australia. Meanwhile, the number of students enrolled in universities throughout Australia rose from

57 672 in 1961 to 83 320 in 1965 and had almost doubled to 109 682 by the end of the decade; and staff numbers had more than doubled, from 3396 in 1961 to 7069 by 1969.[5] It all seems like Camelot, from the perspective of some 40 years later. Camelot didn't last long either.

But the Golden Years were not finished yet. Menzies was still Prime Minister and he was showing no signs of having lost his personal interest in higher education: a Minister for Education assisting the Prime Minister in the Prime Minister's Department was appointed in 1964, and a separate Department of Education and Science was established in 1967. Academic planners might well be encouraged to explore the full implications of Crawford's report. His primary concern had indeed been the provision of vastly enhanced library facilities to remedy what he considered to be 'the inability of our libraries to support advanced research in more than a few limited fields such as Australian history.' But something also needed to be done about the problem of finding time for research. The 'long vacation,' he observed with feeling, was 'a hollow mockery' for those in charge of Departments. Nor was sabbatical leave

> a full answer to the problem because one is always torn between incompatible objectives. One must establish and renew contacts with scholars overseas, see what is being done in various places, and take the rare chance of digging in archives and libraries. But this can be done only by using up the one opportunity in seven years that might allow uninterrupted thinking and writing.[6]

Library plus fellowships equals some form of establishment in academic terms. A committee appointed by the Faculty of Arts at The Australian National University to consider the future development of the Faculty 'gave early attention to the question of research in the humanities in the hope that, if agreement in principle was reached, detailed planning could proceed, and preliminary steps be taken possibly in the 1970-72 triennium.'[7] The Committee reported on 13 August 1968 that there was

> a clear need for a research school in those areas of the humanities not already covered by the Research School of Social Sciences and the Research School of Pacific Studies ... Such a research school would, moreover, be of national importance as there is no centre for research in the humanities elsewhere in Australia.

It was considered that 'physical location should be as close to the Haydon-Allen building as possible,' presumably so as to be within easy walking distance of the University Library (J.B. Chifley Building), the Union Block and the heart of the University in general. There should be

> a relatively small staff (though we would not envisage a number below 20) made up of a small number of permanent appointments, a number of temporary appointments . . . and a number of short-term, high-level appointments from Australia and overseas. All of these should, unless they wish otherwise, be free of teaching commitments (though we would hope that individual members might give seminars and/or public lectures in their own fields).[8]

The ultimate definition, inspiration and mission statement for the Humanities Research Centre came in May 1969 from Professor Richard St Clair Johnson, Professor of Classics in the School of General

Professor Richard St Clair Johnson.

Studies and Dean of the Faculty of Arts at ANU, in another eloquent Report to the Vice-Chancellor, Sir John Crawford, this time on 'The development of Humanities at the A.N.U. . . . together with a view of the place of the humanities in higher education in the U.S.A. and Canada.' It was Sir John, Johnson later recalled, who encouraged him to undertake a research trip in 1968/69 on a Carnegie Fellowship to look at approaches to the humanities in North America, but primarily in the United States. He visited over 16 campuses from Harvard to UCLA. Johnson prefaced his Report with two resounding declarations from the Report of the Royal Commission on National Development in the Arts, Letters and Sciences, 1941-1951, Ottawa, and the Report of the Commission on the Humanities, New York, 1954. The first proclaimed that:

> If we as a nation are concerned with the problem of defence, what, we may ask ourselves, are we defending? We are defending civilization, our share of it, our contribution to it . . . Our military defences must be made secure; but our cultural defences equally demand national attention; the two cannot be separated.[9]

And the second responded to the question, 'Is it then in the interests of the United States and of its federal government to give greater support to the humanities?' with the affirmation that:

> Upon the humanities depend the national ethic and morality, the national aesthetic and beauty or the lack of it, the national use of our environment and our material accomplishments . . . On our knowledge of men [sic], their past and their present, depends our ability to make judgments – not least those involving our control of nature, of ourselves and of our destiny. Is it not in the national interest that these judgments be strong and good?[10]

Such statements left little more to be said. Their North American origin was moreover fundamental to Johnson's basic argument. 'An examination of the position of the humanities in North America,' he considered, 'has, I believe, more relevance to their situation in Australia than has an examination of their position in any other country. The U.S.A., Canada and Australia are all broadly similar societies . . . ' It was therefore appropriate that Australian educationalists should take note of the decisions of their North American counterparts, particularly with regard to their view, especially in engineering schools and in places like M.I.T. and Cal. Tech., that the study of humanities is an essential part of the vocational preparation of their graduates . . . It would take a bold man to claim that Australian management was particularly well educated or needed no improvement. If American top management sees values in the humanities; if schools of management like Harvard's are happy to accept humanities graduates for professional training; then I suggest that Australia might reasonably follow these models.

It would have taken a very bold man indeed to dispute the issue in the context of the times. But one might not have had to be all that bold to have misgivings about Johnson's other reason why Australia should be advised to follow North American models in regard to the teaching of the humanities. 'It is often loosely said,' he continued,

> that Australia is part of Asia. Australia is no more part of Asia than is Greece or Alaska or Egypt; like those countries, we are close to Asia; but we are a nation of Europeans. This is not to deny the importance of studying, understanding and where appropriate adopting Asian culture and attitudes; but inevitably we do these things as Europeans situated between the Pacific and Indian Oceans in an unstable part of the world. The cultivation of the European heritage, "the common background from which have grown the character and way of life of our fellow countrymen," is for Australia an element of national security and strength, just as it is for the Canadians or the Americans . . . It is an element of national security that Australians should appreciate as deeply and as widely as possible the traditions and ideals which are expressed in their society, in its political and legal structures; these ideals are perceived in the history and literature and works of art of various kinds of those nations which are our intellectual and ethnic past, from Greece to Iceland. The study and teaching of these is the work of the humanities, at all levels.[11]

It was brilliant, it was elegant, it was witty; it was no doubt a line of argument eminently congenial to a classicist like Johnson; and it reflected a world view which Johnson himself would alter over the years as the world he was viewing altered. Nobody should be condemned for not possessing the gift of prophecy. It might well have seemed reasonable at the time to suppose that Australia would continue to be at least as European in its ethnic mix as Canada or the USA. There were nonetheless some fundamental problems with Johnson's basic premise. Nobody ever suggested that Egypt was part of anywhere except Africa. And it might be argued that Egypt, Greece and Alaska were closer or as close to Asia as Australia was. But Greece was even closer to Europe and Alaska to North America than either was to Asia; and all were far closer to Europe than Australia was. Nobody was indeed further from Europe geographically than Australia except New Zealand; and Australia was far closer to Asia than it was to anywhere else.

Moreover, Australia's defence planning had been intensively focussed on Asia since 1950; Japan had been by far Australia's most important export market since 1966; and Australia was in the process of extricating itself from a seven years' military involvement in Vietnam, which had cost 532 Australian lives and divided Australian society as no other issue had ever done, and which had been entered into in pursuance of a total misconception of Chinese and Vietnamese history, perceptions and intentions. The question whether Australia is or is not a part of Asia was and always would be meaningless. What would never be in question was that Australia was inextricably and vitally involved in Asian affairs, more than in those of anywhere else, and of necessity always would be; and that meant that a better understanding of Asian issues was what Australia needed more than anything else, and the sooner the better. It was indeed a time of all others when Australia should cease to fight against 'the reality of its own geography,' as perhaps the greatest and most intellectually gifted of Australian Foreign Ministers put it two decades later.[12]

But Johnson's real point was that Asian studies were already starting to make increasingly impressive advances at ANU. The Faculty of Asian Studies, established in 1961, was still devoted to historical rather than contemporary East Asia. But Heinz Arndt began to expand the frontiers of Australian scholarship to include contemporary Indonesia in 1963; Anthony Low, soon to succeed the renowned Professor Oskar Spate as Director of the Research School of Pacific and Asian Studies (RSPacS) and to become Vice-Chancellor of the ANU two years later, introduced South Asian History in the School in the same year; and Wang Gungwu was appointed Professor of Far Eastern History there in 1968. But students in a still essentially Anglo-Celtic Australia were not likely to gain much comprehension

Professor Anthony Low.

of Asian cultures unless they had some comprehension of their own culture first. What was really engaging Johnson and his colleagues in the Faculty of Arts was that there was still no formal provision at ANU for research in the humanities at all. The delay in providing such facilities had already created a serious problem. Research Schools had been proliferating like rabbits: the John Curtin School of Medical Research, the Research School of Physical Sciences and the Research School of Pacific Studies had all been established in the 1950s; the Research School of Chemistry and the Research School of Biological Sciences followed in 1967; and the Research School of Earth Sciences was approved to be launched in 1971. But there was still no Research School of the Humanities: it was apparently assumed, as the first Director of the Humanities Research Centre put it later, that 'people in the humanities simply wrote their books in the intervals between giving lectures, needing no further institutional stimulus or support.'[13]

Nor did it appear that there was likely to be such a Research School in the foreseeable future: the Australian Universities Commission had concluded that seven Research Schools were enough for the time being, in view of the heavy investment they incurred in staffing, facilities and administrative support. It was accordingly decided as a temporary measure to pursue expansion through the more modest development of small centres and units. It proved to be not just a pragmatic decision, but a life-or-death one for the Humanities Research Centre, as ANU would soon be facing the utterly unanticipated prospect of trying to avoid contraction rather than pursuing expansion. A project for the study of the humanities would get off the ground at all only if it were a very small operation indeed. It would become a classic catch-22 situation: the Humanities Research Centre would always be too small to achieve what it was meant to achieve and could indeed achieve what it did only by placing quite extraordinary demands upon its personnel. But it might not have survived to achieve anything at all if it had been any bigger, as Anthony Low in his capacity as Vice-Chancellor was later to observe.

Johnson was well aware of all this. He had also found, in the course of his visits to the United States, institutions which he regarded as 'an inspiration and a partial model' for his project for the humanities in Australia. 'Some of these institutions,' according to the first Director of the HRC Professor of English Charles Ian Edward Donaldson, formerly Chairman of the Faculty of English at Oxford and Professor of English at ANU since 1969,

> had been established by wealthy European refugees who fled to America in the 1930s, and wished to create quiet sanctuaries of knowledge which they hoped would perpetuate the liberal values they'd seen so dramatically endangered in Europe. Concealed in quiet corners of Washington DC or Los Angeles, flanked by luxurious gardens, these institutes served as secular monasteries of the mid-twentieth century. Other kinds of humanities centres had developed at private and state universities during the fifties and sixties, and were often more actively linked to the particular needs and resources of the institutions to which they were attached.[14]

Canberra certainly was not lacking quiet corners and luxurious or at least abundant gardens to provide appropriate settings for a similar sanctuary to perpetuate liberal values, which it would be within the resources of ANU to maintain. 'Perhaps the simplest procedure administratively' to follow the North American models, Johnson suggested, would be 'to establish a Research School in Humanities. However, in discussions overseas I found no support anywhere for such a proposal,' any more than he had found in Canberra itself. 'Nor was there much support for an institution staffed to any large extent by permanent appointees. What scholars in this area want is, first, books ... then, time ... then, contacts and discussion with like-minded people in the university, with others around Australia, with colleagues overseas, and with students. Given these factors,' he considered, 'Canberra could prove attractive, especially for periods of one, two or three years, to scholars from all over the world.' As for the actual structure of the proposed institution, he suggested, making a virtue of necessity, that 'a Research School of Humanities on all fours with the existing Research Schools is not the best way to encourage the highest level of work in this area.'

Neither would there be much point in setting up the proposed institution as a Social Sciences or Pacific Studies centre, as these areas already had excellent research facilities at ANU. Rather,

> some combination of the advantages of a Research School – the freedom for study, the opportunities for travel, the generous provision of resources – with some teaching and with relatively rapid turnover of personnel would seem to be the best formula ... Fellowships with terms between six months and three years would be much sought by present staff in Australia and, I believe, by overseas scholars.

Some central themes should be pursued, to 'avoid dissipation of effort and of library resources over the whole range of the humanities.' These could include, not surprisingly,

> the expansion of Europe (the study of the spread of European cultural influence around the globe, and its interaction with other cultures) ... twentieth-century humanities ... nineteenth century studies (the period of our national formation and the European background to it); Mediterranean studies (the meeting of Asia and Europe ...)

'It surely does not need to be said,' he concluded,

> that we should seek, as senior Fellows and as permanent staff (if permanent staff are desired) leaders in the study of humanities from any part of the world, [of] the highest calibre obtainable; our object is to bring to Australia whatever other nations enjoy.[15]

It was a noble project, compellingly presented; and it was a well-nigh exact forecast of what the Humanities Research Centre was to become.

A First Meeting on 3 June 1969 of The Australian National University Humanities Research Committee, consisting of Johnson and Professor Percy Herbert Partridge, President of the Australian Council for Educational Research and formerly Director of the Research School of Social Sciences (RSSS), 1961-68, agreed that the 'study of European humanities receives weakest attention in Australian universities. While the study of science, Asian studies, etc., receives considerable effort, there are large gaps in work on European literature, history, philosophy and art,' as well as 'too much emphasis on Australia and her environs' and a 'tendency among universities to concentrate too much on Asian and Pacific studies.'[16] The immensely prestigious Professor Oskar Spate agreed that the idea of a new Research School was

> almost ruled out because . . . we just haven't the volume of books (not to mention MSS) needed for such work on the scale of a School . . . Your preference for a Centre is quite right . . . It would not be Eurocentric in the bad

Professor Percy Herbert Partridge.

Professor Oskar Spate.

> sense; in the good sense, it would provide a much-needed corrective to other people's ethnocentricities, now in the ascendant,

he added in a generous observation from one who had been so extensively and intensively involved with varied ethnicities and was now indeed Director of the Research School of Pacific Studies (RSPacS).[17] Their definitive proposal was circulated after repeated re-draftings in September. It proclaimed that in adopting its plan for a Humanities Research Centre 'Australia will do no more than adopt a pattern which is already all but universal in the civilised world,' and that Canberra would be 'the ideal site for the proposed centre.' Nor would the University be undertaking a particularly substantial commitment: 'the report recommends that the permanent staff will be always small, and in the beginning should consist of only two permanent academic appointments, the Director and the Librarian.'

This of course raised the crucial question,

> what kind of man or woman should be sought to be the director of the centre. Two kinds are perhaps possible: one would be a senior academic, with the status and salary of a director of a research school in the Institute; the alternative might be a younger, less prestigious, more executive type of academic, appointed at the standard professorial salary.

'Possibly,' the report speculated, 'the university should try to get a person who combines both characteristics,' thus, presumably, being both senior and younger, scholar and executive, more highly paid and less highly paid. At least, nobody thought that it was going to be an easy job. The issue of the appointment of senior permanent staff would indeed continue to bedevil the operation of the Centre over the years, even after it was recognised that a full-time Director was going to need a full-time Deputy, working together on the job, as an active partner and not just to come off the bench in the absence of the Director. But this entailed logically the presence of yet a third academic to come off the bench in such a situation as an active partner of the Deputy who would then be functioning as Acting Director. At the time, however, the only other academic appointment to be considered was that of the librarian, in accordance with Max Crawford's vision of the Humanities Research Centre as what Ian Donaldson would describe as 'a centre in a library,' on the assumption that what was needed to get good men in and keep them was first and foremost a library adequate for their scholarly needs.[18] It was accordingly recommended that 'the University could seek a director and a librarian;' and that 'in 1973-75, the centre should become fully established. This full establishment comprises a director, a librarian, a business manager, and secretarial and clerical assistants . . . The total cost of the centre would be about $909 000 in the first triennium, phased over the three years.'[19]

It was appropriate that the most pertinent response to the draft proposal came from the man who would come as close as possible to Johnson's hypothetical ideal Director for the HRC. Donaldson wrote perceptively to Johnson that he liked

> the sound of the Centre for Research in Humanities – a really first-rate scheme . . . the only query of any kind is whether by "man". . . you mean a masculine man or a person of either sex? . . . it might be a pity to deter an able woman from applying for either job?[20]

It might indeed, not only because ANU was not all that flush with women in high academic positions, but also because it was likely to prove singularly difficult to get the right person for either job, regardless of gender.

Ian Donaldson would always be noted for acute insight and realism. So also to an extraordinary degree was Professor Dale Trendall, currently Master of University House and a classicist of world distinction. He had also been Librarian at the British School in Rome, which gave a particular significance to his observation to Johnson that his

> initial reactions . . . are not entirely favourable, as I do not quite see what a Librarian could do in this particular context, since the fields of study are indeterminate, still less why a business manager should be needed. The whole project seems to me to need working out a good deal more fully – as it stands your director would be little more than an organiser.[21]

That of course was exactly why it was going to prove so difficult to persuade the kind of academic desired for the position of Director to accept that position. Trendall might have underestimated the need for a business manager to ensure that the Director should have the opportunity to be something other than just an organiser, but he had detected the fundamental problem with the continuing emphasis on the need for a librarian in the proposed Centre: there was realistically little likelihood of the Centre's ever acquiring enough books of its own to need the services of a full-time librarian. Nor was it obvious that it needed to: the University Library had already acquired about half a million books and was expanding rapidly, and there was also the National Library, which had finally been integrated from its diverse locations in arguably the most beautiful building in Canberra in 1968.

Max Crawford himself recognised both that the original concept needed some modification and that modification needed to be aimed in the first instance at making life easier for the future Director, if there were to be any chance of getting the kind of Director whom the Centre would need if it were to fulfil the hopes of its creators. 'Your Committee' he wrote in May 1970 to his brother Sir John Crawford, formerly in the course of a career of remarkable brilliance Director of the Research School of Pacific Studies and then Vice-Chancellor of ANU, 'thought of the Warburg Institute,' a famed English Institute for the cultural and intellectual history of Europe from Classical Antiquity to modern times, which indeed possessed a massive library of 300 000 volumes in its own right, 'presumably, because it justly enjoys great prestige, is primarily engaged in research and succeeds in cutting across a number of stultifying departmental barriers. But the differences between the Warburg and the Centre proposed . . . are important.' Chief of these was that the Warburg 'has a permanent academic staff of seven . . . Your Committee proposes only a Director and a Librarian on the permanent academic staff.' But, as Crawford argued with total realism, the issue that had to be resolved before all else was that the Director would 'need at least one companion of comparable ability in a related field – someone to talk to about his own subject and to protect him,' or presumably her, 'from the subtle temptations of isolated mastery.' These also were most percipient and relevant comments; but the test of battlefield experience was to show that a Director of the Centre would need a Deputy of considerable ability for reasons even more compelling than having someone to talk to or as a defence against the subtle temptations of incipient paranoia or megalomania: the simple fact was that at least two senior academics would be required on the job, full-time, to operate a Centre which aspired to be 'without parallel in the world,' or even without too many parallels in the world.

Crawford was not however yet prepared to abandon entirely his concern that the Centre should be distinguished in the first instance for its attractions as a resource facility. His solution was for the Director to be able to appoint, 'either as research fellow or as an academic librarian, a first-rate scholar ready to make the building up of a strong library collection his main and absorbing task for the first few years.'[22] But somebody whose prime interest was that of a librarian would not necessarily be somebody who could function as an alter ego for the Director. And there were also problems about the actual implications of Johnson's requirement that the focus of the Centre's activity should be 'the cultivation of the European heritage.' This was now restated as 'the expansion of the European intellectual and cultural tradition,' which might sound even worse to non-Europeans as having a certain savour of cultural imperialism.[23] It was agreed at length that the broad theme of the centre

> involves the study of the major elements in European culture, past and present; it also involves the study of their impact on Australian intellectual life and gives scope for study of the European impact on other societies, both of European heritage (e.g. America) and non-European, such as the Asian nations.

It was not apparently to consider the impact of non-European cultures on European societies, nor was it considered that America might have also had a non-European heritage, even if by 'America' were meant only that part of the hemisphere north of the Rio Grande and south of the 49th parallel. These lacunae and distortions of perspective might fairly be regarded as symptomatic of the intellectual climate of the time. The real matter for concern was the extent to which this initial mandate might affect the capacity of the Centre to adjust to the demands of a different intellectual climate. The fact of the matter and the whole burden of the story is that it did so adjust, in the most imaginative and responsive manner, and has continued to do so, responding to challenges that could not possibly have been imagined at the time of its genesis.

Even academics cannot sensibly be blamed for failing to foretell the future. And equally symptomatic of the time was the triumphal affirmation of belief that 'Australia is excellently placed for such a centre which so far as we know would be without parallel in the world.'[24] It was the twilight of the Age of Optimism, but of course nobody knew it at the time. Meanwhile, the creative process of The Australian National University rolled on enthusiastically, if not wholly consistently. An Addendum to the Report of the Working Party: Centre for Research in Humanities insisted that the Centre would consist first 'of a library which will attract scholars from abroad,' and that the 'very small permanent nucleus' of the Centre should be initially 'probably a Director, a Librarian and appropriate secretarial and administrative assistance,' although it was surely difficult to imagine how such a library could be established anywhere in Australia except in very specialised fields, or how it could be established in ANU except at the expense of the libraries already on campus.[25] Notes prepared for the Vice-Chancellor for discussion with the Australian University Commission urged that 'advanced work in the development of European thought and culture in this part of the world' was 'as important a part of the task of understanding ourselves and our neighbours as any study of modern economies and science.'[26] Maybe it was. Advanced work in the development of the thought and culture of our neighbours might have been even more important a task. But perhaps it was thought that RSPacS would be doing enough in that line already.

What was not open to argument was the recommendation of Deputy Vice-Chancellor David Noel Dunbar that 'it would be essential to have a Director appointed as early as possible . . . in order to establish lines of future development, to advise on library acquisitions, and to give some stimulation to the project.'[27] This would seem to be axiomatic, but appointing a Director was in fact to prove perhaps the most perdurable and vexing of all the problems the HRC would have to confront.

But the great decision was taken. Sir John Crawford announced on 5 September 1972 that The Australian National University 'with the approval of the Australian Universities Commission proposes to establish a Humanities Research Centre in the 1973/75 triennium.' The proposed Centre, he advised,

> will consist first of a library which will attract scholars from abroad; second, of a programme of visiting fellowships to support them over several months; third, of programmes of Australian fellowships and of conferences to enable scholars from all parts of Australia to benefit from the stimulus provided by the Centre . . . The prime objective is to encourage the co-ordination and stimulation of research in certain aspects of the humanities amongst all Australian universities.[28]

He wrote to Donaldson the following week to invite him formally to serve on the Advisory Committee to be appointed for the proposed Centre. Its role would be to 'advise the University generally on the development of the Centre and in particular will have as one of its first tasks the preparation of a statement which might be used in

Professors Manning Clark, A.D. Hope, Anne Paolucci at the HRC, 1970s.

seeking applications for the headship of the Centre . . .'[29] Johnson would naturally be the chair, and the other invitees besides Donaldson comprised of course Max Crawford; Director of the Research School of Social Sciences [RSSS] Professor W.D. Borrie; Professor of Fine Arts at the University of Melbourne and President of the Australian Academy of the Humanities Joseph Burke; the august historian Professor Manning Clark; Professor of English at the Flinders University of South Australia Ralph Elliott; Dean of the Faculty of Arts Dr E.C. Fry; Professor of Philosophy in the School of General Studies Peter Herbst; Professor of Germanic Languages Hans Kuhn; Professor of Philosophy in the Institute of Advances Studies John Passmore; Director of RSPAS Oskar Spate; Power Professor of Contemporary Art and Director of the Power Institute of Fine Arts at the University of Sydney Bernard Smith; Professor of Economic History in the Faculty of Economics Graham Tucker; Professor of Far Eastern History Wang Gungwu; and by invitation Acting Vice-Chancellor and Professor of Physics Noel Dunbar. It was an awesome assembly of many of the most honoured and exciting names in Australian academe, drawn not only from the ranks of ANU, as was appropriate for what should be an institution truly national.

The prospects for the new centre could not have seemed more auspicious. What nobody could have known was that it would instead have its origin at the least auspicious time for such a project since the outbreak of war in 1939. But times were never going to get more auspicious for Australian universities.

Notes

1. Raymond Maxwell Crawford, 'The Future Development of the Humanities and the Social Sciences in the Australian Universities', Dec. 1963.
2. R.M. Crawford to Sir Leslie Martin, 4 Dec. 1963.
3. P.G. Tivers, *The Liberal Party: principles and performance*, Milton, Jacaranda, 1978, p. 119.
4. R.G. Menzies, 'The place of a university in the modern community', Address delivered at tenth annual commencement, Canberra University College, 26 Apr. 1939.
5. Australia, Bureau of Statistics, *Commonwealth of Australia Yearbook, 1970*.
6. Crawford, 'Future Development,' pp. 13, 22-23.
7. Faculty of Arts Meeting no. 6, 1968, 14 Aug. 1968.
8. ANU, Faculty of Arts, Proposal for a research school in the humanities, 13 Aug. 1968, 3035/1968.
9. Report of the Royal Commission on National Development in the Arts, Letters and Sciences, 1949-1951, Ottawa, Canada, pp. 274-275.
10. Report of the Commission on the Humanities, New York, 1964, p. 7.
11. Richard St Clair Johnson, Report to the Vice-Chancellor on 'The development of Humanities at the A.N.U. . . . together with a view of the place of the Humanities in higher education in the U.S.A. and Canada', May 1969.
12. See, *inter alia*, Seymour M. Hersh, *The Price of Power: Kissinger in the Nixon White House*, New York, Summit Books, 1983; Glen St.J.Barclay, *Friends in High Places: Australian–American diplomatic relations since 1945*, Melbourne, Oxford University Press, 1985; Gareth Evans and Bruce Grant, *Australia's Foreign Relations in the World of the 1900s*, Carlton, Melbourne University Press, 348. For an authoritative and contemporary commentary on the 'Australia part of Asia' issue, see in particular Richard Woolcott, *The Hot Seat: reflections on diplomacy from Stalin's death to the Bali bombings*, Sydney, HarperCollins, 2003.
13. Charles Edward Ian Donaldson to the authors, 25 June 2002.
14. 'Reconfiguring the Humanities:' a public lecture by Professor Ian Donaldson at the National Library of Australia. 12 Sept. 2002.

15 Richard St Clair Johnson, 'The development of humanities at the ANU. A report to the Vice-Chancellor, together with a view of the place of the humanities in higher education in the USA and Canada,' May 1969.
16 The Australian National University Humanities Research Committee: notes on first meeting, 3 June 1969.
17 Oskar Spate to Johnson, 19 June 1969.
18 Ian Donaldson to all members of HRC Advisory Committee: Post of Deputy Director and Bibliographer, 12 Apr. 1977.
19 Australian National University, Centre for Research in Humanities, 3345A/1969, 7 Oct. 1969.
20 Ian Donaldson to Johnson, 29 Sept. 1969.
21 Dale Trendall to Johnson, 16 Dec. 1969.
22 Maxwell Crawford to Sir John Crawford, 4 May 1970.
23 Meeting of Vice-Chancellor, Directors and Deans, held on 3 June 1970, 1973-75 triennium: 2216/1970.
24 The Australian National University, Humanities Research Centre, Summary of Proposals: 2274/1970, 8 June 1970.
25 The Australian National University Addendum to Report of Working Party: Centre for Research in Humanities, 3354/1969, 18 June 1970.
26 The Australian National University Vice-Chancellor's Notes for Discussion with Australian Universities at the Australian National University, 12 July 1971.
27 David Noel Dunbar to Johnson, 12 Aug. 1971.
28 J.G. Crawford, The Australian National University, Humanities Research Centre: 2957/1972, 5 Sept. 1972.
29 Crawford to Donaldson, 11 Sept. 1972.

2 The Centre's Work Is Gathering Momentum (1972–1975)

The world may or may not have changed essentially after 11 September 2001. There is no doubt that it did so after October 1973. US President Richard M. Nixon had effectively unleashed the world-transforming phenomenon of globalisation on 25 August 1971, when, in the words of former Vice-President of the Council on Foreign Relations Ethan Kapstein, he

> announced that the United States dollar could not be converted to gold, thereby ending the era of fixed exchange rates and ushering in a system of floating rates . . . Floating exchange rates encouraged intense speculation on currencies . . . mobile capital was finally free to roam, giving it tremendous influence on countries' economic policies.[1]

Then Egypt and Syria attacked Israel on 6 October in an attempt to force the Israelis to negotiate a withdrawal from the territories which they had seized after a pre-emptive strike in May 1967, and retained in defiance of UN Security Council resolutions. But the Arab attacks were defeated after the United States rushed military aid to Israel, to avert the catastrophe of an Israeli resort to nuclear weapons. The last chance for the Arab states to achieve a military balance in the region was lost. Their only remaining means of retaliation was economic. The Organization of Petroleum Exporting Countries had been established in 1960. Ten members announced on 17 October that they would agree to an Iranian proposal to raise the price of oil on the world market by reducing their oil production forthwith by not less than five per cent of the September 1973 level, with a similar reduction to be applied each successive month until such time as the total evacuation of Israeli forces from all Arab territory occupied during the June 1967 war was completed, and the legitimate rights of the Palestinian people restored, in other words, until Israel chose to comply with UNSC Resolution 242. This was followed a few days later by an embargo by the Arab states on supplies of oil to the United States. Both endeavours failed, of course. What they did achieve before the embargo was finally lifted on 18 March 1974 was to quadruple the price of oil on the world market, thus creating what has been described as the greatest transfer of wealth in world history. It also precipitated a paradigm shift in social and economic policies in the world outside. Inflation and unemployment soared, placing impossible strains on the benign structures of the welfare state as experienced in most western countries since 1945. Governments ran scared, abandoning Keynesian doctrines of state intervention in favour of cost-cutting exercises that were still being explored and expanded over 30 years later. It was a new world and an essentially less humane one.

All this was still in the future. Horizons were still bright in the last quarter of 1972, all the more so perhaps because Labor was sweeping closer to office, albeit at the worst possible time, under the leadership of the most conspicuously erudite of Australian politicians, of whom it was indeed said that he gave the impression that there was not a book that he had not read, by contrast with some others, who might have given the impression that there was not a book that they had read. The immediate task for the founders of the Humanities Research Centre had naturally been to form a committee. This was done with commendable speed. The Australian National University Humanities Research Centre Advisory Committee invited by Sir John Crawford on 11 September 1972 held its first meeting on 22 September 1972, chaired appropriately by Richard Johnson. It recognised the most urgent task as being that of finding a Director. How far optimism still reigned among the planners of Australian academe was illustrated both by the qualifications expected for a Director and the amount of support which it was assumed could be provided for the appointee.

The Head of the Centre 'should be pre-eminently a distinguished scholar, with much less emphasis being placed on administrative ability; a Graduate Assistant,' it was confidently noted, 'would be available to look after most of the detailed administrative work (although one member suggested that a more senior post might be warranted). In any case,' the Committee considered, 'it was essential that the Head should be kept as free as possible of detailed administrative work so that he [sic] could concentrate on his scholarly activities and on general policy matters.' All this would indeed depend on 'the effectiveness of the Graduate Assistant and on the way in which the person appointed to the Headship preferred to work;' but 'it would be sufficient to tell any prospective appointee to the Headship that substantial administrative assistance would be available – exactly how this assistance would be used could be decided later.'[2] Future Directors and Deputies labouring under the Sisyphean burdens of administrative minutiae might well react to such cheerful expressions with bitter laughter; but the 1970s had just begun, and senior academics were not yet expected to type and file their own official letters, collect their own mail, maintain their own bring up systems, make their own work related appointments and travel arrangements, not to mention other even more unfamiliar chores such as moving furniture for seminars and lectures and keeping up with myriad University policy changes and endless minutes of University committees via the internet.

An obvious problem was that a Graduate Assistant could hardly be the kind of senior academic of comparable status which Max Crawford had recognised as being a necessary counterpart to the Director. Neither would it be appropriate for a senior academic counterpart to be lumbered with the detailed administrative work that the Director was apparently to be exempted from. And the requirements for the Director were becoming ever more exacting. He or she was to be not only a distinguished scholar but also an impressive linguist: five members of the Advisory Committee, including Johnson and Hans Kuhn, wrote to Donaldson and Herbst, rejecting the 'monstrous assumption . . . that what has not been translated into English is not worth reading,' and declaring that they did not 'think it extravagant to ask that the future director should be conversant with Latin, French, German and, preferably, another major language.'[3] Certainly, Johnson, Kuhn, Donaldson and Herbst themselves would have had no difficulty meeting such selection criteria. A draft advertisement for the Director proposed that the successful applicant 'should be a person of substantial scholarship in some field of European thought and culture; he should also have a sympathetic awareness of developments in fields and disciplines other than his own.' There would be 'adequate support staff' to count on; and the Centre was 'expected to comprise about ten academic staff' when developed, the tenured members to be 'the Director and one other with primarily bibliographical responsibilities.'[4]

Some reservations were beginning to be expressed about the explicit Eurocentricity of the project, if not about its implicit gender-exclusiveness. Pacific historian Hartley Grattan told Sir John Crawford that to learn that the HRC 'was actually to come into being was a great pleasure for while it won't be THE monument to your Vice-Chancellorship, it will be remembered as one of the most creative ornaments of it.' However, he noted in the advertisement in the *Times Literary Supplement* that 'there is a reference to European cultural orientation. I hope this is not interpreted restrictively. I hope it will be recognised that too intense focus on "Europe" will narrow the mind.'[5] Dale Trendall advised Sir John Crawford's successor as Vice-Chancellor Robert Williams that he had gathered from Johnson that

> it had now been more or less agreed that [the HRC's] immediate aim should be research into the impact of the European way of life and thought upon Australia and the Pacific. This seems to me a laudable proposal ... but it of course differs to some extent from the suggestion I made to you that the Centre might concentrate upon the rather broader theme of the impact of European culture upon Asia and the Pacific and the reverse process.

However, he supposed that it might be 'as well to start on the narrower topic ... since it could be capable of expansion later.' The trouble was that there was no reason to imagine from Johnson's original proposal, the terms of the advertisement or anything that had been discussed by the Advisory Committee that it was at all in contemplation that the Centre should also examine the reverse process of the impact of Asian and Pacific culture upon European civilisation, although Trendall had raised the possibility for such a readjustment, observing that it did not matter greatly 'whether the Director's own particular field of study lies in the European or the Pacific sector, provided he has some understanding of both.'[6]

Grattan in fact hoped that the HRC might develop as an Australian Studies Centre. He suggested as someone pre-eminently qualified in both European and Pacific fields the author of *European Vision and the South Pacific*, the great Marxist art historian and classicist Bernard Smith. The Committee did indeed consider Smith, who had expressed interest in the position, but noted that he 'would not be available before January 1975, when he would be 58. This raised the question

Professor Bernard Smith,
Director of the Power Institute,
University of Sydney.
Photo courtesy The Australian Academy of the Humanities.

as to whether it was desirable to appoint a person at this stage of his career to set up a new Centre . . . the duties could be physically taxing.'[7] Smith was to become at the age of 60 President of the Australian Academy of the Humanities, a position not incapable of being taxing, and was still in unwearied creative flood at the age of 85, publishing his latest book and posing boldly nude for the Archibald Prize.

The Committee had already resolved on 9 April 1973 to appoint retiring University Librarian J.J. Graneek for a period of 12 months 'to compile a bibliography of desiderata for the Centre,' while C.A. Burmester from the National Library of Australia would compile specialist bibliographies.[8] This dealt with the bibliographical side of the business. However, the quest for a Director was becoming more urgent, as 34 applications for Visiting Fellows had already been received by August 1973. This number had been reduced to a short list of 17, reduced further to nine and fellowships finally offered to only two, but something would still have to be done with them and somebody would have to do it.

Johnson had written to Professor J.B. Trapp, Director of the Warburg Institute, back in September 1970, explaining that 'we will need a director – a scholar of distinction, a man [!] of wide academic contacts, steeped in Europe, yet not unfamiliar with antipodean or North American society,' and hoping that he would 'suggest the name of J.B. Trapp.' This would certainly have gone far to cement the Centre as a locus of European studies.[9] But Trapp had not responded to the lure. Donaldson for his part had been most impressed, both personally and intellectually, by Bernhard Fabian, Professor of English at the University of Münster. Donaldson had met him at the second David Nichol Smith seminar on the eighteenth century in Canberra in 1970, when they had discussed the issue of critical concern to both of them, 'what hope for the humanities?' while 'walking together through The Australian National University's gum groves, watching the grass parrots, and guarding ourselves against the occasional predatory swoop of nesting magpies,' as Donaldson recalled. Fabian had insisted in the comprehensive German manner that 'we needed . . . to organise ourselves much better; to set up research institutes; to establish information networks; to attract more generous funding, both public and private. Just look at the scientists! And take a leaf from their book.'[10] A visiting appointment was arranged for Fabian in the English Department at ANU for the third term of 1970. They 'had all enjoyed teaching together,' Donaldson recalled; and Fabian had acquired a strong liking for Australia, especially as Canberra 'had a growing reputation at this time as a centre for eighteenth century studies' through the series of seminars and later conferences, inaugurated in honour of the renowned Professor David Nichol Smith, in recognition of his immensely valuable donation of eighteenth century English and French works to the National Library. Fabian's own particular field of interest was admittedly the somewhat specialised one of the history of the book trade in Germany, and in particular the dissemination of English books in Germany during the eighteenth century, on which he became a European authority. However, he also 'had a good knowledge of cultural institutions and research centres throughout Europe'; he 'was an up-and-coming scholar of international distinction'; he 'had ideas about the role the new Centre in Canberra might play'; and he manifestly 'fitted the Warburgian model.'[11] He seemed just the man for the job.

The Electoral Committee accordingly approached Fabian, advising him that the purpose of the Humanities Research Centre was 'to stimulate and advance in Australia generally the study of the humanities, especially the literature, philosophy and art of Europe.' Fabian for his part reassured the Committee that

> he did not see the Centre becoming a centre of 18th

> century studies as might have been feared by his own interests and those of others in Humanities in the ANU; the range of work had to be much wider ... One of the Centre's functions might be, he felt, to encourage greater co-ordination in the humanities among the Australian universities ... The first task,

however, 'would be to build up the library; one way of obtaining expert advice would be to invite out a scholar-librarian.'[12]

This was how Max Crawford had seen the Centre developing. It was however appearing increasingly unlikely that the Centre would actually develop this way: the University Library and the National Library were continuing to expand; their librarians were unanimously opposed on principle to multiplying separate holdings instead of consolidating them; and growing budgetary constraints were unfavourable to the creation of yet another collection. The Advisory Committee was now convinced in any event that the most pressing task was to find temporary accommodation for the first intake of Visiting Fellows who would be arriving in 1974. The Committee did not feel that there would be any 'real danger that the traditions and character of the Centre could be pre-empted' if Fellows were appointed before the arrival of the Director; but where to put them was the problem: it had been hoped that the new A.D. Hope Building might be available by August, but it was not going to be ready for occupancy for over six months and it could be difficult to find

> space in the Arts buildings, although it might be possible to use the rooms of people on study leave. This would mean however that Fellows would be dispersed; it would be desirable to have them in adjacent rooms. Other possibilities might be to seek space in the Childers Street buildings or in the Chifley library.[13]

Neither would have been wholly satisfactory, however: the Childers Street buildings were undeniably basic though eminently durable prefabs, which had been put up over 20 years before as temporary accommodation for the workers engaged in constructing ANU, and are indeed still enduring, more or less, accumulating evermore historic quality and rustic charm thanks to encroaching greenery, graffiti and barbed wire. All very 1960s Canberra, and doubtless therefore to be heritage listed. And the Chifley was an excellent place to do research, but it was not equipped to provide distinguished visiting academics with private offices or even such technological support as telephones.

Meanwhile, the search for a Director had suddenly gone awry. Fabian was formally invited to take the post in November 1973. However, Donaldson had suspected that Fabian was having some reservations about the venture when he visited him in Münster early in 1974. A severe bout of illness finally decided him to decline on 26 March 1974. This, as Donaldson put it, 'came as a bit of a bombshell. The first batch of HRC Visiting Fellows was about to arrive, and the first HRC conferences were about to take place. Someone had to look after the new Centre.'[14] He wrote graciously at the time of Fabian's retirement in 1996 that it had been 'Australia's great loss and Germany's gain that he eventually decided instead to remain at Münster.'[15] Perhaps it was. But a person far less modest about their own abilities than Donaldson might have felt that it could have been Australia's gain after all. Then Graneek resigned on 16 April, creating another staff vacancy. Burmester's appointment was due to conclude on 9 July, but the Committee agreed that he should be invited to continue until 31 December. Johnson urged that 'it was essential to have someone in charge of the Centre very soon. There was a budget and visitors were coming.' The Committee 'was convinced by arguments that an appointment, even if a temporary one, must be made soon and it was agreed that the Vice-Chancellor should ask Professor Trendall whether he would be willing to accept the headship for a period of up to two years.'[16] Trendall was then 65, the compulsory retirement age in that ageist era, and seven years older than Smith had been when the Committee had doubted that he would have the stamina for the job. Trendall would no doubt have been a superlatively adept and scholarly choice nonetheless. But he had too much on his plate already, like most distinguished academics in early retirement: he was 'appreciative of the offer,' but 'made it clear that he was not free to take on this work.'[17] Hopes were entertained of Professor Ralph Elliott who at 53 was in the mid-tide of a most distinguished career, Foundation Professor of the School of Languages and Literature at the Flinders University of South Australia and Emeritus Professor of English there since 1974, world authority on Chaucer and Hardy and remarkable in addition to all that as the only German to have received the Sword of Honour at the Royal Military College, Sandhurst, before joining in the invasion of Germany with the Leicestershire Regiment. Australian Chief of the Defence Force General Peter Cosgrove seemed to find it all rather puzzling when Professor Elliott told him the story.

But Ralph Elliott had just accepted Trendall's old position as Master

Professor Ralph Elliott, Acting Director, 1977–1978; Honorary Librarian, 1998– .

of University House and was accordingly not available either. He would however remain most closely involved with the Centre for longer than anybody else, serving it at duty's call as Chair of the Advisory Committee, as Acting Director and later as Acting-Acting Director, Visiting Fellow, guest speaker, Honorary Librarian, and generally guide, philosopher and friend, earning the affection and respect of colleagues as Godfather of the HRC, to which he would continue to bring a breadth of vision and scholarship wholly necessary to such an institution.

But what the Centre needed immediately was not a Godfather but a father or even a mother. The first contingent of Visiting Fellows had arrived and with them the problems which had to be expected. Assistant Registrar of ANU Robert Horan told the Advisory Committee that they would really 'have to try to avoid repeating the experience we are having' with one of the Visiting Fellows 'who is disillusioned with the Centre and is considering leaving before the end of his term.' His complaints, Horan informed the Committee,

> seem to lie around the following ... He cannot understand what the HRC, even in its undeveloped state is about – he is isolated in the Chifley Library without a phone, as we failed to find a room for him in a congenial department ... He has not found anyone with academic interests close to his own.

Horan suggested that the academic in question carried some blame, since the Visiting Fellows had been advised beforehand that 'because of our failure to appoint a Director, the Centre has, as yet, no visible presence.' However, the complainant 'is coming to the conclusion that he has been misled, and I should not want this to happen with the other Visitors – if only for the reason that they could give us a "bad press" when they return home.' It was all too likely that this would

Prefabricated building, Childers Street.

be the case, just as it would be all too easy for any academic coming to the Centre from anywhere in Europe or North America to come to the conclusion that they had been misled when faced with such conditions: it would be hard indeed for them to suppose that The Australian National University could not do better than that.

The academic in question came to terms with the current deficiencies of the Centre to the extent that he gave a presentation in the first of its Conference series later in 1974. But Horan's concern in the meantime was that he was not sure that ANU could do better than that. 'Obviously the best thing to do with these people,' he continued, 'is to accommodate them in some Department where they will find a matching interest, but this seems to be impossible. As a last resort, I have reserved some rooms in Childers Street to be available to HRC until Arts V [the A.D. Hope Building] is completed. This is a last resort,' he emphasised, 'as I am not looking forward to telling Visiting Fellows from overseas that this is the best accommodation the ANU can offer them'.[18]

The Childers Street prefabs were of course by no means without charms of their own: there was food and entertainment to hand at The Street Theatre and a truly historic pie cart nearby for emergency supplies; and Visiting Fellows had the added attraction of contact with graduate students in the same building, assuming that they wished to have contact with graduate students. One Department indeed found the Childers Street precinct so engaging that 'they refused to leave their huts for a smart new brick building that had been provided for them,' as Donaldson recalls. Nothing more could be done about accommodation in any event until the A.D. Hope Building was finished. But something had to be done about the other desperate deficiency of the HRC, its lack of a Director, and done at once. The University at last made a decision which it might well have made to advantage earlier: the urbane, sophisticated and perceptive Ian Donaldson was 'hauled out of the English Department' in August 1974 'on a two-year secondment to take care of the Centre' in the capacity of Director until a permanent appointment was made.[19] This may well have been a great loss to English studies at ANU, as Professor of History Ann Curthoys later observed; but it was the greatest possible gain to the HRC.

The HRC Advisory Committee also decided in September that steps should be taken to advertise a single senior post for Deputy Director and HRC Bibliographer, in case the original and fading concept of the HRC as 'a centre in a library' might yet be realised. It never was, but the necessity for a Deputy Director was becoming more evident all the time. It would be two years before one was appointed and seven years before one actually assumed the duties of the office. Donaldson's appointment was confirmed by the University Council in October. They could have looked far longer and farther and not done nearly as well. Donaldson commented genially a year later that he had been acting 'on what has unofficially been described as a "caretaker" basis. The term is perhaps rather more exact than any of us at first realised,' he added, alluding to the extraordinary burden of cares that he would have to take.[20] Fortunately, Donaldson was then a youthful 39 and able to carry the load.

The first Annual Report of the Humanities Research Centre presented in January 1975 recorded that the HRC had 'made a modest but useful start with its activities this year, despite encountering unexpected difficulties.' The first had been Professor Fabian's inability to accept the position of Director due to ill health. The second of course was accommodation. The A.D. Hope Building had not been ready for occupancy at the proposed time, and present estimates were that the Centre would not be able to move into its designated accommodation on the top floor before May 1975. 'Throughout 1974,' in consequence,

> members of the Humanities Research Centre have been variously located in the Coombs building (Department of Philosophy, RSSS), in the Faculty of Law, in the Haydon-Allen building (Departments of English and Philosophy, SGS), in the Dedman Building (Departments of Romance Languages and Germanic Languages), and in the Chifley Library, while the Centre's Administrative Officer, Mr R.J.C. Horan, whom the Vice-Chancellor had released from his duties at the Chancelry to fulfil that role, along with his secretary and typist, have remained in the University Chancelry.

This too was in practice not quite as bad as it sounded: the Coombs building was indeed somewhat detached, but the others formed a not too inconvenient triangle around the Union Block. However, there could be no doubt that what Donaldson considered the 'wide dispersal of members of the Centre . . . created problems for a new Centre attempting to establish its identity, and for Visiting Fellows hoping to maintain day-to-day contact with the Director, the administrative staff, and with one another.'

Professor Ian Donaldson, Director, 1974–1990, 2004– .

At least they would now have a Director to maintain contact with. And contact with Directors and their Deputies was going to prove perhaps the single most important factor in what would prove the amazing, not to say incredible success of the HRC, nationally and internationally. Nothing satisfactory could be done about accommodation and concentration until the A.D. Hope Building was available: the Centre in the meantime would be located in the run-down and possibly haunted precincts of Childers Street. But even that was not too bad, as Donaldson recalled it: he, Horan, Ms Jennifer Kelly the secretary and Ms Beverley Ricketts the typist, 'along with the first batch of Visiting Fellows, shared Hut C with a group of PhD students from the Faculty of Arts. There was a good atmosphere, with students and visitors mixing in a central tea-room.'[21] There always would be the blissfully welcoming aroma of simmering coffee about the HRC during the Donaldson years: one of the administrative staff recalled later that her first responsibility on entering the Centre was to put the coffee on. It was a gracious, civilised and hospitable tradition which would always represent the essence of the HRC, which was also establishing impressive academic credentials right from the start. 'Several distinguished overseas scholars,' as Donaldson observed, had 'accepted invitations to visit the Centre in the near future'; the Centre's work was 'gathering momentum, and should soon be in full swing'; and five Visiting Fellows had already been working at the HRC during 1974. First had been Professor Eric Gould, of the Department of English at the University of Denver, who was preparing a book on the development of Australian poetry from 1890 onwards. Professor Stewart Sutherland of the University of Stirling was engaged on atheism and belief in *The Brothers Karamazov*. Dr Tilo Schabert of the University of Munich was examining the existential and philosophical foundations of the modern age. Other areas of study ranged from existentialism and seventeenth

Professor Peter Herbst.

Dr Robert Brissenden.

century metaphysics to the place of property in political thought.

Two aspects of significance were apparent already. One was that the Centre was right from the beginning attracting interest from the very top levels of academic talent. Sutherland for example would become Lord Sutherland of Houndswood, Vice-Chancellor of the University of London, Principal of Edinburgh University and President of the Royal Society of Edinburgh; and Alan Ryan, who in Donaldson's words, 'was knocking about with us in Childers Street in the very earliest days of the Centre' was to become Warden of New College, Oxford. The other was that the Centre had begun already to display an impressive capacity to range widely in the virtually boundless field of the humanities. This would be evidenced ever more conspicuously by the great annual sequence of conferences, initiated most impressively as well as appropriately by Peter Herbst in August 1974 with a four-day conference on 'The impact of seventeenth and eighteenth century philosophy on modern thought,' followed by a one-day seminar on Australian lexicography on 30 October.[22] Thirty people attended from New Zealand as well as Australian universities. The eighteenth century was a natural area of involvement for the HRC, as the period in which European influences of every kind expanded most vigorously into the world outside, and Donaldson agreed that the Centre should assume co-sponsorship and organisation of the triennial David Nichol Smith seminars on eighteenth century issues, under the guidance of their convenor, Dr Robert Brissenden.

So far, highly satisfactory. But there were still the fundamental and associated problems of what kind of institution the HRC was supposed to be, and how it was to be staffed. 'Right from the outset,' Donaldson told University Librarian R.A. Simms, 'the HRC has been conceived as a Centre with a library of its own.' This of course was not the same as a library with a Centre of its own, which was really what Max Crawford had originally envisaged; but this was not a practical proposition any longer. 'The University of London's Warburg Institute, with its own self-contained library, has been cited as a partial model for the HRC,' Donaldson continued; and 'the Vice-Chancellor and the Centre's Committee . . . agreed that "The quality of the library collection more than any other single factor would attract scholars to the Centre" . . . It was also agreed that the Centre should have a Working Collection housed either wholly or partly in the building in which the Centre was located;' and the original plans for the A.D. Hope Building, in which the Centre would eventually be located, had made provision for a substantial separate library within the HRC.[23] But the [University] Librarian

> argued strongly against the establishment of a separate collection of books housed within the HRC . . . After some debate, this argument was accepted. It was agreed that

Colin Steele.

> within its own Reading Room the HRC should hold only a small collection of reference materials . . . and a few books of general academic interest.[24]

It was the only practical decision, given that the shades of the prison-house of government cutbacks in education funding were already beginning to close upon the infant HRC. Donaldson had been assisted in arriving at it through consultations with Robert Rosenthal, Keeper of Special Collections at the University of Chicago Library, who had come to Canberra to advise the Centre on whether efforts should be made to establish a significant library, and if so, what its areas of specialisation should be. Rosenthal would

> say that it was still perfectly possible to build up a world-class specialist collection in Renaissance literature (for example) if that's what we really wanted to do, and wanted the HRC to be, and wanted to spend our money on. But aren't there perhaps other things that are important now – like buying yourselves research time, bringing visitors to Australia, getting your act together?

Donaldson recalled that these 'teasing conversations with Bob Rosenthal . . . were probably more influential on my own thinking about the possible future shape and direction of the HRC than anything else.'[25] Former University Librarian Colin Steele recalls Rosenthal asking what the other academics might feel about the Centre's acquiring a substantial library of its own, 'when [at some time in the future] there were 4 million books in the Chifley and Menzies Libraries,' and the heartfelt response of historian Professor Barry Smith of the Research School of Social Sciences: 'Euphoria!'[26] As well it might have been. But it wasn't going to happen: the University Library is still two million volumes short of the four million volumes that Rosenthal envisaged. However, the HRC retains its small scholarly collection, constantly augmented by donations from grateful Visiting Fellows and situated currently in the charming, comfortable and appropriately named haven of the Ralph Elliott Library. Colin Steele, [former Director, Scholarly Information Strategies], reflects on the change:

> When I arrived in Australia from the Bodleian [Library] in August 1976, one of my first activities was to attend a major presentation in the HRC by Bob Rosenthal, the Curator of Special Collections who was a visiting

fellow at the HRC. His vision of a four million volume University Library sadly never came to pass but his vision of the importance of research collections to the scholarly community, particularly in the Humanities, is still as relevant today as it was then. Since that time, Professors Ian Donaldson, Graeme Clarke and Iain McCalman have all encouraged local and national discussions on library and information initiatives. The debate still continues in the digital era. On a personal note, it gave me great pleasure, with Ian Donaldson's support, to organise what the cultural history books have now called Australia's first academic conference on Science Fiction. The conference 'Speculative Fiction: The Australian Context' was held in July 1981 and featured some of Australia's leading SF authors such as George Turner and Damien Broderick, as well as critics such as Bob Brissenden, Van Ikin and Michael Tolley.

The future of libraries themselves has indeed become a matter for speculation in the new century. But that was all in the future, and Donaldson was as ever looking for a compromise which would allow for flexibility of response: he hoped that 'it would be possible some day for the HRC to find its home in the University Library, and that future library planning could take account of this.'[27] The HRC senior staff did have an influence on humanities collections in the ANU Library through serving on Library acquisition committees for the next thirty years. Future planning for an HRC library of the type envisaged was alas still in the future thirty years down the track. Experience had shown in any event that it was not the quality of its own library collection that would ever be the major or even a minor factor attracting scholars to the Centre: it was the quality of its Director and the other senior academic staff.

But the Centre could never be a one-person show. It had been presumed hitherto that the other tenured academic position in the HRC would be that of the Bibliographer or Librarian, who 'would be a person of very considerable importance in the Centre'.[28] But what really mattered in existing circumstances was finding effective support for the Director. Donaldson told Pro Vice-Chancellor Professor Geoffrey Sawer that there was 'at present administrative work in the Centre equivalent to about a half-time position. But we also need someone to help on the research side.' He accordingly proposed 'the establishment of a new post which combines administrative and

The A.D. Hope Building.

research duties.'[29] The University agreed without hesitation that there seemed to be 'no obstacle to the creation of a powerful <u>administrative</u> position in the Centre, whose incumbent would in fact spend part of his time engaging in academic research . . .'[30] An advertisement was duly published in April 1975 for a Research Secretary to

> advise and assist the Director in all administrative matters relating to the work of the Centre. It is expected that the Officer, in consultation with the Director of the HRC and the Business Manager of the HRC, will handle all detailed financial questions concerning budgets, estimates, recommended grants to visiting fellows, purchase of capital equipment . . . assist the Director and members of the University Registrar's staff in matters relating to the

> arrival, accommodation, and general welfare and activities of Visiting Fellows . . . help with the detailed organization and day-to-day running of conferences and seminars . . . serve as secretary to the Advisory Committee of the Centre and also to smaller Steering Committees. From time to time he may be called upon to advise and assist the Centre's bibliographer on administrative and financial questions.

That covered the administrative side. On the research side, the appointee would be

> expected to assist the Director, Bibliographer, and the Centre's Visiting Fellows in their research, and to help survey, and make recommendations upon, proposed conference and seminar topics. Applicants should ideally have had some administrative experience, and have good academic qualifications in an area of the humanities relevant to the Centre's work.

They should also necessarily possess competent shorthand and typing skills and experience in secretarial work, and a 'knowledge of foreign languages would be an advantage.'[31] Those were the days.

The services of such an infinitely precious assistant would presumably free the Director to maintain the level of academic research which would have qualified him or her for the position in the first place, and to concentrate on issues of high strategy for the Centre. There were more than enough of those demanding urgent attention even before the research secretary from Heaven could arrive. There were for example the technical questions of how far the Centre should attempt to bring Visitors of similar interests together at one time, and whether special encouragement should be given to research which crossed the boundaries of more than one of the conventional academic disciplines. Then there was the fundamental question of how Visiting Fellows should be selected, particularly with regard to disciplines like music and art, leading practitioners in which might not always be academics. There was also of course the sensitive question of age. The Committee was not deterred, however: it was agreed on 11 April 1975 that 'the Centre should be prepared occasionally to offer Fellowships to people who might not merit them solely on grounds of academic qualifications.' The distinction drawn was between composers or practitioners in the Fine Arts, who might be considered more appropriately for Creative Arts fellowships; and 'artists who drew their inspiration from the inter-play of ideas and the intellectual atmosphere which the Centre could supply.' It was also agreed that 'there should be no rigid age limits, but that older scholars . . . would as a general rule only be invited if the Committee was satisfied that they were still productive, of unusual eminence, and that they were still flexible enough to communicate with other scholars.'[32] Which was fair enough, and it was only a general rule, anyway.

That defined issues of doctrine sufficiently for the time being. Material issues were also being resolved. Horan was able to report on 3 July that 'all HRC staff and visiting fellows to the Centre are now located in the A.D. Hope Building.'[33] Accommodation consisted of eleven study-offices for the Director, Bibliographer, Research Secretary and up to eight Visiting Fellows, two secretarial rooms, a seminar room and a reading room, described as 'a generous open area to house its Working Collection.' The new premises were said to 'provide agreeably both for privacy and sociability, and have contributed to the centre's growing sense of identity.'[34] However, Donaldson felt required to warn the Dean of the Faculty of Arts that he was 'perfectly happy that HRC Fellows be free to enjoy the western view during the winter months'; but 'some sort of screening will clearly be essential later in the year,' when the occasionally broiling heat of the Canberra summer would make a western view much less enjoyable. 'I must add that I feel some dismay at the thought of yet another uncompleted item on this building,' he added with feeling.[35] He would have felt even more dismay if he had known that that particular item was never to be wholly completed: the seminar space would be airconditioned eventually, but the Director and the Deputy Director would be left to sweat it out for another 25 years.

Donaldson also reported that he was 'continuing his search for a Permanent Director for the Centre.'[36] But there was already compelling evidence that the Centre had in its Acting Director the Permanent Director it needed: Kenneth Garrad, the Professor of Spanish from Flinders University informed the Committee that he wished

> to place on record my profound respect and admiration for Professor Donaldson, as Director of the Centre, as a scholar and as a man . . . the attentions and hospitality which he and his wife have given to myself and all the Visiting Fellows alike have exceeded any conceivable norm of duty. He has, in fact, made everybody feel welcome and at home, and I am sure the other Fellows will be as emphatic as myself in thanking him and congratulating the Committee in its choice of an unsurpassable Director.[37]

Attentions and hospitality were in fact what the HRC would become famous for internationally in the years that followed: a continuing flood of testimonials left no doubt that there was at least one quality in which the HRC might well be without parallel in the world, and that was its capacity to provide a welcoming and congenial research environment for visiting scholars. Nor was there any doubt that it would be the Directors and their stand-ins, in Anthony Low's phrase, who were responsible for that environment. It had not been one of the selection criteria prescribed for the positions; but it was in a real sense what the HRC was all about.

Notes

1. Jerome Binde (ed.), *Keys to the 21st Century*, UNESCO Publishing, Paris, 2001, pp. 352-358.
2. The Australian National University Humanities Research Centre Advisory Committee Meeting No.1, 3434/1972, 50.4.1.1, 22 Sep. 1972.
3. Hans Kuhn and Johnson to Herbst and Donaldson, 25 Sept. 1972.
4. Draft advertisement, The Australian National University Humanities Research Centre, Director, 3618/1972, 29 Nov. 1972; Draft Further Particulars . . . 3619/1972, 29 Nov. 1972.
5. Hartley Grattan to Sir John Crawford, 5 Mar. 1973.
6. Trendall to Robert Williams, 21 May 1973.
7. The Australian National University Director of the Humanities Research Centre Report of Electoral Committee Meeting No. 2, 3024/1973, 13 Aug. 1973.
8. TANU HRCAC 1305/1973, 17 Apr. 1973.
9. Johnson to J.B. Trapp, 10 Sept. 1970.
10. Donaldson, 'What hope for the humanities?' *Zukunftsaspekte der Geisteswissenschaften: Herausgegeben von Bernhard Fabian*, Georg Olms Verlag, Hildesheim, 1996, pp. 41-62.
11. Donaldson to the authors, 25 June 2002.
12. Director of the Humanities Research Centre, Report of Electoral Committee, No. 3, 3332/1973 2.10.73, 12 Sept. 1973.
13. 3rd Meeting HRC Advisory Committee, 21 Sept. 1973.
14. Donaldson to authors, 25 June 2002.
15. Humanities Research Centre, *Bulletin*, 83, Dec. 1996, pp. 39-40.
16. TANU Director of the HRC Report of Electoral Committee Meeting No. 6, 1496/1974, 14.6.74, 7 June 1974.
17. Director of the HRC Electoral Committee Meeting No. 7, 2168/1974, 12.7.74, 7 June 1974.
18. Richard Horan to Chairman, Advisory Committee for HRC [Johnson], 18 July 1974.

[19] Donaldson to authors, 25 June 2002.
[20] Donaldson, 'The Future of the Humanities Research Centre: a personal view,' 31 Oct. 1975.
[21] The ANU, HRC, *Annual Report 1974*, 96/1975.
[22] Donaldson to the authors, 25 June 2002.
[23] Donaldson to the University Librarian, 10 Feb. 1975.
[24] Donaldson to all members of the HRC Advisory Committee: Post of Deputy Director and Bibliographer, 12 Apr. 1977.
[25] Donaldson to the University Librarian, 18 Mar. 1975.
[26] Colin Steele in conversation with authors.
[27] Donaldson to authors, 15 June 2002.
[28] Donaldson to HRC Advisory Committee, 12 Apr. 1977.
[29] Donaldson to Professor Geoffrey Sawer, 26 Feb. 1975.
[30] Sawer memorandum, 28 Feb. 1975.
[31] HRC, *Research Secretary*, 1, *Duties*, 1975.
[32] Meeting of HRC Advisory Committee, 11 Apr. 1975, 1024/1975.
[33] Horan to Staff Office, Chancelry, 3 July 1975.
[34] HRC *Annual Report 1975*, 100/1976.
[35] Donaldson to Dean, Faculty of Arts, 13 May 1975.
[36] Donaldson to Dean, Faculty of Arts, 13 May 1975.
[37] Kenneth Garrad, Report for Humanities Research Advisory Committee, 15 May 1975.

3 A Source of New Energy and New Ideas (1975–1981)

The HRC could certainly be said to have established its own identity by mid-1975. It had already received the most convincing accolade of international recognition. Richard Johnson had visited the United States in the late 1960s and early 1970s to find inspiration and models for the HRC in the varied and proliferating research centres there. But Donaldson found on visiting the USA himself after 1975 that it was the HRC which was now providing inspiration and a model: 'it had attracted the attention of a group of American academics who hoped to establish a similar national humanities centre in the United States; one of whom . . . came as a Visiting Fellow to Canberra to observe at close quarters how the HRC worked'.[1] The Harvard luminaries who consulted Donaldson did not as yet know for certain where their proposed National Humanities Center would be located, how it would be funded, or who its Director would be. They were however very interested to know where the money for the HRC had come from, how it had got started in the first place and how it operated as a national centre. Characteristically, the Americans moved fast. The National Humanities Center was established at the Research Triangle Park in North Carolina in 1976 and opened for business in the autumn of 1978. Nearly 300 humanities research institutes of one kind or another would be operating throughout the United States by the late 1980s. One of the National Humanities Center's Founding Fathers was the Harvard medievalist Professor Morton W. Bloomfield, who was an HRC Visiting Fellow in 1978 and wrote to Ralph Elliott on his return from what he referred to as 'that *locus amoenus* redolent of

Professor Ralph Elliott, top row, extreme left, and staff and Fellows of the US National Humanities Center, 1981

the Golden Age: The Humanities Research Centre of ANU. . .'[2] Elliott himself attended the National Humanities Center as a Visiting Fellow in May 1981, after his second term on the Advisory and Steering Committees of the HRC. There was no question by then that the HRC was recognised nationally and internationally. What would continue to prove a seemingly intractable problem was how to establish its identity within the structure of The Australian National University itself. It was a question to which several plausible answers have been proposed, and are indeed still being proposed at the time of writing. It was also one which would inevitably be bedevilled by the spectre of the HRC's identity being sacrificed on the altar of administrative convenience.

A Joint Committee had been set up to examine the status within the University of unaffiliated centres and units, such as the HRC. It concluded in May 1975 that such bodies suffered collectively from a 'lack of identification with the main sections of the University', and recommended accordingly that all centres and units be affiliated with a Research School or a Faculty.[3] Horan was not too impressed: he wrote to the Deputy Vice-Chancellor that the main proposals of the Report of the Joint Committee, 'and the premises from which they stem, seem to me to take little account of realities within the University'. One of the main problems, as he saw it, was the Committee's assumption that a number of disparate bodies will have significant common characteristics because they are described as "centres" or "units" . . . I am not convinced that a board or group comprising the units assigned either as IAS [Institute of Advanced Studies]-type or Faculty-type would be capable of mustering the community of interest, the mutual understanding of subject matter or, at least, methodology, which would enable it to engage in worth-while discussion and scrutiny of the affairs of its component parts. And to take what is perhaps an extreme, but a possible example, could the concerns of the Humanities Research Centre be adequately appreciated and represented on the Board of the Faculties by the heads of the Centre for Continuing Education, ORAM [Office of Research on Academic Methods], and Federal Financial Relations?

The impact of the proposals could in fact be counterproductive: they would 'lead, through the abolition or depreciation of Advisory Committees, to a reduction in the opportunities the Centres enjoy for contact with other parts of the University'.[4]

Donaldson's style was ever to pursue the normally more rewarding road of conciliation and compromise rather than confrontation: he was, as Graeme Clarke put it admiringly, 'adroit' in dealing with the 'Byzantine machinations of university bureaucracy'; and Clarke as a great classical scholar knew a Byzantine machination when he saw one. Thus Donaldson was ready to agree that 'a genuine problem exists concerning Centres and Units'; and he accepted that, 'for example, proposals for new appointments in Centres and Units need to be scrutinized as vigorously as they would be in other parts of the University', and that 'where a sense of isolation is really felt to exist, steps should be taken to create appropriate links with other University bodies'. However, he insisted, 'I don't believe that the problem of isolation exists for the HRC'. He then listed in support of this position the formal and informal links already existing between the HRC and other parts of the University: the Director was a member of the Boards of the Institute of Advanced Studies (IAS) and the School of General Studies (SGS); the HRC's Steering Committee included members from various other parts of ANU; Visiting Fellows usually had close ties with Departments both in the IAS and SGS; the Centre tried actively to keep in touch with other parts of the University through its *Bulletin*, its lecture series and its seminars and conferences;

and Donaldson himself still taught in the Department of English. Isolation was hardly the problem in these circumstances. The problem was likely rather to be one of over commitment through excessive involvement. Moreover, the HRC's position was rather different from that of the other Centres and Units, in that it was not supposed to be identified solely or even specifically with ANU: the Australian Universities Council had made clear in its Report of May 1972 that 'the operations of the Centre should be of a kind to benefit directly teaching and research in the humanities throughout the country.' The net result of the Joint Committee's proposals could accordingly be to

> weaken important existing links within and outside of the University; to place the HRC with a group of Centres and Units towards which it feels great goodwill, but which have little in common with it; to create, consequently, the very "isolation" which the Committee alleges it is trying to remove; and to add very considerably to the time already taken up by administrative procedures within the University.[5]

Administrative procedures within the University would ever be the subject of every senior academic's lament. But this was not the only intractable and vexatious problem besetting the HRC. It had always been recognised that the Director and whoever his alter ego might be had to be academics of the highest distinction. It was also becoming irresistibly evident that Donaldson's inspiring and congenial personal qualities were critical to the continuing success of the HRC. But academics of high distinction need periodical sabbaticals for serious research (as the HRC was providing for its Fellows); and academics of high distinction with inspiring and congenial personalities are always going to be in great demand from other institutions as academic visitors. It was therefore inevitable that people like Donaldson would be absent from their posts from time to time. But Visiting Fellows who were attracted to a Centre in the first instance largely because of the reputation of its Director would be justified in feeling disgruntled if the Director were not around when they came. The only answer was that the Director would have to have a Deputy who would possess as far as possible similar qualities to attract visitors and make them feel welcome. But the HRC did not yet possess a Deputy of any kind. It did not even yet possess a permanent Director.

Donaldson took a brief term of absence from 26 August to 25 September 1975, to deliver a paper at the English Institute at Harvard and visit

Ian Donaldson and others in HRC Reading Room. *From left*: John Hardy, Jack Graneek, Ian Donaldson, Manji Kobayashi, Peter Herbst, Ted Dorsch, Emily Lyle, Kay Dorsch, 1970s.

research centres in the USA, leaving Horan to fence with the bureaucrats and regale the visitors. Donaldson summarised the results of his observations a month after his return in a paper entitled 'The future of the Humanities Research Centre: a personal view.' The aspect that he considered of greatest importance to the future of the Centre was naturally its philosophical structure, of which he judged there had originally been 'no firm or close definition . . . The Centre's committee agreed . . . that the Centre's general concern was to be with "European thought and culture and their influence overseas"'. He had decided to take 'a broad construction, interpreting the second "and" to mean in effect "and/or" . . . I should want to stick by that interpretation.' It might seem that what he really had in mind was a construction so broad as to allow for a virtual reversal of the original mandate. He averred that he did 'not think that the Centre should be less ready to sponsor work on aspects of European thought and culture which have not at any stage substantially affected the consciousness of ex- or non-European people'; and he would say that normally 'the study of indigenous non-European cultures is not the H.R.C.'s business.' For example, he did not 'think that we should sponsor an ethnomusicologist who wants to come here to study Aboriginal music, or an anthropologist whose work has been with African peoples.' Both might seem thirty years later just what the HRC's offshoot, the Centre for Cross-Cultural Research, might very much wish to sponsor. In fact the HRC would over the years sponsor continuing and very substantial work in the area of the study of Indigenous Australian issues. Donaldson in any case emphasised that he 'should not wish to ignore the influence of the New World on the Old . . . "The impact on Europe of the discovery of Australia" would seem to me a proper topic for the H.R.C. one year to explore.'

As for the physical future of the HRC, Donaldson affirmed the view of the Universities Commission, that the HRC was to be 'thought of as a national centre, stimulating and advancing research in the humanities throughout Australia.' It should accordingly grow, if not into a Research School, with its departmental structure and large numbers of tenured academic appointments, at least into a Research Centre on a truly national – indeed, international – scale, with a programme of Visiting Fellowships which might compare with those of some of the larger American research centres, and serving 'a genuine national need.' He had originally felt that 'we should choose as Visiting Fellows those whose research projects were in some way close to other sorts of work already going on within the H.R.C.; that we should be cautious of bringing to the H.R.C. people from the fields of (for example) Music or Fine Arts, as they find no-one to talk to, and limited library resources.' However, he now felt that 'the Centre should try to attract, *inter alia*, a good many visitors who are doing work that is *not* being done at the A.N.U., or perhaps even elsewhere in Australia . . . The Centre would thus take something of a provocative, rather than merely a supportive role in relation to existing studies in the humanities:' it should 'act as something of a catalyst.'

Donaldson's choice of the term 'provocative' is at least intriguing: the superfluous and imprecise term 'proactive' had not yet made it into the dictionaries, so one may presume that Donaldson was using 'provocative' in the sense of 'tending to rouse, incite, tempt or allure', rather than in its other dictionary definition of 'intentionally irritating'. His intention was no doubt to affirm that the mission of the Centre could be to challenge, as well as to complement academic activities elsewhere in ANU. For the rest, he had effectively given up on the original conception of the HRC as

> a library-centre, with a substantial collection of books of its own. The Warburg Centre was often mentioned as a

> model for the H.R.C. I should like nothing better than to see the Centre develop in this way, but feel that such a development is unlikely to occur without very large and (at present) unlooked-for benefactions.

However, he understood that 'the University Librarian has accepted my suggestion that eventually the H.R.C. ought to move from its present home in the A.D. Hope building to a special area within the proposed new University Library building, with immediate access to the humanities collection'.[6] There were indeed plans for a large Humanities and Social Sciences Library adjacent to the Student Services Building on a still vacant area on the site of the Chancelry, to be named in honour of Sir Keith Hancock, former Professor of History in RSSS. It failed alas to get approval from the Universities Commission and was never built. Hancock's name was eventually assigned to the new Science Library, a most handsome and congenial building, but not actually one serving the discipline for which Hancock was noted.

In the meantime, the HRC Advisory Council was happy to agree at once to Donaldson's proposal that the Centre should take a special interest in the fields of Music and the Fine Arts, and that the Centre might accordingly commit up to 25 per cent of its funds for Visiting Fellowships in these areas during the current period. The emphasis on Music, Art and the Arts generally was to be a very productive direction for the HRC in subsequent years, leading to exhibitions at the University and joint research projects and exhibitions with national cultural institutions. In fact it was foreshadowed in one of the first HRC conferences held in 1975 when Donaldson, along with Dr A.G. Serle from Monash and ANU's Professor Manning Clark, organised a conference on cultural developments in Australia in the 1890s which was attended by 60 people.

Complementing the large numbers of Fellows in Classics, History, Philosophy and other humanities disciplines in the years 1974-1981 (106 Fellows, 25 Conference Visitors and 12 short-term Fellows), the research subjects of those visitors reveal a strong focus on Literature, Music and the Arts. For example, Professor Leon Edel from the University of Hawaii came to work on Henry James, Professor J.V. Bony from the Department of Art at the University of California, Berkeley on Gothic architecture, Professor D.H. Green from Cambridge on Medieval German and Comparative Literature, Professor J.M Holquist from Yale on nineteenth century Russian novelists, Dr Rüdiger Joppien of the Department of Fine Arts,

University of Cologne came to do research on drawings and paintings from eighteenth and nineteenth century maritime voyages to Australia, Professor Manji Kobayashi from Kobe University to work on modern Australian poetry and its translations into Japanese, Professor Chung Chong-Wa from Korea University on D.H Lawrence, Professor André Lefevere from the University of Antwerp on literary translation, Professor L.L. Albertsen from the University of Aarhus, Denmark on German poetry since Schiller, Professor C.K. Abraham from the University of California on seventeenth century satirists, Professor L.A Dittmer of the Department of Music at the University of Ottawa on motets of Adam de la Halle, Australian musicologist Dr John Meyer on the history of the piano concerto, Professor Victor Lange from Princeton on German literature, Professor J.R. Lawler of the University of Chicago on Baudelaire, Professor M. Dufrenne from Paris-Nanterre on aesthetics, Professor Saul Novack from the Department of Music at Queen's College, City University of New York on chromaticism in triadic tonality. Helen Topliss from Monash worked on her catalogue raisonné of Australian artist Tom Roberts, Professor B. F Dukore from the University of Hawaii on Ibsen, Shaw and Brecht, Professor Marilyn Rose from the State University of New York (SUNY) at Binghamton on literary translation, and Professor Leo Treitler from the Department of Music of the SUNY at Stony Brook on musical literacy in the Middle Ages. Australian poet Dorothy Green from ANU was at the Centre too as were English art educator Neville Weston, South Australian art historian Robert Smith, graphic artist Jorg Schmeisser from Hamburg (later to work in Australia); and Australian-born but English-domiciled poet Peter Porter and English artist David Blackburn were short term visitors along with English theatre administrator Elizabeth Sweeting, who came at the HRC's invitation to advise on the proposed new Arts centre. This is but a sample of the cultural research interests of the Fellows in the first seven years and in future years there would be many more Fellows in the Arts. Their impact on ANU and on the other Australian universities, where most Fellows from overseas also went to lecture as standard practice from the mid-seventies in line with the HRC's aim to be a truly national centre, could only have been considerable.

In 1977, Patrick McCaughey, then Professor at Monash and later to be Director of the National Gallery of Victoria and the Yale Center for British Art, convened a conference on Poetry and Painting, at which a number of well-known Australian painters and poets discussed their work. Sasha Grishin, later to be Professor of Art History at ANU, then a young Fine Arts and Russian graduate, took up a twelve-month Visiting Fellowship at the HRC early in 1977 to work on Byzantine Art. He declared later that

> Ian Donaldson's HRC was one of the most imaginative and dynamic weapons available to academics and intellectuals to enable the Humanities to have a voice in Australian cultural life. Without the assistance of the HRC, I would never have been able to get the Fine Art Programme off the ground at the ANU in 1967, and this directly led to the creation of the Department of Art History about a decade later.[7]

It was the first of the new departures in cultural studies which owed their origin at ANU to Donaldson's vision and support.

Unsurprisingly, the University now decided to invite Donaldson to accept appointment as Director for a period to be 'determined by the Vice-Chancellor in consultation with you. A period of 5 years in the first instance has been suggested with the possibility of

HRC Common Room. *Back row*: John Casey, Jim Grieve, Bob White, Chris Cordner, Sasha Grishin and John Jensen. *Front row*: Mary Theo, Ian Donaldson and Dorothy Nicholls, 1970s.

re-appointment'.[8] It was the only possible response to the flood of unrestrainedly laudatory testimonials that was continuing to pour in praising the qualities of both Donaldson and Horan. Academics understand the meaning of words, whatever else they may or may not understand; and academics of such distinction would not use words expressive of such enthusiasm if they had not meant them to be taken seriously. Professor J.E. Morpurgo, Professor of American Literature at the University of Leeds and a former Chief Editor of Penguin Books, who lectured on radio and television during his visit, for example, reported that:

> Through the generosity of the HRC I have achieved far more than I could have hoped for . . . the only sour note that I must admit to in this report is not so much a criticism of the HRC as a comment on my own folly in not appreciating, in advance and in full, the vast opportunity that was being offered to me . . . my work and my comfort during these last months, as indeed my happy view of Australia, has been consistently supported by Mr Horan and by the wisdom, energy and unflagging enthusiasm of Professor Donaldson.

It had been 'one of the most useful and stimulating experiences of my life.' English composer Christopher J. Lyndon-Gee, from the Department of Music at Ellesmere College (who lectured on the ABC during his stay and in Sydney and Adelaide on contemporary music), was

> certain that the A.N.U. has long been aware that it has in Professor Donaldson an academic, an intellect, an administrator and a personality in every respect of rare qualities, and that the H.R.C. has in him as its first Director a person of exceptional vision . . . None of the projects I undertook while in Canberra would have been possible without his selfless co-operation, constant advice, tact and diplomacy . . . well beyond the call of duty . . . My impression is that the Humanities Research Centre . . . is exemplary of its kind.

And Professor C.L. Price from Swansea who came to work on eighteenth century drama found 'conditions at the HRC ideal for work of this kind . . . I have met with friendliness and kindness everywhere.' Not bad for an establishment of one academic, a research secretary, a departmental secretary and a relief stenographer. Professor Price was another example of the widespread influence of the HRC: during his stay of six months he lectured in the English Department at ANU and at New England, Newcastle, Adelaide, Flinders and Monash Universities.

What was of course quite obvious was that this establishment had to be increased if the Centre were to have any prospect of living up to the reputation which it had acquired so early. And the first addition to the establishment had to be a full-time academic Deputy for Donaldson. The position was awarded in June 1976 to Grahame Johnston, a New Zealander, Professor of English at the University of New South Wales' Faculty of Military Studies based at the Royal Military College, Duntroon, with special interests in bibliography, lexicography and medieval, Celtic and English and American literature. Johnston had been a brilliant teacher at ANU in the sixties and Robert Wallace Professor of English at Melbourne and later concentrated his researches in the areas of bibliography and linguistics, including an Oxford Pocket Dictionary of Australian English. However, no separate budgetary provision was made for the post, which meant that the Centre would be receiving a substantial relief in terms of workload at the cost of a substantially greater burden in financial terms: it would be able to afford to do less at a time when it would be physically able to do more. It must nonetheless have seemed to Donaldson and his excessively overworked colleagues to be the greatest relief that they could have looked for. It was to prove their most tragic disappointment.

Meanwhile the agonising reappraisal continued over how the HRC should be situated within the overarching structure of the University, despite Donaldson's reassurances that isolation was not really a problem in the case of the Centre at least. The problem was one that had never been anticipated at the time when the proposal for the HRC had been accepted by the University. It had then seemed reasonable to assume that the resources available to ANU would continue to increase by around five per cent annually. Now it appeared that they were more likely to decrease by at least that proportion. The Joint Committee on the Centres and Units of the Boards of the Institute of Advanced Studies and the School of General Studies noted that the former had observed in a previous report in 1973 that there was then an 'increasing tendency for developments which provide facilities important to the academic work of the University, to be established outside the main IAS/SGS structure in various centres and units.'

Professor Grahame Johnston, Bibliographer and Deputy Director, 1976.

But 'the existence of the centres outside the main IADS [sic]/SGS structure is unsatisfactory from the point of view both of the centres and the University as a whole, particularly in the situation of little or no growth now confronting the University.' Professor Anthony Low, the former Director of RSPacS, had already warned early in 1975, on becoming Vice-Chancellor, that the years of expansion were over, and the University would have to be prepared to make reductions and even deletions in its programmes. He had also insisted that it would therefore be all the more necessary to take new initiatives, if only to maintain morale; and the Centres would seem the natural dynamos to generate new initiatives. But the Joint Committee observed ominously that centres were 'using a rapidly increasing share of the University's overall resources (in 1973 5.7% of total running expenses, in 1974 7% and in 1975 approximately 8%).' It was necessary for the University to consider seriously whether this trend should be allowed to continue. The Committee indeed believed that *'without the understanding and support of the main sections of the University, not only the future development, but perhaps even the survival of the centres may be at risk'*; and that *'an essential step in the process of endeavouring to secure that support and understanding is for the activities and plans of the centres to be subject to the same procedures of peer scrutiny and discussion as those of their colleagues in the Institute, the School or the Central Areas.'* [italics in the original]

The question was thus with which of these main sections of the University the HRC should be associated. The Committee recognised that close academic links existed between the HRC and the Faculty of Arts and that these should be continued and extended. It had been at the initiative of members of The Faculties that the HRC had come into being in the first place, as the only way in which the Humanities might acquire some counterpart to the great Research Schools established for the pursuit of other disciplines. But the whole climate of education funding had changed drastically since then, and there was a certain unease to say the least within The Faculties at the fact that HRC was still able to bring in Visiting Fellows while certain Departments were having to reduce lecturing staff. Funding for the Centre would by contrast look very modest in the context of the Research Schools. The Committee accordingly saw 'benefits in the association of the Centre with the Institute [of Advanced Studies] for the purposes of resource allocation,' and suggested accordingly that the HRC 'should explore the possibility of affiliation with the Research School of Social Sciences'.[9]

Ralph Elliott would later consider the option of affiliation with RSSS as an opportunity lost for the HRC, as holding greater prospect for expansion or at least outreach than affiliation with The Faculties, which might have seemed more appropriate to the origins and tradition of the Centre. Donaldson for his part recognised that the HRC would have to be fitted into the University structure somehow. He told the members of the HRC Advisory Committee, that it should be noted in any case that 'the proposed affiliation of the HRC with the RSSS is for <u>resource allocation purposes only</u> ... The net effect of the HRC being affiliated with the RSSS would thus not mean that we severed in any way our existing links with the School of General Studies.'[10] But now the RSSS Faculty Board themselves appeared to discover difficulties in the way of the affiliation of the Centre with their School: it was argued that it would be too difficult to separate the HRC's budget from that of the School, and that the HRC's academic interests were too far removed from those of other Departments of the RSSS for effective peer scrutiny to be possible. This might have seemed rather surprising, since the RSSS at the time included two former Presidents of the Australian Academy of the Humanities, as well as two former Secretaries and a number of Fellows of the Academy. It was hardly likely that they would find the activities of the Centre too arcane for them to fathom. The main problem was rather that the role of the Centre might be seen to overlap or even compete with that of the History of Ideas Unit within the RSSS. Negotiations involving Donaldson and RSSS Professor A.J. Youngson failed to resolve the issue. The Board therefore decided not to pursue the proposal of affiliation with the HRC. However, it was apparently not going to be any easier to affiliate the Centre with any other section of the University: the 14th Meeting of the HRC Steering Committee acknowledged that 'some means of allowing the centre's proposals to be scrutinized by an academic body had to be devised, but fears were expressed that affiliation with either IADS [sic], SGS or the faculty of Arts created problems'.[11]

So the issue of affiliation was back in the too-hard basket, where in fact it was still winding up thirty years down the track. Donaldson of course did not mind. He thought that the best course for the HRC for the time being would be to seek to achieve some form of independent status within the IAS, but it was by no means a matter of urgency. He soon had a far more serious problem on his hands, in any event: the year which had progressed so promisingly ended in tragedy, not only causing severe emotional distress to the personnel of the Centre, but also plunging it back into the organisational problems that they had hoped to escape from. Grahame Johnston had joined the HRC as Deputy Director on 1 December 1976. He died suddenly on 21 December. Professor A.D. Hope observed in a characteristically graceful eulogy that

> With his wide-ranging skills, his great bibliographical experience, and his deep and mature scholarship, it is peculiarly tragic that [Johnston] did not live to take up

the post in the Humanities Research Centre for which his various gifts and wide knowledge of the workings and personalities of the world of the Humanities would have made him an ideal appointment.

Hope also referred to Johnston's 'cheerful and companionable nature,' which experience had already shown would have been not only ideal but in fact quite essential qualities for effective service as Director or Deputy.[12]

So it was necessary to try once again to find an academic partner for the Director. Johnston's tragic death at least provided an opportunity for the Centre 'to look again with an open and critical mind at its total needs,' as Donaldson told the Advisory Committee. What this meant in particular was reconsidering the issue of requiring the appointee to be both Deputy and Bibliographer. That position had been seen originally as one of 'very considerable importance in the Centre,' while the concept of the 'Centre in a library' was still being entertained. It was apparently still being entertained in 1974, when the Advisory Committee agreed that 'steps should be taken to advertise a single senior post of HRC Bibliographer and Deputy Director.' However, it had now been agreed that 'within its own Reading Room the HRC should hold only a small collection of reference materials ... and a few books of general academic interest.' So the position of Bibliographer was now a less essential matter, while Donaldson felt that it had 'become increasingly apparent ... that the post of deputy Director is an essential one.' He accordingly suggested that 'we would do better if we divided the job in two ... It may be relevant also to consider here the question of the position of Research Secretary.[13]

All this made complete sense to the Advisory Committee. It was 'considered essential to the academic standing of the Centre that the Director should be allowed the opportunity of pursuing his own research and also that he should have in the Centre a senior colleague.' A Deputy should therefore be sought with interests in European studies, since this was Donaldson's own area of expertise and presumably the area on which the HRC was still expected to concentrate. The Committee also agreed that the bibliographical needs of the Centre could 'be met with the appointment of someone at a level lower than that of Professor,' and that the person appointed 'should be entrusted also with certain editorial functions.[14] However, the Vice-Chancellor had warned that it was unlikely that the HRC could expect an increase in its budgetary allocation for 1977, so any new additions to the staff would have to be paid for out of its existing

Professor Hans Kuhn.

allocation, which meant that the Centre would have to look forward to functioning with more staff and much less money.

This would seem to mean that the Centre would have to be satisfied with doing fewer things better, or at least more easily. But the only areas in which the HRC could reduce its activities in practice was the Visiting Fellows programme, which was exactly what it was understood from the outset would be the primary focus of the Centre, and perhaps the Conferences, which would be a primary function of any academic institution. The strategic vision was clear from the outset: the Centre, it was explained in its Annual Report to Parliament for 1975, had 'given special attention to certain areas of study which are at present not strongly established in Australia, for example, interdisciplinary studies, music and fine arts'.[15] It was decided for 1976 to stimulate work in a wide area of subjects in the humanities. The results were impressive. Hans Kuhn convened an *Old Norse Workshop*, devoted to the twelfth century Icelandic polymath Snorri Sturluson, which drew 40 participants, all the more remarkable because the name and fame of Snorri Sturluson were not all that familiar this side of Sydney Heads; another conference on *Shakespearean Comedy* had attracted 100 visitors, a third on *Phenomenology* drew 80, and a fourth on *Parody* drew 60, or over 280 visitors in all; and the associated David Nichol Smith conference, which the HRC had co-sponsored since 1974, convened by poet, literary critic and Reader in English at ANU Dr Robert Brissenden, was attended by a further 114 people.

The quality of the Visiting Fellow applicants was not in question, as Donaldson was able to confirm when Anthony Low observed that 'we haven't yet got the Isaiah Berlins to the HRC,' perhaps alluding to the fact that the History of Ideas Unit of RSSS had actually been honoured with a visit by the great historian of ideas. Donaldson recalls Anthony Low's strong support of the HRC. He took the remark on the half-volley: he admitted that 'Isaiah Berlin we have not invited,' but for the reason that he 'has recently been a visitor in the History of Ideas Unit.'

> Moreover, the fact was that we have quite deliberately tried to avoid filling the Centre solely with distinguished septuagenarians . . . I believe that the intellectual health of the Centre depends upon our mixing younger scholars with older scholars, mixing those who are writing their first major book with those who have many major books behind them.

The Advisory Committee had indeed resolved back in 1973 to invite old, not to say very old scholars only if they were of unusual eminence and were 'still flexible enough to communicate with other scholars.' But the Centre had had, 'and shall soon have, some very eminent visitors from within the humanities.' He then proceeded to list some, none of whom had yet reached septuagenarian status:

> John Shearman, Deputy Director of the Courtauld Institute and one of the most distinguished art historians in Britain today . . . Jean Bony, described by Niklaus Pevsner as without doubt the internationally leading authority on Gothic architecture, Roy Strong, Director of the V & A wants to come, J.A.W. Bennett, one of the greatest living English mediaevalists; Leon Edel, without doubt the world authority on Henry James; Northrop Frye, a legendary figure in the literary world . . .

All except Sir Roy Strong had indeed come to the Centre in those years, Edel providing a report which evoked the varied delights of his sojourn at the Centre in truly Jamesian style. 'My sense of nourishment,' he told Donaldson,

> was great . . . For me, the natural beauty of the surroundings, the fascinating bird-life, the opportunity to explore the flora and fauna of the land, the sense of the bush, the taste of Australian wine, the savouring of local expression and manners – and a thousand other impressions of the mind and senses linger with me and make me nostalgic even as I write . . . I cannot resist telling my story of holding a motherless baby kangaroo I came upon in the bush (unforgettable the delicacy and tenderness of the little creature).

Happily, he found a supply of Australian wines when he returned to his home to refresh his nostalgia. The subsequent fate of the baby kangaroo is not recorded, unlike that of the young wombat whom the great philosopher Richard Rorty encountered in similarly forlorn circumstances.

Quantity had been achieved along with quality: in the three years of its existence the HRC had had 'nearly fifty Visiting Fellows . . . and a lot more short-term visitors of one kind and another. From the beginning of 1976 . . . to the end of second term 1977, nearly two hundred papers will have been given in the Centre, in conferences, lunchtime talks, and work-in-progress seminars'.[16] There had also been an array of a dozen assorted conferences and seminars held since that first critical four-day conference on 'The Impact of 17th and 18th Century Philosophy on Modern Thought', organised by Peter Herbst in 1974.

It was an incredible record for an organisation which still consisted basically of only a Director, a Research Secretary, a secretary, a part-time bibliographer and a typist. It might well have been suggested that seldom had so much been done for so many by so few with so little. It was also, to say the least, inconvenient that the Visiting Fellowships posed an increasing financial burden, as the University made no provision for necessary increases in their grants in the way it did for academic salaries. What was most remarkable was that the Centre had already achieved marked growth, and there was evidence that its activities had been appreciated not simply in Canberra but throughout Australia. Nor was Donaldson concerned merely to try to defend the HRC on the basis of its record of past achievements: he was more than ready to propose ways in which the Centre might adapt appropriately to changing and increasingly unfavourable circumstances, and in particular how it could better serve the interests of ANU, as well as those of the general world of the humanities. He accordingly set himself to prepare a massive discussion paper, 'The HRC: the next phase,' for consideration by the Advisory Committee. The HRC had been in existence for three years. It was, he suggested, 'an appropriate time to take stock of what we have done so far, and to think critically about the next phase of the Centre's development.' The first thing to think about was clearly the extent to which the original vision of the Centre had been affected by the way in which the economic climate had altered for the worse. The HRC was facing hard times, like the rest of the University. But the present financial cutbacks affected the HRC

> more than many other parts of the University . . . because they come at such an early stage of the Centre's history, at a time when we had hoped for rapid growth. Schemes and dreams that looked realizable five years ago, three years ago, even eighteen months ago, may now look altogether less plausible.

The problem of finance was compounded by the fact that 'the larger notion of publicly subsidized research in the humanities has never been firmly established in Australia': there was 'nothing in this country equivalent to the National Endowment for the Humanities in the United States,' and 'only a small proportion of funds disbursed by the ARGC and bodies such as the Myer Foundation goes to the humanities . . .' These financial constraints made all the more important the role of the HRC in 'beginning to take on the role of catalyst and nurse to other activities in the humanities throughout Australia.' It was indeed 'in a unique position to help and be helped by other centres, institutes and societies, which are normally more highly specialised and less well funded.' He might have added that they could not, practically speaking, have been more exiguously staffed.

This role was made possible by the fact that the HRC had been 'working on a pretty broad front,' as a consequence 'not of irresolution but of deliberate policy.' But the legitimate question had to be asked 'what the Australian National University is actually getting out of the HRC, apart from the general stimulus of visitors and conferences.' These themselves were of great importance: the deteriorating financial situation meant that there was 'altogether less mobility in the universities,' with a real risk of 'consequent intellectual stagnation or ossification. In such a situation, a centre like the HRC, with its strong emphasis on a visiting fellowship scheme, becomes more important than ever. It is a potential source of new energy and new ideas.' But there were more practical things that might be done: he was concerned that 'the HRC and its visitors have not been as closely integrated with the actual work of the University as they might have been; they have existed rather as a pleasant overlay to it.' He himself had continued to 'do some undergraduate teaching and supervision of postgraduate students in the Department of English; and Visiting Fellows often give occasional lectures and classes at undergraduate and graduate levels for Departments within the faculty of Arts.' The HRC could not enrol undergraduate students, because it simply 'did not have the resources to cope with them.' However, a 'decision to enrol postgraduate students in the HRC would bring us into line with the other main research areas of the ANU.' The Faculty of Arts had recently established undergraduate and postgraduate courses in Modern European studies, with a coursework MA; and Donaldson thought that the HRC 'might usefully play a major part, especially at graduate level, in these courses or in courses like them.' Since many of the Fellows were in fields of European Studies or were from distinguished European Universities this was a logical conclusion. Among other things this would 'allow us at once to build upon and to boost a developing interdisciplinary activity within the University.' Some changes would need to be made: Visiting Fellows would have to be asked to make a contribution to postgraduate teaching and also, 'if they wished, occasionally to undergraduate teaching.' There was 'a further important consequence of these proposals. If we are to entertain the possibility of a close academic relationship of this sort with the Faculty of Arts, it seems logical to think also of a close administrative relationship.' Donaldson admitted that he and other members of the Advisory Committee 'were once apprehensive' of such a relationship; but it 'might now be both workable and desirable'.[17]

All this was naturally welcome to the Committee, particularly Donaldson's proposal that the HRC should become involved in the teaching of Modern European Studies: fears had been expressed that 'the present faculty of Arts course in Modern European studies was weighted towards the Social Sciences,' and it was suggested that 'the Centre might redress the balance towards the humanities, especially literature, music, fine arts . . .' It was also suggested that the Centre 'should have a continuing project to which it would devote a substantial part of its resources'.[18] All of which was most appropriate for the HRC, except that its financial resources were becoming increasingly limited and its human resources literally could not have been more limited. Nevertheless, without question, the HRC was to add immeasurably to the quality of European studies and to the teaching of the humanities generally at ANU. However, it was not until 2002 that the HRC would gain any financial recognition for its substantial teaching contributions to ANU across many disciplines when the Vice-Chancellor, Professor Ian Chubb, allowed the Centre (after nearly thirty years of operation) finally to enrol its own graduate students and to receive funding for them.

Donaldson took a year's study leave from 11 August 1977 to 4 August 1978, to visit the United Kingdom, Poland and Vienna and to complete a book on Lucretia and the establishment of the Roman Republic. The indefatigable Professor Ralph Elliott agreed to serve as Acting Director, as well continuing to sit on the Advisory and Steering Committees. The year 1977 had been most satisfactory for the Centre all round. Dr J.C. (Chris) Eade had joined the team in March as Research Fellow, with special responsibility for bibliography and editorial work. He inevitably acquired other responsibilities as well, contacting future Visiting Fellows in order that their research requirements might be met as far as was practicable by the time they arrived, assisting in the planning of the proposed Directory of Research in the Humanities within Australia and New Zealand and helping to run the fifth David Nichol Smith seminar. It would always be a case of all hands to the pumps at the HRC, but at least there was another pair of hands to pump with.

This was also the first year when Donaldson's new strategy was put into effect of adopting an annual theme for the activities of the Centre, naturally to be announced well in advance for the benefit of prospective applicants. It was a decision at once critical, defining and long-pondered. It had originally been contemplated that 'the HRC, once established, would mark out for itself a particular patch of academic territory, a special field of research,' Donaldson recalled, 'within which it would seek to achieve international distinction. The most frequently canvassed options were Byzantine studies; Renaissance studies; and eighteenth-century studies; but these were just examples. It might have been anything. The library would reflect this concentration, and be a specialized collection within a clearly defined field.' It was to be left to the first Director to make the determining choice. Donaldson however had felt when first appointed that such a decision was not appropriate to his initial 'caretaker' role. He was also by no means sure that this was the most rewarding way for the HRC to develop. He felt in particular that specialization might often be necessary in a country like the United States 'because there were already such a lot of competing humanities research centers that each had to develop an individual character, while here there were no centers of this kind at all; we hadn't even started. If the HRC were to become (let's say) a Byzantine Centre it might well achieve international distinction within that comparatively narrow brief, but it wouldn't fulfil the hopes and expectations that people held for it, and might in time become an academic backwater.'

Donaldson had been relieved to discover during his visit to the United States in 1977 that not all the humanities research centers there had in fact followed the pattern of specialisation. Some had instead 'developed a system of changing specialisms, by nominating a different theme for each year. Director of the Humanities Research Center at Wesleyan University Professor Hayden White proposed to Donaldson that such a strategy would, *inter alia*, respond to the besetting problem that 'academics were wholly unreliable people, who when applying for a fellowship would swear that they were working on a topic related to the theme, but would have dropped that idea and moved on to something else by the time they arrived at the Centre; but that I shouldn't worry about that. Whatever the Fellows were actually working on when they came, the theme provided a sense of community, a central conversational topic to which they'd pledged themselves, and in which they could all engage.'

And so it proved: conversational engagement and a sense of community would always be the essential features of the HRC and the ones recalled most fondly in the testimonies of past Fellows. There was also the great advantage of adaptability in a time of exploding innovation in Australian intellectual circles. It enabled the HRC 'to play an innovative role, rather than entrenching itself in a traditional scholarly corner.' The Centre would be greeting the future from the very outset. And the future could never have looked quite so unpredictable, nor the pace of change quite so disconcerting. Flexibility had never been quite so manifestly the key to relevance.

The theme chosen to inaugurate the new approach was that of translation, which, Donaldson explained, 'involves problems of central interest to literary criticism, linguistics and to certain areas of the social sciences,' and was therefore eminently suited to both the literary emphasis and the broad outreach of the Centre. Three conferences on the theme were organised by J.D. Frodsham, Foundation Professor of English and Comparative Literature at the School of Human Communication, Murdoch University, and were hailed as the first occasion in Australia when literary translation had been considered in such depth. There were 40 papers presented; the ANU Arts Centre performed for the first time in English the play *Amputation* by Norway's foremost contemporary playwright Jens Bjørneboe with a translation by ANU scholar Solrun Hoaas; and there were readings of poetry in translation and an opera workshop of Benjamin Britten's *Albert Herring*. There was also a non-thematic conference on Mannerism convened by Professor of Musicology at Adelaide Andrew McCredie, which drew 40 participants; and five seminars were 'convened and planned by members of other Australian universities, in keeping with the Centre's claim to hold a national status in addition to its special responsibilities to The Australian National University.' Indeed, it could be said that it was now 'acknowledged as a strong influence in humanities studies throughout Australia' and was 'achieving recognition overseas,' as Donaldson reported happily.[19]

Comments of the latest intake of Visiting Fellows were at least as laudatory as those of their predecessors. John Shearman, the renowned Deputy Director of the Courtauld Institute, wrote to Donaldson

> to thank you most sincerely for the invitation and warmth of your hospitality but also to congratulate you on the success of the enterprise. I dare say that the idea of an interdisciplinary conference on Mannerism raised a few eyebrows in Australia – it certainly did here – but the intellectual adventure was fully justified by the real stimulation that was produced . . . this was something different and much more productive . . . Such events at the H.R.C. must contribute something unique to scholarship in Australia and I am perfectly certain . . . that their effects percolate through the whole academic system, lifting the level of research and debate. I forgot to enquire who invented the H.R.C.; it would be nice if all academic engineering was as rational . . . All predictions of Australian hospitality were confirmed at every part of my journey, but no-one had told me of the excellence of Australian staff-work.[20]

Nor had the Visiting Fellows been merely enjoying themselves: they had delivered in all some 50 lectures in the course of the year, and the fact was that the Centre was creating an unmistakable impact as well as an impression of intense and efficient scholarly enterprise. Professor McCredie told Anthony Low that he felt

> impelled to . . . congratulate the Australian National

University on their creation of a Humanities Research Centre, now able to handle a rapid succession of important scholarly events with such apparently effortless expertise, and authoritative yet sensitive professionalism. For Australian studies in the humanities, the Centre is clearly destined to assume the function as the catalyst of advanced interdisciplinary studies, frequently providing academic leadership where it is most urgently needed, and generating new directions and perspectives in humanist scholarship. But apart from regenerating the humanities throughout Australasia, the Centre will project Australian scholarship abroad in a fashion almost unparalleled anywhere. The achievement of the Centre is already such that it deserves special consideration in the future planning of Australian universities. I sincerely trust both public and private instrumentalities will be made to recognize the importance of the Centre to the development of the humanities in Australia.[21]

It is prima facie sound policy to bring such considerations to the notice of the person at the top. However, the danger with such plaudits was that they could be taken to imply that the HRC was doing such a splendid job with the resources available to it already that there was no need to give it any more. The imperative necessity to relieve the pressure on personnel was made more urgent when Horan resigned in March 1978, to live happily in the Cotswolds and enjoy once again the social life of Oxford, as he had enjoyed most happily that of Canberra. He had been a most congenial presence at the HRC, especially in what had become the most significant role of making Visiting Fellows feel welcome. It would indeed hardly be possible to replace Horan's combination of style, scholarship, administrative flair and warm sociability. 'He loved the milieu in the HRC,' Donaldson recalled; 'and enjoyed meeting the visitors, and attending seminars . . . He had a large house off Melbourne Ave with a big garden and swimming pool,' something of a rarity in Canberra, 'and gave some wonderful parties.'[22]

The HRC Steering Committee 're-affirmed the importance of the post of Deputy Director to the Centre's proper functioning and its participation in planning and teaching European Studies in collaboration with the Faculty of Arts,'[23] which in effect meant asking the one person to do two jobs, which could only be a serious deterrent to anyone who might otherwise have been attracted by the prospect

Robert Horan, Mary Theo and Julie Barton in the HRC Reading Room, 1970s.

of doing either. To assist the Director prior to the appointment of a Deputy, James Grieve was seconded from the Department of Romance Languages as Research Secretary, with his time to be divided equally between research and administration, as indeed was Donaldson's time supposed to be. During his time undertaking administrative duties at the HRC he worked also on his own research and translations of Proust as well as continuing to teach in French studies in the Faculty. Eade, who had been appointed as Research Fellow in March 1977, continued his historical researches in astronomy and astrology as well as his bibliographical work editing an Early Imprint series and editing Centre publications. But the division was becoming ever more unequal as academics found themselves lumbered more and more with the minutiae of management. It appeared that the Deputy Director's time would have to be divided too.

Some progress at least seemed to have been made on the question of incorporating the Centre within the ANU administrative structure: the University Council decided on 14 July 1978 that the HRC should 'be associated with the School of General studies for resources allocation purposes and affiliated with the Faculty of Arts,' which was the kind of relaxed arrangement that Donaldson preferred as least imposing on the independence of the Centre, even though it offered the least opportunity for any kind of expansion.[24] The Council also resolved that steps should be taken at last to fill the post of Deputy Director, which had for practical purposes never been filled. The post was to be advertised at professorial level, consideration being given to applicants with a special interest in Modern European studies. It was 'likely that the successful applicant will work closely with colleagues in the School of General studies,' which was consistent with the decision regarding the affiliation of the Centre.[25] Donaldson advised the Steering Committee, now chaired by Ralph Elliott on Donaldson's enthusiastic recommendation, that the position of Deputy should be 'seen primarily as a research chair,' which would mean that the appointee would be expected to spend most of his or her time doing research. The appointee would also of course 'be required to assist the Director . . . in the day-to-day running and long-term planning of the Centre, and to deputise for him from time to time,' which is just what a deputy would expect to have to do. 'Day-to-day tasks in the Centre,' Donaldson explained,

> include the organization of conferences, seminars, talks, exhibitions, readings, and other activities, and supervision of the welfare of Visiting Fellows and other short-term visitors to the Centre, and of the centre's secretarial and administrative staff. Long-term planning is done in conjunction with the HRC's Advisory and Steering Committees, of which the Deputy Director (like the Director) is *ex officio* a member . . . Both the Director and Deputy Director are also *ex officio* members of the Faculty of Arts.

In addition to all this the lucky incumbent would also be a full-time Professor of Modern European Studies, 'required to assume over-all responsibility for postgraduate and undergraduate programmes in Modern European Studies run in conjunction with the Faculty of Arts'.[26]

The implications of Donaldson's report were clear: it was being proposed that the present pressure on the Director should be relieved by appointing someone who would in their turn be subjected to the unreasonable pressure of having to do at least two full-time jobs. This factor would be sufficient to discourage anybody who was capable of doing either properly. Nor was the University prepared even to give assurance that there would be adequate administrative support available, as it had been confident enough to do when advertising the post of Director seven years before: Donaldson reminded Low that no separate budgetary provision was being made for the present position, just as none had been made when Grahame Johnston had been appointed, so it would hardly be possible to appoint additional secretarial staff. There was however no doubt of the necessity for the HRC 'to begin to consolidate and for the Director to have a senior colleague,' even though the Centre had been 'overtaken by financial economies at a crucial stage of its early growth'.[27] They would have to keep house somehow, as Abraham Lincoln observed of the Union, just before the Civil War began.

It was not surprising that the advertisement should have had the deterrent effect that Donaldson anticipated: more than 20 applications were received for the position, but only two made the short list, and 'doubts were raised as to whether either candidate was perfectly suited to handle the two main areas of the job.' Donaldson asked the obvious question: 'are the two halves of the job really compatible? Are we not asking too much of a single person, to look after the Modern European Studies (and so some teaching in these courses) and at the same time give guidance to the HRC? There will,' he continued, reiterating the obvious, 'be frequent, and occasionally long, periods when the Deputy Director will have to stand in for the Director. In addition,' he continued, again reminding the Committee of a fundamental consideration which all concerned would always need reminding of, 'this is thought of as essentially a research position. Some of the applicants expressed the view that the job already looked as heavy as (if not heavier than) a normal teaching professorship.' No applicant who had actually read the advertisement could indeed have possibly thought otherwise. Donaldson had accordingly proposed to the Electoral Committee

> that we think of re-advertising the Deputy Directorship in different terms, dropping the Modern European studies component, and not specifying any particular field of interest. The position would be that of Deputy Director and Professor in the Humanities Research Centre. We should simply try to get the best available person: classicists, mediaevalists, musicologists, and others who may have been discouraged from applying last time around could now put in if they wished.

He would however still like 'to explore ways in which the centre might contribute in a positive and continuing way to the Modern European Studies programme . . . We may (for example) be able to plan some of our conferences and choose some of our visitors with Modern European studies needs in mind . . . On this whole question,' he concluded typically, 'it is important to think constructively'.[28] That was the strategy adopted with considerable success in terms of ANU's developing European studies programmes and the HRC's contributions to European studies were acknowledged years later when ANU made a successful bid to the European Union for funding for a National Europe Centre. That new Centre began as an affiliate of the HRC which had done so much to make the University a focus for European scholarship.

Donaldson's style of negotiation was always that of US Secretary of State George C. Marshall, who implored his officials 'Don't *fight* the problem, gentlemen: *solve* it!' He had in fact already been doing some constructive thinking on ways in which the Centre might be seen to contribute more effectively to the University at large: he had reminded the Advisory Committee back in October 1978 that the original planning committee of the HRC had agreed early in 1970 that 'the new Centre's theme should be broadly defined as "The Expansion of European Intellectual and Cultural Traditions."' The Centre had continued to declare since its establishment that its general concern was with 'European thought and culture and their influence overseas,' which meant much the same thing. 'So far, however,' he considered,

> this formula has been very loosely interpreted and applied, and it must be asked whether the spirit of that 1970 resolution has really been met. Many of the projects of Visiting Fellows and many of the Centre's conferences have in fact been concerned with topics that may be described not unfairly as 'Eurocentric'.

They certainly might be so described, and it might have seemed that it had been the intention of Richard Johnson, Partridge, Spate and the other founders of the Centre that that was just what the HRC should be doing. However, Donaldson had been impressed while in the United States by reports of a conference on the impact on the Old World of the discovery of the New. The application of such an approach to Australia would achieve a distinct shift from the original Eurocentric conception of the Centre; it would declare unambiguously what the role of the HRC actually was; and it would undoubtedly be more appropriate to Australian realities, geographic, economic and increasingly social. In any case, Donaldson argued, the fact was that only a handful of Visiting Fellows 'have been looking at problems relating to the transmission and transformation of European ideas overseas . . . It would seem that the time has come for the Centre either to abandon its declared theme or to make a more determined effort to work within it.' He accordingly recommended that the Centre 'take its general brief more seriously, devoting a year quite specifically to an Australian/European theme . . . the various ways in which the discovery of Australia affected European ways of thinking, perceiving, and creating'.[29]

The theme of 'Australia and the European Imagination' was accordingly approved for 1981. Meanwhile, there had been further gratifying success with the five major conferences organised in 1979 on the theme of 'Drama', particularly with respect to the critical factor of collaboration with other Australian universities and cultural institutions: two of the convenors were from the University of New South Wales, Donaldson reported; there had been theatrical workshops with local and invited actors; and displays had been supplied by the cultural services of some foreign embassies and the Centre presented a postgraduate course at ANU in methods of literary scholarship. A certain public relations problem seemed to have developed with the great metropolitan centres, however: there were reports that some academics in Sydney felt that the distinguished Visiting Fellows from overseas were wasted in the isolation of ANU, and would be much more profitably stationed in Sydney where they would have maximum contact with the maximum number of undergraduates. There was of course the consideration that some at least of the distinguished Visiting Fellows had chosen to come to Canberra precisely in order to have contact with the minimum number of undergraduates, and there were plenty of students around ANU for those who did wish to have contact. The Centre had been encouraging its Fellows to visit other universities around Australia in any case.

This did not mean that there was not a problem or that it should be ignored. One of the most fascinating and endearing features of the Australian scene has always been the scorn of the two great metropolitan centres for their federal capital, matched only by their distaste for each other. But the issue of jealousy and resentment in such quarters was too serious to be overlooked. Donaldson asked Professor Peter Herbst towards the end of 1979 if he would 'care to go to Melbourne to talk to people about the HRC.' Herbst 'went in January, and spent some days in discussion, mainly with members of the German Department at Monash and with [the] History of Ideas Unit.' All the people with whom he spoke were 'interested in the work of the HRC and keen on co-operating with us, but none of them thought that we had succeeded in making adequate contact with our colleagues in the State Universities or that we had made much of an impact on the Australian academic community in general.' It seemed that the *Bulletins* of the HRC 'were not widely read, and that most scholars in the humanities in Australia regarded the HRC as a "Canberra show"', which was of course exactly what the Universities Council had intended the HRC should not be: its operations were to be, on the contrary, 'of a kind to benefit directly teaching and research in the humanities throughout the country.'

Herbst recognised that it was inevitable in the nature of Australian society that many people at the State Universities should be 'envious of Canberra, and resented an alleged advantage of the ANU in being able to invite and monopolise overseas visitors.' Two colleagues to whom Herbst spoke in Melbourne argued that the existence of the HRC, far from being a boon, was a positive disadvantage to them: they said that

> the HRC was regarded with awe by University administrators, as a sort of national pinnacle of research in the humanities, and also as quite rich, and so we in Canberra were expected to facilitate and to fund research projects of which the State University administrators were then happy to wash their hands. In effect the academic administrators said to members of the faculties: "if your work were of sufficient merit and if it satisfied a genuine academic need, the HRC would by now have supported you. They have not supported you: ergo, your work is not worth supporting, so you won't get any help from us".

This was a real problem with the most serious implications for the HRC: nothing could be more ominous for a tiny institution with overworked personnel and facing ongoing financial constraints than to be viewed generally as lavishly funded and resourced. However, Herbst could be counted on to have some practical suggestions to remedy this alarming state of affairs: he proposed that the HRC should 'improve its communications network by finding a suitable person in each university, or at least in each major university city . . . to act as our agent and informant': the Centre should in other words 'compile a list of "Friends of the HRC"'. It should also act as 'a centre for co-ordinating and perhaps facilitating some of the work being done by members of the chapters in the State Universities'; give 'serious thought to the possibility that some of our conferences might be conducted in cities interstate'; and 'have more contact and friendlier relations with the History of Ideas Unit [in RSSS], and . . . plan a common activity.'[30]

Herbst's suggestion was promptly taken up: the Steering Committee resolved that Donaldson, Herbst and Grieve should be 'charged with proposing the names of people to act as "local agents" for the Centre in other Universities'.[31] Sympathetic academics were accordingly invited to explain to those other universities the mutual benefits to be achieved by collaboration with the HRC. The response was enthusiastic: liaison groups were established over the next fifteen years in virtually every institution of higher education in Australia and New Zealand; and Ann Curthoys, later Professor of History in The Faculties, who acted as convener at the University of Technology, Sydney, during the 1980s considered that they were 'extremely valuable then both for the "other universities" and the HRC itself'.

It had been possible to do something about improving communications. Nothing much could be done about the pervasive distrust and resentment of Canberra inside as well as outside academe. It was no doubt most gratifying to be regarded with awe by the great State Universities, but the notion of the HRC as being 'quite rich' must have struck Donaldson as more than a bit rich, especially when the financial situation was about to be made even more challenging by the long-awaited appointment as Deputy Director in May 1981 of Graeme Wilber Clarke, Professor of Classical Studies at the University of Melbourne since 1969, a classical scholar of imposing international distinction and another New Zealander, like his ill-fated predecessor. He at least was not going to be required to teach and manage a full-time course as well as performing the functions of Deputy; but the Committee's response to Herbst's report meant that 'in addition to his other duties, Professor Clarke will act as the central convenor of the HRC's Liaison Groups, and co-ordinate visits by HRC Visiting Fellows to other Australian universities'.[32]

Clarke was 47, a year older than Donaldson, energetic, fit, enthusiastic and supremely equipped for the role. He was indeed one of only three academics during Anthony Low's tenure as Vice-Chancellor to be appointed without advertisement. His arrival must have seemed like a gift from heaven to Donaldson, despite the increased financial stresses it incurred. It was not just that he had at

Professor Graeme Clarke, Deputy Director, 1982–1990; Director 1990–1995; Associate Director, 1995-2000.

last acquired an academic colleague of the very highest distinction, after nine years of doing without one at all. Clarke would in fact prove to be in Donaldson's own words, 'an absolutely wonderful colleague: a superb administrator, calm, quick, wise, unruffable; a top scholar in his field; an excellent friend . . . Graeme's arrival dramatically increased the scope of the Centre, and gave us new strength'.[33] It was praise fully deserved. Clarke would demonstrate during a term at the

HRC even longer than Donaldson's the ideal managerial combination of authority and approachability: his hand was felt in every aspect of the Centre from decisions on future directions to arrangements to have visitors met at the airport or the bell which summoned all present to the collegial morning and afternoon coffee; an unending stream of yellow stickers in his small, exquisite and beautifully legible handwriting kept staff apprised of his decisions; but his door was ever open for genial, courteous and decisive discussion on any aspect of HRC business. It is interesting in this connection that Clarke later referred to Donaldson in almost exactly the same terms of admiration, affection and respect which Donaldson had used to describe Clarke. It was in effect a perfect partnership. That always helps.

Donaldson had meanwhile taken another short break, this time to attend a conference in Germany from 26 June through 13 July 1981. Ralph Elliott had just returned from six months at the National Humanities Center at Research Triangle Park, North Carolina, and duly took over as Acting Director during Donaldson's absence, with James Grieve to 'look after the day to day affairs of the Centre'.[34] Clarke however made his presence felt at once, even though he was not required officially to assume his duties as Deputy until January 1982: he, Donaldson and Grieve met with the Dean of the Faculty of Arts in June 1981 to discuss the 'increasing volume of work in the Centre . . . the spreading of the Centre's reputation and the consequent increase in the number of applicants and in the number of good candidates who are rejected,' not to mention 'the growth of projects like the recently formed liaison groups.' All this meant that the Centre could 'justify the need for one and a half academic-cum-administrative staff, in addition to the Director and Deputy Director.' A likely need for secretarial assistance was also seen 'in view of the centre's acquisition of a word-processor and the volume of work this would generate,' no doubt in consideration of the invariable effect of technology to increase work rather than diminish it.

Donaldson proposed accordingly that an approach should be made to the Deputy Vice-Chancellor,

> arguing the opportunities for change in the Centre, given the changed circumstances, in particular the Government's and the University's concern with "centres of excellence", with a view to having the Centre's salaries budget increased by the small proportion that would be necessary to enable this proposed staffing growth to occur.

Nor did it seem unreasonable that the HRC should be regarded as qualifying as a 'centre of excellence' in anybody's language: the International Association of University Professors of English, for example, referred in its *Bulletin* for summer 1979 to the HRC as 'the main beacon for visitors to Australia', and declared that 'the Centre is beginning to provide for Australia something akin to the attractions and amenities of the great American foundations like the Huntington', which of course enjoyed far more lavish funding. Donaldson anticipated that this might raise the question in the administrative mind, 'Why then should a Centre of this kind, which is apparently functioning successfully on its present resources, be thought deserving of additional funding?' And he had the answers ready. Australian universities were becoming 'increasingly static and immobile places' as academic funding throughout the nation continued to be reduced year by year. They were indeed already 'suffering from a kind of siege mentality.' A major problem for Australian universities generally and for the humanities in particular was 'how to introduce an element of change and growth during the present period of sharp recession.' Here, he proposed, the HRC, 'like its North American counterparts, can play a vital role.'

But it could hardly play such a role under its current budgetary constraints. 'Scarcely had the HRC come into existence,' Donaldson reminded the Committee, 'when the financial climate in Australian universities changed dramatically. As a result, the HRC has been able to reach what ANU's Vice-Chancellor [Anthony Low] has described as "no more than an absolute minimum size". One could not indeed have a more absolute minimum size than one academic, as was still the case at the time and would be the case on not infrequent occasions in the future: the fact was that the only continuing appointment in the Centre had been that of Director, who had been assisted by a Research Secretary and a Research Fellow, both of whose appointments were to terminate that year, as indeed was Donaldson's. A Deputy Director was to assume his multifarious duties in January 1982, 'but no additional funding is available to the Centre for this post'. Hence, that appointment, 'while strengthening the Centre very materially,' would 'nevertheless necessitate a reduction in certain of its present activities.' This applied particularly to the Visiting Fellows program, which was essentially what the HRC had been created for in the first place. And here the HRC was literally the victim of its own success: 'as the Centre's international reputation dramatically grows,' Donaldson concluded, 'so does the annual number of Visiting Fellow applications. But many applicants already had to be turned away, including some of the highest distinction, such as a Fellow of the British Academy and the Immediate Past President of the British Historical Association'.[35]

Donaldson's appeals were given added cogency by the fact that the conference programs for 1980 and 1981 had witnessed a significant advance in what might be described as the catalytic, interdisciplinary and generally interactive roles of the Centre. Five conferences on Romanticism and Revivals had been conceived in 1980 by the ever-resourceful Hans Kuhn, convenors for which had been drawn from the Faculty of Arts, the Canberra College of Advanced Education and RSSS, with the assistance of the National Library of Australia, the Australian Academy of the Humanities and the Australian Historical Association, with contributions to funding for visitors from the British Council, the Faculty of Arts and the Pro Helvetia Association. The six conferences in 1981 on the theme of Australia and the European Imagination had 'brought together sociologists, anthropologists, cartographers, film-makers and geographers together with the philosophers, linguistic and literary scholars, musicologists and historians who are the usual denizens of the HRC'.[36] But perhaps most significant and certainly most satisfying to Donaldson's mind was that 'Rhys Jones's chapter on "Seeing the First Australians" that came out of the HRC meeting perfectly captured the kind of Montaignian perspective that I'd hoped the conference as a whole would achieve (an Aboriginal view of the chaotic nature of white Australian social and cultural behaviour).'[37] There could be no question any more of the HRC's range of activities being constrained by an inappropriately Eurocentric perspective: it was truly 'working on a pretty broad front,' and most certainly as a result of deliberate policy, not of any irresolution.

The Centre could hardly have embraced the humanities more widely or interacted with other organisations and institutions more broadly, given the resources available. The problem was how to make greater resources available while the HRC remained a centre unto itself. Ralph Elliott had been considering some possible options during the months he had spent in what he would later describe as 'the shady groves', 'the blessed sylvan seclusion' and 'idyllic working environment' of the National Humanities Center in North Carolina. He delivered some of the fruits of his reflections on his return in a deeply thoughtful as well as eloquent article on the possible future of the HRC. The establishment of the Centre, he observed, had been

> seen as acknowledgement that the humanities still mattered and that their well being depended upon sound scholarship pursued in congenial surroundings. But the gap between them and the natural and social sciences remained unbridged as long as humanists continued to work in isolation, not from each other, but from their peers in other realms. It was the recognition of this fact,

he continued, 'which prompted what is probably the main difference in policy between the HRC and its American counterpart, the National Humanities Center . . .' This difference was

> summed up in the NHC's aim 'to seek as fellows humanistically inclined scholars in the natural and social sciences and the professions as well as scholars in fields conventionally identified with the humanities . . . Even the architecture of the Center's building, situated in the heart of a North Carolina forest, is designed to foster the combination of private study and participation in wide ranging discussion. There are no outside distractions except walks among the pine trees.

It might have been retorted that ANU was set pretty substantially in bush, if not precisely forest; that there was more than adequate provision for walks among the gum trees; and that few visitors to Canberra were wont to complain about an excess of outside distractions. However, Ralph Elliott's fundamental argument was that ANU attracted 'many scientists, social scientists and other visitors to the research schools', but

> few of them interact with the HRC . . . Perhaps the possibility of regular joint fellowships at the HRC and other ANU research centres should be explored . . . A rare opportunity was missed when the HRC was affiliated with the Faculty of Arts, with which it has obvious affinities, rather than with the Research School of Social Sciences or that of Pacific Studies, which would have fostered the kind of interchange so fruitfully pursued in North Carolina . . . The HRC has not been neglectful in some of its sister disciplines outside the traditional humanities . . . but perhaps its horizon might be widened still further.

And he concluded with the resounding declaration that

> The more the humanities are assailed in contemporary society as irrelevant, anachronistic, and expensive luxuries, the more should humanists be prepared to look beyond their own disciplines and beyond the humanistic disciplines themselves. This is essential if the humanities are to play a continuing, and fruitful role in a society increasingly uncertain of inherited values and seemingly incapable of solving the problems posed thereby . . . The basic aim of both centres is to encourage the writing of good books,

he added as a salutary reminder of the bottom line.

Elliott noted that the NHC could offer three times as many fellowships as the HRC and had had as many fellows in three years as the HRC had had in seven. However, he considered that this was 'purely a function of size and of the American custom of "thinking big."'[38] Elliott's breadth of vision always represented the essence of what the HRC was about. It was a breadth of vision shared by Donaldson and Clarke. But it was not alas the case that it was just a matter of thinking big. It was also a matter of money. And the fact was that there was to be no extra funding for the Centre: indeed, as Grieve sadly informed the Committee the HRC had to expect a cut of five per cent in its budget for 1982 by comparison with the previous year's, which 'represents a substantial reduction in funding'.[39] It seemed as if the Centre was to be denied even the word processor needed to generate more work than its staff could handle: the Business Manager reported to the Bursar on 22 September that 'the special bid of $15 000 to meet the cost of the purchase of a wordprocessing facility for the H.R.C. has been deferred'.[40] But a word processor was in fact forthcoming in October. It was 'second-hand and on hire'.[41]

Notes

1. Donaldson, 'Reconfiguring the Humanities', 2002.
2. Morton W. Bloomfield to Ralph Elliott, 3 Dec. 1978.
3. Report of the Committee of Review of the HRC, ANU, 295/1988 22 Jan. 1988.
4. Horan to DVC, 11 June 1975.
5. Donaldson to E. Helgeby, 11 June 1975.
6. Donaldson, "The future of the Humanities Research Centre: a personal view," 11 Oct. 1975.
7. Sasha Grishin to the authors, 23 July 2003.
8. Letter of appointment to Donaldson, quoted in M.G. Bouquet to Mr Dicker, 'Director of the Humanities Research Centre *Consideration of extension of appointment*,' 25 June 1980.
9. The ANU Board of the Institute of Advanced Studies, Board of the School of General Studies, Joint Committee on Centres and Units, 2525/1976, 8 Sept. 1976.
10. Donaldson to all members of the HRC Advisory Committee: Report of Joint Committee on ANU Centres & Units, 30 Sept. 1976.
11. 14th Meeting of HRC Steering Committee, 25 Oct. 1976.
12. A.D. Hope, HRC *Bulletin*, No. 6, Mar. 1977.
13. Donaldson to all members of HRC Advisory Committee: Post of Deputy Director and Bibliographer, 12 Apr. 1977.
14. 13th Meeting, HRC Advisory Committee, 12 Apr. 1977.
15. Annual Report to Parliament 1975, 100/1975, 13 Feb. 1976.
16. Donaldson to Anthony Low, 4 July 1977; Leon Edel to Donaldson, 9 Nov. 1976.
17. Donaldson, 'The HRC: the next phase', discussion paper for the HRC Advisory Committee Meeting, 8 Aug. 1977.
18. Horan to Steering Committee, 16 Aug. 1977.
19. HRC *Annual Report 1977*, 46/1978.
20. John Shearman to Donaldson, 22 June 1977.
21. Andrew D. McCredie to Low, 29 June 1977.
22. Donaldson to authors, 15 June 2002.

23 22nd Meeting of Steering Committee, 11 Apr. 1978.
24 Extract from minutes of meeting of Council, 14 July 1978.
25 HRC *Bulletin*, No. 13, Sept. 1978.
26 Donaldson to Steering Committee, 15 Sept. 1978.
27 Donaldson to Low, 11 Dec. 1979.
28 Donaldson to members of the HRC Steering Committee, 11 Dec. 1979.
29 Donaldson, discussion paper for Advisory Committee, 18 Oct. 1978.
30 Peter Herbst to Donaldson, 14 Apr. 1980.
31 33rd Meeting of Steering Committee, 3 June 1980.
32 HRC *Bulletin*, No. 27, Mar. 1982.
33 Donaldson to authors, 15 June 2002.
34 M. E. Bouquet to Ralph Elliott, 3 June 1981.
35 Grieve to all members of the Steering Committee, Report on discussion between the Director, the Deputy Director elect, the Dean and the Research Secretary, 23 June 1981.
36 HRC *Annual Report, 1981*, 48/1982.
37 Donaldson to the authors, 14 June 2003.
38 Elliott, 'HRC: its aims and activities deserve close study', *ANU Reporter*, 14 Aug. 1981, p. 3.
39 Grieve to Advisory Committee, 28 Oct. 1981.
40 Business Manager to Bursar, 22 Sept. 1981.
41 41st Meeting Steering Committee, 9 Oct. 1981.

4 A Unique Institution in the World of the Humanities (1981–1991)

Words may be cheap, but they can make good reading: the litany of praise lavished on the HRC by former Visiting Fellows made a striking contrast with the decidedly unlavish funding bestowed on it by the University. Charles Fantazzi, Professor of Classical and Modern Languages at the University of Windsor, Ontario, testified that the HRC was, *inter alia*, 'a unique institution in the world of humanities.' It was 'comforting to know that such strongholds of humanistic and humane learning exist and exert their influence in a tangible way.' The Director and Deputy Director 'set the tone of excellence and industry, tempered with affability, that characterises the Centre,' which provided 'the ideal atmosphere for learning and the sharing of knowledge.' This testimonial was supported by another foreign academic who declared that no words were 'adequate to describe the sensitivity, tolerance, kindness and consideration' with which Donaldson and Clarke treated their Visiting Fellows. Professor J. Goldberg from the Department of English, Temple University 'found working conditions at the HRC ideal.' Professor Stephen Orgel, Sir William Osler Professor of English Literature at Johns Hopkins, found them 'superlative.' His only regret was 'the puzzling lack of connection between the HRC and the teaching departments,' which would indeed be noted by Donaldson as a continuing puzzling aspect. Professor Charles W. Fornara of the Department of Classics at Brown University recalled the Centre as 'a place of civility and grace.' His words were echoed by Dr Thomas Wheaton Bestor of the Department of Philosophy at Massey University, New Zealand, who felt similarly that the most beneficial effect of the Centre 'was not any "on paper" accomplishment... It was more in the nature of being reassured that there *do* exist places in the world where humanities research is taken for granted as an acceptable form of human endeavour and, indeed, where it is conducted in the most civilized and gracious atmosphere. I felt isolated and embittered upon arrival; I leave encouraged and enlivened.' Professor F.C. Inglis of the School of Education at the University of Bristol wrote that

> the breadth of reference and the catholicity of definition with which the pursuit of humanities is sustained here, have together been the occasion of the most exhilarating three months of my life... I hope it will not seem invidious to identify both the Director and Deputy Director as signally ensuring that in their small corner of the universe Newman's idea of a university is kept splendidly alive.

And Fellow of the National Library of Australia Helen Topliss, recorded that 'my faith in academic pursuits has been renewed... The Centre is a place of true integrity, wit and intellect... a model of its kind – it ought to become the original form of places for research... such a splendid model of Humanitarian enterprise and discourse.' She even compared it favourably with academic life in Melbourne. And you can't say better than that.

It was the ritual morning and afternoon coffee that evoked some of the most poignant recollections for past Visiting Fellows. Professor Guy Fitch Lytle of the Department of History at the University of Texas at Austin, thought that his time as a Visiting Fellow was

> probably among the most productive three months of my life thus far – and among the most pleasant... I have never worked with nicer people... When you add to that the quality and congeniality of the Visiting Fellows, it is hard to restrain the utopian adjectives and metaphors ... I could go on for pages, but it is 10.30 and I think I will go have a cup of coffee alone and hear echoes of Pearl [Moyseyenko]'s bell and all of your voices.

Dr Peter J. Hempenstall of the Department of History at the University of Canterbury, New Zealand, had

> for the HRC and its system of Fellowships... only the warmest feelings, tinged with envy... the ritual morning and afternoon tea [and coffee] sessions (which I

found actually did lead on to productive things) so caught my imagination that I have carried a mission home to introduce it among my colleagues here.

Director of the Institute of Advanced Study in the Humanities at Edinburgh Professor Peter Jones judged that the facilities in the HRC were 'ideal in almost all respects', and that 'the daily coffee and tea assemblies' were 'central to the happy intellectual atmosphere'. Donaldson recorded that Jones' visit

> helped to cement good links between HRC and IASH . . . There was an IASH Fellowship, tenable each year at Edinburgh, fully funded from Australian sources, the candidate selected by a committee organised through the HRC . . . I wondered if we couldn't do a similar thing for the HRC itself in Canberra . . .[1]

Dr Cicely Howell from York University, reported that an 'ex-fellow once told me that in retrospect he saw the HRC as an "oasis of civilization" and I tend to agree . . . the regular coffee and tea breaks provided just the right amount of human interaction'. And Professor K.S. Guthke of Harvard found that: 'My thinking about my project benefited greatly from the informal (and addictive) conversations over tea and coffee (from now on there will be gaps or blanks in my life at 10.30 a.m. and 3.30 p.m.' It is worth noting that the nostalgia was quite literally for the very economical pleasures of coffee, company and especially conversation. Anything more extensive or expensive would only be provided privately by the Director and Deputy Director: lavish entertainment was not an item in the budget of the HRC. Such a tradition as the coffee and tea and associated opportunities for discussion which evoked such nostalgia among people of such professional eminence was not to be set aside lightly. It was, for a period during the late nineties, after the departure of Donaldson and Clarke. But it came back with the beginning of the new century under Graeme Clarke's successor as Deputy, augmented by Friday afternoon get-togethers for drinks after seminars, with significant others specifically invited, in line with a welcome and enlightened suggestion by an earlier visitor.

Visiting Fellow in the 1980s John Docker evokes the vision of the 'urbane cosmopolitan culture of the European Enlightenment' as described in Jonathan Israel's *Radical Enlightenment and the Making of Modernity 1650-1750* to convey a sense of the HRC scene in the first and second decades of the Centre's existence. There was during the century of the Enlightenment, according to Israel, '"freedom of conversation between men and women, in a kind of new Epicureanism. In such a libertarian culture and Enlightenment public sphere ... what mattered was not membership of a particular family or noble group, but a new kind of meritocracy of mind and of attitude, given to philosophical knowledge, irreverent writing and refined pleasure seeking." Well, I'm not sure about Epicureanism as a specific presence in the HRC "culture"', Docker observed, 'or refined pleasure-seeking, but at morning and afternoon break times there was excellent coffee served in an urn which added conversational fluency as visitors and scholars sat about the central tables; and after the weekly seminar, wine and cheese would be wheeled in to assist in mulling over issues raised in the seminar that had just ended.' Perhaps the most significant contribution of all this civility and grace was that it constituted, in Docker's opinion,

> a sophisticated and gently irreverent intervention into an ANU that, as I recall from the 1970s and 80s was formidably gerontocratic and perhaps even openly misogynistic ... In the archipelago that is ANU, the HRC as it shaped and refined its practices and tone was an island of Humanities cosmopolitanism and interdisciplinarity.

This was all the more important 'because of the distinction then and still at ANU between Humanities and the Social Sciences, so that one was always made to feel that the Research School of Social Sciences ... could be clearly distinguished from Humanities ...'[2]

Canberra itself evoked more modified rapture. Professor Alexander P.D. Mourelatos of the University of Texas at Austin declared that in 'a world in which cities (including the city of my birth, Athens) have become ugly and oppressive, Canberra is a jewel of beauty and humaneness.' On the other hand, a visitor from the metropolitan sophistication of Waikiki saw 'nothing in Canberra to recommend it,' apart from the HRC. 'This city is a major disadvantage for the HRC', he concluded. Not however a sufficiently major disadvantage to deter overseas academics from pursuing Visiting Fellowships at a rate beyond the capacity of the HRC to sustain. Highly distinguished among such Fellows in 1982 was Richard Rorty, Professor of Humanities at the University of Virginia, acclaimed as one of the most influential philosophers of the late twentieth century. Professor Rorty's primary academic mission was to continue his work on the intriguing if somewhat equivocal philosopher Martin Heidegger. It

Rainy, Professor Richard Rorty's orphaned wombat, 1982.

Professor Richard Rorty at the HRC, 1982.

was nonetheless, he reported, 'an idyllic period for me and my family . . . the nicest sabbatical I've ever had'. And it was Rorty's unreserved and authoritative endorsement of the HRC that might well have carried the most weight at the time of its most critical review thirteen years later. He also provided a major contribution to the mythology of the Centre when he and his wife adopted or were adopted by a forlorn young wombat, which they found in its dead mother's pouch and named Rainy. Rorty and Rainy became inseparable during the great philosopher's visit, giving rise to genial academic speculation as to whether the philosopher perceived the wombat as a very small philosopher, or the wombat perceived the philosopher as a very large wombat. Rorty indeed consented to make return visits to the Centre in 1992 and again in 1999 only after he had been assured that he would be able to renew his association with Rainy.

One of the most interesting HRC policies was the 'Open Door', reiterated in HRC *Bulletins* from the mid-seventies until the mid-nineties:

> The HRC does not wish to become merely a small and closed society of privileged scholars. Many of its Visiting Fellows will quite properly be looking for one thing only from the Centre: a period of uninterrupted time which allows them to get on with their own work in peace.

> This they will be able to find. Nevertheless the Centre hopes that its activities will have some impact upon the Australian National University as a whole, and upon Australian universities generally, and that they may also be of interest to a wider public. Members of the University and the general public are welcome to attend HRC conferences, lectures, readings, and work-in-progress seminars. Information about such activities is available from the HRC Secretary.[3]

(and later from an electronic mailing list and the web). The HRC maintains its open door and attendees at HRC events range from undergraduate students to retired members of the public.

It was naturally the conferences which achieved the most *éclat* and demonstrated most vividly the degree to which the HRC was fulfilling its mandate as a catalyst for the study of the humanities, both nationally and internationally. The HRC style of conferences was set very early and consisted of an emphasis on new and critical research presented in an atmosphere of collegial debate and within a programme which was constructed to allow plenty of time for discussion and which eschewed parallel sessions then becoming the bane of academic life. Conference participants were carefully selected and conference conveners were expected to apply rigorous selection and develop an overall intellectual conception which broke new ground. Fellows participated in the conferences, but the fact that they stayed at the Centre before and after meant that intellectual exchange and 'conversations' began before and continued well after the conferences ended. The extent of scholarly collaborations begun at the Centre cannot be estimated, but without question many major research projects and books resulted. And many younger Australian academics owed much to the Centre in terms of opportunities provided by the HRC to participate in and even convene conferences and saw their careers benefit substantially from the contacts made in those conferences.

There were three conferences in 1982 on the general theme of 'Insight and Interpretation', two of them convened by the invaluable Peter Herbst, attracting an impressive 175 people, including 'sociologists, anthropologists, textual scholars, political scientists and philosophers, as well as the linguistic and literary scholars' whom the Annual Report that year considered to be 'the mainstay of the HRC'.[4] The spread of the scholars had become considerable: eminent historian Professor Lawrence Stone gave 17 papers while an HRC Visiting Fellow in

1983 in Canberra at ANU and at the Universities of Sydney, NSW, Queensland, Adelaide, La Trobe and New England.

The 1983 series on the theme of the 'Renaissance' had set a benchmark which could not have been dreamt of even in the optimistic days when the Centre was first conceived. In selecting this theme, Donaldson reported, 'the HRC Steering Committee was aware of the existence of several small but flourishing Renaissance groups and societies in Australian universities, and of the particular international distinction of a number of Australian Renaissance scholars.' It had been resolved that the first of the three conferences should take place at the University of Melbourne, the first time that an HRC conference had been held outside Canberra, while a display on the Renaissance garden was held at Monash University, all of which Donaldson considered 'benefited the three Melbourne universities.' The second and third conferences were held in Canberra, convened by Dr William Ramson of the Department of English at ANU and formerly President of the Australian and New Zealand Association for Medieval and Renaissance Studies (and who played a major role in HRC Steering Committees over the years); by Dr Sasha Grishin of the Department of Fine Arts at ANU; and by Mr W. G. Craven of the Department of History in The Faculties. Concerts of appropriate music were held in University House; Visiting Fellows gave special lectures

Dr William Ramson.

at the University of Sydney, the University of Western Australia, the University of Adelaide and the Victoria University of Wellington, New Zealand; 50 papers were given and over 400 participated, including in the words of the *Annual Report* 'economic, social, historical and musical historians as well as the linguistic and literary scholars who are the mainstay of the HRC',[5] as distinct presumably from the other scholars listed among the 'usual denizens' of the Centre in the previous year's report.

But nobody needed to feel left out. In 1983 the Centre hosted sociologist Professor Zygmunt Bauman, in 1989 political scientist Professor Quentin Skinner, in1985 anthropologist Professor Michael Herzfeld, in 1987 anthropologists Professor James Boon and Professor Clifford Geertz, in 1989 anthropologists and ethnographers such as Professor Faye Ginsburg, Professor George Marcus and ethnographic film makers David McDougall as well as Mihály Hoppál from Budapest, the latter an expert on Hungarian ethnographic film, and in future years would host many anthropologists such as Dr Deborah Bird Rose or Professors Margaret Jolly and Howard Morphy. Writers on Indigenous issues like Professor Peter Read and on new media and philosophy like Brian Massumi all had a continuing association with HRC conferences and events. Later years would also see scientists, medical experts and lawyers as HRC Visiting Fellows as the Centre took on even broader interpretations of the humanities and interactions within society. Scholars in older fields of study which were sadly starting to disappear from Australian universities, such as classical languages, Russian, Scandinavian and Slavonic studies and even more sadly by the nineties Modern European languages, continued to come and keep the flame alive in Australia. Scholars were also coming in new fields such as Dr Stephen Bann (1984) from Modern Cultural Studies at Kent working on contemporary landscape theorists or Professor Mary Jacobus from English at Cornell (1985) who while at the Centre completed a book on feminist literary criticism and psychoanalysis and began one on Wordsworth's *Prelude* and De Quincey's *Confessions* and managed in a very busy lecture schedule to lecture at most Australian universities and two in New Zealand. There were independent scholars, artists and writers such as Dr Ursula Hoff, Humphrey McQueen and Robin Wallace-Crabbe. Art scholars like Dr John House, Dr John Gage and Dr Marilyn McCully came as conference visitors in association with new links developed in the 1980s with the National Gallery of Australia and later Asian art historians such as Professor Michael Sullivan, Helen Jessup and

Professor John Hay in association with Asian Studies and film theorist and writer on women's film E. Ann Kaplan, Director of SUNY Stony Brook Humanities Centre, a Visitor in 1989 and 2000 who was doing critical work in feminist film and literary studies and was much in demand from other universities on both occasions.

The fact was that the Centre was welcoming scholars in well-nigh every conceivable field of the humanities, while the scope of its conferences was evidently extending beyond the Eurocentric confines contemplated at its outset. An example was the work of Gayatri Spivak, then Andrew W. Mellon Professor of English at the University of Pittsburgh and still one of the foremost figures in the study of world literature and its cultural consequences. She came to the Centre in 1987 to work on a major manuscript on master discourse and native informant and interacted with the English Department scholars at ANU as well as lecturing at Deakin, Monash, Melbourne and Adelaide and was interviewed on multiculturalism on the ABC. In her report she noted: 'I found my stay at the Centre most enjoyable and, indeed, quite seriously wish I was there now'. Eminent scholars in new fields like Spivak and those in 'subaltern' studies and multiculturalism made a major impact through their lectures and teaching as would Professor Dipesh Chakrabarty in future years.

However, all this record of achievement and all this continuing applause from distinguished visitors might even have added to the financial problems of the HRC by providing support for the argument that the Centre was doing so well with so little of everything that there was no point in giving it anything more. The Centre of Excellence submission was not favoured because ANU was 'uncertain whether the HRC was strictly eligible to apply for additional funding under this scheme, or whether it would be considered, like the ANU Research Schools, as already constituting a centre of excellence'. This would, the Advisory Committee considered, be 'a flattering judgment that might nevertheless work to the Centre's financial disadvantage', because this could result in the Centre's 'being grouped with The Faculties for the purpose of budgetary cuts in 1982, and with the Institute of Advanced Studies for ineligibility under this scheme, thereby losing on both the swings and the roundabouts'. The Committee felt that this would leave the HRC 'in an unfortunate and anomalous position'.[6] That could only be taken as a superlative example of scholarly understatement. And in the meantime there was the persisting problem of just what the position of the HRC was, in terms of its location within the structure of ANU, in other words whether it was '"associated with" or "part of"' the Faculty of Arts, as William Ramson queried.⁷

Donaldson recognised in statements to the HRC Committees that the HRC was entering its tenth year and had not grown very much apart from acquiring a Deputy Director. Visiting Fellows were 'now coming for three to four months on average or for even shorter periods'. The problem was very simply that 'At the time of the Centre's establishment, universities had begun to contract financially, and the Centre had really never reached its full projected growth, now operating with a staff consisting of Director, Deputy Director, Research Officer', and of course as Donaldson recorded graciously in his Annual Report, a supporting secretarial staff now consisting of Miss Mary Theo, Mrs Pearl Moyseyenko and Mrs Jodi Parvey

> which cheerfully accepts periodic overwork and the difficulties inherent in an enterprise such as ours. Under the efficient direction of the Secretary, Miss M. Theo, they are used to serving not only as typists, stenographers and clerical assistants but as tea and coffee-makers, travel agents, errand runners and at times as chauffeurs for a large and changing population of visitors (some

Left to right: Graeme Clarke, Mary Theo, Ian Donaldson, Pearl Moyseyenko, Chris Eade, Jodi Parvey, in the late 1980s.

with dependants) whose demands can be numerous and unforeseeable.[8]

Donaldson would testify later that it was the secretaries who 'really do hold the place together and help make it what it is'; and Graeme Clarke observed that 'the academic staff relied heavily on the goodwill and dedication of the secretarial and administrative staff; without them the Centre simply could not have functioned'. Clarke mentioned in particular how Jodi Parvey

> mastered the growing technicalities of the computing world – as well as getting at the same time a first-class degree part-time in the Faculty of Arts, specialising in Mediaeval Studies and Art History. Her competence proved invaluable in producing our quarterly Bulletins and the series of HRC monographs ... Jodi edited through the entire process from typescript to published form.

Pearl Moyseyenko had initially been assigned as Clarke's secretary when he arrived at the Centre at the beginning of 1982, but 'had other duties especially with organising conferences and looking after the domestic sort of details with the Visiting Fellows' and dealing with 'the entertainment side of the job . . . which helped greatly to oil the HRC machine'. Jennifer Kelly had been 'the first of the HRC secretaries in 1974–75. She was there from the very beginning in Childers Street . . . [and] oversaw the Centre's move to the A D Hope Building'. She was married to a British diplomat and 'had many of the diplomatic skills and graces herself', which would indeed have been a significant asset in her role at the HRC. And Mary Theo had 'a big laugh and immense energy, always at the centre of things',[9] which are significant assets in any role at all.

An additional problem had to be faced immediately: the new political philosophy that university units had to be self-funding meant that by 1985 the Centre could not afford to allow Visiting Fellows more than a stay of six months. Donaldson and Clarke put up three proposals to the Vice-Chancellor to try to relieve the pressure on the Visiting Fellows programme, which was of course the main reason for the existence of the HRC in the first place. They were

> (1) for a topping up of the existing Visiting Fellowship (short-term) vote to enable Visitors to come for slightly longer periods of time; (2) for the creation of Research Fellowships (with support staff) of 3-4 years' duration,

> to enable the Centre to operate on a continuing project
> ... and (3) for the establishment of 2 senior Research
> Fellowships and 2 junior post-doctoral Fellowships with
> tenure of 1-3 years in undesignated fields.[10]

These approaches achieved some marginal relief: Donaldson reported to the Steering Committee 'the good news that the submission to the Vice-Chancellor for additional funds, although not approved in toto, had realised a budget supplementation for 1985 and subsequent years of $50 000 per annum'. This meant that two people 'on the reserve list for 1985 Visiting Fellowships ... had been written to in the hope that they would be able to accept late offers for 1985'.[11]

The Centre would, however, henceforth only be able to provide a stipend to cover basic costs to assist self-funded scholars to survive, rather than financing accommodation. There was no question that the Visiting Fellowships programme had been a spectacular success: the Centre had received '152 Visiting Fellows, 44 Conference Visitors and 27 Summer Fellows' by the end of 1984, as well as holding 45 conferences. Donaldson expected that 'more than 250 visitors would have been through the Centre and 50 conferences would have been held' by the end of 1985. These had been marvellously varied, and sustained at an average strike rate of between three and five annually. There had been six in 1981, on the general theme of 'Australia and the European Imagination', which had seen conferences on *The Roman Family, Transmission in Oral and Written Traditions and Speculative Fiction: the Australian Context*, as well as a workshop in honour of the illustrious Marxist historian of the English Revolution Christopher Hill, who assured Donaldson and Clarke that he found it 'difficult to imagine a more friendly, tolerant and luxuriously appointed environment for working in'. Donaldson reflected that it had been 'quite a catch to bring to Canberra simultaneously the three leading historians of seventeenth-century England, Christopher Hill, Keith Thomas and Lawrence Stone'. And the summer school organised in relation to Hill's visit was the precursor of the summer school for teachers of history organised in 2001 in conjunction with the Emeritus Faculty of ANU and the ACT History Teachers Association.

There were three conferences in 1982: *Understanding Texts, Interpreting and Understanding,* and *Creativity and the Idea of a Culture.* It had always been Donaldson's concern that the new research presented in HRC conferences and seminars should be published and accordingly the HRC began its own monograph series in 1983 and also had a publications agreement with Macmillan begun in the same year which

A Unique Institution in the World of the Humanities (1981–1991) 99

Visiting Fellow office, A.D. Hope Building, 1980s.

The HRC Reading Room, A.D. Hope Building, 1980s.

resulted in several books. (See Appendix F: Publications.) Donaldson reported in 1984 that the joint series of publications with Macmillan had been terminated, but 'it was expected a new contract with OUP would be signed quite soon'. Short runs of fewer than 1000 copies were planned, with the HRC 'to do all copy editing in-house, wordprocess the material, and deliver hard copy or disc to OUP for compositing and printing'. Doing so much with so few inevitably took its toll, here as elsewhere: the Committee 'showed concern that the Centre's wordprocessor operator had contracted RSI'.[12] This would not have been surprising if the wordprocessor in question were still the second-hand one acquired on hire in 1981. However, the RSI outbreak was not in fact 'confined to the HRC but was a pan-ANU epidemic accompanying the introduction of computers in the early eighties', as Donaldson observed, and was 'a major source of industrial and medical anxiety within the University'.[13]

A contract was in fact signed late in 1984 initiating a new publishing series with Oxford University Press. The new series was designed for monographs prepared by members of the Centre and for composite volumes deriving from the HRC conferences. Thus the first volume in the series was to be a book of essays from the 1983 conference on *Patronage, Art and Society in the Renaissance,* and a volume deriving from the 1984 Landscape conferences was being prepared by Helen Topliss and Eade. 'We tried to get a permanent record of HRC achievements by encouraging and facilitating publication', Clarke told the authors.

> We strongly felt that the publication programme chalked up research achievements for the *Centre* apart from those of the individual Visiting Fellows & would constitute one of the academic measures by which the HRC might be judged internationally. A great deal of effort, accordingly, went into this aspect of the life of the HRC & many of the conferences were actually planned around the books that were intended to follow.[14]

It was remarkable that Donaldson and Clarke could find the time and energy to put a great deal of extra effort into anything, given the heroic demands of the record of achievement listed above. It was certainly difficult to imagine how such a level of performance could possibly be sustained without significant support in terms of both finance and personnel. But that depended to a degree on the still unresolved issue of where the HRC best fitted into the University structure in the interests of both ANU and itself. A renewed proposal for the HRC to be affiliated with the Faculty of Arts was not perceived as being likely to be productive of practical benefits to either: the Faculty Working Party on Relations with Other Areas and Institutions had complained in December 1983 that Visitors to the HRC 'often establish closer links with relevant departments in other Australian universities than they do with departments in the ANU Faculty of Arts, perhaps because they have no alternative base of support within other universities'. Furthermore, the HRC budget was

> part of The Faculties budget, but the Director of the HRC is virtually autonomous with respect to its allocation and in responsibility for HRC staff and visitors. This on the one hand insulates the HRC from scrutiny and the need to co-ordinate with the Faculty but also deprives it of direct access to forums such as the Resources Committee.[15]

However, the situation was that the HRC was still being regarded officially by the University as a component of the Faculty of Arts, as indicated by the Registrar's letter to Ralph Elliott on 29 September 1986, expressing pleasure that he had 'accepted the appointment as Visiting Fellow in the Humanities Research Centre, Faculty of Arts, for the 1987 calendar year'.[16]

The University duly resolved to undertake a full review of the HRC in 1987. Donaldson set himself to prepare a full submission, so the University would be in no doubt as to what it was reviewing. His position was enhanced substantially by the fact that the Centre had staged a series of conferences over the past four years that had both been spectacularly successful in terms of numbers participating and had also demonstrated the will and capacity of the Centre to go boldly where no Research School had gone before. They were both blockbusters and forays at the cutting edge of academe. Helen Topliss had convened two conferences on the theme of 'Landscape and the Arts' in 1984 with the support of the National Gallery of Australia, which had drawn nearly 300 participants. There had also been a seminar to discuss the work of the vastly honoured Adams University Professor of American History at Harvard and Pulitzer Prize-winner Bernard Bailyn who was a Visiting Fellow that year. Bailyn gave a public lecture at ANU and lectured at five other Australian universities. He wrote that he had enjoyed his stay at the HRC 'enormously' and had begun an involvement with Australian history and historians he hoped to pursue. There were four conferences on the theme of

Conference on Hellenism. Dr Dick Green; Dr Jean-Paul Descoeudres; Dr Gino Rizzo, The Hon. Neville Wran, Premier of New South Wales; Professor Dale Trendall; and Professor Graeme Clarke, 1985.

'Hellenism' in 1985, *Byzantium and Hellenism* convened by Elizabeth Jeffreys, now Bywater Professor of Byzantine and Modern Greek at Oxford and by Dr Ann Moffat of the Department of Classics at ANU and *Greek Colonists and Native Populations*, convened by Dr Jean-Paul Descoeudres from the University of Sydney, now Professor of Classical Archaeology at Geneva, constituting the first Australian Congress of Classical Archaeology, appropriately honouring Dale Trendall. Then in 1986 came the first of what would be a whole series of 'Great Leaps Forward', when the Centre would provide a forum for the examination of topics of major contemporary interest and concern not so far strictly within the purview of the Research Schools.

Over 600 participants crowded three conferences on Feminism and the Humanities, convened by Dr Susan Sheridan of the Department of the Humanities at Deakin University and Dr Susan Magarey of the Department of Women's Studies at the University of Adelaide. Donaldson described the event moderately as 'a record in the history of the Centre'.[17] It was indeed a resounding *démarche* in terms of scholarly examination of a critical contemporary issue. And it remained a record in the history of the Centre 25 years later in terms of the number of participants it attracted. The first conference, *Feminist Criticism and Cultural Production*, encompassed feminist work on film, theatre, dance, literature and urban architecture, exploring connections and discontinuities in feminist criticism in all these areas of cultural production. It also involved two sessions of readings, one by the Canberra Women Writers Group organised by the National Library, and one by visiting Canadian poets Nicole Brossard, Daphne Marlatt and Betsy Warland and translator/critic Barbara Godard; a film and video programme arranged by Helen Grace; and an exhibition of works by women artists from the National Gallery, 'Picturing the Difference', through images of body and mothering. Well over 300 participants attended these various functions.

This was only the beginning: the second conference, *Feminism and the Humanities: Enrichment, Expansion or Challenge*, examined the impact of feminist thought on the Humanities and the manner in which feminist thought was itself being shaped by its critical function. It was accompanied by another exhibition of Australian women artists, this time held at the National Library. Speakers included Professor Joan Scott from Princeton, Professor Alice Jardine from Harvard, Dr Lenore Davidoff from the University of Essex and Professor Marilyn Butler from Cambridge. The HRC third conference on *Feminist Enquiry as a Transdisciplinary Enterprise* was held at the University of Adelaide and included scholars in anthropology, art history, education, English literature, geography, history, philosophy and sociology. Overseas speakers included Professor Catherine Stimpson from Rutgers, Dr Rosi Braidotti from Paris and Dr Anthea Callen from the University of Warwick. At the same time, 60 people attended a seminar held with the collaboration of the Canadian Government and the University of Sydney in honour of the Canadian scholar Northrop Frye, Professor of English at the University of Toronto, hailed in his *Festschrift* as a father figure to the present generation of literary theorists and esteemed widely himself as the most systematic and brilliant of literary theorists and as the proponent of symbolist literary criticism in English.

Feminism and Northrop Frye were hard acts to follow. But the 1987 activities on the theme of 'Europe and the Orient' were also highly successful in terms of popularity as well as brilliantly successful in illuminating new areas of scholarship by endeavouring to reverse the conventional Eurocentric and Orientalist view of Asia. The timing was singularly opportune: postwar Japanese economic triumphalism was at its height, with the Ministry of International Trade and Industry

(MITI) more or less seriously floating projects for constructing a second Panama Canal, cutting a new one across the Kra Isthmus, damming the Congo, greening the Sahara, Sahel and Arabian deserts and colonising outer space; the Australian economy was lurching into the recession we had to have, with Australian trade representatives plaintively asking their Japanese counterparts for economic advice, which a Queensland official suggested was in that context like a lamb asking a lion if it knew a good use for mint sauce; and Japanese Ministers in Canberra had proposed in January establishing in Australia a Japanese enclave in the form of a 'Multi-Function Polis', a 'city of the 21st century'.[18] It never happened, of course, any more than any of the other grandiose visions of MITI; its most aggressive exponents went bankrupt or became invisible shortly after; and it was Japan that was to enter a prolonged economic twilight. But it was without question a most appropriate time for Australians to essay the salutary experiment of trying to view the world outside through Asian eyes, or at least trying to appreciate what Asians saw through their own eyes.

The two main conferences convened jointly by Dr Tony Milner of the Department of History at ANU, later Professor and Dean of

Cover of HRC monograph *Europe and the Orient*.

the Faculty of Asian Studies and by Dr Andrew Gerstle of the Japan Centre at ANU, drew over 400 registrations. It had been intended that Edward Said would be a guest but alas at the last minute he was prevented from travelling, due to the illness of his mother. However, there were many eminent participants in many disciplines including Professors Clifford Geertz from Princeton, John Hay from New York University and Michael Sullivan from Oxford. The first, on *Europe and the Exotic*, brought together Europeanists and Asianists from various disciplines, engaging with the central theme of Asian influence on European artists in the late nineteenth and early twentieth centuries and the contrasting ways in which the exotic was perceived and depicted by artists and scholars. The second conference, *The Occident and the Orient*, continued the debates initiated in the previous conference, shifting the focus from European artists to contemporary scholars of Asia. An extensive exhibition 'Europe and the Orient' was organised by the National Library; the National Gallery hosted exhibitions of Chinese woodcuts of the 1930s and 1940s, Indonesian textiles and Buddhist sculpture; the Department of Foreign Affairs and Trade sponsored a concert of Indonesian music at the National Gallery Theatre; the Japanese Consulate in Melbourne loaned a small collection of Japanese woodblock prints; the School of Music arranged a concert of Asian influenced music; the Altenburg Gallery at Braidwood presented an exhibition of Japanese-influenced Australian pottery; there was an exhibition of Asian films at the University Library (R.G. Menzies Building); the Faculty of Asian Studies arranged another exhibition on E. Kaempfer, a seventeenth century German physician who wrote extensively of his experiences in Thailand and Japan; the Nolan Gallery at Lanyon Homestead arranged a special viewing of Nolan's 'Chinese' paintings; and the Japanese Embassy sponsored a traditional bamboo shakuhachi flute recital by Mr Riley Lee. Milner still speaks warmly of the impact of this series of interdisciplinary events on Asian Studies and scholars at ANU. There were also two non-thematic conferences, to add something more to this wonderful year, so to speak: one on the *History of Books*, and another on *Literary Journals;* and a Seminar in October convened for the HRC by Director of RSSS Professor Paul Bourke in honour of the very highly distinguished Sterling Professor Emeritus of History at Yale Edmund S. Morgan, the historian of popular sovereignty in England and America in the seventeenth and eighteenth centuries, who declared that his three months at the Centre had 'been among the most memorable and rewarding of a lifetime. Never before have

I been subjected to such a variety of stimulating experiences, while at the same time being made to feel completely at home'.

There was no doubt that the year's activities of the HRC had 'reached far outside the ANU campus' as Milner and Gerstle observed with moderation.[19] Nor was there any doubt that the Centre was functioning admirably as a clearing house of information about current work and conferences in the Humanities in Australasia, as Donaldson noted in the *Annual Report* for 1987. Donaldson could thus afford to continue to approach the Committee of Review with his customary blend of confidence and realism. The basic situation, he reminded the Committee, was that the HRC had been 'originally established in 1973-4 as an unaffiliated Centre within the ANU'. The Director was a member of the Board of the Institute of Advanced Studies and also of the Board of the School of General Studies. This meant that 'proposals relevant to the Centre would be discussed by both Boards or . . . dealt with summarily by their Chairmen'. The arrangement had worked well as a whole, he thought, and 'allowed the Centre . . . to play something of a bridging role between the Institute and the SGS'. However, it had the very serious drawback for the HRC that it 'had no direct representation on the Resources Committee, and was correspondingly disadvantaged when bidding for funds'. In addition, the Joint Committee of the IAS and the SGS had concluded in 1976 that 'the ANU's Centres and Units collectively suffered from, *inter alia,* 'a lack of identification with the main sections of the University', 'a sense of isolation', 'absence of clear lines of communication with the academic board and other bodies', 'lack of understanding and appreciation . . . by the main sections of the University', and so on. Donaldson however thought that the Review Committee had 'failed to perceive or to acknowledge the full extent of co-operation between the Faculty and the HRC'. Nor was any lack of co-operation solely the fault of the HRC in any event: the Centre informed Faculty members and Department heads in detail of visitors coming each year and encouraged them to make contact with these visitors. But on the whole, he noted, the Faculty response was disappointing: it was 'as if many members of the Faculty have not perceived the existence of a resource that is available to them, or are too busy with their own teaching to take advantage of it'.

This, Donaldson noted, was 'a long-standing problem, which has so far defied solution'. It would continue to defy solution because of the very simple factor of endemic and increasing burden of overwork on academic personnel, especially in the teaching departments: the advent of the wordprocessor meant in capitalist logic the departure of typists; the ratio of teaching staff to students continued to deteriorate, so academics found themselves with progressively more to do and less time to do it in; and attendance at seminars tended ever more and more to be viewed as something beyond the call of duty, even when there was time to attend.

Isolation had never really been an issue for the HRC, however. Relations with RSPacS had been 'on the whole fairly casual and *ad hoc*', but there had been some important formal links; the Faculty of Asian Studies had been working closely with the Centre during 1987; 'a good working relationship' had been developed with the Canberra Schools of Art and Music; and 'a close and cordial relationship' had grown with the National Library and the National Gallery. And the range of services performed by the Centre extended far beyond Canberra itself. It was still 'the only institution of its kind in Australia (and indeed in the Southern Hemisphere).' Some more specialised humanities centres had been established at other Australian universities, but many of these had to 'function on minimal (or zero) funding'. It was therefore appropriate that 'several have looked to the HRC . . . for co-operation and support. The HRC's potential sphere of activity and influence', Donaldson continued, 'is in one sense greater than that of, say, the National Humanities Center at North Carolina: for that large and handsomely-funded institution exists in a country that already has about fifty humanities research centres of varying sizes and specialisations'. The HRC had attempted to fulfil this national role in a number of ways: by encouraging Visiting Fellows to travel to other universities in Australia and New Zealand; by organising conferences both in and outside Canberra in conjunction with other institutions; by acting as a clearing-house for information about current research in the humanities in Australia and New Zealand; by establishing links with other humanities centres and national bodies throughout Australia; and by helping to initiate new projects of national importance.

The year also saw the publication of the first in the new monograph series with OUP, *Patronage, Art and Society in Renaissance Italy*, edited by F.W. Kent and Patricia Simons, with J.C. Eade. Eade in addition edited the fourth in the Centre's own series of monographs, *Projecting the Landscape*, derived as Donaldson and Clarke had planned from the 1984 conferences on *Landscape and the Arts*.

The main role of the HRC was however necessarily as a conference centre and a haven for research: the Centre was 'now known internationally, and Visiting Fellowships are keenly competed for by applicants from many parts of the world. Since 1974, it has appointed 230 Visiting Fellows, 65 Conference Visitors, and 51 Summer Fellows, Visiting Scholars and Short-term Visitors'. Of the Visiting Fellows 92 were from the United Kingdom, 53 from Australia, 48 from the United States, 15 from Continental Europe, 12 from Canada, three from New Zealand, two from Hong Kong and one each from Korea, Japan, Israel, China and Ireland. Something might be said about the distribution, and indeed would be said; but there was no denying the global reach of the Centre or the monumental amount of sheer work that it was accomplishing.

Which of course raised the obvious issue of who was doing the work. Donaldson's analysis of how the Centre functioned in practice is a classic prescription for the organisation of all available resources for the achievement of a predetermined goal, such as would have gladdened the hearts of the German General Staff. 'The Director and Deputy Director', he explained,

> are together responsible for the day-to-day running of the Centre . . . The Deputy Director oversees the HRC budget, whose detailed management is in the hands of The Faculties' Business Manager. The Deputy Director also looks after the agenda for the Steering and Advisory Committees; HRC liaison committees, travel by Visitors to other Australian and New Zealand universities. The Director handles most of the correspondence and paper work. All incoming mail addressed to the Director or to the Centre is initially read and registered by the Secretary before being passed to the Director, who shows it to the Deputy Director before replying (or asking the Deputy Director or someone else in the Centre to reply). The Secretary places copies of all outgoing mail on a Day File, which the Director, Deputy Director and Research Officer read at regular intervals. The Secretary, the Director and the Deputy Director are thus all theoretically knowledgeable about everything that is happening in the Centre, and are able to deal quickly with enquiries on any matter. The Research Officer and the Deputy Director's Secretary . . . are also well-informed about the running of the Centre, as is the Word Processor typist . . . Everyone knows their way around the files, and knows how to set about answering a problem . . . The six members of (academic and general staff) work essentially as a team.

This was the touchstone of the success of the HRC, not to say its survival: an organisation as small as that could do what it did only if all members did indeed work as a team. It was also the essence of Donaldson's personal contribution: a team does not exist without a captain, and captaincy was a talent that Donaldson possessed in an exemplary degree.

It is also the essence of a team that its members can play different roles as required. And this versatility was called for particularly in the less academic functions of the HRC. 'The total administrative workload in the Centre is heavy', Donaldson told the Review Committee. 'The Director and Deputy Director spend too much of their time arranging furniture for seminars, carrying typewriters from one room to another, waiting at airports, and driving out to University houses in distant parts of Canberra to await the connection of gas or electricity'. They would also in later years be expected to make the coffee, carry out the dishes and operate the dishwasher. But these activities were not what they were actually paid to do: the Centre was, Donaldson pursued,

> badly in need of another member of administrative staff who might (for example) look after the HRC's budget, liaise with University House and the University Housing Office, meet visitors at the airport, be responsible for equipment and furniture in the Centre, arrange for the hire of buses and vehicles and booking of venues, and so on. The social demands in a centre that is host to thirty or forty visitors each year are also considerable,

especially as the generosity which Donaldson, Horan and Clarke had always shown to visitors had given rise to the very highest expectations in that area on the part of new arrivals. But the fact was that the Director and Deputy Director were there to

> do more than carry typewriters and wait at airports. Their jobs are extremely varied, extremely rewarding, and increasingly onerous. For a centre like the HRC to operate efficiently, it is essential that the Director and Deputy Director are able to maintain their own research, keep abreast of new developments in the humanities, talk in some depth to HRC visitors about the research projects which they have come to Canberra to pursue, stay in touch with former HRC visitors (whose number increases yearly) and with the local and overseas institutions mentioned

earlier in this submission. Ironically, the more successful the HRC becomes, the harder it is to do these things, and the greater the demand upon the Director and Deputy Director to act as assessors, reviewers, advisers, etc. on a variety of matters around the country and internationally.[20]

Just what the Director and Deputy Director had to do beside carry typewriters and wait at airports might be gathered from a record of their academic activities during 1987-89, for example. In brief, Donaldson continued his research on Ben Jonson and his general editorship of the Oxford University Press/HRC monograph series; taught regularly in the Department of English at ANU; lectured for the Department of History and supervised graduate students from the Departments of English and Modern European Languages at ANU; was on the Review Committees for RSPacS and the Canberra School of Arts and of course participated extensively in the HRC's own review in 1987; lectured and gave papers at the Australian Defence Force Academy, the Universities of Melbourne, Adelaide, Macquarie and Oxford, in Lausanne and at the twentieth anniversary symposium of the Australian Academy of Humanities; served on various ANU committees and committees of the Australian Academy of Humanities; chaired the National Committee of the Arthur Boyd Australian Centre in Italy; was on the Advisory Committee for the National Dictionary Centre, the Australian Encyclopaedia Britannica Committee and the University of Edinburgh's Australian National Fellowship Committee; was a Visiting Professor at Cornell and lectured extensively in the US in 1988; was elected in 1987 a Corresponding Fellow of the British Academy and in 1989 to the Executive Committee of the International Association of University Professors of English. Clarke, in 1987-1989 prepared chapters on early Christianity in the Roman World for Volumes X and XII of the Cambridge Ancient History as well as a translation and commentary of the letters and fragments of Dionysius the Great; taught regularly in the Department of Classics and supervised graduate students for that Department; gave seminars in the Centre and in the Department of Prehistory and Anthropology; served on numerous ANU academic committees; chaired the Library committee; was a member of the Council of the Australian Institute of Archaeology in Athens, Treasurer of the Australian Academy of Humanities (serving on several of its subcommittees – publications, finance, language, library); was a Member of the National Committee for the Arthur Boyd Centre in Italy and advisory boards for *Medi-*

terranean Archaeology and *New Documents Illustrating Early Christianity*; co-led archaeological digs in North Syria; provided entries for the Anchor Bible Dictionary; and completed the editing of a volume of papers on *Rediscovering Hellenism* for Cambridge University Press. The Arthur Boyd Centre, incidentally, had originated in consequence of massive efforts by Donaldson and Clarke to get an Australian Centre established in Rome. Professor William Kent of Monash University finally succeeded in establishing a Centre at Prato, outside Florence, of which he became the Director.

There was one feature of this amazing record of achievement which might be regarded as an anomaly rather than a problem. It was certainly much easier to identify it than to suggest anything effective to do about it. Professor David Roberts of the department of German at Monash University told Donaldson that the composition of visitors was 'clearly unsatisfactory, e.g. 92 visitors from the U.K. as compared with 3 from France or 4 from Germany. Oxford and Cambridge alone have provided 23 visitors compared with 15 from continental Europe as a whole. You can hardly be surprised if one concludes that the H.R.C. has confined its interest to Anglo-America e.g. 210 of the 230 visitors', or 91.3%; and 'has made no serious attempt to attract visitors from elsewhere'. Roberts considered that 'positive discrimination is clearly indicated' to break this pattern: the United States and Continental Europe 'should provide about equal percentages of visitors, the U.K. should drop from over 40% to about 10%, Asia and Latin America should be actively targeted etc. In other words, a spread based on regional percentages should be worked towards'.[21]

Easy to say, not so easy to do: affirmative action or positive discrimination is always a delicate operation in academe; it was hardly surprising that European scholars might prefer to pursue European studies in Europe itself; it was not exactly a disadvantage that the HRC should be located in an English-speaking country, since probably more academics spoke English than any other language; and there was not much that could be done in the way of targeting scholars who preferred to work among people who spoke languages they were more familiar with. Twenty-five years later, 90.3% of all visitors to the HRC still came from the United States and the United Kingdom, and the proportion coming from Continental Europe had actually fallen. However, the HRC had attempted to redress the balance by devoting special theme years to Africa, Latin America and the Asia-Pacific, with the result that the number coming from Asia had significantly increased; there were far more New Zealanders; and the total now included eight Latin Americans and seven Africans, the latter admittedly all from Anglophone Africa.

What really mattered was the report of the Committee of Review in 1987. This was as satisfactory as could reasonably be hoped for in an economic and political climate so much more unfavourable to the humanities than Max Crawford or Richard Johnson could have contemplated in the comparatively benign sixties. The Committee described its terms of reference as being '(a) to consider and advise the Vice-Chancellor on future developments of the Humanities Research Centre on the assumption that the present level of resources devoted to the HRC continues'; '(b) to report on the relationship of the Centre to the Faculty of Arts and to the Research School of Social Sciences at the Australian National University'; and '(c) to comment on the international standing of the Centre and its relationships with universities and other organizations within Australia'. The option of increasing the present level of resources was not on the agenda. It was recognised that 'Evaluation of enterprises such as the HRC pose special problems . . . it is difficult to know what should count as success in a venture based substantially on activities such as sponsoring visitors, conferences and seminars'. A count of participants and publications might have seemed as good a way as any to start. In any event, the Committee concluded that in general 'the HRC has been an outstanding success. It has fulfilled its stated goals admirably and, in so doing, has at modest cost brought much credit and visibility to the Australian National University. The testimony before us from distinguished former Visiting Fellows of the HRC was quite striking on one central point viz. That the HRC has become known internationally in a wide range of fields of the humanities for the distinction of its academic staff and for the quality of the intellectual environment it has provided for work at the highest level'. This high standing 'rested substantially on the academic leadership of its Director, Professor Donaldson, very ably assisted since 1982 by Professor Clarke as Deputy Director'. The conference programme of the HRC, the Committee recorded, 'has maintained a high standard of excellence and scholarly relevance . . . providing a national forum for the exploration of major issues within its mandate'; had 'given a notable stimulus to humanities scholarship within Australia'; and had 'in general, established itself as a national resource and the focus of a national network in the humanities'.

There were problems, of course; but these could not be said to be of the HRC's own making, except in the sense that some were the price to be paid for its success. It was evident that the Committee had painstakingly studied Donaldson and Clarke's submission, and virtually accepted it *in toto*. The Committee noted that the total administrative workload in the Centre was substantial, and that the Director and the Deputy Director appeared 'to be obliged to spend an excessive amount of their time in the routine administration of the Centre'. It was considered appropriate to emphasise as part of the success of the Centre, as Donaldson and Clarke had done, 'the long standing contribution of the support staff', the 'bibliographic work of the Research Officer, Dr J.C. Eade', and especially the efforts of the Secretary, Miss Mary Theo. Indeed, her position was 'crucial to the efficient running of the Centre', but was 'particularly demanding', and the Committee believed it 'almost certainly to be under-classified'. The Centre had 'an acute need for another member of administrative staff' who might, for example, in Donaldson's own words, look after the HRC's budget, liaise with University House and the University Housing Office, meet visitors at the airport, be responsible for equipment and furniture at the Centre, arrange for the hire of buses and vehicles, the booking of venues, etc., etc. The Committee also noted that role of Research Officer had 'special responsibility for publications', did the 'executive editing for the Centre', and produced the *Bulletin* and the brochure 'as well as engaging in in-house editing'. However, the Committee noted the anomaly that 'Dr Eade seems to have more time for research than either the Director or Deputy Director'; and recommended accordingly that Donaldson, Clarke and Eade 'should seek to reallocate routine tasks and resubmit their case for an expanded staff only after a period of some revision of the present situation'.

The Committee then addressed the issue of where the HRC should be located within the structure of ANU to the greatest benefit of the Centre itself and the University as a whole. There was no doubt that many of the Centre's activities related 'to disciplines housed in the Faculty of Arts and, accordingly the formal affiliation has proved of benefit to both sides'. However, it was also evident that the Centre 'has its obvious intellectual links with RSSS and, to a lesser extent with RSPacS'. It was accordingly considered that 'significant advantages to the HRC may follow its being established as a structure within the IAS [Institute of Advanced Studies] and attached to the Research School of Social Studies'. The logic was compelling, prima facie at least: the HRC was not a teaching institution, although Donaldson had always given time to teaching in The Faculties; and it was conspicuously a forum for advanced study. The Committee accordingly concluded in its final recommendations that:

1. the HRC, in the light of the quality of its performance, be regarded by the University as a centre of excellence;

2. the HRC be re-located within the Institute of Advanced Studies, attached to the Research School of Social Sciences'; and that:

3. consideration be given to funding the activities of the academic staff of the HRC on the basis of membership of the IAS.

It was also recommended that 'the HRC should explore external sources of funding'. This could have seemed ominous. But Donaldson would ever strive to find practical solutions to difficulties, present or conjectural. He was certainly getting plenty of practice. He told the Dean of the Faculty of Arts, Professor R.G. Cushing, that he believed for example, that

> named fellowships sponsored by the business community or the governments of other countries whose representatives are in Canberra might be achieved . . . It may also be worth considering launching an appeal for funds among former Fellows and Scholars for the endowment of a special Fellowship or an annual HRC lecture, possibly given by a former Fellow.[22]

The proposal to relocate the Centre back from The Faculties to the RSSS was in essence an exercise in survival: it was perceived that the rampaging Minister for Education John Dawkins had in mind to amalgamate The Faculties with the University of Canberra. Dawkins' policy, as described in 2002 by his former fellow-Minister Barry Jones, was that 'universities were required to adopt corporate governance models, to see themselves as trading corporations, not just communities of scholars. This', Jones considered, 'pushed many universities towards courses with strong, rising economic demand . . . Fifteen years down the track humanities were down, business and computer studies up. At Monash University in Victoria only 9 per cent of activity was in the humanities, 30 per cent in computers and Information Technology, marketing, management and accounting.' Jones decided that all this added up to 'the greatest mistake of the Hawke/Keating years'.[23] What it certainly had done was accelerate a shift in the nature of academic structures which was presumably irreversible: the number of students grew by 50 per cent between 1980 and 2000, the number of academic staff grew by only six per cent, Commonwealth funding fell by three per cent and the number of senior university managers increased by 300 per cent.

This was in the future, though the implications were clear enough. But the immediate problem was that amalgamation with the University of Canberra was likely to mean that the HRC would lose all independent identity which could mean that the HRC would lose all independence. The Dean of the Faculty of Arts himself supported the move to relocate to the RSSS, advising the Budget Committee of the University that 'the HRC's attachment to the Faculty is only nominal'. None of its business went through the Faculty. And this had the effect of inhibiting any possible growth for the Centre through competition for funds. 'The move to RSSS', by contrast, 'would provide the HRC with a potential growth path that probably cannot be provided by Arts'; he could not 'see the Faculty diverting teaching or research resources to the HRC in a substantial way'.[24] It was also the case that HRC staff would be available for ARC grants if affiliated with The Faculties, but not if they were part of the RSSS. Also, there were shared appointments with The Faculties, some members of The Faculties being non-stipendiary visiting Fellows. Clarke told the HRC Steering Committee that the HRC would 'ideally like to be a Centre having links with both Faculty and the RSSS', although he realised the administrative difficulties. It was accordingly agreed that 'the HRC should keep its options open for the time being'.[25] Cushing appreciated this expression of preference: he wrote to Donaldson that he understood that

> the HRC's preferred option is to stay as it is (in effect an autonomous unit loosely affiliated with the Faculty of Arts), but some mechanism be provided to allow it to compete effectively for funds to foster growth (e.g., to develop longer term projects without winding down existing activities). Strategic Planning may provide the most appropriate route to growth in present circumstances.[26]

Donaldson was quite prepared to accept that an association with the RSSS 'could be of considerable benefit to the HRC'; and that 'the HRC might in turn have something positive to contribute to the RSSS at this transitional time', as he told Director of the RSSS Professor Paul Bourke. It was true that the Board of the RSSS had decided in

October 1976 against having the HRC affiliated with that School, on the grounds that it seemed too difficult to separate the Centre's budget from that of the School; and that it was thought, rather improbably, that the Centre's academic interests were too far removed from those of other Departments in the School for effective peer scrutiny to be achieved. There had also of course been the problem that the HRC might seem to be competing with or at least duplicating some of the operations of the History of Ideas Unit already within the RSSS. The Centre had accordingly been affiliated with the Faculty of Arts in 1977. This had the effect that the budget of the HRC was 'administered by the Business Manager of The Faculties in consultation with the Centre, but normally without reference to the Dean of Arts', who 'nevertheless represents the HRC on the Faculties' Resources Committee'. The disadvantages of this arrangement flowed mainly from 'the HRC's anomalous status as a research-only Centre located within The Faculties'. Bourke himself was however genuinely in sympathy with the role being played by the HRC and could see advantages in its playing this role within the School. The Review Committee accordingly recommended that the HRC be relocated within the IAS, attached to the RSSS, as had been proposed at the very outset. What made it particularly attractive this time around was that the RSSS had at present 'a number of Departments and Units... whose work lies partly within the broad field of the humanities'; and several of the HRC's recent themes 'might profitably have been undertaken in close conjunction with the RSSS... the HRC', Donaldson concluded, was 'especially interested at the present time in the possibility of undertaking joint projects and appointing shared visitors with the RSSS itself'.

Donaldson was at pains to reassure his colleagues that the 're-location of the HRC that is envisaged is not geographical but administrative and budgetary'.[27] There would be limits to the extent of the administrative and budgetary relocation as well. Bourke explained to the Advisory Committee that it was 'not proposed that the HRC be fully incorporated as a new department or division within the RSSS with access to the research funds of the School and Institute. Rather, it was proposed that the HRC's separately identified budget be managed through the Joint School's Business Manager Office. It was hoped that the HRC and RSSS would thereby come into a closer academic relationship'. But closer to the RSSS would presumably mean further from The Faculties. Concern was expressed that the withdrawal of the HRC from The Faculties 'would involve, or be thought to imply, a further weakening of the already-imperilled humanities disciplines within the Faculty of Arts'. Withdrawal might of course never have been an issue if there had not been 'some indifference towards the HRC by the Faculty of Arts within the ANU', as Donaldson and Clarke observed. It was conceded in any case that 'it might still be in the Centre's own best interests to pursue an RSSS affiliation'; and the Committee 'agreed that the question of RSSS affiliation should be cautiously but actively explored'.

What made the whole question of affiliation peculiarly urgent for Donaldson and Clarke was the fact that the terms of reference of the Review Committee had seemed to assume that the HRC would 'continue without any apparent growth'. There was certainly little opportunity under the existing arrangement 'for the HRC to benefit financially, e.g. by the Faculties coming to the HRC's financial rescue . . . if there was to be any growth, the HRC had a strong chance to fare well in competing in a bid for funds within the RSSS'. But this 'would not be possible if the Centre continued with the Faculties owing to competition with teaching enterprises'. Richard Johnson warned gloomily from long and bitter experience that 'it would not necessarily be that a relationship with the RSSS would be any different': the Centre 'should take into account that there was a general suspicion of research for its own sake in the Australian community'. Things had not improved for the Humanities since 1969. They had got much worse.

But perhaps something could even be done about that. Graeme Clarke thought that 'it seemed timely for the HRC now to consider adopting a slightly different style of life . . . organising, alongside its annual themes and short-term fellowships, a project of slightly longer duration (three/five years), which might attract a few additional appointments at Research Fellow/Senior Fellow level'. Such a project might be 'some quite current topic in the humanities (e.g. defence of research funding)'. He and Donaldson were concerned at the disjunctions which were emerging in the seventies and eighties between what was being done by the staff of the Research Schools and what students were doing or rather wanted to be doing. They accordingly set out to visit other universities, attend lectures by other academics and in general attempt to discover for themselves what students were really interested in. Their aim was ever to discern the wave of the future, in order to keep the HRC at the cutting edge of academic investigations. This could mean investigating topics such as, for example, sex or religion, which were not regarded as areas of appropriate investigation by the Research Schools, and which also could not be encompassed within the Eurocentric boundaries within which the HRC was still supposed to be confined.

Their first spectacular success in this provocative as well as proactive role was the resounding conferences on Feminism in 1986, which had attracted over 600 participants. But extending the activities of the HRC in this manner would inevitably mean more work, and more work had to mean more appointments, given the conditions of overstretch which the Centre was already enduring. Donaldson told the Review Committee that he 'felt that the administrative work-load for all staff of the Centre had grown remarkably in recent years. He himself had explored (unsuccessfully) the possibility of a two-year respite from administrative duties in order to begin a large research project. There seemed a growing tension between administrative and research expectations for the staff of the Centre'. All this dedicated effort was however still bearing superb fruit, especially with regard to one of the prime objectives of the Centre, its interaction with other national institutions: '1987 had been a very successful year with regard to co-ordination with the [National] Gallery'; the National Library had 'diverted sums of money to various exhibitions in connection with the Centre's conferences'; the Centre had also 'enjoyed a close relationship with the School of Art and Music . . . often sharing speakers'; and relations with the Australian Academy of the Humanities were 'quite close'.[28]

The year 1988 proved another excellent one for the Centre, although the Director was able to spend the first six months in the United States as Visiting Professor at Cornell and directing a seminar on Ben Jonson for the Folger Shakespeare Library in Washington. He also lectured at the Universities of Chicago, Stanford and Princeton and campuses of the University of California (Los Angeles, Irvine, Santa Barbara and Berkeley) and at the California Institute of Technology.

The year 1988 had been the first year without a set conference theme since 1976. It was however naturally dominated by the bicentenary celebrations, and the Centre was fully involved in the planning and running of the Academy of the Humanities' bicentennial conference in Sydney *Terra Australis* which was designed as a sequel to the 1981 conference series *Australia and the European Imagination*. It also provided however a further example of the facility of the HRC to interact with other universities: the Terra Australis conference was held in both Sydney and Canberra, a seminar was devoted to *The Use of the Past* which attracted 70 participants, and a second conference on *The Roman Family* drew 65, which was twice as many as had attended the previous airing of that topic in 1981. Participants noted the developments in the field since the first conference and even since the important book resulting from that conference had been produced by Professor Beryl Rawson. There was in addition a seminar held in honour of the distinguished literary critic and Fellow of King's College Cambridge Professor Frank Kermode, later Sir (John) Frank Kermode.

More new contacts and advances were made in 1989. The theme was 'Film and the Humanities', convened by Dr Roger Hillman of the Department of Art History and Film Studies at the School of Humanities, ANU, who considered later that the HRC had been 'indirectly responsible for launching the current Film Studies Program at the ANU', as Sasha Grishin had said of Donaldson's support for the Fine Arts Programme in 1977. 'Ian Donaldson and Graeme Clarke', Hillman recalled, 'boldly enlisted local, but largely inexperienced convenors, Leslie Devereux and myself, rather than going with

Professor Beryl Rawson.

established figures from outside. The dramatically steep learning curve ultimately generated momentum. New courses were established in the Arts Faculty building up to a major available as of 1995 . . . I for one, but I'm sure many others too, will remain grateful for the wonderful start made possible by the HRC'.[29] The documentary film festival associated with the conference drew 100 viewers over four days, while the conference itself extended the field of interaction of the Centre by drawing on the National Film and Sound Archive and AIATSIS, as well as the National Library and the National Gallery. The named seminar was in honour of Professor of Political Science at the University of Cambridge Quentin Skinner, as a tribute to Skinner's very considerable impact on the study of political theory of the whole early modern period. In 1990 Skinner was to write: 'You really did me proud, I at once reflected in inviting me to the Centre last year. I had a wonderful time, and I also learnt a lot. In fact it sent my work off in a new and I think very fruitful way'. And Graeme Clarke triumphantly recorded the appearance in print of the fourth volume of his monumental study of *The Letters of St Cyprian*, as well as editing *Rediscovering Hellenism: the Hellenic Inheritance and the English Imagination*, deriving from the 1985 conference series on *Hellenism: Rediscovering the Past*.

Professor Kermode had given the Centre what would surely have been to his mind the ultimate accolade, assuring Donaldson and Clarke that he did not think that he had 'encountered higher standards anywhere on my travels, or for that matter in Cambridge'.[30] There were of course still administrative matters to be tidied up, as always, of which the most pressing was the vital issue of funding, also as always. Advice was sought from Professor Don Aitkin, Chairman of the Australian Research Council. Aitkin was told that it was 'not proposed that the HRC move from its present physical location within the A.D. Hope Building. Nor is it proposed that the HRC be fully incorporated as a new department or division within RSSS with access to the research funds of the School and Institute', though this might have seemed almost the whole purpose of the suggested arrangement. Apparently what was in contemplation was merely that 'the HRC's separately identified budget henceforth be managed through the Business Manager's Office in the Joint Schools'. It was hoped that 'a re-location of the HRC on these terms would carry a number of administrative and academic advantages, and encourage a closer collaboration between the HRC and the RSSS'. The critical issue was whether it would carry any financial disadvantages. Aitkin was asked to rule on 'how such a re-location would affect the eligibility of HRC staff for ARC funding'.[31] His response was that staff of the Centre would remain eligible to receive ARC grants 'if their salaries come from that pool of funds within the University subject to the diversion of funds to the Australian Research Council for competitive re-allocation'. However, they would not be eligible to receive ARC grants if their salaries came from 'that pool of funds which goes to support the activities at the Institute of Advanced Studies'.[32]

It looked as if any advantages accruing from relocation were going to be mainly administrative and academic. However, Donaldson had meanwhile been 'giving a good deal of thought recently to the possibility of obtaining additional outside funding for the Humanities Research Centre', as the Review Committee had advised. He told the University Treasurer that he was 'attracted by the possibility of establishing a few Visiting Fellowships endowed through private or foreign national funds, and of creating perhaps an annual "named" lecture, similar to the annual Esso lecture of the Academy of the Humanities . . . Fund-raising of course', he pointed out, 'takes time, skill and energy; and the reason we have not pursued these possibilities before is that the HRC is extremely short-staffed: neither Graeme nor I have felt that we could take on the job single-handed'. However, Ralph Elliott had been appointed Chair of the HRC Finance Committee, and Donaldson wondered if he 'might now have time and inclination to act as the HRC's chief negotiator in these matters'.[33]

Ralph Elliott would seemingly always have time and inclination to further the interests of the HRC, and not just by serving on committees: he had served as Acting Director while Donaldson had been overseas briefly in 1981 and 1983; he had regaled the Centre with talks on the English of Thomas Hardy and on runic writing and mythology; he had been a most welcome Visiting Fellow in 1987; he performed effortlessly the role of Acting Director again when Clarke was absent on his annual two-monthly archaeological researches in Syria in May-June 1988; and he would assume the responsibilities of Librarian at the Centre in 1990, when that post was filled at last. His managerial style was also eminently suited to the Donaldson-Clarke regime: courteous, charming, prompt and unambiguous in defining priorities for the Centre. The human resources available to the HRC were limited in the extreme but they could not have been better suited to their mission.

The University Council had meanwhile resolved that 'the Humanities Research Centre be affiliated with the Research School of Social Sciences and that for administrative purposes the Centre be regarded as an entity within the Institute of Advanced studies'. However, the Centre was also to 'take steps to strengthen its important relationship with The Faculties and in particular with the Faculty of Arts and to operate more effectively within the University as a whole'.[34] It might have seemed that any steps in that direction would have to be taken by the University as a whole rather than the Centre. And there were other recommendations, perhaps easier to conceive than to implement: the Steering Committee agreed that 'it seemed additionally important not to invite visitors exclusively from North America and the United Kingdom', which indeed had never been the practice of the Centre, 'and not to forget the question of gender balance'.[35] How much the latter needed to be addressed was indicated by the fact that women accounted for just under 28% of some 608 visiting academics over the first 30 years of the Centre's operations. Perhaps the only real solution was for universities worldwide to employ more women. Certain processes of evolution were however in train in academe: the Advisory Committee decided to vary the wording of the brochure of the Centre to read that the HRC

> interprets "the humanities" generously, recognizing that new methods of theoretical enquiry have done much in recent years to break down the traditional distinction between the humanities and the social sciences; recognizing, too, the importance of establishing dialogue between the humanities and the natural and technological sciences, and the creative arts. The Centre encourages interdisciplinary and comparative work, and seeks to take a provocative as well as supportive role in relation to existing humanities studies in Australia. It aims to give special attention to topics and disciplines which stand in need of particular stimulus in Australia at any given time.[36]

Donaldson himself expressed the true *raison d'être* of the HRC in what was to be his last public address as Director of the Centre. Graeme Clarke and Dr Sue-Anne Wallace of the National Gallery convened a two-day symposium to coincide with the opening at the Gallery of *Civilization: Ancient Treasures from the British Museum*, at which National Gallery Director Betty Churcher welcomed Acting Director of the British Museum Jean Rankine. Not surprisingly it attracted 250 registrants. More than 100 others attended a conference on *Shaping Lives* addressed by Philip Ziegler, and another 72 registered for a symposium on *Working outside the Academy*, described as being presented

> for a section of the intellectual proletariat, comprising both those who were securely placed inside the academy but wanted to reduce to part-time employment or quit altogether and those who had found an academic career-path closed to them, such as women with children or those who came to university courses relatively late in life.

It was at this symposium that Donaldson told how

> In the early 1970s a German friend of mine, deeply troubled by what was happening in universities throughout the Federal Republic and much of the western world, told me with some bitterness that he believed the only "real" work in the humanities would from now on be done outside the academy... I wasn't at all sure that the Humanities Research Centre we were trying to create in Canberra should be seen as lying wholly *outside* the academy, as constituting a kind of bunker within which scholars comfortably nest down and brood, unruffled, upon the eternal issues.

Such certainly never had been the case for the academic staff of the HRC, and in all conceivable likelihood never would be. Donaldson and Clarke had to this end established workshops for scholars working outside the academy, to advise them on how to survive by contract writing and other sources of non-academic income. As for research centres such as the HRC itself, Donaldson continued in words which conveyed everything that the Centre was ever designed to do and the utmost that it could ever aspire to do,

> seem to me vital agencies of change for the universities, a principal avenue through which, even in times of great financial hardship, new people, new ideas, new ways of thinking are constantly introduced into the academy... The architecture of such centres carries further symbolic messages about the relationship they seek to maintain with the rest of the world, the heavily fortified Humanities Research Center at Austin, Texas, with its armed security guards representing a kind of ultimate in the art of high-rise scholarly bunkering down (or up, or in, or out)... The

> Centre here in Canberra is located in a building that has an openness and accessibility to the kind of role that we've hoped the HRC would play . . . The A.D. Hope Building stands at what is officially designated the entrance to the Australian National University . . . So here in the HRC we work not outside the academy but inside and alongside.[37]

It might be hoped that this vision would not be affected excessively by the eventual relocation of the Centre to an equally unfortified and far more gracious and welcoming but also far less open and accessible building at the opposite end of campus to the designated entrance to the University, perhaps alongside the academy but certainly not inside it.

But the time had come at last for handing over the baton. Donaldson and Clarke had agreed that they should alternate positions every five years. The Steering Committee sadly recorded on 31 July 1990 that Donaldson had announced that he would be relinquishing his position as Director on 3 August to take seven months' Outside Studies Leave. He would then return to the Centre for another seven months before formally resigning in September 1991, to take up the post of Regius Professor of Rhetoric and English Literature at Edinburgh. Meanwhile, Clarke had similarly been granted leave for an Outside Studies Program in Syria from 15 August 1991 through 30 June 1992. Approval had been granted 'subject to satisfactory arrangements in relation to appointment of an Acting Director of the Centre' during Clarke's absence. That of course meant Ralph Elliott, now Emeritus Professor, whom Clarke proposed be given the job 'as from 15 August 1991 until the end of the calendar year in the first instance, the precise period of appointment being subject to review depending on the successful appointment (or otherwise) of a candidate to the presently vacant second Chair in the Centre'.

Elliott had always been agreeable to acting in Clarke's stead for brief stints on previous occasions, on the understanding that there would be no remuneration with such appointments. However, this was to be for a term of six months at least; and Clarke accordingly advised Professor Geoffrey Brennan, Director of RSSS, that it 'would be proper for Professor Elliott to receive an appropriate salary-loading during his period as Acting Director'.[38] If only things were so simple. Elliott raised with Brennan

> the question of the honorarium to be paid to me as Acting Director of the HRC. It now appears that Deryck

Schreuder will assume duty as Acting Director in early February 1992. This makes my own term a round 26 weeks. At the figure of $2000 which you suggested, this means a gross payment of $77 per week, which is reduced to $53 net after taxation. In other words, the proposed honorarium would be around $1380 net. As I am not in receipt of a professorial salary but of superannuation, Graeme Clarke's suggestion that I receive "an appropriate salary-loading" during my period as Acting Director hardly applies. In view of the fact that I am carrying out all the duties of the Director, may I suggest that a more appropriate figure be arrived at . . .[39]

It is a sound principle of both theology and the Labour Movement that the labourer is worthy of his/her hire. However, Brennan was constrained to explain to Elliott that 'the University cannot, as I understand it, pay salary to its own retirees'. So a more appropriate figure was not on the board. The official solution was for the University instead to invite Professor W. S. Ramson to 'act formally as the Acting Director, nevertheless I hope that it will be possible for you to assist him in the day-to-day management of the Centre'.[40] That of course meant, as Elliott informed Clarke, that 'Bill Ramson is de jure, while I am de facto. I do all the work, and I suspect that Bill is getting all the wages! Never mind!'[41] Ramson was also able to see the funny side, which indeed he was in a position to see: he told Elliott that he was 'happy to authorise payment to you to attend the "Histories in Culture" conference, in your capacity as Acting-Acting'.[42]

Donaldson's term was coming to an end. It had been a reign of seventeen years as Acting Director and Director, interrupted only by a year's study leave in 1977-78, six months in 1988 and this seven months' break. It was also a record of service and achievement that deserved to be celebrated in the most civilised and eloquent terms. And there was no more civilised and eloquent voice in the University than that of Ralph Elliott, that 'stalwart symbol of continuity' as Donaldson delightfully termed him. Elliott began by applauding Donaldson's scholarly achievement, for which the most appropriate term was 'tireless' and of which the pinnacle at that moment was his '1985 Oxford Authors edition of [Ben] Jonson, all 787 pages of it'. But there was also his record as 'stimulating, much respected, indeed loved, teacher'; he had 'given invited lectures at about 40 universities and numerous conferences in Australia, Europe, the People's Republic of China and the United States of America'; he 'held visiting appointments, acted as member of electoral committees for fourteen chairs of English, and served in various editorial capacities from his Oxford days as Co-editor of *Essays in Criticism* to the present day'; and his 'involvement as chairman or as member of numerous committees both at Oxford and in Canberra, ranging from the Oxford Experimental Theatre Club to the Australian National Dictionary project' testified to 'his willingness to serve in any capacity in which his wisdom and his wide academic experience could be usefully employed'. His achievement in so many and varied fields in the Humanities has been justly recognized by his Fellowships of the Australian Academy of the Humanities and the British Academy. 'But it is here, at the HRC', Elliott observed gracefully,

> that Ian Donaldson will be most affectionately remembered – and missed. There was no model in Australia, and not many overseas, to which he could turn when appointed Foundation Director of the Centre. But he had his vision of a haven where scholars in the Humanities from Australasia and overseas could pursue their work in congenial surroundings, take part in informal discussions as well as in more formal seminars and conferences, and return to their homes or home institutions refreshed and invigorated. His vision never left him – and it was amply fulfilled. Seventeen years and nearly eighty conferences later, some 260 Visiting Fellows as well as almost 400 Conference and other Short-Term Visitors from places as far apart as Warsaw and Wellington, Binghamton and Beijing, have been welcomed to the HRC . . . From all around the world grateful tributes continue to arrive from scholars who have successfully completed projects begun or continued at the Centre . . . The HRC is still the only one of its kind in Australia. Its reputation and that of its Foundation Director have made it, in the words of a former Vice-Chancellor of the Australian National University [Professor Peter Karmel], "the Jewel in the University's Crown".[43]

It had achieved that distinction because Donaldson and Clarke had made it a place where Visiting Fellows were assured of every encouragement to pursue whatever it pleased them most to pursue: 'the main thing', Donaldson had told John Docker, 'is to enjoy the research you'll be doing in your time at the HRC'. Such a libertarian

Professor Peter Karmel, Vice-Chancellor, 1982–1987.

approach could be deployed effectively only in an atmosphere of superlative scholarly standards. It was. Docker recalls that he 'always felt a little nervous' talking to Donaldson, to the extent that he wondered at times if he was getting his use of the subjunctive in English right.[44] Anybody who can make Australians feel concerned about getting their subjunctives right would have to project a rare aura of scholarly refinement.

But perhaps what John Henry Newman would have called the real *note* of Donaldson's directorship had been that he had made it his aim always to be there: there to hail and farewell visitors, there for the camaraderie of every morning and afternoon coffee break, there to chair every seminar and to ask the first question; and Ralph Elliott or Graeme Clarke would always be there when he could not be. That was what inspired all the multitude of tributes to the hospitality, civility and grace that had become the identity of the HRC. That was the tradition he had created. That was the legacy he left.

Notes

[1] Donaldson to the authors, 2 Nov. 2003.
[2] John Docker to authors, 9 June 2003.
[3] HRC *Bulletin*, Nov. 1984, p. 7.
[4] HRC *Annual Report 1982*, 47/1983.
[5] HRC *Annual Report 1983*, 29/1984.
[6] 18th Meeting Advisory Committee, 16 Nov. 1981.
[7] Dean of Faculty of Arts to Registrar, 10 Mar. 1982.
[8] 53rd Meeting Steering Committee, 11 Aug. 1983; Donaldson to Advisory Committee, 12 Dec. 1983; HRC *Annual Report 1981*, 48/1982.
[9] Donaldson and Clarke to the authors, 21 July 2003.
[10] Donaldson to Advisory Committee, 12 Dec. 1983.
[11] 59th Meeting Steering Committee, minutes, 30 Oct. 1983.
[12] Advisory Committee minutes, 20 Nov. 1984.
[13] Donaldson to the authors, 20 Aug. 2003.
[14] Graeme Clarke to the authors, 19 Aug. 2003.
[15] Report of the Working Party on Relations with Other Areas and Institutions, Extract from Arts Faculty Paper, 2600/1983, 12 Dec. 1983.
[16] R.V. Dubs, Registrar, to Ralph Elliott, 29 Sept. 1986.
[17] HRC *Annual Report 1986*, 14/1987.
[18] See *inter alia* Barclay, 'The *Oyabun* does not dance on stage', *Meanjin*, p. 49 (Summer 1990), 689-708; Gavan McCormack, 'Pacific Dreamtime and Japan's new Milleniarism', *Kyoto Review*, 22 (Spring 1989), 80-81; R. McTaggart Murphy, 'Power without Purpose: the crisis of Japan's financial dominance', *Harvard Business Review*, Mar.–Apr. 1989; Sheridan Tatsuno, *The Technopolis Strategy – Japan, High Technology and the Control of the 21st Century*. Prentice-Hall, New York, 1986; Karel van Wolferen, *The Enigma of Japanese Power*, Macmillan, London, 1989.
[19] HRC *Bulletin*, 49, Sept. 1987, p. 7.
[20] Submission to Review Committee by Ian Donaldson, HRC Review Submission *Item 9*, July 1987.
[21] David Roberts to Donaldson, 19 Aug. 1987.

22. Report of the Committee of Review of the Humanities Research Centre, Australian National University, 28 Oct. 1987.
23. Catriona Jackson, 'Dawkins changes a mistake, says Jones', *The Canberra Times*, 30 Nov. 2002.
24. Professor R.G. Cushing, Dean, Faculty of Arts, to Mr B. Unwin, Budget Committee, 1158/1988, 22 Apr. 1988.
25. Minutes of the 85th Meeting of the Steering Committee, 26 Apr. 1988.
26. Cushing to Donaldson, 9 June 1988.
27. Minutes of the 24th Advisory Committee, 24 Nov. 1988.
28. Donaldson to Paul Bourke, 1 Nov. 1988.
29. Roger Hillman to the authors, 28 May 2003.
30. Frank Kermode to Donaldson, 24 Nov. 1988.
31. Max Neutze to Don Aitkin, 14 Apr. 1989.
32. Aitkin to Neutze, 14 Apr. 1989.
33. Donaldson to A.D. Barton, 3 May 1989.
34. Extract from Minutes of the 236th Meeting of Council, 2055/1989, 11 Aug. 1989.
35. Minutes of the 100th Meeting of the Steering Committee, 21 Nov. 1989.
36. Minutes of the 26th Meeting of the Advisory Committee, 30 Nov. 1989.
37. Donaldson, Address to Symposium in the Centre on *Working outside the Academy*, Apr. 1990.
38. Clarke to Geoffrey Brennan, 8 Aug. 1991.
39. Elliott to Brennan, 10 Sept. 1991.
40. Brennan to Elliott, 16 Sept. 1991.
41. Elliott to Clarke, 26 Nov. 1991.
42. W.S. Ramson to Elliott, 23 Sept. 1991.
43. Ralph Elliott, 'Ian Donaldson', HRC *Bulletin*, No. 65, Sept. 1991, pp. 1-2.
44. John Docker to authors, 9 June 2003.

5 In Australia there is *Only* the HRC (1991-1995)

Ralph Elliott described Graeme Clarke towards the end of 1991 as 'standing among the remains of the Acropolis Palace at Jebel Khalid . . . smiling broadly, under a cloudless sky, in light working clothes, his left hand resting proprietorially on what looks like a huge stone hamburger'.[1] It was a happy picture and one which no doubt owed much of its happiness to the fact that work on his archaeological digs on the Euphrates was rather less exacting than was required of Clarke in his other capacity as Director of the Humanities Research Centre in Canberra. Maybe the weather was better too.

But it was also more importantly a picture that conveyed Clarke's unique contribution to the HRC. He himself insisted that he merely continued the aims of Donaldson after the departure of the first Director. Ann Curthoys confirmed that 'the gentlemanly style of Ian Donaldson continued and developed' under Clarke, and that 'Graeme's emphasis was always on developing a community of scholars'.[2] But Clarke's archaeological researches had the effect of linking the HRC with a great tradition of classical scholarship evoked by John Docker in his reference to Clarke's being a 'classicist of international repute', whose presence as such 'added great depth to the HRC as a scholarly centre', with his 'extraordinary width of knowledge about so many topics, his cosmopolitan ease of knowing different cultures as diverse as ancient Greek and modern Syrian'.[3] Clarke indeed described himself as being really 'just a simple-minded ancient historian and field archaeologist'. But that was a tradition that was not without a certain element of the heroic, as Donna Merwick

Graeme Clarke at Jebel Khalid, North Syria, 1991.

and Greg Dening observed: undertaking archaeological researches on the banks of the Euphrates in the Syria of Hafiz al-Assad the Terrible in the 1980s and 1990s was rather more demanding than a stroll across campus to the University Library. It involved a real degree of dedication, discomfort and danger.

Graeme Clarke inherited Ian Donaldson's terms of contract, being appointed for a five-year term from 4 August 1990. What he did not inherit was a deputy like Graeme Clarke, or indeed any deputy at all. Donaldson himself had remained with the Centre until September 1991, but he had been necessarily preoccupied with winding up his work at the HRC and preparing for his departure to Edinburgh and the new responsibilities he would be assuming there. He had however been able to oversee the launching of another superb, innovative and interactive sequence of conferences, themed and unthemed. The theme was Histories, and the conferences associated comprised *From Materials to Representations, Heritage and Memory and Histories in Cultural Systems*, convened at the University of Melbourne by Max Crawford Professor of History Greg Dening. Dening's academic contributions would always be noted for their flair and originality. A member of the HRC administrative staff was nonetheless slightly taken aback when she was greeted on arriving at the University of Melbourne to prepare for the conference with the remark 'Oh, you're the conference that needs the dead body'. But it was just a slight confusion: it was a medical conference being held at the same time that actually needed the cadaver, not the discipline of history.

Another striking advance was made with the extra-thematic conference on *Modernism and Post-Modernism in Asian Art*, convened by Dr John Clark, Art Historian and Associate Professor in Asian Studies at the University of Sydney, the first conference to be jointly sponsored by the HRC and the Department of Art History, with funding from the Japan Foundation and the Cultural Relations Section of the Department of Foreign Affairs and Trade. It followed up the 1987 conference on the Occident and the Orient, continuing the very salutary experiment initiated on that occasion of endeavouring to look at Asian art from the inside out, rather than from the outside in, as hitherto, eschewing a Eurocentric and Orientalist gaze. Many regard this as a seminal event in Australia. Caroline Turner remembers that modern and contemporary Asian art was only just beginning to be seen in exhibitions in Australia (the first museum-based exhibition of contemporary Asian art had been organised by Turner for the Queensland Art Gallery in 1989 and the Museum of Contemporary Art Sydney followed in 1991 with the stunning 'Zones of Love' from Japan). 'At the Queensland Art Gallery', she recalls,

> we had just resolved to commit to a ten year program of contemporary Asian and Pacific art and John Clark's HRC conference brought to Australia very significant Asian scholars whose papers, presented from non-EuroAmericentric perspectives, made an incredible impact on Australian art professionals at the time and introduced us to the debates about art going on in Asia.

The tradition of the Named Seminar in honour of a leader in world academe was continued, this time giving tribute to Irish-born Philip and Beulah Rollins Professor of History at Princeton Peter Robert Lamont Brown, credited by his peers with having literally created the study of late antiquity, i.e. 250-800 CE, and hailed by an anonymous student in the unofficial Princeton *Full List of Awesome Courses* in terms which must excite wild envy in every academic heart: 'Peter Brown is a God, folks . . . Take this course'.

Graeme Clarke took a year's study leave in August 1991, his first long absence from the Centre for 10 years, to continue his archaeological excavations in Northern Syria, before proceeding to the National Humanities Center in Research Triangle Park, North Carolina, to experience the pleasures of being himself a Visiting

Professor Deryck Schreuder, Associate Director, 1992-1993.

Fellow, relishing the hospitality and relief from stress which his own Centre had provided to so many others, but not to its Directors. Constraints of time and funding had delayed any attempt to obtain a permanent Deputy Director. William Ramson, then Director of the Australian National Dictionary Centre and Chairman of the HRC's Advisory and Steering Committees, was accordingly appointed as Acting Director as an interim measure, with the indispensable and indefatigable Ralph Elliott attending to the day-to-day running of the

Centre. And support was coming, in a form as committed, energetic, enterprising and resourceful as could well have been hoped for. Professor Deryck Schreuder agreed to be seconded from the Challis Chair of History at the University of Sydney in March 1992 to become what would be termed Associate Director of the Centre. During his time at the HRC he continued his research into nineteenth century European history as well as the history of migrant settler societies and was on a formidable array of national academic committees including chair of the Australian Research Council Grants panel on the Humanities and Social Sciences as well as chair of the ARC's Priority Panel on 'Australia's Asian Context'. Schreuder was on his way to the very highest echelons of Australian academe. He was however determined that his contribution to the HRC should be far more than that of merely a caretaker role. Nobody could be more aware of the significance of the Centre for cultural life, internationally as well as nationally, the need for that significance to be recognised and the need for the activities of the Centre to be expanded to ensure this recognition. He threw himself immediately into the task with a splendid expression of the Centre's essential contribution, past achievements and future plans, delivered appropriately on Canberra Day, 19 March 1992. 'The HRC', he announced with perfect truth,

> has been a remarkable intellectual success story. With only two tenured academic faculty and a small general staff, it has devoted its modest budget to bringing the very best of humanities scholars to Canberra ... Little wonder that in an age of increasing utilitarian and economic rationalism one distinguished scholar of literature [Professor Ken Ruthven] termed the HRC our "sacred site" for the humanities in Australia.

However, he continued with equal percipience, the 1990s threatened to be an even harder environment for the humanities. Schreuder then outlined what the Centre was going to do to counter these graver challenges. 'The Directors and Steering Committee of the HRC', he said, 'are very well aware of this unfavourable climate for the Humanities and have been considering new roles and functions in the Centre'. These would include New Visiting Fellowships which would 'welcome "sabbatical scholars" to the HRC, to enjoy the special features of centre and campus, but above all to *write!*'[4]

Write they did indeed: the many volumes presented by grateful former Visiting Fellows to the Ralph Elliott Library represent only the tip of the iceberg of works begun or completed during sojourns at the HRC. Graeme Clarke listed HRC publications up to the beginning of 1997 as comprising four monographs produced in the joint imprint series with Oxford University Press, six with Macmillan, 16 HRC publications with other houses, 16 more published through the HRC, nine special issues of journals and nine major works in preparation. That was only getting a bit further down the iceberg, for the list of publications worked on by Fellows while at the Centre was enormous. (See Appendix F.) Nor did they only write: they gave work-in-progress seminars, delivered lectures, visited other Australian or New Zealand universities, interacted with one another and with staff and students and in many cases set about seeing more of the continent than most of its citizens would probably see in a lifetime: they showed in particular, Clarke noted, 'a curious tendency all to want to have invitations from the campus of the James Cook University of Northern Queensland'.[5] Bernard Bailyn revised 14 of 16 chapters in final form of a major book while at the Centre; Professor E. Ann Kaplan visited four universities, delivered 12 lectures and substantially completed the revision of her book *Motherhood and Representation*; Professor of History at UCLA Anne K. Mellor delivered 18 lectures and Professor of Sociology at the University of New South Wales David M. Halperin no less than 23 lectures; Professor and Chair of Political Science at Johns Hopkins William Connolly, hailed by his peers as one of the subtlest, boldest and most intellectually fertile political and moral thinkers now writing in the USA, 'arrived with a few chapters roughed out' and left 'with an entire manuscript ready to go to the publisher'; and Richard Rorty doubted that he would have been able to generate the 10 000 words he produced in reply to his critics if he had hadn't had such 'an idyllic think tank to work in'.

Further fellowships, Schreuder continued, would be

> targeted at young "new Researchers" – to come and work in the Centre as they move in to post-doctoral research and publication. Post-graduate student summer visitorships will be expanded to welcome those entering advanced research. An annual "Summer School", in a major area of theory in the humanities, is being explored for February of each year.

And he concluded with a credo at once authoritative, admonitory and inspiring for all with any concern for the future of the Humanities. 'We do ourselves absolutely no good', he declared, 'by claiming varieties of "relevance" in terms of national needs . . . the Humanities will always be relevant if we speak to the fundamental issues which concern human life'.⁶

Schreuder's primary concern was to achieve the widest possible recognition for the Centre. Membership of the HRC Advisory Committee had included, in Clarke's words, 'Directors, or their representatives, from the National Gallery and usually from the National Library . . . RSPacS (as it then was), RSSS, President of the Australian Academy of the Humanities, Dean ANU Faculty of Arts, Director Institute of the Arts and from around the country in various Humanities fields . . . The Committee was . . . a useful, if a little cumbersome, way of informing a number of influential people and institutions of forthcoming activities and visitors, and enabled the national profile of the HRC to be raised'.⁷ Schreuder now wrote to Deputy Vice-Chancellor Professor Max Neutze, urging that 'the University give approval to the disbanding of our current Advisory Committee . . . It is my view . . . that we should rather have a panel of Advisors drawn from a broad range of educational, cultural, publishing and media organisations'.⁸ He also oversaw a highly interactive series of conferences. The designated theme was 'Europe', and conferences on *The European Moment, Europe: Representations of Change* and *Intellectuals in Europe today* were convened by Professor Brian Nelson and held jointly with the Centre for European Studies at Monash University. Then there was an extra-thematic conference on *The Articulate Surface: Dialogues on Painting Between Conservators, Curators and Art Historians*, sponsored by the HRC and the National Gallery; and on *The Changing Idea of an Australian University*, convened by Schreuder himself and Director of RSSS Professor Geoffrey Brennan and sponsored by the Centre, RSSS and Macquarie University; and a one-day symposium on the decidedly relevant topic of *The Idea of a Republic*, with the Australian Defence Force Academy. But what was in preparation for 1993 would be something which even the 'Feminism' year could hardly match for sheer vision and *éclat*.

Schreuder himself was soon called to fight the battle for the humanities on an even higher plane, being elected President of the Academy of the Humanities in November 1992 and appointed the following month Deputy Vice-Chancellor (Academic) of Macquarie University, operative as from Easter 1993, subsequently becoming Vice-Chancellor of the University of Western Sydney, and later Vice-Chancellor of the University of Western Australia. He announced his acceptance of the 'warm invitation' from Macquarie along with a reiterated warning that the humanities were under challenge in Australia. 'There is a widespread spirit of utilitarianism about – partly symbolised by economic rationalist theory, more still through technocratic models of society and development'. The humanities nonetheless had 'never been more relevant in our troubled world ... And yet the technocratic vision is adopted uncritically by government. A recent Commonwealth paper, entitled *Developing Australian Ideas: a blue-print for the 1990s* ... offers a set of ideas entirely devoid of the Humanities'. That was in 1993. The spirit of utilitarianism in government was just beginning to spread its wings. Schreuder expressed his resolve to 'continue to be associated with the HRC over the years ahead, and especially in relation to the 1994 and 1995 themes on "Freedom" and "Africa"'.[9] Clarke returned to the Directorship in July, quite convinced as to what was the greatest service that institutions like the HRC could provide for the world of learning. He had just discovered for himself what it was like to be a visiting academic at a hospitable and congenial research centre, and the experience had been wonderful. He had spent

> a blissful seven months ... in the tranquillity of the National Humanities Center in the Research Triangle Park of North Carolina. My experience there has reinforced my considered view that what will make most Visiting Fellows happiest is a quiet office, a blank wall, a desk with a p.c. or writing pad, and a peaceful atmosphere after all the noisy static and argumentative competitiveness of their everyday academic lives... The National Humanities Center was wonderfully equipped and efficiently run to meet this Platonic ideal: the experience spurs the HRC to emulate, so far as our resources allow. In essence we must ensure that the HRC continues as a precious resource because of its very capacity to provide a place for undisturbed senior scholarship.[10]

There was a fascinating irony in the fact that the Director of the HRC had to go as a visitor to another research centre to enjoy the opportunities for serious and relaxed academic study that his own centre was famed for providing for its visitors. But there was no question as to the gravamen of his address. Donaldson too had been reflecting since his return to the United Kingdom on the implications of the ever more constrained resources available to the HRC, although he characteristically reflected that even this might not be 'altogether a bad thing'. 'Placed alongside the ANU's powerful Research Schools', he wrote,

> the HRC was a tiny affair: only two tenured academic positions were contemplated, that of Director and Deputy Director, and the remainder of its budget was reserved for visiting appointments. Privately, however, it was hoped that the HRC would transform itself in due course into a small Research School with its own departmental infrastructure and range of tenured appointments and long-term research projects. In the idealistic projection of the Melbourne historian Professor R.M. Crawford, the HRC would in time develop a substantial research library which would enable it to operate in the manner of the Warburg Institute at the University of London, as a centre housed within its own specialist Collections.

But 'what none of these dreams predicted was the severe contraction of University funding that was to occur throughout Australia during the 1970s and 1980s which not only prevented the HRC from ever evolving into a Research School, but held the number of its tenured academic staff to one (a Director) during the first eight years of its existence. In retrospect', however, 'I believe this failure to fulfil the earliest hopes for the Humanities Research Centre may not have been altogether a bad thing. It forced the HRC to be flexible and resourceful during a period when the ANU's Research Schools themselves became increasingly anxious about their own comparative inertia.'[11]

This was looking on the bright side with a vengeance. But the HRC could hardly have survived at all if it had not been guided by people who were prepared to look on the bright side and make virtue out of hard necessity. It was this kind of tough-minded optimism which had made the Centre such a superb place to work in and to work for. It was precisely the need to do as much as possible with what might have seemed as little as possible that had inspired Donaldson and Clarke to go beyond the original mandate of the Centre into fields outside the areas of operation of the Research Schools. They had already achieved a spectacular success in this line with the Feminism programme in 1986. Clarke had already prepared a programme for 1993 that promised to be at least as spectacular and even more provocative. But the power of positive thinking can accomplish only so much without adequate resources. And the most effective way to expanding the exiguous resource base of the Centre seemed to be for it to take on an expanded role. Clarke and Schreuder put it flatly to the Advisory Committee that HRC activities were 'currently restricted by the budget within which the Centre must work'. They had accordingly tabled a proposal for an expanded HRC which the Committee 'noted and generally endorsed'. Its basic argument was that 'an argument for an increase in the budget could be made from the breadth and diversity of the Centre', and 'the diverse use made of the Centre's facilities, e.g. as a conference area'. The Directors observed that 'successful fund-raising will depend on the HRC's profile'. There was 'a need for publicity not only within the university but also outside academia', such as Schreuder had been tirelessly promoting, 'of the kind afforded by the Centre's involvement in one-off conferences such as *Republicanism* and *The Idea of an Australian University* [1992]. They were convinced that 'not only the constant variety and change of activities in the HRC but also the desirability of undertaking longer projects justified a larger budget'. Larger premises might also be justified: the HRC 'should not necessarily be tied to the AD Hope Building if larger more suitable accommodation could be provided. If the Centre is to expand, it might be preferable that new space be specially designed for its activities'.

Clarke and Schreuder maintained that the HRC in fact played a genuinely national role in Australian cultural life. It was also one that it was critical to maintain and augment in the national interest. The Centre, they argued, had

> a unique status in Australia. There is no other cross-disciplinary humanities centre, and it is highly unlikely that such a research resource could now be created . . . It is therefore all the more crucial in the 1990s that the HRC both continue its work for the broad area of the 'humanities' in Australia, with its major international linkages, and also ensure that there is at least one resource dedicated to humanities enquiry and publication within an educational environment that has become increasingly utilitarian in policy outlook and emphasis. The United States of America has many centres for humanities research . . . But in Australia there is *only* the HRC.

And he repeated Ken Ruthven's comment about the HRC being 'a sacred site for the humanities.' It was a good phrase and it was worth repeating.

But all this entailed of necessity an expansion of resources, physical as well as human. 'Ideally', the Directors continued,

> the Centre should be able to accommodate:
> a) The Directorate
> b) Centre Administration
> c) Publications and editorial room
> d) Seminar/Reading Room
> e) Rooms for Visiting Fellows/Sabbatical Fellows etc.
> f) Library of reference works and periodicals; and fellows' works
>
> Plus, have a good modern kitchen, to support the social side of its seminars/conferences, and possess adequate storage resources . . . Whilst it would be desirable to keep the permanent senior academic staff low (two is an absolute minimum) there is a great need for an academic assistant to the Directors (say a lecturer/senior lecturer on secondment for a specified term). This person,

they represented with feeling,

> can mop up a great deal of routine correspondence on behalf of the Directors, deal appropriately with a series

James Grieve, Krystyna Szokalski, Leena Messina, Graeme Clarke, Jodi Parvey and Stephanie Stockdill, 1993.

> of queries from the Visiting Fellows . . . have authority for deciding on a number of budgetary items, and make decisions of a reasonably routine sort that crop up with running seminars, work-shops and conferences. A lot of this flack needlessly intrudes, at present, into the daily lives of the Directors.[12]

Schreuder could testify with feeling on that subject: he confided to Clarke when the latter returned from his blissful term of release that he had 'found his job as Acting Director, when I took a period of leave, as "impossible", being torn between the administrative demands of the position and the need to get on with research', as well as fulfil his responsibilities as a member of the Australian Research Council.[13]

But one appointment could not be delayed any longer. An absolute minimum of two academics entailed in reality a permanent staff of three, since one of the two was certain to be absent from duty for part of the time, for one reason or another. But first it was necessary to get the two. It was decided in March 1993 that applications should be sought for a Professor and Associate Director in the HRC. The paragon who would combine these functions should be

> a distinguished scholar with wide-ranging intellectual sympathies and special expertise in any area of the humanities relevant to the work of the Centre. The person appointed will be required to pursue research in his or her field of interest and to assist the current Director . . . in the administration and long-term planning of the Centre, and in the promotion of its work nationally and internationally.

Essential prerequisites for the job would include skills which would 'complement those of the current Director (whose interests lie primarily, though not exclusively, in Greek and Roman history, literature, religion and archaeology)'. Clarke's interests had already been shown to extend far wider than this very classicist list might imply and they would be seen to extend far wider yet. 'A readiness to deal with a wide range of people' was stipulated and was essential without question; and a 'familiarity with several European languages and cultures would also be an advantage', although, it was observed realistically, 'not essential'. The appointee might also 'be asked to take special responsibility for certain day-to-day tasks in the Centre, which include the organization of conferences, seminars, talks, exhibitions, readings and other activities'. Clarke and Schreuder had proposed

Wendy Antoniak.

that these functions should be the responsibility of the senior academic on secondment for whom they discerned a great need. Much was in fact being undertaken by the devoted administrative staff, Jodi Parvey, Wendy Antoniak, Stephanie Stockdill, Krystyna Szokalski and Leena Messina, whose services would be recognised in a continuing flow of testimonials. But this did not mean that another academic was not absolutely essential, to be 'the Director's closest senior colleague and adviser on matters of general policy and long-term planning'.[14] That was indeed how it had been in the past with Donaldson and Clarke and again with Clarke and Schreuder. It was how it would have to continue to be if the Centre were to function at all in the future.

Clarke was never in any danger of suffering from the dreaded condition that Lenin identified as 'dizziness with success'. However, the plaudits of Visiting Fellows might have been a temptation in that line, had circumstances been less sobering. Professor John D'Emilio from the University of North Carolina at Greensboro said that the Centre had 'proved an almost utopian work environment'. Professor David M. Halperin, from the exalted heights of the Massachusetts Institute of Technology, testified that the Centre offered 'an ideal venue for research'. It possessed 'the right proportion of social and intellectual life, on the one hand, and solitude, on the other', which might well be said of Canberra in general. Further, the 'combination of rich opportunity and untrammelled freedom is exactly as it should be, and in that respect', he concluded authoritatively, 'the HRC is on a par with the world's best research centres in the humanities. (The HRC's chief disadvantage is financial.)'[15] He would get no argument there.

Clarke now declared the quantum shift in the mission of the HRC which he and Donaldson had been subtly introducing since 1981. 'The centre', he later told a Canadian audience, 'consciously strives to "de-Europeanise" humanities studies, breaking down the separation between European and Asia/Pacific scholarly theories, methods and approaches and takes care to include in its themes, if possible, antipodean, Pacific and Asian perspectives and experiences'.[16] The central function of the Centre, he affirmed in 1993 was 'to stimulate research in the humanities (broadly interpreted) within Australia'. One of the ways in which the Centre could foster this aim was 'to concentrate from time to time on an area of research which, while important, happens not to be well represented within the Australian Academy'. He and Donaldson had already achieved such a breakthrough with their 1986 conference on Feminism. Plans were 'now maturing for our 1995 year with "Africa" with this aim in mind'.[17] Africa was Schreuder's own idea, having himself been born in South Africa and educated in Zambia and Cape Province before leaving for Oxford. It was an idea that in Clarke's words

> fitted in with one of the declared objects of the Centre – to reinforce an area of study, established within Australian academia, which could do with strengthening and encouragement . . . This was a conscious policy and fitted in with the concept of the Centre as a National Facility for the Humanities. The other broad category for the annual

Regimes of Sexuality Conference. Professors Margaret Jolly and Graeme Clarke in first row.

Forces of Desire Conference. Dr Jill Matthews (convener) with Professor Graeme Clarke and Dr John Ballard.

themes, with a similar vision as national facilitator, was fields of study which were ripe for critique . . .[18]

Plans had also been matured for a conference on an area very important indeed and even less well represented within the Australian Academy.

Some 1300 participants attended the sequence of HRC events in 1993 associated with the nominated annual theme of 'Sexualities and Culture'. The Centre, 'knowing itself to be an unparalleled national resource', Clarke reported on the event, 'has put much effort into collaborating with other institutions . . . A most notable feature of this collaboration was *Lips of Coral – Sex, Violence and Surrealism*, the conference held in conjunction with the National Gallery of Australia's major international exhibition *Surrealism: Revolution by Night*'.[19]

Notable hardly conveys the impact of the Sexualities series of conferences. The marvellously entitled 'Lips of Coral' had been sponsored jointly by the Centre and the National Gallery, convened by Dr Ted Gott of the National Gallery and Dr Ken Wach and presented jointly by the National Gallery and the Museum of Contemporary Art (MCA) in Sydney. The NGA Theatre was crowded with 270 art specialists, which was in fact all that it could hold. *Breath of Balsam: Reorienting Surrealism*, the second conference, was held at the Museum of Contemporary Art Sydney and the Art Gallery of New South Wales

Lips of Coral Conference. Dr Ted Gott (convener) with Mrs Betty Churcher, Director, N.G.A.

(AGNSW) and delegates were welcomed by MCA Director Leon Paroissien and Chief Curator Bernice Murphy and AGNSW Director Edmund Capon and addressed by Assistant Director National Gallery of Australia Dr Michael Lloyd who had co-curated the exhibition. The conferences, *Regimes of Sexuality and Forces of Desire*, and other associated events attracted more than 600 participants, almost as many as the great Feminism exercise, bringing together artists, performers, curators and writers. Among the keynote speakers was Professor Trinh Minh-ha from the University of California at Berkeley. There was also a named seminar in honour of Professor Jane Gallop convened by Dr Jill Matthews, Women's Studies ANU.

Enthusiastic audiences attended public lectures by Jane Gallop, Distinguished Professor of English and Comparative Literature at the University of Wisconsin and without question one of the leading figures in contemporary Feminist discourse; and by Professor of History at the University of California at Berkeley and Director of the Doreen B. Townsend Center for the Humanities Thomas W. Laqueur, vastly published historian of, *inter alia*, literacy, death and masturbation. Clarke had selected his distinguished visitors most appropriately for the occasion. The fact that academics of such international eminence would always be ready to make the long trip to Canberra was proof positive of the distinction which Donaldson and Clarke had earned for the HRC.

There was also an extra-thematic conference on *The Dawn of History* convened by Dr Julian Thomas and Professor Stuart McIntyre of the University of Melbourne, and another on *Music and Musicians in Australian Culture 1930-1960,* convened by Dr Peter Read, Dr Nicholas Brown and the composer Larry Sitsky with the Canberra School of Music, the National Library and the National Film and Sound Archive. Among the distinguished speakers at the latter conference was Professor Malcolm Gillies, later Deputy Vice-Chancellor (Education) at ANU. The First HRC Summer School on 'Colonial and Post-Colonial Humanities in a Post-imperial World' was convened by Dr Nicholas Thomas of the Department of Anthropology at ANU and Professor Dipesh Chakrabarty of the University of Melbourne and held in conjunction with the Ashworth Centre for Social History at that university. The aim was to comprehensively explore issues of post-colonial criticism in literature, history, anthropology, cultural studies and feminism, challenging prior understandings of colonial history and representations. It was indeed all very notable.

And it was indeed noticed. Clarke's *démarche* had been provocative in every sense of the word: it had excited, inspired, enticed and also incited irritation or at least perturbation within and without academe. The Sexualities conferences had naturally attracted numbers of enthusiastic and demonstrative gay and lesbian researchers and practitioners from California whose activities attracted the disapproval of the United States Ambassador, one of the more conservative appointees to a post the incumbents of which have scarcely ever been anything else.[20] It had also been the target of reiterated denunciation in the columns of *The Canberra Times*. Nor was it only outside academe that reservations were expressed: 'we were much derided', Clarke recalled,

> for putting on what was called a "whips and chains" year, and many scholars and gentlemen thought this was a rather messy and inappropriate topic for scholarly inquiry. But the scholars showed quite differently and they came in their hundreds, particularly younger scholars . . . from a huge range of disciplines.[21]

Ann Curthoys had no doubts at all: the Sexualities year had 'certainly played a role in foregrounding Australian scholarship in sexuality and forging links between Australian and international scholars in the field which remain to this day. It is certainly a key link in the history of the HRC'.[22] Her judgement was endorsed by Cindy Patton, Professor of Lesbian/Gay Studies at Emory University, who told Graeme Clarke that, rather surprisingly,

> those of us working on sexuality in North America work in isolation . . . and under conditions of considerable hostility in our respective locales. The atmosphere of the [Humanities Research] Centre and the [Australian National] University – so far as I could tell, at any rate – was one of enthusiasm and openness to the range of innovative and often controversial scholarly inquiries.[23]

There could however be no question that 1993 had triumphantly fulfilled the ambitions of Clarke, Donaldson and Schreuder to extend the frontiers of the Centre, publicly and intellectually: the conferences had, as Clarke put it, 'helped to fulfil more than we had anticipated one of the goals of the Centre – to be a *national* facility for the Humanities'.[24] The Advisory Committee noted that the year's conferences and weekly seminars had been extremely successful, attracting the largest attendances ever. The diversity of participants throughout the year showed that the HRC had reached a wider audience than usual. There had also been broad coverage in newspapers and radio, laudatory and otherwise. The Committee noted the HRC's involvement with the National Gallery of Australia and the Museum of Contemporary Art as well as the University Gallery, School of Music and National Film and Sound Archive. There had also been 250 applicants for the 1995 Visiting Fellowships. And the Committee was pleased to welcome the new Associate Director, Professor Iain McCalman, who would take up his appointment on 1 January 1994.[25]

McCalman might well have been expected to engage with the notion of expanding horizons and greeting the future: he was only 46, about the same age that Clarke had been when he was appointed Deputy Director; he could be described as being like Clarke and Schreuder of colonial or at least post-colonial origin, having been born in Malawi and subsequently trained, wholly against his will, with the legendary Rhodesian Light Infantry in the days of the Ian Smith regime; had degrees from ANU and Monash University, had held previous appointments at ANU, Monash, Melbourne, Macquarie, University of Canberra and Charles Sturt University; had received the Vice-Chancellor's Award for Teaching Excellence in 1992; and had developed a particular interest in the fruitful fields of the more arcane, louche and *rastaquouère* areas of English literary studies: he had published *Radical underworld: prophets, revolutionaries and pornographers in London, 1795-1840* in 1988 and *Horrors of slavery: the life and writings of Robert Wedderburn* in 1992; and was engaged at the time of his appointment as Chief Editor along with three associate editors, two assistant editors, 43 essay contributors and 120 entry contributors in a mammoth 500 000-word, 780-page *Oxford Companion to the Romantic Age: British Culture 1776–1832*. And this was only one of the plethora of literary ventures in which the new Associate Director and future Director would be involved.

McCalman had already made his impact at the Centre when he impressed James Chandler, the very eminent Director of The Franke Institute for the Humanities at the University of Chicago, as 'of course impresario of the HRC', who would emerge 'not only as a force in his own field of Romanticism, but also, building on the strong record of Ian Donaldson, as a leader in the international development of humanities institutes and centres'. Chandler had also been continually amazed by 'the breadth, depth, and sheer invention of the activities that the Centre sponsors every month. Now that I direct a Humanities Institute myself', he wrote in 2002, 'I appreciate Iain's example more than ever – his exemplary combination of ease of manner, generosity of spirit, and rigor of scholarship'. This was for the future: what McCalman found that he was required to display most at the outset of his career was fortitude, fancy footwork and a profound sense of survival. He was indeed no sooner in the job than he and Clarke were called upon to face the usual financial crisis. And financial crises would always mean crises of survival for an institution funded as exiguously as the HRC. It had been agreed in December 1988 that the Centre should be 'affiliated' with the RSSS in the Institute of Advanced Studies, 'with the proviso that enquiries concerning research fund eligibility for members of the HRC should be satisfactorily answered'. But it appeared that they had not been answered all that satisfactorily. 'We have been given to understand – indirectly –' McCalman wrote to Vice-Chancellor Deane Terrell,

> that the University has shifted the HRC funding from a one-line item on the Faculties' budget to that of the Institute. Whilst there may well be advantages to the University in such a change, there are at present very considerable disadvantages to the Centre. In the short term we cease to be eligible for FRF and ARC funding and we also cease to be claimants on Faculties' new funding for travel grants, conference leave, equipment, space, small works, etc. If we are to be fully established as a Centre

within the Institute, then we not only need access to all the prerogatives and privileges of membership in the Institute (currently denied to us as being of "ambiguous" status), and the basis of our affiliation to one of the Research Schools (eg. RSSS) needs to be spelt out specifically, but we also need to be established with adequate support infrastructure . . . At the very least the Director and Associate Director should be able to have the annual level of research funding they could expect to receive from FRF and ARC . . . In total . . . a funding base of $140 000.

Then he unmasked a proposal which was to lead to the HRC acquiring a new direction, a new philosophy, a new managerial structure and a new location, with the challenges inherent in a revolution of that order.

Donaldson, Clarke and Schreuder had been committed to the point of passion to extending the horizons and impact of the HRC, as so of course had Ralph Elliott. But McCalman's vision went beyond the boundaries of the HRC itself. 'Graeme Clarke and I', he told Terrell, 'believe that the HRC is also uniquely placed, both nationally and within ANU, to develop a Centre for Advanced Cultural Studies. Like it or not, cultural studies is a burgeoning field which impinges on the concerns of both the traditional humanities and social sciences, and is here to stay'. Survival for academic institutions was coming more and more to mean getting more students in; and the problem was that 'students coming to the ANU are showing increasing interest in the interdisciplinary fields of cultural studies yet it has no institutional expression here . . . Rival universities such as the University of Canberra have benefited enormously from meeting this demand'. The HRC appeared to be 'ideally placed for developing a concomitant postgraduate degree in cultural studies with a strong coursework component'. But what was needed to put this into practice was 'someone to act as a graduate teacher and coordinator within the HRC in order to prepare an examinable program in Advanced Cultural Studies . . . We believe', McCalman concluded,

> that an important opportunity exists at a crucial transitional time for the HRC. We are prepared to commit ourselves to the effort to make it work, but we cannot do so without an adequate research establishment, measured in physical resources such as rooms and computer facilities, and personnel such as research assistants, postdoctoral fellows

and possibly a graduate teacher/coordinator . . . If the Centre [for Advanced Cultural Studies] is to become an integral part of the Institute, cognisance will have to be taken of our legitimate aspirations for a more complete establishment as a research unit.[26]

Geoffrey Brennan wrote to the Vice-Chancellor in support of McCalman's appeal. 'There is no doubt in my mind', he told Terrell,

that both Clarke and McCalman could reasonably have expected continued ARC funding to the tune of probably $140 000 between them – and conceivably rather more if Iain's cultural studies "companion" volume captured ARC imagination . . . the facts are: first, that the HRC was moved to the IAS (without being consulted as far as I know) for reasons of the perceived financial interests of The Faculties; second, that this move cost the HRC about $140 000 pa in expected research funding (assuming *no* development); and third, that the faculties did indeed gain from the move to the tune of about $2m. It seems clear to me that simple justice requires compensation to the HRC.

However, Brennan argued, this compensation should not come from the IAS budget, and

a fortiori not from RSSS's budget. Perhaps in the long run, the HRC personnel should have their research plans financed competitively against other IAS claimants . . . But for the time being, some way will have to be found to meet the true cost of the HRC transfer out of the benefits that The Faculties obtained thereby.[27]

This seemed only fair, although it is not usually difficult to find reasons why justice should be served by someone else's footing the bill. What needed prompt attention was the fact that spending on conferences in 1993 had exceeded budget by the not too exorbitant sum of about $60 000. This was not indeed surprising, considering the phenomenal spread of visiting scholars and conferences that had been held that year. Clarke and McCalman advised the Steering Committee that had 'been in part occasioned by shifting monies from their customary allocations . . . and this . . . had led to overspending on conferences and publishing'. The Committee for its part noted that 'the HRC could only support with difficulty large conferences that exceeded its infrastructure'. The lack of a publications officer was also 'placing severe pressure on the administrative staff'.[28]

Important conferences had certainly been the distinguishing mark of the HRC's contribution to the humanities, nationally and internationally. The tradition continued in 1994 with three major conferences devoted to the theme of Freedom: one on 'Ideas of Liberty' convened by Professor Barry Hindess, Director of the Political Science Program at RSSS; another on *Asian Paths to the Idea of Freedom*, convened by Professor of Southeast Asian History at RSPAS A.J.S. Reid; and a third on *Commitments to Representation and Freedom*, again convened by Dr Sue-Anne Wallace, in conjunction with the National Gallery and the Museum of Contemporary Art. There was also a special public lecture and colloquium convened by Professor Conal Condren on *The Republican Conception of Freedom* to mark the second visit to the HRC of Professor Quentin Skinner of the University of Cambridge and acclaimed as the world's leading historian of early modern political thought; a Summer School devoted to *Feminist Theory and Women's Studies in the 1990s* convened by Associate Professor Barbara Caine of the University of Sydney with Associate Professors Rosemary Pringle and Elizabeth Grosz, for which an expanded quota of 60 participants proved to be not expanded enough with many applicants disappointed by not getting a place; an extra-thematic conference on writing and editing had been convened by Professor Paul Eggert jointly with the Australian Scholarly Editions Centre; and *The Roman Family,* a topic in which the HRC had taken a leading world role thanks to the efforts of ANU academic Professor Beryl Rawson of the Classics Department, an expert in this field, was revisited in a third conference convened by Professor Rawson and Professor Paul Weaver of the University of Tasmania and with speakers from France, Canada, Denmark, England, New Zealand, Germany, the US and Australia.

But the question was as always how long this kind of effort could be sustained. Clarke reiterated the obvious problem: the Centre

> runs on a very slim budget and its establishment is lean – just two senior academic appointments and a small secretariat (barely adequate for the Centre's needs). This is by deliberate design so that we can put as many resources as we can possibly manage into our Visiting Fellowship programme . . . Ideally, the Centre would wish to be involved in a long-term humanities project of national significance . . . but at present funding any such involvement would drastically reduce, if not eliminate, the humanities constituency we are currently able to serve.

But hope springs eternal.[29]

That had always been the motto of the HRC. The immediate question was whether it was going to be its epitaph. The University had decided to conduct a Review of the RSSS. This would involve a Review of the HRC, as a centre attached to the RSSS, although Clarke and MacCalman made the point that the HRC was 'very conscious of its role as the only centre in Australia established for research in the Humanities generally'; and that it did 'not make sense, given its mission, to be *either* of The Faculties *or* of the Institute but rather a Centre of the University, with membership of both'.[30]

Clarke went on research leave to supervise a dig in Syria, planned originally when he had thought that Deryck Schreuder would still be in place, leaving McCalman as Acting Director, with major responsibility for the planning of the activities of the Centre over the next two years. McCalman saw the issue as being one of whether there was going to be a Centre to have any activities: he warned his readers that the 'next few months are likely to be portentous for the HRC. The context is an impending review of the Institute of Advanced Studies (the research-only side of ANU) conducted jointly by the University and the Australian Research Council. The HRC has been included in this review', he suggested,

> primarily, it seems, in order to resolve its ambiguous status as a research centre located neither in the teaching Faculties nor the Institute . . . our reviewers will naturally be keen to assess whether we have been successful in meeting our avowed national and international mission to promote research excellence in the humanities at large.[31]

Behind the scenes many believed that the purpose of including the HRC in the Review was to produce an outcome which would lead to the HRC being assimilated as a Department of RSSS. The Director of RSSS, Professor Paul Bourke, had recently closed down the History of Ideas Unit in that Research School, a move that had provoked much criticism and it was widely discussed that the HRC could perhaps replace it. The danger for the HRC was that it could lose its identity and independence. And criticisms were being expressed by some unsympathetic to the HRC that a Visiting Fellows programme was less productive than long-term fellowships. Such criticisms probably reflected the competition for resources beginning to affect every part of the University and failed to take into account that the HRC had a different mission and a different funding structure from a Research

School and that the Visiting Fellows and conference programmes had served as the public face of ANU and of the humanities in Australia for many years. As for research output the list of publications of the Centre was indisputable evidence of the research done there.

One of the means by which McCalman planned to satisfy enquiries on the score of the Centre promoting excellence in humanities research nationally and internationally in particular was by rallying support from pre-eminent national and international scholars in the Humanities who could speak from personal experience of the Centre and its achievements. The strategy was totally successful: even the few negative comments were positively advantageous in that they related entirely to technical issues like the lack of IBM equipment and air conditioning resulting from inadequate funding; and the positive comments were all that could have been desired and more than could well have been imagined.

Perhaps in a technical sense the most compelling testimonial came from Judith Ryan, Professor of German Languages and Literature at Harvard, who had been appointed Assessor into the HRC. She reported with appropriate judicious moderation that the Centre

> stands extremely well by comparison to other high quality research centres, particularly those I am familiar with in the United States . . . it functions as a model for other

Dr Sandra Buckley, Dr Gayle Rubin, Dr Roseanne Kennedy and Dr Carol Vance.

> tertiary educational ventures . . . The Centre's unique combination of historical and contemporary studies makes it far less isolated than many other Humanities centres, which often focus on cultural studies without the broad informing framework of social sciences that is palpable in [the] work of the ANU Humanities Centre.

Other distinguished overseas academics were quite immoderate in their expressions of support. Professor Peter Jones, Director of the Institute for Advanced Studies, The University of Edinburgh, testified that the HRC had 'established a unique and enviable reputation, worldwide, for the quality of its Fellows', and 'the innovative character of its thematic meetings and conferences'. Harold F. Linder, Professor of Social Science at Princeton, declared that he himself worked in 'a research institute, somewhat comparable to the HRC, and have spent time, both in this country and abroad, at others. There is none, including my own, which is more effective in pursuing its mission with direction, dedication, and a broad range of interests'. His accolade was endorsed by Dr Carole Vance, Associate Research Scientist, Anthropology and Public Health, Columbia University who reported that of the many scholarly centres she had visited 'in the United States and in several other countries, the Humanities Research Centre is by far the most outstanding. The HRC provided an exceptional environment for scholarly research and exchange, particularly at the international level'.

Australian academics could give their own national perspective, all the more impressive for evincing no trace whatever of the inter-institutional and inter-state rivalry symptoms of which some observers claimed to have detected earlier. Associate Professor Patricia Crawford of the Department of History at the University of Western Australia, reported that the conferences which the HRC organised

> played a significant part in the research scene in Australia. The Centre has selected conference themes of widespread scholarly interest and succeeded in making the Australian academic scene part of the international circuit. It is hard to overemphasise the value of this to Australian research. Individual scholars . . . have attended the Centre, but in addition, visitors have come to Western Australia . . .'

Ian Templeman, Assistant Director-General, Cultural and Educational Services Division at the National Library of Australia testified to the success of the Centre's policy of networking with other cultural institutions. 'In a period in which the National Library has begun to build a more active program of outreach and collaboration with the Australian intellectual community', he told the Committee, 'the relationship with the Humanities Research Centre constitutes a natural partnership which offers considerable benefit to both parties'. He observed that the 'distinguished international and Australian visitors which the Centre has attracted through its Fellowships program have given great charisma both to the Humanities Research Centre itself and to the Australian National University as its host body'. Dr H.V. Brasted, Associate Professor in Indian and Islamic History at The University of New England went even further: he was

> convinced that what the HRC represents is of considerable value to the ANU in a number of ways:
>
> - As the only research centre of its kind in Australia it must play a part in raising the profile of the University, both nationally and internationally.
> - In a sense the HRC is the visible shop front of the Humanities at the ANU, its ability to bring to Canberra a galaxy of the finest scholars across the disciplines is the envy of other universities, and is a testament to its high standing in the academic world.'

And he concluded that:

> - Doubtless the Research Schools house an equally impressive array of international scholars but they do not seem to be nearly as visible or as accessible to the academic community beyond Canberra.

For Professor Wilfrid Prest of the Department of History at The University of Adelaide there was no question: the HRC was

> unique, and not only in Australian terms; to the best of my knowledge no other humanities/social science research institution in the UK or USA has had a comparable impact on such a broad national constituency . . . There is simply no other institution in Australia which offers Australian and foreign scholars opportunities to pursue research and writing across the whole range of humanities and social sciences in a congenial, productive and stimulating intellectual environment.

But no testimonial could be more authoritative and conclusive than that of Professor Richard Rorty, friend to wombats and acknowledged as one of the pre-eminent philosophers of the age. 'The HRC', he stated flatly, 'has been the principal means of communication and collaboration between Australian scholars in the humanities and their colleagues throughout the world. It has an absolutely impeccable reputation in the international scholarly community, and is thought to be one of the most successful think-tanks in the world'. There was nothing more that needed to be said.

McCalman recorded that he had found the Review experience 'extraordinarily wearing'. He was however happy to report that he had been

> told that the Committee's broad conclusions and recommendations . . . are everything we could have wished . . . the Committee has suggested that the HRC remain autonomous, commended the excellence of our programs under straitened circumstances, and recommended budgetary increases to enable us to support longer-term Fellowships and more sustained research projects . . . for the exhausted HRC staff this is a wonderful affirmation of the Centre's mission.[32]

It was no more than the truth. The Report of the Review Commission congratulated the HRC on:

- the success of its extensive Visiting Fellows' program which 'increases the profile of Australian work in the Humanities and also helps to foster important networks with Australian universities. The Committee commends the excellent job the HRC has done in the past, particularly given its budgetary constraints.'
- its 'pivotal position and future potential in the nation's work in the Humanities.'
- its research achievements: 'the University acknowledges that the Centre is an important component of its research and outreach profiles and a major contributor to the indicators which are reflected in the University's quantum rating.'

The Committee also noted that 'the Centre's continuing success was seriously imperilled by its ambiguous administrative location and the long-term erosion of its resources. It accordingly stressed that:

- even to maintain its current activities, the HRC required more space and improved equipment, especially adequate computer resources.
- the HRC requires an urgent increase in funding level: the Centre's budget being basically unchanged for many years despite a significant growth in its activities and a significant erosion in its infrastructure.
- if the Centre is to be put on a sound basis for maintaining and extending its valuable and important national role, it must have clear avenues for funding within the University.

All this was an admirably lucid summary of the enduring problems faced by the Centre since its inauguration. And the Review Report was just as lucid on what needed to be done to resolve them. It urged the University to begin with

> a significant expansion of the HRC's research and administrative resources in order for the Centre to fulfil its greater potential as a national centre for research on culture with a strong focus on Australian culture and multicultural issues:
>
> - the HRC must be strengthened in order to allow it to focus more on research while keeping its strong collaborative efforts, its visitors' program, and its conferences. In particular, it would require substantially more research staff members. It would also require increased administrative staff, and an administrative officer.
> - given the Centre's pivotal position and future potential in the nation's work in the Humanities, and the general lack of comprehensive research units in this broad field when compared with the social and natural science fields, the University must make an approach to the Government and appropriate advisory groups for a special increment to its funds to enable the Centre to fulfil an enhanced international role.[33]

It was indeed a wonderful affirmation of what was being done, how it was being done and who was doing it.

Notes

1. Ralph Elliott, 'Graeme Clarke', HRC *Bulletin*, 66, Dec. 1991, p. 1.
2. Ann Curthoys to the authors, 8 Sept. 2003.
3. John Docker to the authors, 1 Sept. 2003.
4. Deryck Schreuder, 'From the desk of the Associate Director', Canberra Day, HRC *Bulletin*, Mar. 1992, 67, pp. 4-7.
5. Graeme Clarke, 'Who cares about the humanities?' Deryck Schreuder (ed.), *The Humanities and a Creative Nation: Jubilee Essays*, Canberra, Highland Press, 1995, pp. 280-282.
6. Schreuder, 'From the desk of the Associate Director', *supra*.
7. Graeme Clarke to the authors, 23 June 2003.
8. Schreuder to Max Neutze, 8 Apr. 1992.
9. Schreuder, 'Hail and Farewell', *Bulletin*, 69, Dec. 1992, p. 2.
10. Graeme Clarke, 'From the desk of the Director', *Bulletin*, July 1992, 68, p. 3.
11. Donaldson, 'From the desk of the ex-Director', *Bulletin*, Dec. 1992, 69, pp. 6-10, reprinted from *The Cambridge Review*, June 1992, 113, 2317.
12. 'An Expanded NRC – Position Paper. NATIONAL ROLE', 30th Meeting Advisory Committee, 26 Feb. 1993.
13. Clarke to the authors, 29 Sept. 2003.
14. *Bulletin*, Mar. 1993, 70, p. 9 (ed. by Leena Messina).
15. Graeme Clarke, 'From the desk of the Director', *Bulletin*, June 1993, 71, p. 1.
16. Clarke, 'Directing a National Humanities Research Centre in Australia', paper delivered to a conference in Vancouver on 'Practising Interdisciplinarity', Mar. 1997.
17. Clarke, 'From the desk of the Director', *supra*.
18. Clarke to the authors, 29 Sept. 2003.
19. HRC *Annual Report*, 1993.
20. Some indication of the attention which Washington traditionally devotes to its diplomatic relations with Australia may be gathered from the fact that the first US Ambassador in Canberra got the job because (a) he needed to get back on the public payroll, and (b) because President Harry S. Truman was advised to send

him as far away as possible. One of the few true professional career diplomats ever appointed as Ambassador to Canberra was the equivocal Marshall Green, whose role in the fall of the Whitlam Government is still a matter for debate and likely to remain so indefinitely. It has been reliably suggested that he was sent to Canberra in the first place as punishment for having displeased Secretary of State Henry A. Kissinger. Green certainly never held an important post afterwards.

[21] Clarke, 'Who cares about the humanities?'
[22] Ann Curthoys to the authors, 1 Sept. 2003.
[23] Cindy Patton to Clarke, 13 Sept. 1993.
[24] Clarke, 'From the desk of the Director', *Bulletin*, Sept. 1993, 72, p. 1.
[25] Advisory Committee, minutes, 25 Nov. 1993.
[26] Iain McCalman to Deane Terrell, 28 Feb. 1994.
[27] Geoffrey Brennan to Terrell, 1 Mar. 1994.
[28] 134th Meeting, Steering Committee, minutes, 26 July 1994.
[29] Clarke, 'From the desk of the Director', *Bulletin*, Sept. 1994, 76, p. 1.
[30] McCalman and Clarke, 135th Meeting, Steering Committee, Item 8: HUMANITIES RESEARCH CENTRE STRATEGIC PLAN 1995-2005, 25 Oct. 1994.
[31] McCalman, 'From the desk of the Acting Director', *Bulletin*, Mar. 1995, 77, p. 1.
[32] McCalman, 'From the desk of the Acting Director', *Bulletin*, June 1995, 78, p. 1.
[33] *Joint Review of the Institute of Advanced Studies, May 1995: Humanities Research Centre Response to Section 10 of the Report of the Committee Which reviewed the Research School of Social Sciences . . . The Role and Location of the Humanities Research Centre*, Sept. 1995.

6 Endings and Beginnings (1995–2000)

Graeme Clarke's five-year term as Director came to an end in mid-1995 and Iain McCalman took over as Director. Clarke remained as Associate Director and continued to have a very significant intellectual input into the HRC. In a characteristically gracious 'Welcome to the Director' penned by Clarke to McCalman and published in the Centre's June 1995 *Bulletin* Clarke wished Iain well and thanked him for serving as Acting Director for seven months during the very stressful period of the HRC Review 'when Iain demonstrated how well the Centre is going to fare under his Directorship. All who use the Centre now and in the future are in his debt'.[1] One might add that they were also in considerable debt to Graeme Clarke for his extraordinary contributions over such a lengthy period of service.

The Report of the Review Committee had been enormously supportive of the Centre and admirable in its vision of future strategy. There was however still the problem of tactics. The Steering Committee 'noted the excellence of the HRC Review had now been acknowledged by the University, but apart from being separated from the Review of the Institute [of Advanced Studies], no further action had been taken by senior University administration in regard to the future funding of the HRC'. In fact this was what everything else depended on: it could not be expected that the HRC could attempt to do more than it was doing already without more staff and more funding. Director of the RSSS Professor Geoffrey Brennan had 'expressed his concern that the work of the Centre at times placed unrealistic pressure on the

Professor Iain McCalman, Associate Director, 1994–1995; Acting Director, 1994–1995; Director, 1995-2003; Federation Fellow, 2003– .

Directors, when one was on leave, due to the lack of academic support staff'. Indeed for a time while Clarke was on leave the HRC had consisted for practical purposes of McCalman and Leena Messina. The fundamental problem was still that the Centre 'had to finance any additional academic staff directly from its own budget', which meant that more staff meant less money and therefore less capacity to host the activities which the increased staff would be responsible for managing.² It was still the classic catch-22 situation. And what was worse was that the University had made it clear, despite the accolades received by the Centre during the Review process, that money for sustained or new research programmes had to be sought outside, such as through competition for ARC grants. Thus new and innovative ways of attracting such funding would have to be found if the Centre were to move forward. The next five years would see McCalman undertake an energetic and indeed visionary series of initiatives to achieve some spectacular results for the Centre, ANU and the humanities.

The HRC had continued its outreach profile and conference programme through all the turmoil and distractions of the Review. Visitors included Dr George Abungu from the National Museum of Kenya, Professor Dipesh Chakrabarty from the University of Chicago, Dr Julian Cobbing from Rhodes University, Dr Saul Dubow from the University of Sussex, Professor Toyin Falola from the University of Texas at Austin, and Ms Alinah Segobye from the University of Botswana. And the accolades kept on coming: Professor Julian Cobbing declared that the 'facilities and atmosphere at the HRC were everything promised by the Director, Professor Graeme Clarke . . . It has been my first visit to Australia, and it has been a captivating experience'. 'Can the humanities humanise?' Professor Toyin Falola asked.

> My answer was always negative until I came here. Now I can at least say yes and illustrate with the HRC, ANU. The HRC has changed my mind by showing that scholarship can be pursued in a congenial and peaceful atmosphere. The staff is friendly and dedicated. The Director and the Associate Director are true leaders . . . Centres like this one are rare. If I were to rate it internationally, I would rank it as the best for its facilities, quality of staff, quality of fellows and conferences, and its accessibility to learning resources.

Such an accolade might have seemed sufficient on its own. But there is no such thing as too much appreciation, and there were many testimonials just as impressive in terms of what was being said and who was saying it. Dr John Lonsdale of Trinity College, Cambridge, could not 'remember a more productive and collegially enjoyable time . . . My abiding impression is the friendly efficiency of the place, with your superb staff always ready to help . . . So many thanks to Graeme and you – especially for attending and contributing to sessions way outside your fields'. Professor Bruce J. Berman of Queen's University, Ontario, was

> happy to report that the HRC has provided me with the most stimulating and congenial intellectual community of my academic career . . . I think that you and Graeme have set a most admirable standard of intellectual discourse and hospitality at the Centre . . . The HRC is a unique institution. Long may it flourish!

Dr Joanna Casey of the Department of Anthropology, University of South Carolina, did not know 'where to begin to praise the staff at the HRC. I have never received such warm, and professional treatment as I have at HRC . . . I cannot imagine two more excellent Directors than you and Graeme . . .'

Clarke and Schreuder had agreed in 1993 that 'Africa' should be the theme for 1995. It was all the more appropriate now that the HRC had an African-born Director. The theme also allowed the HRC to continue its strongly established policy of examining critical issues of contemporary societies. Events commenced with an important workshop on HIV in Africa organised by Director of the United Nations HIV Program Elizabeth Reid. Large numbers of experts,

Cover of HRC monograph *Africa Today*.

especially from Africa, attended to discuss the terrible human crisis on the Continent. The three major conferences planned earlier also went ahead. Professor of Archaeology and Palaeoanthropology at the University of New England Graham Connah convened one on the seminal aspect of *Africa: Precolonial Achievement* which aimed to draw attention to the growing data on social, economic and technological attainments of Africa prior to European colonisation. Dr David Dorward from the Department of History at La Trobe convened a second on *Out of Africa: Texts for Understanding the African Past*, (focussing on the uses of 'texts', written and oral and material culture as evidence of the past) with both international experts and ANU Africa specialists including Professor Anthony Low giving papers. This was held in conjunction with an exhibition at the Drill Hall Gallery, 'Objects of Adornment: Personal Art in Africa' (an exhibition of Sub-Saharan jewellery, snuff boxes and other items from the Christensen Collection and that of David Dorward); and Schreuder and Professor Peter Alexander convened a third on *What is Happening in Africa Today*. Iain McCalman later recalled:

> The Africa year exercised a profound impact on me and all those who participated, an impact that went well beyond the intellectual, important though that was. We did not attract huge crowds but the collective enterprise did so much good. Black African scholars in so many countries were utterly starved of resources that our humblest students would take utterly for granted – things like photocopying, computers, telephones. Many of them . . . were being hounded by authoritarian governments. Their classes were closed down and their pay withheld unless they toed some dictatorial line. The opportunity to travel overseas, to meet scholars from both their own continent and the rest of world was unique. Most of them knew and acted as if this was the one chance of a lifetime. They threw themselves into the year with an enthusiasm, exuberance and intensity that was quite breathtaking. Many of them also later reported that the prestige of coming to the HRC had transformed the attitudes of those who ruled their universities. They were promoted and given better resources. Equally, African studies was finding itself increasingly beleaguered here in Australia as we turned more and more inward culturally and focussed on more and more utilitarian kinds of teaching and research. The

HRC gave the field a stimulus that has probably been the chief reason it has survived in Australia to this day.[3]

There were important out-of-theme conferences in 1995 including McCalman's joint conference with the History Program at ANU and the Research School of Social Sciences on *New Directions in British History* and the first Freilich Colloquium on Tolerance Studies: an examination of *Diasporic and Multicultural Approaches to South East Asian Studies* convened by Professor of South Asian Languages and Civilizations at the University of Chicago Dipesh Chakrabarty and Dr Kalpana Ram (Gender Studies RSPAS ANU). Thus began one of the HRC's most important adjunct programmes made possible by a generous donation from Herbert and Valmae Freilich to allow public programmes and research into intolerance, the causes of bigotry and how such intolerance might be combated through education. Herbert Freilich, a retired doctor from Sydney, and his wife Valmae had decided in 1990 to make a significant bequest to ANU for this purpose but little had been done until Iain McCalman and the HRC took up the proposal. Herbert Freilich wrote later:

> We knew of the ANU only as being the name of a University in Canberra. The reason for selecting the ANU was because we had in mind two aspects to a study of bigotry. One was an academic programme of study and the other was to use the results of such a study to advise and perhaps influence policy. The academic study did not

Signing the Deed and Charter of the Foundation. *From left to right*: Dr Herbert Freilich, Mrs Valmae Freilich, Professor Deane Terrell, Vice-Chancellor of the University, Professor Peter Baume, Chancellor of the University, Ms Maureen McInroy, Acting University Secretary, Professor Iain McCalman, July 1999.

need Canberra but the "advise and influence" part seemed more appropriate in the national capital; the Parliament, the Ministries, the national archives, the national gallery and national film centre to portray aspects and effects of bigotry, etc.[4]

In the same year the HRC also presented a Summer School on 'Modernist and Postmodernist Perspectives on Religion, Literature and the Arts' held at the School of Studies in Religion at the University of Sydney and convened by Associate Professor James Tulip and Dr Raymond Younis; and a special public lecture and Named Seminar, *The Making of a Public Intellectual,* convened by Associate Professor Tim Bonyhady and Dr Tom Griffiths, organised by the HRC, RSSS and the Sir Robert Menzies Centre for Australian Studies, and sponsored by the Australian Academy of the Humanities, the Academy of Social Sciences in Australia and the National Museum in honour of Emeritus Professor John Mulvaney, formerly Professor of Prehistory in The Faculties and recognised as Australia's most distinguished prehistorian. Mulvaney had done much to change understanding of Australia's past and contributed to developing policies related to heritage, archaeological and museum and conservation practice. He was in every sense a public intellectual *par excellence:* Secretary of Australian Academy of the Humanities, President of the Australian Institute of Aboriginal Studies, Australian delegate to the UNESCO Committee on World Heritage, among other services to scholarship and the community. Mulvaney was also a member of the critical Piggott Committee review of Australian Museums and National Collections and a key figure in the debates surrounding the establishment of the National Museum of Australia with which the HRC was to be extensively involved in future years. Papers were given by many specialists, among them Professors Isabel McBryde, Ken Inglis and Greg Dening as well as younger scholars such as Tom Griffiths, Bain Attwood, Howard Morphy, Deborah Bird Rose and Marcia Langton, Chair of the Australian Institute of Aboriginal and Torres Strait Islander Studies and later Professor of Australian Indigenous Studies at the University of Melbourne. Thus the HRC continued its long tradition of focus on Indigenous history and culture in Australia as well as European and settler culture.

The HRC's 1995 programme had been an imposing display of outreach and it had been accomplished amidst all the storm and stress of its most critical review. Meanwhile the University had resolved that the HRC should be 'deemed a University centre, associated for administrative purposes with The Faculties and accountable to the council through the Board of The Faculties'.[5] What this meant in practice was that the formal location and administration of the Centre was to be transferred from RSSS to The Faculties Business Office after 8 March, 1996. Professor Iain Wright of the Faculty of Arts and Chairman of the HRC's Steering Committee thus stepped in as Acting Director while McCalman was on leave to RSSS in late 1995 and until the return of Graeme Clarke from a dig in Syria. McCalman had also been successful in obtaining a grant from Quality funds of $50 000 for equipment upgrade and a junior Academic for a three-year period to assist with administration, graduate teaching and developing the HRC's electronic capacities. Dr Benjamin Penny, a specialist in Chinese religion, was appointed in 1996 for three years as a result as Project Officer (Academic). His role would be essentially to edit the new journal, facilitate the web site and new electronic mailing lists, organise conferences and later to manage the Freilich colloquia. He was appointed Executive Officer of the Freilich Foundation in 1999. This did not really provide support for the Visiting Fellows programme or allow assistance for research projects. However, Penny also assisted for a time with developing the Australian Studies Graduate teaching programme begun by Dr Sylvia Kleinert which McCalman was developing for the Graduate School as a focussed HRC commitment to teaching through another grant he received for this purpose. Kleinert also undertook two offshore developments including conferences and exhibitions of Aboriginal art to Yogyjakarta, Indonesia and Potsdam, Germany. The Australian Studies programme continued for three years with a board of studies that included Professor Bruce Bennett from the Australia Defence Force Academy, and from ANU, Dr Nicholas Brown from Urban Research, Professor Ann Curthoys who became Convener, Professor Francesca Merlan from Anthropology, Mr Nigel Lendon from the School of Art, Dr David Parker from English, Professor John Warhurst from Political Science, Dr Jennifer Rutherford from Australian Studies, Mr Neville Perkins from the Jabal Centre and later Professor Joan Kerr. A number of students were successful graduates through the programme and a series of colloquia were held by the HRC to stimulate Australian Studies at ANU.

Donaldson, Clarke and Schreuder had in their time proposed at least partial solutions to the besetting difficulty of lack of funds and academic staff by expanding the role of the Centre to undertake teaching responsibilities and introducing named lectures. McCalman's answer was by contrast literally revolutionary in that it would involve changes, anticipated and unanticipated, which would alter the structure and even the physical location of the Centre. The basic concept had been foreshadowed in his letter of 28 February 1994 to the Vice-Chancellor, in which he had raised the possibility of developing a programme for Advanced Cultural Studies within the structure of an expanded HRC. It was a brilliant, even visionary, solution of the problem of how to expand the HRC's reach and scholarly projects which McCalman was also able to inspire others to support: he discussed the idea of a bid to the Australian Research Council for a Centre of Research Excellence during 1995 with Dr Nicholas Thomas of the Department of Archaeology and Anthropology, and also with Professor Ann Curthoys, now with the Department of History in The Faculties in terms of a submission to the Australian Research Council. Ann Curthoys had had a long association with the HRC, at least since 1986 as a Visiting Fellow during the 'Feminism' year. She had served as well as a member of the contact group encouraging collaboration between the Centre and other universities; had been a conference organiser in 1991 and a member of the committees which had appointed Deryck Schreuder and later Iain McCalman; had served on an assessment committee in 1994 for the ARC Key Centre on Media Policy at Griffith University; was now a member of the HRC Steering Committee and would later be Chair of the National Advisory Board of the new Centre. She 'knew what such committees looked for'.[6]

Thomas and Curthoys gave their strong support. However, the ARC had never funded such a Centre in the humanities and some extraordinary work would have to be done by McCalman to achieve what many thought was impossible. Thus the concept for what would finally be called the Centre for Cross-Cultural Research (CCR) was born. At the subsequent inauguration of the CCR several metaphors related to conception and birth were utilised. The two Centres would eventually be described as 'sister' institutions. But however their relationship was later described and phrased the CCR was without doubt the child of the HRC and McCalman was without doubt the father.

McCalman and Thomas's resulting submission to the ARC forecast a Centre focussing on long-term fellowships and research projects to complement the HRC's focus on short-term fellowships and conferences and joint research projects. There would be three integrated individual work streams, comprising Studies of Australia in the Asia-

Professor Deane Terrell, Professor Nicholas Thomas and Professor Iain McCalman at the CCR opening, 1997.

Pacific region in the eighteenth and nineteenth centuries, which would be McCalman's field; Anthropology, Archaeology and Art History, which would be Nicholas Thomas's; and Ethnographic Film and CD-ROM Anthologies, to be handled by Dr David MacDougall. Later Professor Joan Kerr of the University of NSW joined to work on visual culture. Bringing two such distinguished scholars in their respective fields as the latter to ANU and into the CCR was an enormous boost. The proposed new Centre for Advanced Cultural Studies would be complementary to the HRC, as one third of the future projects of the HRC would fit into the subjects nominated. The new Centre would of course require a full-time Director, and McCalman proposed Nicholas Thomas for that role. It was however the intention that the Director of the new Centre would be supervised by the Director of the HRC. This relationship between the two Directors was thus fundamental to the whole strategy: the new institution was to be a centre within a centre which would generate new sources of funding to provide for the expansion of the HRC and thus allow the HRC to take on long-term research projects by the appointment of funded postdoctoral scholars to work on such projects. It soon became apparent that this concept was not going to be acceptable to the ARC, so it seemed that the new Centre would have to operate as an independent unit, which would obviously pose potential administrative problems. However, it was intended to get around this by having Iain McCalman play a leading role in both Centres.

The HRC Steering Committee recorded on 30 July 1996 that the submission for the new centre, to be called the Centre for Cross-Cultural Studies

> had developed to a site visit on 8 August [by the ARC]. The relationship of the Centre with the HRC was discussed and it was noted that several activities would be carried out jointly, ie, conferences, summer school, sharing visiting fellowships. The Director of the HRC would also devote 1/3 of his time to research in the new Centre'.[7]

This produced a significant temporary financial benefit to the HRC, in that a third of McCalman's salary for a period of time was to be paid out of the ARC funding for the CCR.

Future prospects seemed extraordinarily exciting: optimism at the HRC had been buoyed by another wide-ranging conference series in 1996 under the theme year of 'Culture and Science'. *Re-Imagining the Pacific: A Conference on Art History and Anthropology in Honour of Bernard Smith* was a joint venture between the HRC and the National Library and attracted more participants than any other save the 'Feminism' and 'Sexuality' blockbusters, Bernard Smith's opening public lecture being attended by around 450 people. The Conference resulted in a major publication edited by Nicholas Thomas from ANU and Dr Diane Losche from the College of Fine Arts, University of NSW and was also sponsored by Qantas, the Canberra School of Art at ANU, the Faculty of Arts at ANU, the Power Institute of Fine Arts, University of Sydney, the Wenner-Gren Foundation for Anthropological Research, and the Australian Foundation for Culture and Humanities. Its intention was to review Bernard Smith's fundamental contributions to understanding colonial art and settler colonialism as well as the representation of non-European peoples in the Pacific. It examined new ways of understanding how representations of the Pacific were constructed by Europeans and Indigenous peoples and then looked at settler and Indigenous traditions in Australian art. Key speakers included Professor Anne Salmond from New Zealand, Dr Bronwen Douglas, then at La Trobe University, Dr Jocelyn Hackforth-Jones from Richmond College London, Professor Jonathan Lamb from Princeton, Margo Neale, then Curator of Indigenous art at the Queensland Art Gallery, Professor Fred Myers, New York University, Dr Howard Morphy then at the Pitt Rivers Museum, Dr Michael Rosenthal from the University of Warwick, Professors Terry Smith, University of Sydney and Joan Kerr, University of NSW, and Dr Sylvia Kleinert, Professor Margaret Jolly, Nigel Lendon, and Professor Nicholas Thomas from ANU, with artists Judy Watson from Australia and John Pule from New Zealand participating as keynote speakers.

The themed HRC conference on *Science and Other Knowledge Traditions* held at James Cook University in Cairns, and convened by Dr Henrietta Fourmile of Bukal Consulting Queensland, Dr David Turnbull from Deakin University and Associate Professor (later Professor) Paul Turnbull from James Cook University, drew a remarkable 100 or so people a day, including secondary school teachers from North Queensland. A highly significant feature was the attendance of Indigenous scholars, Elders and Knowledge Custodians from North Queensland Murri and Islander communities. Mick Dodson, now a Professor at ANU and then Aboriginal and Torres Strait Islander Social Justice Commissioner, opened the conference. Other speakers singled out as truly memorable by participants were Hori Parata of the Ngati Wai Trust and his colleagues and Aurukun Elder Mrs Gladys Tybingoompa. Important papers from this Conference were published in a special issue of the HRC's journal *Humanities Research* in 2000. The tenth David Nichol Smith seminar *Margins and Metropolis: Literature, Culture and Science, 1660-1830* convened by Dr Ian Higgins and Dr Gillian Russell, both of the Department of English, Faculty of Arts, ANU, provided an important impetus for eighteenth century scholarship in Australia and New Zealand. This conference marked the return of the DNS seminar to Canberra after a thirteen-year absence and was jointly sponsored by the HRC, the National Library, the Australasian and Pacific Society for Eighteenth-Century Studies (APSECS), Qantas and the British Council.

Another HRC major themed conference in 1996 was *The Natural Sciences and the Social Sciences* convened by Dr Dorothy Porter from Birkbeck College, University of London with a number of overseas speakers, and a Colloquium on *Enlightenment, Religion and Science in the Long Eighteenth Century* in conjunction with the Research School of Social Sciences at ANU and convened by McCalman with again a number of overseas specialists. There were over 60 visitors to the HRC in 1996 and a number of shared seminars and lectures including a poetry reading by Les Murray (shared with RSSS), lectures by Professors Clive Emsley and Peter Gay (with the Department of History) and Professor Evelyn Fox Keller (with Women's Studies and the John Curtin School of Medical Research). Visiting Fellows in 1996 included Professor David Okpako from the University of Ibadan, Nigeria, Dr Michael Rosenthal from Warwick (who began his important book later published by Yale University Press in 1999 on the art of Thomas Gainsborough while an HRC Visiting Fellow in 1996), Dr Nick Haslam from the New School of Social Research, Dr Martin Fitzpatrick from the University of Wales, Professor Claude Rawson from Yale and Professor Marilyn Butler, Rector of Exeter College, Oxford, who declared in her report: 'The conferences have been superb'.

There were also non-themed HRC conferences: *Mad Cows and Modernity: the Crisis of Creutzfeldt-Jakob Disease,* at that time massively increasing the distaste of continental Europe for things British, convened by McCalman and artist and author Robin Wallace-Crabbe to consider an epidemiological crisis in contexts including historical contexts. This conference originated as the first intellectual collaboration of the new National Academics Forum which combined all four Learned Academies. The topic had originated with Professors Paul Bourke and Sir Gustav Nossal. It was appropriate, interesting and a testimony to the HRC's formidable reputation that it was the Centre that was asked to run this science/social sciences/humanities conference at very short notice. It was undoubtedly an outstanding success – so much so that there was great demand for a book. Speakers

Cover of HRC monograph *Mad Cows and Modernity*.

included medical experts like Dr Charles Guest from the National Centre for Epidemiology and Population Health, ANU. The resulting monograph edited by McCalman with Benjamin Penny and Misty Cook (who had joined the HRC as Publications Officer) is still one of the Centre's most popular sellers. Other non-themed conferences were *Questions of Time and History*, convened by Dipesh Chakrabarty and Penny; and *The Discovery of European Sources in Australian Libraries*, convened by the University Library in conjunction with the Gladys Krieble Foundation. Dr Alastair MacLachlan and Professor Ross Poole organised a summer school on *Nationalism and National Identity*, which brought together participants from History, Philosophy, Cultural Studies, Literary Studies, Women's Studies, Aboriginal Studies, Legal Theory and Comparative Religion, among other forms of intellectual exercise. Margo Neale convened an Indigenous Curatorial Workshop with 30 participants in August 1996, followed by *Transcultural Exchanges: the Asia-Australia Art Connection*, a colloquium convened by McCalman and Professor Anthony Milner of Asian Studies. Speakers included Drs Nicholas Thomas, John Clark and Geremie Barmé from the ANU and one of the present authors, Dr Caroline Turner, then Deputy Director of the Queensland Art Gallery. This seminar considered the dramatic changes taking place as Australia sought in the 1990s to become more Asia-focussed and Asia-literate.

The HRC was preparing the way for the new Centre by exploring intellectual areas of great relevance to the proposed new Centre. These were, of course, also areas which had, particularly in recent years, been central to the HRC's programmes. It was intended the two Centres would operate in such areas in intellectual partnership while taking on different roles. McCalman was also extending the horizons of the HRC's philosophy and the geographical focus of activities. 'In truth', he told the Delmas Colloquium on The Future of European Studies in November 1996, 'we are not Europeans in other than the broadest outline . . . As antipodeans it is not only our feet that point the wrong way, but our minds as well . . . I have tried', he continued, 'to recontextualize European studies within the HRC's annual thematic program . . . Somewhat to my surprise I discovered that my perspective on the subject was close to that of the original founding charter of the HRC . . . As enunciated by Professor Dick Johnson in 1973, the Centre proposed to focus particularly

> on aspects of European thought and culture . . . which have had a substantial impact on the thought and life of . . . Australia, New Zealand, Oceania and Asia. By

stressing that this must entail a two-way process of cultural exchanges and adaptations, we arrive at a contemporary vision of how European studies can be revitalised within humanities research. Accordingly the HRC has over the last three years sought: i. To break down the separation between Asia-Pacific and European scholarly theories, methods and approaches . . . ii. To reconfigure traditional Western analyses of European cultural traditions so as to include Antipodean, Pacific and Asian perspectives and experiences . . . We aim not only to take European studies out to Australians but also to take Australia and the Pacific out to Europeans.[8]

This was, of course, continuing the strategy that Donaldson and Clarke had initiated in 1981 and that Clarke's work on the Middle East in particular had further extended, but in the context of the Keating push into Asia in the 1990s and Australia's long overdue recognition that it was not only geographically but potentially in many other ways a part of the Asia-Pacific, McCalman had taken it further. And McCalman acknowledged that it was more than a focus on Asia and the Pacific and entailed 'working on a pretty broad front', as Donaldson had put it, doing what only the Centre could do, moving beyond the Eurocentric horizons of the original mandate of the Centre to encompass a global perspective, which naturally included an Australian one. It was a strategy which McCalman proposed that the new Centre for Cross-Cultural Research, now at last a reality as a result of a great deal of hard work, should be able to augment.

McCalman's last message to the readers of the HRC *Bulletin* in 1996 hailed the New Year as

> an historic moment for the HRC; from January 1997 we will be working in close co-operation – symbiosis might be a better way to describe it – with a new sister research centre in the humanities . . . The new Centre for Cross-Cultural Research is the first SRC [Special Research Centre] . . . to be awarded in the field of the humanities. The Director will be Professor Nicholas Thomas, of Archaeology and Anthropology, The Faculties. I will work part of the time in the Centre as Deputy Director . . . While the HRC will continue to foster and expand our broad mission to serve as a national catalyst for the humanities, the Centre for Cross-Cultural Research will concentrate on exploring

the "formation of cultural identities and cross-cultural relations in Australia and the Asia-Pacific region".[9]

At the inauguration of the CCR in January 1997 the then ANU Vice-Chancellor Deane Terrell pointed to the enhanced opportunities for international collaboration provided by the new Centre and Hilary McPhee, Chair of the Australia Council, spoke of the potential for the new Centre in policy and publishing while launching the HRC's latest three publications: *The Articulate Surface: Dialogues on paintings between conservators, curators and art historians* edited by Dr Sue-Anne Wallace, Jacqueline Macnaughtan and Jodi Parvey; *National Biographies and National Identity* edited by Iain McCalman, Jodi Parvey and Misty Cook and *Africa Today* edited by Peter F. Alexander, Ruth Hutchison and Deryck Schreuder. But the success of the bid to the ARC meant more than research outcomes and intellectual possibilities. The bottom line in crass terms was that McCalman's efforts would result in over $10 million coming into ANU for the CCR alone from the ARC over a period of nine years and there would be other significant financial successes to follow in other grants and external funding for both Centres.

The HRC was further strengthened in the late nineties and early years of the new century by individual ARC research grants won by Clarke and McCalman and by a strategy of McCalman's to attract Australian Research Council Fellows for periods up to five years as well as Visiting Scholars and adjunct academics who stayed longer than the by now typical period for Visiting Fellows of three months. Their contributions helped augment the HRC's long-term research profile. Senior art scholar Dr Helen Topliss, who as a Visiting Fellow had also made many contributions to the programmes of the Centre, was an ARC Research Fellow from 1994–96. Dr John Docker was an ARC Research Fellow for five years to 1998 and then an Adjunct Senior Fellow and made a considerable impact on the HRC's activities in English and philosophy and on its intellectual life, convening several major conferences as well as maintaining an extraordinary publications output. Leading historian Professor Bill Gammage joined the HRC in July 1998 as an ARC Senior Research Fellow to work on the critical history of Aboriginal land management and also made a most significant contribution. As he noted, the HRC provided a unique environment for a scholar such as himself working in an interdisciplinary way across fields as disparate as history, anthropology and botany. His book *The Sky Travellers: Journeys in New Guinea 1938–1939* (Melbourne University Press) published in 1998 won the

Dr Helen Topliss, ARC Fellow.

Dr Trin Minh-ha and Dr Brian Massumi.

1999 Queensland Premier's Literary Award for Best Non-Fiction. Dr Brian Massumi was an ARC Queen Elizabeth II Research Fellow in the nineties working on ways of theorising vision, a project 'aiming to inject alternate philosophical perspectives into current debates in cultural studies, the status of the body and cultures of vision' and was an inspiration to many young scholars in philosophy, art, science and cultural studies. Dr Libby Robin completed an ARC Post Doctoral Fellowship in 1998 after publishing her important and much praised book *Defending the Little Desert: The rise of ecological consciousness in Australia*, (Melbourne University Press). Her second book also begun at the HRC, *The Flight of the Emu*, later won the 2003 Victorian Premier's Literary Award for Science. Dr Paul Duro joined the HRC as a Visiting Scholar in 1998 working on French nineteenth century painting and was a stimulating presence at the Centre. Renowned historian of subaltern studies, Professor Dipesh Chakrabarty of the University of Chicago was appropriately an HRC Australian Studies Graduate Programme Eminent Teaching Fellow in 1997.

The HRC was delighted to have distinguished scholar in American history Dr Donna Merwick, who had recently retired from Melbourne University, and former Director of the National Gallery of Australia Mrs Betty Churcher, who became adjuncts shared between the HRC and CCR in 1997/1998. Dr Paul Pickering began a five-year ARC

Dr John Docker, ARC Senior Fellow.   Dr Libby Robin, ARC Fellow.

Queen Elizabeth II Research Fellowship in 2000 and was immediately an energetic and invaluable presence at the HRC. Dr (later Professor) Tim Bonyhady became a shared CCR, CRES and HRC Fellow and published his prizewinning book *The Colonial Earth* at that time; and Dr Roger Benjamin later Power Professor of Fine Arts at the University of Sydney was an HRC/CCR shared Visiting Researcher in 2002 completing his major book on Orientalism. Dr Alastair Maclachlan continued a long-term association with the HRC contributing to seminars, summer schools and conferences when he moved to Canberra in 2002 and was attached to the HRC as a long-term Fellow, as were Professor Amareswar Galla, shared with RSPAS, and Dr David Pear, shared with the School of Music, who both joined in 2002. They greatly enhanced the HRC's focus on heritage and sustainable development and creative arts respectively. The focus on heritage was enhanced when Professor Stephen Foster joined the HRC as a shared appointment with the National Museum of Australia and the Faculty of Arts at ANU in 2002/2003 to work on developing Museum Studies, and Emeritus Professor Ken Taylor became a Visiting Fellow in 2002. A number of specialist researchers also came in order to work with Iain McCalman on eighteenth century projects including Dr Clara Tuite (Associate Editor with Dr Jon Mee and Dr Gillian Russell of McCalman's *An Oxford Companion to the Romantic Age*), Kate Fullagar (Assistant Editor), and Dr Christa Knellwolf, who came on a Swiss Government grant and co-convened the 2001 David Nichol Smith colloquium and edited subsequent important publications with McCalman. Eminent literary scholar Professor Bruce Bennett became an Adjunct Professor of the HRC in 2003.

Many of these appointments were still to come in 1997/98. In the meantime the CCR appointments were beginning to be made and to offer opportunities for enriching exchanges.

Symbiosis between the two Centres was the keyword. But the prospects for continuing symbiosis were rendered more difficult from the outset by the refusal of the ARC to endorse the concept of 'a centre within a centre', fundamental to McCalman's vision. A new position of Executive and Liaison Officer was created in January 1997 with a view to facilitating consolidation of the links between the two Centres. It was filled by Julie Gorrell, who had been at the Research Office and was highly experienced with ARC grants and had been extensively involved in assisting McCalman throughout the process with the successful bid to the ARC for the CCR. An early initiative of the two Centres was the introduction in 1997 of a joint refereed journal *Humanities Research*, replacing the *HRC Bulletin* and edited until 1999 by Dr Benjamin Penny assisted by Misty Cook. The first issue of the journal contained essays by Nicholas Thomas, Greg Dening, Dipesh Chakrabarty and Sasha Grishin. It was remarkable to say the least that the HRC should have expanded its own conference programme during this time of setting up the new Centre. The HRC theme for 1997 was 'Identities', peculiarly appropriate at a time when the Centre was undergoing a significant transformation of its own identity. Activities included a seminar in honour of the work in urban research of Patrick Troy convened by Dr Tim Bonyhady and Dr Mark Peel. Dr Margot Lyon of the Department of Archaeology and Anthropology and Dr Jack Barbalet of the Department of Sociology at ANU convened the conference *Emotion in Social Life and Social Theory*, which attracted 100 participants. Another 200 attended a conference on *Indigenous Rights, Political Theory and the Reshaping of Institutions* convened by Dr Will Sanders of ANU and Dr Paul Patton of the University of Sydney and supported by RSSS and the Australian Foundation for Culture and the Humanities, which brought together Aboriginal and non-Aboriginal activists and political theorists. A seminar on *Identities in the Eastern Mediterranean in Antiquity* to honour the work of Fergus Millar, Camden Professor of Ancient History at Oxford, drew 57 people. The HRC's particular strength had always been a broad spread and these events demonstrated continuity with classical traditions and history combined with a focus on critical contemporary issues.

An exhibition at the Drill Hall Gallery, *New Australian Images through British Eyes,* featuring the work of British-born artists David Blackburn, Mary Husted and John Wolseley, curated by Dr Sasha Grishin and supported by the British Council, IDP Education Australia, ANU, the Hart Gallery London and Goanna Print, was visited by around 1800 people over a month and enhanced already excellent relations with the Director of the Drill Hall Gallery, Mrs Nancy Sever. The main non-thematic conference, presented by ANU and AIATSIS on the ever-relevant topic *Is 'Racism' Un-Australian?* attracted 130 participants and offered 12 papers which were published by Monash University as *The Resurgence of Racism: Howard, Hanson and the Race Debate.* Dipesh Chakrabarty of the University of Chicago and, at the time, an HRC Australian Studies Graduate Programme Eminent Teaching Fellow convened a workshop on *The New Australian Racism,* co-sponsored by the HRC and the Research Centre in Intercommunal Studies of the University of Western Sydney, attended by 60 people and addressed by Professor Ien Ang of that University and by Dr Ghassan Hage of Sydney University, with Professor Ann Curthoys and Dr Meaghan Morris as discussants. In all, three conferences, a workshop, a seminar and an exhibition. One would not have thought that the staff of the HRC could have had much else to keep them busy. Meantime other

Attendees at the Is Racism Un-Australian conference, with Professor Ann Curthoys in the front row, second from left, in 1997.

Launch of *Oxford Companion to the Romantic Age*. Professor Iain McCalman, Dr Gillian Russell and Dr Clara Tuite.

changes were occurring. Two long-serving members of the HRC left to pursue other career directions. Jodi Parvey, as McCalman noted, had 'worked at the Centre for fourteen years as office administrator and, most recently, publications officer as well . . . and Stephanie Stockdill, who was with us for four crucial years'.[10] Ann Palmer joined Lia Szokalski in the front office. Later Judy Buchanan replaced Lia as Administrative Assistant. Leena Messina took on Visiting Fellows as well as Conferences. There was considerable planning of possible future activities to include the CCR.

Initiatives for strategic planning at the HRC and CCR in 1997 were complicated by the fact that McCalman himself was effectively away from the HRC for several months in the role of Acting Director of the CCR in the temporary absence of Nicholas Thomas, and then away entirely on Special Leave at the University of London and All Souls, Oxford, until February 1998, to complete the editing of his massive 500 000 word multi-contributor, illustrated reference work, *An Oxford Companion to the Romantic Age: British Culture 1776–1832*, for which he was General Editor working, as noted, with Dr Jon Mee, Dr Gillian Russell, and Dr Clara Tuite as Associate Editors, Kate Fullagar and Patsy Hardy as Assistant Editors and an eminent academic advisory board. It was a volume which, when completed in 1999, would add much to the HRC's formidable reputation in the field of European studies and it was the first time that Oxford UK had commissioned a Companion on a British subject outside the British Isles – another feather in the HRC's cap. While in the UK and USA McCalman delivered The Cambridge University Press lecture at the British Association for Romantic Studies conference and The Webb lecture at the University of Maryland, Baltimore, as well as papers at Oxford, at the Institute for Advanced Studies in the Humanities, Edinburgh and at St Andrews University.

Space for the two Centres was now becoming a major issue. The initial arrangement had been for the CCR to be located on the lower floor of the A.D. Hope Building, which had been the home of the HRC for over 20 years. It had been an ideal location in almost all respects save the lack of air conditioning: it was admirably accessible, at the terminus of Ellery Crescent, which made it in effect the public entrance to ANU; there was still at least adequate parking adjacent; it was in the genuine heart of the University, a short stroll to the University Library in the J.B. Chifley Building and R.G. Menzies Building, to all the Faculty Offices, to the Union, the banks and the restaurants, and a reasonably short walk to the School of Arts, the School of Music and not too far a walk to Civic; and it had even acquired its own supernatural resident, according to a female HRC Visiting Fellow, who complained of having been disturbed by a poltergeist, which was probably only the genial shade of Professor Hope himself. What was perhaps still more compelling than all these was the close proximity to The Faculties, which had engendered the Centre and had from the outset regarded it as their very own Research School. 'The HRC', Ann Curthoys considered,

> would never have relocated if the CCR didn't exist – it was fine where it was in the A D Hope building, especially once the new cubicles were built and the Arts Faculty started downsizing, reducing pressure in that building generally. But the CCR was enormous, just endless people not only on the ARC grant but others on various other grants ... It just could not fit into the A D Hope building.[11]

The CCR was indeed enormous by HRC standards: there were only 3.5 academics on establishment, as Nicholas Thomas reported in the 1998 annual report, but the academic staff, including short-term appointments, had already grown to 20 and with the inclusion of administrative, research staff and students (the latter numbering 15) the total was 47 with, as well, 14 Visiting Fellows and 53 visiting scholars (graduates participating in one month courses). ARC funding in that year was over $1 million and the total budget of the Centre was close to $2 million while the HRC remained fairly static at much less than $1 million. The CCR had had an impressive start in areas of publishing and grants for research projects, including several inaugurated originally with McCalman, such as in publications McCalman's Oxford Companion and the Travel series with Cassell, and in research, a major multimedia project with the National Library on Cook's voyages directed by Dr Paul Turnbull.

The space problem had become urgent by the time McCalman returned. A logical solution might have seemed for the Centres to relocate to an existing building and possible space at the Coombs Building was becoming available, just 300 metres or so away, at the other end of Ellery Crescent. But McCalman had a more ambitious solution in mind. The first year of cooperation between the sister institutions, he recognised in 1998, had 'combined some exhilarating new developments with some difficult new challenges. For both Centres the paramount challenge was to cope with existing and future pressures on space'. His aspiration had

> always been to achieve administrative and intellectual synergies, efficiencies and collaborations between the

Attendees at an HRC conference in the A.D. Hope Building Reading Room. Professor Graeme Clarke (*front row, fourth from right*), Professor Iain McCalman (*second row, far right*), Professor Anthony Low (*third row, second from right*), Julie Gorrell (*front row, far right*), in the 1990s.

two Centres, while retaining our distinct missions and identities . . . The possibility that a new or refurbished building on the Acton Peninsula might be made available was exciting both because it promised to resolve our space difficulties and to open up potential new collaborations with the National Museum of Australia and the Institute of Aboriginal and Torres Strait Islander Research, both of which were relocating to new buildings in that precinct. The possibility of this move aroused some anxieties among friends and co-tenants in the A. D. Hope building, who were anxious to retain long-time intellectual and collegial relations, but these concerns were, we hope, allayed by our strong and genuine reassurances that our relations would be retained and even enhanced in various ways.[12]

The concerns of some members of The Faculties would not be so easily allayed. The new facilities would, however, allow the HRC to have more long-term Research Fellows including Faculty staff on sabbatical leave. There were indeed suggestions that pressure for relocation was driven less by academic considerations related to ANU than by considerations involving the two Centres' roles as

Old Canberra House.

national centres. However, others could and did see the outreach possibilities of the new proposal. It was impelled further in any event by the decision of the Commonwealth Government to construct a new National Museum of Australia and an Institute of Aboriginal and Torres Strait Islander Studies on a sublime position at the end of the Acton Peninsula. The most conspicuous University presence on the base of the Peninsula was Old Canberra House, which might well be described as a perfect setting for an Agatha Christie or John Dickson Carr murder mystery, and had functioned first as the residence of the inaugural Administrator of the ACT, then as the residence of the British High Commissioner, then as an annex to the Commonwealth Club and latterly as a staff club and watering hole for ANU staff and students.

What McCalman and Thomas were now proposing was that a purpose-built Humanities Research Building be constructed on the Peninsula beyond Old Canberra House to contain both the HRC and the CCR. 'There is absolutely no doubt', McCalman wrote to the Pro Vice-Chancellor (Administration) Chris Burgess,

> that the HRC and CCR need to be situated contiguously. Not only are there all the advantages of intellectual synergy . . . but ARC advisors have also stressed that the greatest cause of difficulties with Special Research Centres in the past has been physical separation from their host or affiliate institutions. There is no disputing that both the HRC and CCR need a considerably expanded space provision to accommodate their current and future growth. The ANU has in these two centres a humanities research hub that is unrivalled in Australia and envied abroad.

Moreover, a 'crucial intellectual nexus' was 'developing between our centres and the National Museum of Australia, a nexus which seems to me to clinch the logic of situating us in a purpose-built premises on the Acton Peninsula'. 'In practice', McCalman considered, 'resituation on the Acton Peninsula would not greatly diminish our present contacts and relations with schools and departments located around the A.D. Hope precinct'. There was the further consideration which greatly strengthened the case that

> Dr John Gage of the Economics History department, Faculty of Arts, has presented a proposal for a "European Centre," which he hopes will be funded in part by the

> European Union as a gift to Australia in commemoration of Federation. He envisages that such a centre would be located in the Acton Peninsula and would house the HRC, the CCR and other humanities research units.[13]

It was of course entirely logical that the HRC would be heavily involved in the development of such a Centre given its role over 25 years as a major centre of European studies in Australia, and McCalman served on the Advisory Board to set up the Centre. A later administrative review would describe the HRC in management terms as an 'incubator' to the two Centres (the CCR and the National Europe Centre), recognising McCalman's and the HRC's seminal role in the development of both, especially as, when the National Europe Centre did come into being, it was attached administratively to the HRC with McCalman as Chair of the Europe Centre's Board.

McCalman's views were endorsed by the highly influential Building and Grounds Committee of the University Council. Chair Warwick Williams told Pro Vice-Chancellor (Academic) Robin Stanton that the Committee had

> felt for several years that the University should be developing, or at least have a significant presence, on Acton Peninsula . . . The Committee also noted that, given the Government's decision to locate the National Museum of Australia and other bodies on the old Canberra Hospital site, there could be several exciting opportunities for the University to provide cognate facilities to those groups in this area . . . Arising out of the associated publicity and discussions, the HRC and CCR expressed interest in relocating to the Peninsula . . . In recent months there have been discussions about a possible "Europe Centre". . . .[14]

All this positive thinking was however challenged by a storm of anguished protest from staff of The Faculties at being deprived of the presence of what they had reasonably viewed for 26 years as an integral part of their own establishment. The storm culminated in a petition to Burgess signed by no fewer than 52 members of The Faculties, including members of Nicholas Thomas's own old Department of Anthropology and Archaeology. They protested that relocating the HRC and CCR away from the Arts Faculty 'at a remote location on Acton Peninsula represents a significant diminution of the productive intellectual and collegial activity that we have enjoyed with those Centres' and 'make it impossible for us to have close and fruitful association with their staff and visiting fellows'. It would 'diminish the intellectual environment of the Faculty for both staff and graduate students in a wide range of disciplines and remove one of the distinctive features of the Faculty that is an important enhancement of its image and standing across the country'. Furthermore, both the HRC and the CCR 'have grown out of the Arts Faculty itself'. More serious still, the proposal would 'isolate scholars brought in by the University at great expense from around the world by placing them in the least accessible location for easy formal and informal interaction with the University community'.[15] Individual complainants objected that access to libraries would be much reduced on the Acton Peninsula, although 'libraries were utterly essential to humanities research'; that the meeting facilities of the HRC were widely used not just by the two Centres but by many other Departments in 'one of the most efficient uses of such space on campus'; and that the two Centres were after all humanities research centres which should be located adjacent to the existing humanities teaching and research centres in the University to the mutual benefit of all concerned.

These arguments had some force (the new site was approximately one kilometre from the University Library in the Chifley Building), but there was equally no answer to the counter-objections that the two Centres could not be contained within the A.D. Hope Building any longer; that McCalman and Thomas were both insistent that the Centres could not be separated physically; and that there was nowhere else to put them if they were not to be separated, except on the Acton Peninsula. Pro Vice-Chancellor Robin Stanton attempted to assure the critics that

> far from being involved in any process that would banish the HRC and CCCR [sic] to a remote part of campus, my current situation is one of listening to the centres ... [with] ... their acute space problems and noting the considerable planning work being carried out by the Facilities and Services Division to provide options for meeting space requirements of various sections of the University.[16]

Momentum for relocation was unstoppable in any event by now, accelerated by the fascinating prospects that the proposed Europe Centre offered. A meeting in Brussels between the Master of University House and a representative of the European Commission agreed that the Centre would be 'a post-graduate research institute with good capacity to attract senior academics and policy people ... the ANU (and its supporters) were prepared to finance the construction of a quality building on Acton Peninsula to a value of around A$6-7 million'.[17] Pro Vice-Chancellor (Administration) Burgess advised McCalman that

> the University has a tremendous site on its campus, a strong academic and practical interest in matters European and given our strong Asian connections we make for a very stable stepping stone into a currently turbulent but nevertheless exciting and important region . . . If all this were to come about, we would have a very handsome facility with a set of prestigious and very appropriate neighbours in the building as well as a vibrant and worthwhile ongoing activity to mark the coming of the early European settlers and the waves of immigration particularly post 1945. This is an exciting vision to us here in Canberra.[18]

Despite all the great achievements of the past three years McCalman was still finding himself faced with the eternal problem of funding, involved essentially with the other eternal issue of the position of the HRC within the structure of ANU itself. For 25 years, McCalman explained to the then Deputy Vice-Chancellor Professor David H. Green,

> the HRC has truly been a 'University Centre', with its funding not subject to claims by either The Faculties or the IAS. Although conceived originally by researchers in The Faculties and, therefore, having strong academic links to The Faculties, the *raison d'être* of the HRC was to act as a bridge between the two parts of the ANU. Its funding was not channelled through the faculty with which it had strong academic links, i.e. Faculty of Arts, but was separate, although HRC funding was subjected to the same external influences brought on by Commonwealth funding policies, such as the 'clawback'. Since inception, the University has grappled with the HRC's status and what it meant to be a <u>research-only centre</u> that is not located in The Faculties or the IAS. Because it had a very small core staff, it could only survive administratively by assistance from a larger group, i.e. The Faculties (Faculties Resources Office) . . . or a School within the Institute, notably RSSS. Since inception, the HRC has perforce

defied the binary nature of the ANU's structure. For many reasons, but mainly administrative ones, the HRC allied itself successively with one or other of those two parts, although the terminology used to describe the alliance created further ambiguities in its status. "Affiliation" was the term devised to describe its place within the structure and its relationship variously to The Faculties or the IAS (there was simply no other language that could describe its place). This term was then appropriated in ways that led to further ambiguities and confusion, both internally and externally to the institution.[19]

In 1998 McCalman was successful in ensuring that the HRC did acquire a new formal status as a University Centre made accountable to the Pro Vice-Chancellor (Academic) and was also, as McCalman put it in the 1998 Annual report,

> given a voice in a new combined grouping of Deans, heads of Research Schools and University Centre Directors that meets regularly under the chairmanship of the Deputy Vice-Chancellor. This has given us greater autonomy and stature within the University administration, as well as a long sought forum for registering our needs and aspirations.

He went on to say that:

> We have also become members of an informal but important body of University Centre Directors which meets periodically to air common concerns. These changes, alongside our growing connections and collaborations with external bodies, particularly the national cultural institutions, led us in turn to initiate a restructuring of our own internal governance. We have recommended to the Vice-Chancellor that the HRC's governance be restructured to provide a Director's Advisory Group and an Advisory Committee.[20]

The year 1998 had been another demanding yet exciting intellectual year for the HRC. The chosen theme was 'Home and Away: Journeys, Migrations, Diaspora', the catchy main title inspired by a long-running TV soap opera. Anthony Low convened a symposium in honour of Sir Keith Hancock, in conjunction with RSSS and the Australian Academy of the Humanities, on the 100th anniversary of Hancock's birth. Dr

Barry Higman of RSSS and HRC Visiting Fellow from the University of York Professor James Walvin convened a second conference on *Black Diasporas in the Western Hemisphere*. Visiting Fellow from the University of Sydney Dr Deirdre Coleman convened a third on *Re-Orienting Romanticism* with Dr Peter Otto and Dr Clara Tuite from the University of Melbourne. Professor Wilfrid Prest of the University of Adelaide and Dr Graham Tulloch of Flinders University convened a fourth, on *The Scatterlings of Empire*, held at the beautiful bijou Art Gallery of South Australia in conjunction with the University of Adelaide. But the blockbuster of the year was inevitably the *Tenth Irish-Australian Conference* held in conjunction with La Trobe University and convened by Dr Philip Bull of that University, to mark the bicentenary of the Year of the French in 1798. That catastrophe of all catastrophes most dear to Irish hearts was memorialised with poetry readings, music recitals, art exhibitions and film screenings, together attracting some 400 people many of whom endured without complaint as true patriots the tepid food and cold showers consequent on the collapse of basic infrastructure in Victoria. The HRC collaborated with the Art Gallery of NSW in supporting a conference in association with Roger Benjamin's important exhibition on Orientalism: 'The Oriental Mirage: Visions of the East from Delacroix to Klee' and followed this in 1999 by association with Queensland Art Gallery on the Third Asia-Pacific Triennial Conference which attracted nearly 700 delegates from over 30 countries to Brisbane. This conference was convened by Dr Caroline Turner as Deputy Director of the Queensland Art Gallery with Iain McCalman and Dr Russell Trood of Griffith University, supported by Queensland Art Gallery staff.

The following year delivered a rather less frenetic program, albeit in the nature of a temporary slackening of pace. However, the intellectual depth could not be faulted. The HRC theme in 1999 was the formidably serious one of 'Religion, Society and Values'. Professor Robert Goodin and Dr David Parker of ANU convened a Named Seminar in honour of Martha Nussbaum who as public philosopher had interests extending from classical philosophy to reflections on liberal education and human cloning – interests as laudably wide as those of the HRC. Professor Philip Pettit of ANU convened another Named Seminar and workshop in honour of Richard Rorty; Benjamin Penny convened a conference, *The History of Daoism*, in honour of the great scholar Emeritus Professor Liu Ts'un-yan, with support from the Italian Embassy, the French Embassy through the Alliance Française and the Goethe Institut; Professor Robert Holton of

Flinders University and Dr Sandra Holton of Adelaide convened a second conference on *Max Weber, Religion and Social Action*, which attracted a wide range of historians, sociologists, anthropologists, social psychologists and students of religion. The inaugural Freilich Foundation lecture series in 1999 was delivered by Professor Henry Reynolds, and Iain McCalman and Professor John Frow of the University of Queensland convened an un-themed spectacular on *The Humanities, Arts and Public Culture in two Hemispheres* at the Queensland Art Gallery, which brought together directors of humanities centres and institutes in the United States, Canada, Australia and Europe, members of the academic and arts communities and representatives of various relevant funding agencies. This was the inauguration of another innovative strategic plan of McCalman's to bring together humanities centres in Australia with counterparts overseas, the latter already in a formal association known as the Consortium of Humanities Centers and Institutes (CHCI), of which McCalman was an International Board member. The result of this conference was the founding of an Australian chapter with McCalman as President.

Then Graeme Clarke retired. His loss had serious implications for the Centre. Clarke was a renowned scholar and excellent administrator. His administrative expertise had been lauded not only by Ian Donaldson, but also by his administrative staff, who are often the people best placed to evaluate the managerial style of a boss. His meticulous ('immaculate' was the word of one administrative staff member) approach to every aspect of the Centre's endeavours while Director and attention to the human relationships of the Centre had achieved a spirit where administrative staff could feel, as one of them stated, that there were opportunities for growth and change and that the HRC was a family which encompassed not only academics and visiting scholars but also those who worked administratively in the Centre. As Director, he had expanded the 'open door' of the Centre to include colleagues in every discipline and had also expanded the HRC Liaison Committees in other universities to make the HRC even more of a national centre for the humanities. He had broadened the geographical reach of the Centre to many more non-European endeavours and its reach in chronological time through wide-ranging programmes from classical studies to contemporary issues such as sexuality. He had extended its intellectual reach to many younger scholars and those outside the University and Academy while, at the same time, maintaining the highest intellectual and academic standards for the HRC. He had also achieved a prodigious record of scholarship classical in every sense of the word: his publications while serving with the HRC included some 32 articles and seven books, among which might be noted *The Letters of St. Cyprian of Carthage (in four volumes)*, *Rediscovering Hellenism*, *The Hellenic Inheritance and the English Imagination*, *Reading the Past in Late Antiquity* and the first of four projected volumes of *Jebel Khalid on the Euphrates: Report on Excavations*. He had served in addition to all this as Member of the Council of The Australian Archaeological Institute at Athens; the National Committee to establish an Australian Centre in Italy; the Council of the Australian Academy of the Humanities; the Selection Committee, Harold White Library Fellowships, National Library of Australia; Visiting Fellow, the School of Historical Studies, Institute for Advanced Study, Princeton and so on, and so on. But he was now 65, the customary age for retirement; he had served ANU as Professor of Classical Studies (and is credited as a major force in helping to keep Classics alive at ANU) and the HRC as Deputy Director, Director, Associate Director and Acting Director for 18 years.

His departure meant that the animate corporate memory of the HRC now reposed in Iain McCalman, Ralph Elliott and the indefatigable Leena Messina, now being praised more than ever by conference organisers and participants for her 'massive, unfailingly resourceful, and patient assistance'. Then Nicholas Thomas resigned and left for the United Kingdom. His departure was at the very least a grievous loss to the CCR, both because of his enormous contribution as an anthropologist with a remarkable sympathy for and comprehension of the cultures of the South Pacific, and also because of the brilliant synergy achieved between himself and McCalman. This wholly unforeseen development naturally caused a major rethinking of the relationship between the two Centres. In the first place, McCalman was now faced with the physically impossible task of acting as director of two centres, without a full-time deputy in either. He would thus be trying to undertake the responsibilities of what would reasonably be four senior academics and ideally six. Moreover, Thomas's departure also meant that the CCR would perforce be acquiring a new Director, who would have to be expected to have his or her quite independent ideas about the direction that CCR would follow.

Relief came when Dr Caroline Turner moved from the Deputy Directorship of the Queensland Art Gallery to assume responsibility as Deputy Director of the HRC in January 2000, bringing the expertise of a cultural historian and long-term art professional, whose many exhibitions had enabled her to establish excellent relations

Caroline Turner, Deputy Director, 2000– .

with international artists, curators and cultural institutions, thus assisting with Iain McCalman's long-term plans to extend the HRC's cultural collaborations. In the 1999 Annual Report McCalman wrote announcing the appointment:

> the HRC was extremely fortunate in recruiting Dr Caroline Turner as our new Deputy Director. Caroline was formerly Deputy Director of the Queensland Art Gallery (QAG) and a highly respected art history scholar specializing in the fields of modern and contemporary Asian, European, and American art. While at QAG, Caroline was Project Director for the Asia-Pacific Triennial of Contemporary Art, one of the most significant Australian cultural achievements of the late twentieth century. She takes up her appointment at an extremely fortuitous moment for the HRC as we consolidate our expansion of collaborative interests into new relationships with national and international cultural

institutions. Caroline's interests and expertise will help us greatly in our effort to broaden our research interests into Asia.[21]

The Asia-Pacific Triennial had included a major community outreach focus and in three exhibitions in 1993, 1996 and 1999 had attracted audiences of well over 300 000. Turner had also served on the Advisory Board of the CCR and was strongly committed to its philosophy and purpose. At the same time, Professor Howard Morphy, a renowned scholar of Indigenous Australian culture, moved from the Department of Anthropology, The Faculties, to become Director of the CCR.

These appointments relieved the pressure on McCalman, to the extent that he was now able to revert to being director of just one centre, with a deputy at the HRC. As well, Morphy's distinguished scholarship in the field of Indigenous Australian culture, including Directorship of the Pitt Rivers Museum at Oxford University and numerous international publications, held the promise of fruitful collaborations as he had been a former HRC Visiting Fellow, and would continue to facilitate the long-held interests of the HRC in sponsoring research which included Indigenous perspectives. His appointment ensured that the CCR would necessarily continue a

Professor Howard Morphy.

strong focus on Indigenous studies as was most appropriate with the appointment of such an eminent scholar. Indeed, one of the flagship endeavours initiated by Iain McCalman for the proposed CCR and which had convinced the ARC of the viability of the CCR was the monumental *Oxford Companion to Aboriginal Art and Culture* then being brought to completion by General Editors Dr Sylvia Kleinert and Margo Neale with a major grant from the Getty Foundation.[22] Professor Morphy's interests would also encompass art and aesthetics, material culture, visual anthropology and ethnographic film, museums, and human adaptation and the evolution of culture, the history of anthropology and anthropological history.[23]

Thus 1999/2000 brought endings but also marked new beginnings for the HRC. Meanwhile the University Council concluded that it would refurbish the 86-year-old Old Canberra House as a domicile for the Directors and administration of the two Centres, after it ceased to function as the ANU Staff Club in March 1999. As well a purpose built building adjacent to and behind Old Canberra House would be constructed for visiting scholars of both Centres. The choice of Old Canberra House had much in its favour: the building was charming, its history was imposing, the grounds were extensive enough to allow for the building of another structure to provide additional office space and the site was magnificent.[24] Nor did it appear to be haunted, although it certainly looked as if it ought to be: the only revenants which disturbed the peace of its new occupants, initially at least, were living members of ANU, who for months afterwards would wander thirstily up to what had been their traditional watering hole, only to find that it had been transformed into the ultimate Australian tragedy of a Pub with No Beer.

Notes

1. *HRC Bulletin*, June 1995, 78, p. 1.
2. 33rd Meeting Advisory Committee, Minutes, 23 Nov. 1995.
3. McCalman to authors, 8 Nov. 2003.
4. Quoted by Benjamin Penny in Penny, 'The Humanities Research Centre and the Freilich Program', paper presented at CHCI Conference 'The Humanities, Arts and Public Culture in Two Hemispheres', Queensland Art Gallery, July 1999.
5. Minutes of the Meeting of the Board of The Faculties, 23 Feb. 1996.
6. Ann Curthoys to the authors, 27 Jan. 2003.
7. 148th Meeting, Steering Committee, 30 July 1996.
8. McCalman, Address to the Delmas Colloquium, 15 Nov. 1996.
9. McCalman, 'From the desk of the Director', *Bulletin*, Dec. 1996, 83, p. 1.
10. McCalman, *Bulletin*, Mar. 1997, 84, pp. 1-2.
11. Curthoys to the authors, 27 Jan. 2003.
12. McCalman, Director's Report, *Annual Report 1998*, pp. 4-6.
13. McCalman to Chris Burgess, 19 Mar. 1998.
14. Burgess to Robin Stanton, 21 May 1998.
15. Petition to Burgess, 22 June 1998.
16. Stanton to Nicholas Peterson, 18 June 1998.
17. Summary points from a meeting in Brussels between Nicholas Clegg, Minister of the cabinet of Sir Leon Brittain, European Commission and Dr R. de Crespigny, Master of University House, 20 Aug. 1998.
18. Burgess to McCalman, 6 Sept. 1998.
19. McCalman to David H. Green, 15 Sept. 1998.
20. McCalman 'Director's Report', *HRC Annual Report*, 1998, pp. 5-6.
21. McCalman 'Director's Report', *HRC Annual Report*, 1999, p. 4.
22. *The Oxford Companion To Aboriginal Art and Culture*, General Editors Sylvia Kleinert and Margo Neale, Oxford University Press, 2000.
23. Website Centre for Cross-Cultural Research, Staff, http://www.anu.edu.au/culture/ (March 2004)
24. The building had been constructed in 1913 as the residence for the Administrator

of the ACT, David Miller. It had also served as the residence for the British High Commissioner and as the first Commonwealth Club as well as the University Staff Club. Julie Gorrell 'Old Canberra House', *HRC Annual Report*, 2000, pp. 39-42.

7 Greeting the Future (2000–2004)

The move from the A.D. Hope Building took place in June 2000. Visiting Fellows were housed in the cottages located in the vicinity of Old Canberra House (OCH) until the new building located behind Old Canberra House, to be known as the WEH Stanner Building, was ready for occupancy in August 2001. There were fewer Visiting Fellows to be accommodated in 2000; but the HRC academic cohort was enhanced by ARC Fellows Professor Bill Gammage and Dr Paul Pickering and Adjuncts including Dr John Docker. Dr Brian Massumi left in 2000 but returned to run one of the HRC's most successful Graduate courses and conferences on 'the Biophilosophy of Life' in 2003 along with former HRC Visiting Fellow Professor Sandra Buckley. One of the most telling demonstrations of the warmth of commitment to the HRC from Fellows and former Fellows has always been their willingness to return and continue to contribute to the Centre's programmes, especially the teaching programmes in later years.

The theme in 2000 was 'Law and the Humanities', and important collaborations occurred with the Faculty of Law and RSSS, some continuing well beyond that year such as Caroline Turner's 'Art and Human Rights' project begun in 2000 in collaboration with Visiting Fellow, distinguished international jurist and Professor of Law at the London School of Economics, Professor Christine Chinkin. Professor Chinkin came in 2000 to convene a conference on *Feminist Explorations of International Law* with Director of the Centre for Public and International Law at ANU, Professor Hilary Charlesworth, one of Australia's most renowned and respected international lawyers. Other

HRC conferences held under this theme were: *Romancing the Tomes: Feminism, Law and Popular Culture* convened by Professor Margaret Thornton from the School of Law and Legal Studies, La Trobe; *Women and Property in Early Modern England* convened by Dr Nancy Wright from the University of Newcastle and Professor Margaret Ferguson from the University of California; *Those Lasting Alliances of Habits – Law, History and the Humanities in the Imperial World,* convened by Dr Ian Holloway of the Faculty of Law, ANU and Professor John McLaren of the Faculty of Law, University of Victoria, British Columbia; *Natural Law and Sovereignty in Early Modern Europe,* convened by Professor Ian Hunter from the Centre for Advanced Studies in the Humanities, Griffith University; *Constructing Law and Disability,* convened by Ms Lee Ann Marks from the School of Law and Legal Studies, La Trobe and Ms Melinda Jones from the Faculty of Law, University of NSW (this conference leading to the speedy construction by ANU of much needed disabled toilet facilities at Old Canberra House); and *Law in Chinese Culture,* convened by Professor Bill Jenner of the China and Korea Centre, ANU and Dr Benjamin Penny. Non-thematic conferences in 2000 were: *Chinese Art: the Future,* convened by Caroline Turner with the National Gallery of Australia; *Lost in the Whitewash: Aboriginal-Chinese Encounters from Federation to Reconciliation,* convened by Dr Penny Edwards of the CCR and Dr Shen Yuan-fang from the Centre for the Study of the Chinese Southern Diaspora, ANU, (later published as an HRC monograph 'Lost in the Whitewash' in 2003); and *Landprints over Boundaries: Celebrating the Work of George Seddon,* convened by Professor Peter Beilharz and Dr Trevor Hogan from La Trobe. Visiting Fellows included Dr Deborah Rose from ANU, Dr Bryan Ward Perkins from Oxford, Dr Peter Sutton from Adelaide, Professor Brian McKnight from the University of Arizona, Professor Alison Mackinnon, Director of the Hawke Institute University of South Australia, Mr Adam Tomkins, from King's College London, Professor John McLaren from the University of Victoria, British Columbia, Dr Rosalinde Kearsley from Macquarie University, Dr Kevin Knox from the California Institute of Technology, Dr John Gage from Cambridge, Professor E. Ann Kaplan from Stony Brook, Dr Don Watson, Professor Barbara Andaya, University of Hawaii, Dr Barry Godfrey from Keele University, and Dr Ann Genovese from the University of Sydney. Other visitors included Professor Jean Howard from Columbia, Professor Patricia Parker from Stanford, Professor John Sutherland from University College, London and Dr Leslie Witz from the University of Cape Town. The HRC supported six interstate speakers travelling to conferences and held 11 conferences in all, including one in London, with 536 participants, during a year in which the Centre faced all the upheaval of a major move.

The theme for 2001 was 'Enlightenment' and it attracted a very large number of specialist eighteenth century scholars including Professors Andrew Vincent and Martin Fitzpatrick from the University of Wales, Professors Donna and Edward Andrew from Canada, Professor Randall McGowen from the University of Oregon, Dr Joanna deGroot, Professor John Barrell and Dr Harriet Guest from the University of York, Professor Marta Petrusewicz from the City University of New York, Dr Jon Mee from Oxford and Dr Kathleen Wilson from the State University of New York at Stony Brook. Seminars included topics on the underside of eighteenth century life as well as its better-known political and social philosophies. Out of theme Visiting Fellows included Joanna Innes and Renaissance specialist Professor Ian Maclean, both from the University of Oxford, Dr Nicholas Mirzoeff, Deputy Director, Humanities Research Centre at Stony Brook and an expert on art and new media, Professor Gabriele Schwab from the University of California Irvine, Professor Nicholas Rogers from the University of York and Professor Candace Slater, Director of the Doreen B. Townsend Center at the University of California Berkeley, who began a major research collaboration with the HRC on rainforests.

Iain McCalman convened the Consortium of Humanities Centres and Institutes (Australia) conference on the theme of Human Rights with Caroline Turner, the eleventh David Nichol Smith conference with Visiting Fellow Dr Christa Knellwolf and a Round Table Meeting 'Australia: a Knowledge Culture?' with Dr Lawrence Warner of the Australian Academy of the Humanities. Caroline Turner also convened a conference on Indonesian Art with the Asia Society, a workshop on Art and Human Rights with Christine Clark and a conference on 'Postcolonialism and Beyond' with Professor Dipesh Chakrabarty of the University of Chicago. Professor Barry Higman of RSSS convened the *4th Biennial Conference of the Australian Association for Caribbean Studies*. Dr Rosamund Dalziell of the CCR convened a Literature Seminar on 'Selves Crossing Cultures' and the Association of Commonwealth Literature and Language Studies Reading and Lunch with Dr Jacqueline Lo, also of the CCR; 'Humanities Exposure' with Lawrence Warner; and the October Colloquia 'The Year of Reading' with Dr Donna Merwick of the HRC. Drs John Docker and Subhash Jaireth convened a conference on *Adventures of Dialogue:*

CHCI Conference. *Back row*: Professor Iain McCalman and Dr Chandran Kukathus. *Front row*: Professor Alison McKinnon, Professor Mbulelo Mzamane, Dr Caroline Turner, and Professor Candace Slater.

Speakers at the seminar on *Postcolonialism and Beyond*. Professor Dipesh Chakrabarty (*centre front row*), Dr Roger Benjamin (*back row, second from left*), 2002.

New Graduate student intake of the HRC/CCR 2004. *Left to right*: Dr Paul Pickering, Harry Wise, Dr Mandy Thomas, Dr Diana Glazebrook, Rosemary Hollow, Anna Edmundson, Sylvia Marchant, Kirstie Gillespie, Josh Wodak, Nancy Michaelis, Daphne Nash.

Bakhtin and Benjamin, with Professors Katerina Clark from Yale and Meaghan Morris from Hong Kong as keynote speakers. Other activities included a conference on *The Importance of Italy*, convened by Dr Gino Moliterno of the Department of Art History and Film Studies, which attracted a large number of Italian specialists from throughout Australia as participants, with the launching of Dr Moliterno's own book on the subject of Italian culture. Over 90 delegates attended despite the conference taking place in the aftermath of 11 September and the collapse of Australia's second airline Ansett. The conference was supported by the Italian Cassamarca Foundation. The HRC also participated in *Women in Asia*, convened by Dr Kathryn Robinson from RSPAS with Caroline Turner helping to convene a workshop on art with Dr Jennifer Webb of the University of Canberra and other ANU colleagues. As well there were the conferences *Foreign Bodies: Oceania and Racial Science 1750–1940*, convened by Drs Chris Ballard and Bronwen Douglas and 'Constitutions and Human Rights in a

Advisory Board of the HRC. *Left to right*: Dr Robert Edwards, Dr Anna Gray, Mr Andrew Sayers, Professor Graeme Turner, Ms Dawn Casey, Professor David Williams, 2003. (Absent: Ms Jan Fullerton and Dr Gerard Vaughan)

Global Age: an Asia Pacific Perspective', convened by Professor Tessa Morris-Suzuki, all from RSPAS; *Art of Seeing and the Seeing of Art*, convened by Dr Geoffrey Henry of the Research School of Biological Sciences which combined science and humanities approaches and for which Turner served on the planning committee as a visual art specialist; *Spies and Surveillance in the 18th Century*, convened by Professor John Barrell of the University of York with Iain McCalman; *Law and the Enlightenment: the British Imperial State at Law, 1689–1832*, convened by Professor David Lemmings of the University of Newcastle; and *The Libertine Enlightenment*, convened by Professor Peter Cryle and Dr Lisa O'Connell of the University of Queensland and held at the University of Queensland.

The Director noted in the Annual Report: 'For the Humanities Research Centre (HRC) 2001 was without precedent in the pace and depth of change'.[1] He might well have said so: a certain slackening of activity would have been natural in such a time of relocation, dislocation and administrative reorganisation. But the Centre had racked up 12 conferences in the year (over 20 if workshops and Freilich colloquia are included), with a total participation of nearly 600.

Emeritus Professor John Molony, Emeritus Professor John Mulvaney and Richard Gorrell at the inaugural HRC History Teachers Summer School.

Other changes had taken place as well: the Advisory Board was reconstituted, comprising Director of the National Portrait Gallery Andrew Sayers as Chair; Director of the National Museum of Australia Dawn Casey, former CEO of Art Exhibitions Australia Ltd Dr Robert Edwards, Director-General of the National Library of Australia Jan Fullerton, Director of the Centre for Critical and Cultural Studies at the University of Queensland Professor Graeme Turner, Director of the National Gallery of Victoria Dr Gerard Vaughan, Assistant Director of the National Gallery of Australia Dr Anna Gray representing the Director of the National Gallery Dr Brian Kennedy, and Director of the Canberra School of Art, National Institute of the Arts, Professor David Williams.

The Centre also revived its tradition of summer schools in 2001. In 2000 the report of the National Inquiry into School History Teaching entitled 'The Future of the Past' concluded that participation of secondary school students in Australian history was declining. Emeritus Professor historian John Molony believed that there was no better way to respond to the crisis in Australian history in schools than by the HRC sponsoring school teachers from all over Australia to a summer school which would promote new ideas and methods by enabling teachers to have contact with leading history scholars and their research. The project was supported by the Vice-Chancellor Professor Ian Chubb and Deputy Vice-Chancellor (Education) Professor Malcolm Gillies for two years, with great support from the Emeritus Faculty, especially Emeritus Professors Molony and Beryl Rawson. Eminent lecturers such as Professors John Mulvaney, Bill Gammage and Iain McCalman offered their services. The teachers applied in great numbers, and their enthusiastic praise for the project

Above: Professor Bill Gammage (*front right*) and students at the HRC Summer School, 2004. Professor Mulvany at right.

Below: Dr Glen St John Barclay.

Launch of *Gold: Forgotten histories and lost objects of Australia* by Professor Ian Chubb, Vice-Chancellor, ANU, 2001.

at the first Summer School in 2002 encouraged the HRC to repeat the summer school in 2003 and 2004 with the National Institute of Social Sciences as sponsor and Dr Paul Pickering as Convener. HRC Fellows and scholars of history, Professor Gammage, Dr Alastair Maclachlan and Dr Glen Barclay took part.

Iain McCalman was in addition to all this intensely involved in 2000 and 2001 with projects for the National Library and the new

National Museum of Australia. He was appointed to the Council of the National Library and the Library's Committee for Harold White Fellowships, and was commissioning editor of the publication *Cook and Omai: The Cult of the South Seas* as part of a major publication collaboration between the National Library and the HRC to accompany an exhibition of the same name. The exhibition was curated by McCalman with Michelle Hetherington of the National Library and Alexander Cook and Caroline Turner of the HRC, drawing on the Library's superb collections of eighteenth century voyage material, and attracted a very large number of visitors. McCalman was also on the Advisory Committee of the new National Museum of Australia, co-curator for a major exhibition to mark its opening, and general editor with Alexander Cook and Andrew Reeves of 'Gold: Forgotten Histories and Lost Objects of Australia'.

Caroline Turner recalls that one of her most significant tasks as Deputy Director from 2000 was to strengthen links with the rest of the University, inevitably disrupted by the move from the A.D. Hope Building, by working on projects across the many disciplines, especially with the Faculty of Arts, RSPAS and RSSS, both to guard the HRC against isolation on the Acton peninsula and also to include ANU colleagues through consultation in forward planning for activities of the Centre. This had always been one of

Launch of *Gold: Forgotten histories and lost objects of Australia*. Dawn Casey, Director of the National Museum of Australia, Alexander Cook, Emeritus Professor John Mulvaney and Professor Iain McCalman, 2001.

the HRC's most critical roles – to work across the University and to put together interdisciplinary collaborations to achieve important research links and synergies. At the same time a new relationship was being forged with the National Museum of Australia, which had opened in March 2001, through the exhibitions McCalman and later Turner worked on and by means of an ARC Linkages grant in that year for research on Asia-Pacific museums awarded to Turner and a team which included Program Director of the Gallery of First Australians at the Museum Margo Neale and Alison Carroll from the University of Melbourne's Asialink. Director of the National Museum Dawn Casey was deeply committed to research collaborations between the Museum and University scholars, and the HRC became closely aligned to the Museum through her efforts to extend scholarly and public debate about the issues of social history presented in the exhibitions and displays. Much older relationships of the HRC with the National Library and National Gallery were meanwhile maintained and expanded. The directors of those institutions, Dr Brian Kennedy and Jan Fullerton, were especially supportive of the extensive research collaborations being developed with the HRC in the early years of the century. Turner also undertook a highly successful planning workshop for the Department of Foreign Affairs and Trade and the Australia-Japan Foundation on Australia's cultural relations with Japan, and conferences and exhibition development for the Asia Society on contemporary Indonesian art. The resulting exhibition, which toured Australia in 2003, proved more significant than could have been imagined in the planning stages, occurring as it did at a particularly difficult time for relations with Indonesia in the aftermath of the Bali bombing. These projects arose naturally from Turner's previous Australian Government appointments to the Australian Government's Australia-China Council, the Australia-Indonesia Institute and Australia Abroad Council, all based in the Department of Foreign Affairs and Trade and which spearheaded Australia's cultural relations with those countries, and leading an official cultural delegation to China and another to Japan. Her interest in Asia-Pacific art and culture also enabled the HRC to begin extensive new collaborations from 2000 with RSPAS (especially through the collaborations with Professor Amareswar Galla, an international authority on sustainable heritage development) and the School of Art and the Drill Hall Gallery at ANU, the National Gallery and National Museum and to begin a series of new research projects related to visual culture, art and society.

Opening of the WEH Stanner Building, 2001.

The School of Art had been, under Director Professor David Williams, a pioneer in Australia in exhibiting contemporary art of Asia and the Pacific, and had played a major role as an internationally recognised leader in this area through its artist-in-residence programme and exchanges with art colleges and universities. David Williams was now serving on the Advisory Board of the HRC and Turner had previously worked with him on the National Committee for the Asia-Pacific Triennial in Brisbane. Other collaborations between the HRC and the School of Art followed in 2000-2003, particularly in the field of Asian and Pacific art.

The WEH Stanner Building to be shared by the HRC with the CCR, as Old Canberra House was already shared, opened in August 2001 and provided much needed space for staff, Visiting Fellows and students of the two Centres, as well as housing the most congenial Ralph Elliott Library. It was named by Chancellor of ANU Emeritus Professor Peter Baume AO on 30 November after the great anthropologist WEH (Bill) Stanner (1905-1981) whose researches had extended from Aboriginal Australia and the Pacific to East Africa. The ceremony was attended by Vice-Chancellor Ian Chubb, Professor Stanner's widow, Mrs Patricia Stanner, and former Vice-Chancellor

Opening of the WEH Stanner Building. *Left to right*: Professor Deane Terrell, former Vice-Chancellor; Professor Iain McCalman, HRC Director; Professor Ian Chubb, Vice-Chancellor; Professor Howard Morphy, CCR Director, in front of the sculpture 'Winged Harvest' by Fiona Foley, 2001.

HRC staff and Visiting Fellows on the verandah of Constable's Cottage, Christmas 2001.

Deane Terrell. The building was designed by Canberra architects Alastair MacCallum and David Cook and reflected a number of traditional elements to be in sympathy with OCH, enhanced by energy saving innovations such as zonal air conditioning and double glazed windows, needed because of its overlooking a freeway tolerably active by Canberra standards. Budget problems entailed a regrettable reduction of the original space but the building has proved a most admirable design. The European-style gardens of Old Canberra House were complemented by native gardens around the Stanner Building designed by Paul Cox. Queensland-based artist Fiona Foley was commissioned by the public art committee chaired by Warwick Williams to do a public sculpture named 'Winged Harvest' for the area between the two buildings with landscaping inspired by Aboriginal plantings. This referred to aspects of Indigenous history and especially to the Ngunnawal people of the district and elements of their history, particularly feasts for the bogong moths which had brought generations of ancient Aboriginal inhabitants to Canberra. The former chauffeur's cottage at the rear of Old Canberra House was also restored as office space for staff and students, and the HRC retained the use of one of the cottages which had been utilised while the Stanner Building was built – Constable's Cottage, a charming old building overlooking the lake where it was said prisoners had been housed in the outbuildings on their way to gaol in Goulburn and elsewhere. Another important addition to the precinct came when the University, at the instigation of David Williams, declared a Sculpture Park at the foot of the gardens at OCH. Anne Rochette from the Ecole nationale supérieure des beaux arts, Paris, Australian Christine O'Loughlin, Lucia Pacenza from Argentina and Indigenous artist Djon Mundine completed the first sculptural works *in situ*.

Despite the rather cramped conditions until the Stanner Building was ready, the HRC staff continued to receive accolades from Visiting Fellows whose own distinguished careers shed lustre on the HRC, even though one did complain there were now too many non-humanities people at the two Centres. Fellowships continued to be the HRC's 'core public business', and it became apparent that one of the ways in which the HRC Fellows could find the most stimulating atmosphere for their work and interact with other scholars across ANU in the new location was through the conference programme. The conferences introduced the Fellows publicly and they then formed important links across campus, often resulting in new research opportunities for ANU. This was important because the Acton

Peninsula location did make it necessary to put more work into links across campus than had been the case in the A.D. Hope Building.

The Visiting Fellows who came to Canberra to the HRC in the years 2000–2003 continued to praise the HRC for its intellectual milieu and breadth of programmes. For example, Professor E. Ann Kaplan, Director of the Humanities Centre at the University of New York at Stony Brook and an expert on feminist film wrote: 'I do want to thank Iain McCalman and Caroline Turner for inviting me to the HRC and giving me this unique opportunity to undertake my research in an inspiring environment, intellectually, socially and physically . . .' Dr Kieran Dolin from the University of Western Australia similarly wished 'to acknowledge the high level of intellectual engagement which prevails among the staff and fellows of the HRC . . . This interdisciplinary dialogue has taken place in an atmosphere of great friendliness and support nurtured by Iain McCalman and Caroline Turner . . .' Eminent philosopher Professor William Connolly from Johns Hopkins, Baltimore declared that he had 'been inordinately pleased with my visit to the HRC. The staff at all levels have been helpful and supportive. Indeed the hospitality of the Centre combines with its positive intellectual atmosphere to render it distinctive among the centers I have visited including the Center for Advanced Study [at Princeton] . . .' He mentioned John Docker in particular among the Adjunct and Visiting Fellows for his contributions to the positive intellectual atmosphere. Professor Barbara Donagan from the Huntington Library, California, was 'especially grateful to Iain

Dr Benjamin Penny, Executive Officer with Professor Donald Akenson, Queen's University, Kingston, Ontario the Third Freilich Foundation Eminent Lecturer 2003.

McCalman for making my visit possible and for the stimulating milieu he has nurtured and to Caroline Turner for her unfailingly helpful presence . . .' Professor Ian MacLean from All Souls Oxford 2001 similarly reported that the 'Acting Director and Deputy Director [Turner and Pickering] were both extremely attentive to the needs of the Fellows. . .' Almost all mentioned Leena Messina. Accolades continued through the time of writing in 2003. Joanna Innes from Oxford commented particularly on Dr Paul Pickering's intellectual contributions and presence at the Centre and Professor John Keane from the University of Westminster extended 'special thanks to Dr Caroline Turner for her generous and effective support throughout my visit'. Dr Minoru Hokari from Keio University, Japan wrote that:

> I was truly fortunate . . . First I enjoyed and appreciated having such a great opportunity to hold constant discussions with staff and students of the HRC (and CCR) about my research. I especially thank Dr Caroline Turner, Dr John Docker, Ms Christine Clark . . . I do not know how to thank Ms Leena Messina for her expert knowledge and generous support of my first experience as convener.

The Freilich Foundation attached to the HRC proved in the years from 2000 to 2003 an example of very successful philanthropy. The Freilichs were highly committed to expressing their concerns about bigotry and, as Benjamin Penny the Executive Officer pointed out in a talk in 1999, those concerns were not confined to the humanities and they also wished to reach an audience beyond the University. Particularly popular were the annual lectures begun in 1997, with broadcaster and columnist Philip Adams, followed by human rights advocate, lawyer and Jesuit priest Father Frank Brennan on Indigenous rights, then by journalist David Marr on homophobia. An eminent lecture series was inaugurated by Professor Henry Reynolds, who gave four lectures related to issues of Indigenous and settler history and human rights in 1999. The Freilich Foundation programmes were some of the HRC's most successful and the facilities at Old Canberra House allowed for more general public attendance. Benjamin Penny estimates that attendances at conferences and other, always very well attended Freilich events, ranged from 50 to 120 people and that the majority of attendees have been non-University people. He says of the Foundation:

> In the seven years since our first public lecture, the Freilich Foundation has developed into a strong locus for

Staff of the National Europe Centre. Mr John Gage, Deputy Director; Mr Donald Kenyon, AM, Distinguished Visiting Fellow and former Australian Ambassador to the European Union, Brussels and Luxembourg, and former Australian Ambassador to the World Trade Organisation; Professor Elim Papadakis, Foundation Director of the National Europe Centre; Dr Karis Muller, Visiting Fellow; Dr Richard Grant, Research Officer; and Mrs Helen Fairbrother, Centre Administrator, April 2001.

activities that bring the issues of bigotry, prejudice and discrimination to the academic world and to the general public. With our seven annual public lectures, the three lecture series by internationally eminent scholars, and our seven conferences in Sydney, Melbourne and Adelaide as well as Canberra, the Foundation has begun to establish a national profile. Recently, the Foundation has decided to broaden its activities to focus more specifically on the education system through programs for school students and their teachers reasoning that early awareness of the issues surrounding bigotry, prejudice and discrimination is probably the most effective way to elicit positive social change.[2]

The National Europe Centre (NEC) became a reality in 2001 as the European Commission's Centenary of Federation gift to Australia, opening in new quarters close to OCH in 2002, with the potential for another new building if the Commission renewed funding for the NEC. The HRC played a role because of its deep commitment and contributions nationally and internationally to European studies over 30 years; and there was excellent collaboration with Foundation Director of the NEC, Professor Elim Papadakis, Professor of Modern European Studies at ANU, whose areas of research include policy related to environmental movements and the welfare state, political sociology and social theory, and his Deputy John Gage, an economic historian with research interests in international trade and trade policy, the European Union and Latin America, together with Administrator Helen Fairbrother. McCalman and Turner both served on the NEC Advisory Board, each acting as Chair of the Board. However, the NEC had developed its own line of funding from the European Commission and would concentrate on EU policies in relation to contemporary Europe with a strong social sciences emphasis. The HRC programmes with a strong humanities, arts and historical emphasis complemented those of the NEC extremely well, and the two Centres collaborated on many projects in a particularly fruitful manner and in particular in 2001/2002 in planning 'The Europeans' with the University of Western Australia. Collaborations continue at the time of writing with Professor Papadakis' successor as Director, Simon Bronitt, a Reader in Law and expert on European and Comparative Law, Criminal Justice and Human Rights, Terrorism and Cross Border Investigation.[3]

The HRC was remarkably successful in the five years to 2003 in attracting grants and donations to ANU and utilising joint funding with other institutions to realise its projects. The Centre's role and reputation over 30 years in which it functioned as a centre of excellence in the humanities and a national resource was the major factor in this success. It had played the key role in achieving the Centre for Cross-Cultural Research for ANU; an important role in achieving the National Europe Centre for the University; and the key role in bringing to fruition the Freilich Foundation and other donations. The HRC's record in achieving competitive grants remains impressive: in the critical area of competitive research grants the Director and Deputy Director of HRC both held more than one ARC grant. The HRC also attracted a collaborative grant from the Humanities Research Institute, University of California, which funds six senior academics for six month research grants in the USA and Australia. The HRC was in addition very successful in obtaining grants and sponsorships for its events, totalling several hundred thousand dollars including bequests from two retired staff at ANU and substantial in-kind and actual external support.

The new facilities at OCH were superb for conferences and attracted excellent attendances. The premises were much in demand from other University departments for their conferences and meetings, but these naturally were supplied without charge. Indeed the move from the A.D. Hope Building now meant the University was charging the HRC for electricity, cleaning and other costs which, in the past, had been in part subsumed into the A.D. Hope Building budget, and the need for excellent IT and computer services meant employing an IT officer. Glenn Schultz was superb in that role and his services and those of Anna Foxcroft who joined in 2003 were much praised by Fellows. Some of these extra costs were shared with the CCR but the advent of the CCR had not brought any extra funds into the HRC in the long term as Iain McCalman's salary had now reverted to being the HRC's responsibility. The CCR meantime was itself focussed on seeking additional funds to support its own extensive and expanding programmes. The CCR had always stated that the ARC grant would not be sufficient for its programmes. The HRC's core budget from the University in 2003 was not significantly different, except for money earned by the HRC from grants and students, from that allocated by the University in the previous five years.[4]

Any move and changes of the magnitude of those faced by the HRC inevitably lead to a certain amount of dislocation. There were increasing pressures on staff at the two Centres, the HRC and

Staff, Fellows and students of the HRC and CCR 2004 at welcome barbeque for new students.

CCR in 2001 due to expanding programmes. Two reviews were accordingly undertaken to consider 'our changing structural and strategic relationship with our affiliated twin centre [the CCR]', as McCalman reported, resulting in 'a series of organisational refinements to staff positions and responsibilities in order to give greater autonomy to each Centre in line with their different strategic roles, while preserving and enhancing a high degree of collaboration and interaction between them'.[5] Julie Gorrell, who had overseen the CCR ARC bid and the restoration of Old Canberra House, became Assistant Director and Executive Officer for the expanding CCR and Felicity Bowskill was appointed HRC Executive Officer. Her departure the following year when her husband was transferred to Perth was greatly regretted. She was succeeded by Garrett Purtill who left to go to a job in the ACT Government in 2003 and was in turn succeeded as HRC Executive Officer and Business Manager by Michelle McGinness, a much respected and experienced finance officer from RSSS. Georgina Fitzpatrick, a highly qualified researcher joined the staff as Research Assistant to Iain McCalman, replacing Alexander Cook who was awarded a prestigious scholarship to undertake his PhD at Cambridge; and Christine Clark, a curator and art management expert joined from Queensland as Research Assistant to Caroline Turner, all three paid out of ARC grants.

The HRC and CCR of course continued to collaborate, as for example with shared Visiting Fellows, conferences and publications and a joint journal with alternating editors from each Centre and the HRC providing the layout and design through its Publications Officer, Misty Cook and later Lindy Shultz. The HRC gave support to CCR initiatives such as the CCR's important 'Fusion' year of exhibitions and conferences in 2003. The Centres worked together on a new media consultancy CRIO, a concept of McCalman's, a bid for a special research centre in new media and a new highly successful joint Graduate course in Interdisciplinary Cross-Cultural Research. Synergies and intellectual exchanges were possible at all times and HRC Visiting Fellows interacted with CCR staff and students. The CCR had adopted specific and focussed streams of research in line with ARC requirements and had a special emphasis on Australia and the Asia-Pacific region and on contemporary issues. Iain McCalman had stated at the formation of the CCR that in attempting synergies each Centre would retain its distinct identity, and that only one third of HRC projects would coincide with those of the CCR. There continued to be very important shared interests between the HRC and

Graduate Students. *Above, left*: Robert Bell. *Centre*: Chris Blackall. *Right*: Gordon Bull, Angela Philp, Lee-Anne Hall. All at the Graduate Student Chapter Writing Workshop, 2004.

HRC Graduate student Tina Parolin (*left*) and HRC Executive Officer, Michelle McGinness, 2004.

Graduate Students. *Above, left*: Anna Lawrenson and Dr Mandy Thomas (CCR Deputy Director). *Right*: Michelle Antoinette.

CCR in specific specialist areas such as the conference on Aboriginal-Chinese relations in Australia. Shared interests in visual culture and Asian culture between the two Centres also coincided, in particular when Dr Mandy Thomas, an anthropologist with extensive expertise in migrant cultures and especially youth and Vietnam, joined the CCR as Deputy Director in May 2002 from a research position at the Institute of Cultural Research at the University of Western Sydney. Dr Thomas took a strong leadership role in developing CCR programmes, particularly the Postdoctoral and Graduate programmes and in heading the CCR research focus on 'The Cultural Impact of Migration to Australia'.[6]

The mandate of the HRC continued to be to cover the whole of the humanities and work across the entire University in an interdisciplinary manner, such as in the themes years devoted to science and law. The HRC continued to have a wide historical brief (from ancient times to the present) and geographical spread (literally the world). The HRC continued to have European literature, philosophy, art and history as its core disciplines, as well as Australian history and culture and now as well Asia-Pacific history and culture. The HRC, through its themes and conferences, did, of course, also welcome many scholars outside the humanities and social sciences and had embraced with enthusiasm research foci such as Asia, Africa and Latin America as well as interdisciplinary collaborations in science, medicine, environment and the law. Interestingly the non-HRC attendees at HRC seminars continued to come in the main from the Faculty of Arts, RSSS and RSPAS and the Faculty of Asian Studies with some from the National Museum and National Gallery. HRC international Visiting Fellows and conference visitors in those years still tended to come in the main from the UK, USA and Europe. Many continued to come in response to requests from colleagues at ANU or other universities working collaboratively with the HRC. The simple fact was that scholars within ANU expected the HRC to continue its European humanities projects and its leadership role in Australia in the area of European humanities research (despite the recent establishment of the National Europe Centre which, as stated, had a more contemporary policy and social sciences emphasis as required by the European Commission) as well as to respond to ideas for collaboration from across the University in interdisciplinary research projects as it had been doing for more than 30 years. As well the HRC also tried to work in ways which improved the situation of the humanities nationally.

'Latin America' was the theme for 2002, chosen as the Africa year had been to play a national as well as local role in supporting an important field of study under threat in Australia. The HRC had in fact been requested by colleagues to try to provide a stimulus in Latin American studies as it had with African studies. And it is vitally important that parochial narrowness does not tend to exclude such critical stimuli. The year was highly successful especially through the synergies with the National Museum whose staff were particularly keen to work on heritage and archaeology research with several Visiting Fellows brought out by the HRC. It opened dramatically with *Telenovelas*, a lively conference on Latin American popular culture and soap opera, convened by Professor Christiana Slade of the University of Canberra; *Landscape and Symbol in the Inka State* convened by Dr Ian Farrington of the Faculty of Arts, ANU which was a groundbreaking event bringing together the foremost scholars in the world in Inka studies with the papers published in a major book; an *Art and Human Rights in Latin America Workshop* convened by Dr Caroline Turner and Christine Clark; *The Diaspora of the Latin American Imagination* convened by Professor Peter Read of the CCR and Dr Marivic Wyndham of ANU with papers published in the HRC/CCR's new electronic journal in 2003; *National Narratives and Identities in a Global World: The Latin American Case* convened by Dr Barry Carr of La Trobe University, which is Australia's major centre for Latin American Studies and for which this was a major event; and *New World, First Nations: Native Peoples of Mesoamerica and the Andes under Colonial Rule* convened in Sydney by Dr David Cahill of the University of NSW which is also one of the few to espouse Latin American studies. There were also the exhibition 'Tar Babies', the work of artist and HRC Visiting Fellow and expert on Caribbean slavery Dr Marcus Wood at the Canberra School of Art Gallery, and four exhibitions of Latin American Art curated and organised by Mrs Nancy Sever, Director of the ANU Drill Hall Gallery, on the work of Omar Rayo (Colombia), Betsabee Romero (Mexico), Juan Davila, an Australian artist of Chilean background, and the Latin America Drawing Biennale. All these exhibitions received significant help from the Latin American Ambassadors and provided an important public and community face for the year's focus.

Non-thematic conferences in 2002 were: *The Dialectic Interpretation of Religious Phenomena* convened by Emeritus Professor Hans Mol as a result of his bequest to the University; *New Feminist Histories of Gender and Colonialism* convened by Dr Fiona Paisley of ANU and Professor Angela Woollacott an HRC Visiting Fellow from Case

Western University; *Locations of Spirituality: 'Experiences' and 'Writings' of the Sacred* convened by Dr Minoru Hokari an HRC Visiting Fellow from Keio University, Japan; *The Theory and Practice of Early Modern Autobiography* convened by Dr Philippa Kelly of the University of NSW, ADFA; *The Enlightenment World* a workshop convened by Dr Christa Knellwolf of the HRC, and the 2002 History Teachers' Summer School convened by Emeritus Professor John Molony and Dr Paul Pickering. The Freilich Foundation also had one of its most active years with a number of conferences and workshops including for teachers. Visiting Fellows in 2002 included a number of Latin American specialists, several from Latin America: Dr Miriam Estrada, UN Special Advisor on Human Rights, Ecuador; Dr Maria Hernandez-Llosas of the National Council of Scientific and Technical Research of Argentina; Dr Hilda Araujo, Director of the Centre of Research and technology for the Andean Countries, Peru; Dr John Earls from the Catholic University Peru; Dr Marsha Meskimmon from Loughborough University (the latter working on Latin American women artists), UK; Mr Ruben Stehberg of the National Museum, Chile; and Dr Brigida Pastor from the University of Glasgow (a specialist on Spanish literature). Non-thematic Visitors included Emeritus Professor David Fieldhouse and Dr Vic Gatrell from Cambridge, Professor Alan Gross from the University of Minnesota, Professor Peter Jones from

Professor Adam Shoemaker, Dr S. Timothy Maloney and Mr Gaston Barban, Deputy Canadian High Commissioner, at the inaugural National Institute of the Humanities/HRC lecture given by Dr Maloney, 2002.

Edinburgh, and Dr Isabelle Merle from the Centre de Récherche et de Documentation sur l'Océanie, France.

A new initiative of Vice-Chancellor Professor Ian Chubb in 2002 was the establishment of a series of National Institutes which all members of ANU were invited to join. The HRC staff joined several with enthusiasm. These National Institutes were intended to cross the divide between the faculties and research schools and to provide a coherent vehicle for highlighting the research and teaching strengths of the whole University. The project proved highly successful. The Director and Deputy Director of the HRC served on the steering committee of the National Institute of the Humanities (later, in September 2003, to become the National Institute of the Humanities and Creative Arts). The HRC had many connections with the National Institute of the Arts and the National Institute of Social Sciences (later National Institute of Social Sciences and Law), and Turner served on the inaugural steering committee for the National Institute for Asia and the Pacific. Dr Paul Pickering of the HRC worked closely with the National Institute of Social Sciences and Law, especially in teaching programmes, and joined the Board in 2003. Logically, the HRC was particularly involved with the National Institute of the Humanities and its inaugural event was a joint lecture held at Old Canberra House in November 2001. Delivered by an eminent musicologist from the National Library of Canada – Dr Timothy Maloney – the presentation was a fascinating analysis of the contribution of Canadians Glenn Gould, Northrop Frye and Marshall McLuhan to the world of ideas.[7]

The National Institute of the Humanities (NIH) had a splendid start at ANU through 2002-2003 with Professor Adam Shoemaker, Dean of the Faculty of Arts, as convener. Among its achievements were a significant expansion of the number of summer research scholarships in the humanities for third year Australian and New Zealand students and a spectacular range of outreach programmes in which the HRC participated actively. Professor Shoemaker also accepted the challenge of broadcasting and disseminating ANU's research strengths to the wider world through many exciting endeavours which otherwise could not have happened, including a highly successful National Arts Research Showcase held over a two-day period in August 2003 at Parliament House. It was designed to introduce 12 exemplary research projects in the Arts, Creative Arts and Humanities from all over Australia to 130 Senators, members, Research Staff and Parliamentary Officials.[8] The Showcase also acted as a catalyst for a project being pursued by the Academies of Humanities and of Social Sciences which

Professor Bruce Bennett, HRC Adjunct Professor.

resulted in 2003 in funding for a Council for the Humanities, Arts and Social Sciences (CHASS) to act as a lobby group to government on behalf of these areas. The HRC worked highly effectively with the NIH – and, indeed, in harmony with all National Institutes, helped by excellent relations especially with the two conveners, in particular Professors David Williams at the National Institute of the Arts and Professor Adam Shoemaker at the National Institute of the Humanities. This allowed the HRC to concentrate on new long-term research initiatives and new teaching programmes. Professor Shoemaker stated that

> A renewed focus on the centrality of the humanities to national and international life has been one of the signal features of Ian Chubb's Vice-Chancellorship. The depth, breadth and passion of arts and humanities scholars has been given room to move in new ways – such as cultural informatics and the art of documentary film – and the reaction to this movement beyond the borders of the ANU has been tremendous.[9]

Professor Bruce Bennett, an Adjunct Professor at the HRC since 2003 has noted the HRC's continuing role at ANU:

> Under Ian Donaldson's and Iain McCalman's leadership the Humanities Research Centre at ANU has been an

oasis of Humanities scholarship. Supported by enlightened policies which support high-quality researchers, the HRC has attracted outstanding Visiting Fellows from around the world, whose published work testifies to the stimulating and supportive research environment they have found in Canberra.

The HRC remains a beacon for early career and experienced researchers and a strong group of PhD students indicate the longer-term sustainability of Humanities research in Australia.[10]

Cross-university interaction was more intensive than ever for the HRC in 2002. The Centre collaborated with the National Institute of the Arts in an exhibition with joint fellow Dr Marcus Wood and shared international guest lecturers Heri Dono from Indonesia and Nalini Malani from India; with the National Institute of the Humanities in public lectures and a book launch; with RSSS and the Faculty of Arts in a Cross-Campus History Seminar Program (now an annual fixture) and the Tanner lectures; with RSPAS in the 'Women in Asia' Conference and a Masters Course in Sustainable Heritage Development; with the Drill Hall Gallery in five exhibitions on Latin America and planning for a joint exhibition in 2003; with the Centre for International and Public Law in planning the *Art and Human Rights* conference for 2003; with the Faculty of Arts in an Archaeology conference on *Inkas* and three joint sabbatical fellows, and in developing honours and postgraduate programs in Advanced Museology; with the CCR in the *Diasporas of the Latin American Imagination* conference, a shared PhD course, and four shared Fellows; with the National Europe Centre in 'The Europeans' conference programme; and with the Centre for Resource and Environment Studies (CRES) in the joint appointment of Professor Tim Bonyhady.

The Director and Deputy Director both served on the following University committees and boards in the period 2000-2003: the Steering Committee of The National Institute of the Humanities; two Library Advisory Committees; the Academic Board; the Board of the Freilich Foundation; the Board of the National Europe Centre; the Deans, Directors and Centre Heads Group, the Heads of Centres Group. Iain McCalman served on the Education Committee; the Research Working Policy Group; the National Advisory Board of the CCR; the National Dictionary Centre and the Tanner Lectures Committee of the RSSS. Caroline Turner served on the Board of the Institute of the Arts chaired by Emeritus Professor Peter Karmel, the Steering Committee for the National Institute of Asia and the Pacific, the Coombs Creative Arts Fellowship Committee, the Gallery Advisory Committee of the School of Art, and the Undergraduate Review Committee chaired by Professor Malcolm Gillies. External collaborations with national and international cultural institutions comprised: a joint conference, the DNS, joint lectures and symposia, joint Fellows, and exhibition projects with the National Library of Australia; conferences with the National Gallery of Australia; the Museum's Curatorial Committees for several exhibitions, joint conferences and symposia, a joint ARC Linkages grant; and a joint postgraduate programme with the National Museum. Collaboration with other humanities bodies included, apart from those already documented, joint symposia and a young scholars seminar series with the Australian Academy of the Humanities, and convenership and a conference with the Consortium of Humanities Centres and Institutes of Australia.

Meanwhile the Centre was vigorously maintaining its international role: important research projects and research collaborations and links were set in place with the Huntington Library, California; Lingnan University Hong Kong; the Getty; the Yale Center for British Art; and Cambridge University. McCalman was advisor and participant on the BBC and History Channel TV series 'The Ship', and advisor on the BBC TV series 'Nelson and Emma Hamilton'. He travelled extensively on leave to Europe, the United Kingdom, North America and Hong Kong, giving lectures and addressing the British Academy Centenary Conference in London. Caroline Turner served as Acting Director with Paul Pickering as Acting Deputy for several months in 2001, 2002 and 2003 during McCalman's absences; and Turner herself gave a paper at the Consortium of Humanities Centers and Institutes at the University of California Berkeley; was an invited speaker at an International Council of Museums meeting in Shanghai; and consulted with colleagues in China, Korea, Japan, Singapore and Europe as part of her ARC grant research.

Despite all its activities and achievements, the HRC nonetheless faced its thirtieth birthday as it had its first, understaffed, overstretched and underfunded for its international outreach. But there was still so much to celebrate. Donaldson, Clarke, Elliott, McCalman and Caroline Turner gathered with some two hundred guests in the beautiful grounds of Old Canberra House on a typically chilly Canberra spring day of 8 September 2003 to do just that on the occasion of the twenty-ninth anniversary of Sir John Crawford's announcement that The Australian National University proposed with the approval of the Australian Universities Commission to establish a Humanities Research Centre. Vice-Chancellor Ian Chubb reminded the occasionally shivering audience that the HRC was the only centre of its kind in

At the HRC's 30th birthday celebrations. *Left to right*: Dipesh Chakrabarty, Garrett Purtill, Margo Neale (back), Margaret Elliott, Deborah Hart, Grazia Gunn, Paul Pickering, Debjani Ganguly, Donna Merwick, Stephanie Stockdill, Jodi Parvey, Greg Dening, Roger Hillman, Margaret Jolly, 2002.

At the HRC's 30th birthday celebrations. *Left to right*: Professor David Williams, Dr Robert Edwards, Professor Ian Donaldson, Professor Ian Chubb (Vice-Chancellor), Professor Iain McCalman, Ms Jan Fullerton and Dr Caroline Turner, 2002.

Australia, one of the oldest centres of its kind in the world and the model for centres established subsequently in Oxford and Cambridge, as well as a large number in North America. It had been designed to be a catalyst and national focus for research in the humanities throughout Australia, and to that end had attracted in the course of its thirty years of operation over 1000 eminent scholars from Australia and from 39 countries overseas. Professor Chubb referred among the other achievements of the HRC in the past year to the Cook and Omai exhibition at the National Library, which had drawn 30 000 visitors; the exhibitions of Latin American artists at the Drill Hall Gallery during the HRC's Latin America year; the exhibition of 'Oceanic Tarbabies' held with the School of Art; and in particular to the new graduate teaching program, and the two collaborative initiatives in museology and heritage studies to be undertaken by RSPAS and the National Museum. Such a record, he considered, showed that the confidence of the founders of the Centre had been amply justified, and served to establish the Centre firmly as a proud part of The Australian National University. It was what all those who had given their devotion to the HRC in the past and were still giving it in the present most wanted to hear.[11]

Donaldson and McCalman both delivered addresses on reconfiguring the humanities four days later at the National Library, in which McCalman pleaded passionately that

> the knowledge base of the nation not be impoverished, nor the intellectual integrity of the education system undermined, by an excessive focus on science and technology . . . We must recognise the value to the innovative knowledge economy and a tolerant democracy of the contribution of language scholars, historians, authors, anthropologists, poets, playwrights, designers, dancers, composers, musicians, artists and others.

The experience and skills of humanist scholars, he argued, were 'relevant to whether or not this will be a decent, fair, humane and civilised country for all its citizens'.[12] It was the same appeal that Max Crawford had made back in 1963, when the proposal for a Humanities Research Centre had first been mooted. It was the same that had been made by the US Commission on the Humanities in 1954 and by the Canadian Royal Commission on National Development in the Arts, Letters and Sciences in 1951. It was the same that had been made by Prime Minister Menzies in 1939, when Australia lay under the threat of war, as it did again at the time when McCalman was speaking.

The appeal obviously needed making more than ever. Menzies had been a champion of humanities research and had authorised the greatest expansion in government funding for tertiary education in Australian history. But government funding for tertiary education had been falling for decades, to the extent that *The Sydney Morning Herald* estimated that it would have taken a 17 per cent increase above the level in 2002 even to restore university income to the level of the mid-1990s.[13] The question as always was 'What is to be done?' in the words Lenin borrowed from the novelist Chernyshevsky.

What might be done could be suggested by what had been done: over 1000 visiting academics, 422 of them from 39 different countries outside Australia; 16 monographs, with two more in process; hundreds of additional publications produced at and credited to the Centre; the organising of many hundreds of conferences and colloquia, many deemed groundbreaking; several major exhibition projects; a journal with a readership of at least 3000; ongoing collaborations with more than 20 national and many international cultural institutions; national leadership of humanities centres in Australia; an international reputation for its research; the conduit for over $2 million in bequests to the University; well over that sum in ARC grants; Iain McCalman's

Ralph Elliott, Ian Donaldson, Graeme Clark, Ian McCalman in the Ian Donaldson Common Room, Old Canberra House with posters from theme years in the background.

initial achievement of the CCR and the work towards the creation of the National Europe Centre; the Summer Schools for teachers; the Freilich Foundation; ten current ongoing collaborative international and national research projects; service by the current Director and Deputy Director on some 15 University Committees and Boards, and so on and so on. And the international recognition: unreserved is indeed a faint term for expressions in some of the 30th birthday greetings that poured in from Visiting Fellows, some of which would be applicable to a vision of Heaven, assuming that such a vision included the ever-present aroma and ever-available savour of coffee. This was literally so in the case of David Gallop, Professor of Classics at Trent University, Ontario, who was inspired to hail the HRC in verse as 'Heaven – in Oz!' Other plaudits in prose went about as far. Peter Quartermaine, Professor of American and Commonwealth Arts Studies at Exeter, said that his time as a Visiting Fellow in 1974 had provided the happiest memories of his life, which was the more remarkable as the accommodation available for Visiting Fellows then was the somewhat down-market prefabs in Childers Street.

Marilyn Gaddis Rose, Distinguished Service Professor of Comparative Literature at the State University of New York, a Visiting Fellow in 1977, said that the HRC had 'provided a supportive collegial atmosphere, excellent scholarly resources, and a physical environment that will be my life embodiment of Never-Never-Land'. The mighty Professor Edmund S. Morgan of Yale wished that he could relive every moment of the time he had spent at the HRC. For S. Beynon John, Reader Emeritus in French at the University of Sussex, the HRC 'in a word ... was a haven'. Professor Bob White of the Department of English at the University of Western Australia declared that his period at the HRC 'stands out in memory as a beautiful Arcadian interlude, which changed my life in many ways'. Professor Michael Lützeler, Rosa May Distinguished University Professor in the Humanities, Department of German, at Washington University, St Louis, Missouri, found the working conditions at the Centre 'truly ideal'. And Patrick O'Farrell, Emeritus Scientia Professor, School of History, University of New South Wales, announced that he

> would like to bear witness to my personal gratitude for the existence of an academic retreat house where one might refresh the soul. All this is noxious thinking in a utilitarian results-oriented age, but I affirm its absolute necessity and the Centre as being a place where it is, thank God, still possible.

Thank God, indeed. But the immediate issue was how to keep the Centre as such a place. McCalman had a couple of answers. One was the proposal by the National Academy of the Humanities that 'Australia adopt a positive structure by which the public can benefit from the innovative research occurring in the humanistic and creative fields', of which the HRC itself was an outstanding exemplar. This was to be achieved through the development of Collaborative Research Innovative Centres, the core principle of which was that 'participants can achieve their strategic objectives more successfully by working in collaborative and interdisciplinary environments'. Such Centres could 'be mobilised to address problems, needs and opportunities of the sector', including fostering the growth of 'new fields and commercial applications such as new media and informatics . . . documentary film . . . CD-ROM game applications . . . digital immersion technology and so on'.[14] This was excellently forward-looking, high-tech and generally state-of-the-art; and McCalman gave a typically vivid personal illustration of collaborative research in the field of documentary film and also to a degree of immersion with an account of his participation in a historical re-enactment for BBC Television of Cook's voyage up the coast of Australia, which demonstrated for the participants the validity of Uncle Gordon's observation in Robert Louis Stevenson's *The Merry Men*, that 'it's an unco life to be a sailor . . . a cauld, wanchancy life'. McCalman claimed that he had never had a more creative and collaborative intellectual experience. Nor, one would trust from his own account, a more disagreeable physical one.

A less physically demanding approach was for the HRC to pursue the project which McCalman had raised with Deane Terrell in 1994 of 'developing a . . . postgraduate degree in cultural studies with a strong coursework component'. After years of trying, the HRC was in 2002 finally permitted to enrol Graduate students in the programme it jointly developed, 'Interdisciplinary Cross-cultural Research'. By 2003 the Centre had 6.5 graduate students, with numbers increasing to 11.5 by early 2004 and was also supervising a further four PhD students for other programmes. Demand for postgraduate placement at the HRC was high especially in the joint course with CCR but also in traditional disciplines and especially interdisciplinary areas which were the HRC's strength. Students were attracted also by the Visiting Fellows at the HRC and a level of interdisciplinary research that as one stated was just not possible anywhere else, even at ANU. The calibre and contributions of the students are excellent, many being senior or mid-career professionals, such as the former Director of the Canberra Museum and Gallery, the former Director of the Museum of Contemporary Art in Sydney and the Senior Curator of Decorative Arts at the National Gallery of Australia, and a national expert on new multimedia. Their presence quickly made a substantial impact on the HRC's intellectual climate

The HRC also helped pioneer short-course interdisciplinary teaching for postgraduates (proposed to the Australian Government's 2003 Nelson review of Higher Education as a national model of excellence), an example being an HRC philosophy/science short course for Graduate and Honours students 'The Biophilosophy of Life' held at Kioloa Coastal Campus in 2003 for which the HRC received a Joy London Foundation Grant. The HRC continued plans for more short courses, including in 2004 by McCalman on history, television and re-enactment, dubbed by some extreme history. The HRC also launched two major collaborative initiatives to develop postgraduate teaching in advanced museology and heritage studies: a Masters Degree by thesis, coursework and web based delivery with RSPAS on 'Sustainable Heritage Development in the Asia-Pacific,' to begin in 2003 on web based delivery; and a PhD, Graduate diploma and Masters programme in 'Advanced Museology and Heritage Studies' with the National Museum of Australia and Faculty of Arts, to begin in 2004. And it organised and ran three summer schools for teachers of history in January, which have become a national model, while continuing to participate in the Summer Scholarship scheme for undergraduates. Students, of course, as well as academic enrichment meant money in the prevailing academic environment of economic rationalism, and the great benefit of these ventures into teaching was that they would generate an income stream, which would enable the Centre to acquire at last its long-desired third tenured academic: for the first time in its existence the HRC might not have to make an agonising choice between human resources and financial resources. It was, of course, true that students in the humanities attracted far less funding than science students, reaffirming A.D. Hope's complaint, forty years before, that the humanities had come to accept a position that the sciences would not tolerate for a moment, when they could have had all they needed for the cost of a single cyclotron. But the appointment of Dr Paul Pickering meant that the Centre could at last embark on a serious and consistent teaching role to begin when he took up his appointment in early 2004, despite the fact the Director and Deputy Director were then already supervising four PhD students each. It was in fact an enormous reinforcement in every way: he had been an ARC Queen Elizabeth II Fellow at the HRC since 2000; he was the Convener of the Graduate Program in Social Sciences and

HRC staff 2004. *Left to right*: Glenn Schultz, Leena Messina, Christine Clark, Georgina Fitzpatrick, Anna Foxcroft and Judy Buchanan.

Morning tea in the Ian Donaldson Common Room, Old Canberra House. *Back from left*: Bernice Murphy, Dr Alastair MacLachlan, Sylvia Marchant, Dr Paul Pickering. *Front*: Professor Marilyn Lake, Professor Wilfred Prest, 2004.

Dr Paul Pickering, Director of Graduate Studies.

Law and Graduate Academic Advisor for History at ANU; he had published extensively on Australian, British and Irish social, political and cultural history; his articles had appeared in leading academic journals in Australia and overseas; and he was developing a fruitful research interest in an area most important for the HRC of public history, addressing the relationship between public memory, heritage and history. As Paul Pickering said:

> In important respects the HRC is a victim of its own success. Few people realise that so much is accomplished for so little – the place runs on the smell of an oily rag. It is ironic that a Centre that has been more or less constantly threatened by the commodification of the university sector is actually a paragon of efficiency and productivity. The economic rationalists ought to love us much more than they do. Teaching was the logical next step for the Centre and we have embraced the challenge with characteristic fervour. I have no doubt that we have already begun to build a reputation for excellence in teaching as well as research.[15]

Through 2000–2003 the HRC continued to produce the refereed journal *Humanities Research*, jointly with CCR, and edited by Turner since 2000, with a reach of 3000 readers. In 2003 it was also published electronically. Eight issues have been published since commencement in 1997. Its predecessor the *HRC Bulletin* ran to eighty-four issues, publishing conference proceedings and other scholarly papers. The HRC published the fourteenth in its monograph series, 'The World Turned Upside Down', and the fifteenth, 'Lost in the Whitewash', in 2002 and 2003 respectively. The HRC collaborated extensively with outside publishers including most recently Oxford and Cambridge University Presses, and the new ANU E Press. 30 publications in all were approved for Department of Education, Science and Training publications from 2000 to 2002, in addition to considerable output in areas not accepted by the Department, including exhibition curation and catalogues and industry partner publications in areas such as art and museology.

The theme for 2003 was 'Culture, Environment and Human Rights'. It proved to be one of the HRC's most successful years with audiences matching those of the famous Feminism and Sexuality events. The major themed HRC conferences were: *23 Degrees South: The Archaeology and Environmental History of Southern Deserts* convened by Dr Mike Smith of the National Museum of Australia; *Books and Empire: Textual Productions, distribution and consumption in Colonial and Postcolonial countries* convened in Sydney by Professor Elizabeth Webby of the University of Sydney and Professor Paul Eggert of the University of NSW at ADFA; *Art Museums: Sites of Communication* convened by Ms Susan Herbert and Ms Pamela McClelland Gray of the National Gallery of Australia and National Portrait Gallery of Australia respectively; *Frankenstein's Science: Theories of Human Nature from 1700 to 1839* convened by Dr Christa Knellwolf of the HRC and Dr Jane Goodall of the University of Western Sydney; *History Television Workshop* convened in Sydney for the ABC by Iain McCalman; *Forest, Desert, and Sea* convened in Townsville by Professor Paul Turnbull; *Genocide and Colonialism* convened in Sydney by Dr Dirk Moses of the University of Sydney; *Envisaging the Future: Digital Research and Scholarship in the Humanities* convened by Professor Paul Turnbull; *Toward an Ecology of Practices* convened by Professor Brian Massumi of the University of Montreal, Professor Sandra Buckley and Stephen Zagala; *Art and Human Rights* at ANU, the National Gallery and National Museum, convened by Caroline Turner and Christine Clark with Professor Christine Chinkin of the London School of Economics, Margo Neale of the National Museum of Australia, Dr Jennifer Webb of the University of Canberra and Dr Pat Hoffie of Griffith University; *South Africa Focus* convened by Professor Mbulelo Mzamane of the University of Fort Hare and Christine Clark of the HRC with Dr Jennifer Webb of the University of Canberra, supported by the

National Institute of the Humanities and the South African High Commission. The HRC also gave support to the National Institute of the Humanities' conference and film festival *Art of the Documentary*, the inspiration of Professor Adam Shoemaker and convened by him with Dr Catherine Summerhayes of the National Institute of the Humanities. There were the 'Art and Human Rights' exhibitions at the Drill Hall Gallery, the School of Art Gallery, the National Museum, the Canberra Contemporary Art Space and the National Gallery of Australia and the 2003 History Teachers' Summer School convened by Dr Paul Pickering and a Visiting Scholar course 'The Biophilosophy of Life' for PhD and Fourth Year Honours students convened by Brian Massumi, Stephen Zagala and Sandra Buckley with some very eminent speakers including Professors Isabelle Stengers from Brussels, Simon Penny from the University of California, Irvine, Maria Hernandez from Cornell and artist Stelarc, which was held at Kioloa as well as in Canberra. There was also a series of collaborations with the University of Western Australia on a programme 'The Europeans' inaugurated by Deryck Schreuder, now Vice-Chancellor of that University. Visiting Fellows in 2003 included Dr Norbert Finzsch from the University of Cologne, Professor Lily Kong from the University of Singapore, Professor Sidonie Smith from the University of Michigan, Professor Kay Schaffer from the University of Adelaide, Professor John Keane from the University of Westminster, Professor Julie Graham from the University of Massachusetts, Dr Petra ten-Doesschate Chu from Seton Hall University, Professor Ben Kiernan from Yale, Professor Jack Barbalet from the University of Leicester; and, as keynote speakers at the *Art and Human Rights* conference, Professor Barbara Stafford from the University of Chicago, Professor Mbulelo Mzamane from Fort Hare University, South Africa, Dr Charles Merewether from the Getty and Professor Ihab Hassan from the University of Wisconsin, Milwaukee. Professor Hassan is an example of a distinguished scholar who was returning to the HRC on his second Fellowship and continuing links with Australian culture developed on that Fellowship. He had been a visitor also in 1990, when he had come to speak as one of the pre-eminent scholars of post-modernism.

Long term Fellows attached to the HRC between 2001 and 2003 who greatly enhanced its research and outreach included Dr John Docker, Professor Bill Gammage, Dr David Pear, Professor Amareswar Galla, Dr Alastair Maclachlan, Dr Glen Barclay, Emeritus Professor Ken Taylor, with Emeritus Professor Ralph Elliott, Mrs Betty Churcher and Dr Donna Merwick remaining as Adjuncts and being joined by

Professor Bruce Bennett.

The *Art and Human Rights* conference was part of a larger interdisciplinary endeavour begun in 2000 by Turner with Professor Christine Chinkin of the London School of Economics. Its aim was a research collaboration, bringing together international scholars in the humanities, social sciences, arts and law, which is a continuing project and has resulted in an ARC grant. In the first three years of the project there were workshops in 2001 and 2002; an international conference and exhibitions in 2003; and publications, all related to the subject of art and human rights, which has emerged against all expectation as perhaps the most important single issue of the twenty-first century. It was all the more pertinent in an Australian context because of the way in which the *Tampa* and 'children overboard' incidents had inspired artists to express concern for refugees disadvantaged by the policies of the Howard Government. The exhibitions held at the Drill Hall Gallery, the Canberra School of Art, the Canberra Contemporary Art Space, the National Museum and the National Gallery included 15 artists from North and South America, Africa, Australia and Asia. The exhibition was shown at a number of venues and was curated by Turner with Director of the Drill Hall Gallery Nancy Sever, Christine Clark, David Williams and Bronwen Sandland from the School of Art

At the HRC 30th birthday function. *Left to right*: Dr Paul Pickering, Professor Iain McCalman and Professor Greg Dening, 2002.

and Lisa Byrne from the Canberra Contemporary Art Space. Several of the international artists, including Dadang Christanto, Guan Wei, Michel Tuffery and Mella Jaarsma, participated in residencies at the School of Art working with students. The impact of these events is perhaps best conveyed by a gracious letter to the Vice-Chancellor from Director of the National Gallery Dr Brian Kennedy, in which Kennedy said that the conference was, in his opinion, an important one, which had 'reverberated throughout the community with a series of exhibitions, performances, openings and lectures ... It was a great example of team collaboration and inspired leadership'. He went on to say that events such as this Conference and related programs 'take the ANU out of its campus and into the city in such a wonderful way'.[16] Professor Hilary Charlesworth was particularly pleased with the interactions between students in her area of law and the humanities through the Conference. She wrote:

> I think it's the single best conference I've ever attended and was full of interdisciplinary stimulation for me and my law colleagues who attended. Some of my students who came along were euphoric about the papers at the edge of the two areas. It was especially good to hear directly from the artists involved.[17]

The exhibitions and conference were supported by the National Gallery and the National Museum, the Royal Netherlands Embassy, the French Embassy, the National Institute of the Arts and the National Institute of the Humanities and the National Europe Centre at ANU. The National Europe Centre was a major supporter of the art and human rights exhibitions, assisting the HRC in obtaining works of the famed European artists Christian Boltanski and Luc Tuymans, reflecting the strong emphasis of the EU on human rights issues.

A critical issue in these years was the move towards 'research priorities' at a national level, mirrored by the need for these to be developed at a university and local area or centre level. The HRC had always had its own research priorities but government priorities were heavily weighted towards the sciences. Nevertheless the HRC moved to consolidate and define priorities for its longer research projects in line with policy while maintaining as far as possible a broad programme of events and activities outside the more narrowly defined frameworks of the research priorities. Iain McCalman and the HRC took the lead among humanities institutions in Australia including convening a meeting in Adelaide in early 2003 to try to work out national priorities for the humanities and respond to the issues. McCalman was successful in presenting a vigorous case and in having some of the priorities expanded to relate to the humanities. The danger with these moves of course was not only that the humanities would be left out and thus even less funded, but that from the HRC's point of view the priorities would be too narrowly conceived. This concern was naturally shared in other areas of the University as well: one distinguished scientist at ANU pointed out in a meeting that a government-preferred area of science/technology was one in which Australia would now never be able to catch up and that the field had moved on in any case – in other words the emphases could be wrong or unachievable.

All this was of particular concern at a time when in Australia as a whole classics, European languages and now even Asian languages and studies were being cut back due to funding shortages. And many in the humanities feared that this would lead to even greater losses of funded subject areas: as Professor Ralph Elliott put it at an HRC staff meeting when priorities were discussed, 'Does this mean that there would be no room for a medievalist in a future HRC?' The HRC's concerns had always been to nourish the best in human scholarly work in whatever field in the humanities and creative arts as well as to take the lead in bringing forward new fields and ideas. These swirls and eddies were a major preoccupation for the HRC as it attempted to meet University and government guidelines.

The theme 'Culture, Environment and Human Rights' provided the HRC with its headiest year in terms of numbers for almost a decade. It seems that the focus on this theme struck a very strong chord. Visitors had research interests that spread from ancient hunter/gatherer societies, through Medieval and Renaissance studies, theories of human nature in the early modern world, colonial and far more recent genocides, as well as issues of great contemporary relevance in a rapidly changing world related to understanding technological impacts in computer sciences, Bioscience and 'Biophilosophy', new media, the environment and, of course, human rights. By November 2003 the total conference attendance for the year was over 1000, the best overall year's attendances for conferences in the decade since the Sexualities year in 1993 which also had over 1000 attendees. Annual attendances for conferences over the previous decade (attendance records for conferences pre 1991 are incomplete) had previously hovered around 500, except in 1996 where the very large 276 attendance for the Bernard Smith conference sent conference attendances for the year to 790 and in 1998 when the figure of 250 for the Ireland and Australia conference brought the year's total to 746. The most popular conferences in the decade apart from these and a conference in 2003 on Art Museum education which had over 200 attendees, and apart from the blockbusters of the Sexualities year in 1993, *Lips of Coral* (245), *The Jane Gallop Seminar* (114), *Regimes of Sexuality* (250), *Breath of Balsam* (122), *Forces of Desire* (205), were *Indigenous Rights and Political Theory* 1997 (214); *Science and other knowledge traditions* (about Indigenous knowledge) 1996 (153), and *Art and Human Rights* 2003 (151).

There had also been a conference which McCalman and Caroline Turner convened, although it was not strictly only an HRC conference: 'Beyond the Future: The Third Asia-Pacific Triennial Conference' 1999 (700). This was the highest figure for any HRC conference in the 30 years. As well, in 2003 the HRC supported a conference run by the National Institute of the Humanities and the Creative Arts 'Art of the Documentary' which reached 170.[18]

It seems then, apart from the Irish and conferences of specific academic associations such as the DNS, that the most attended conferences were those that connected with issues of critical importance in Australian society or which broke new ground in introducing new ideas particularly in interdisciplinary ways. Unfortunately it is not really

Leena Messina, HRC Programmes Manager.

Professor Adam Shoemaker, Director August 2003–January 2004.

possible to compare attendances with other Australian universities but those held by the HRC at other universities show that the HRC conferences appear to have excellent attendances. Certainly the HRC work-in-progress seminars always had very high attendances by ANU standards even immediately after the move and by 2003 were again averaging 50 while average attendances elsewhere on the campus were often less than 20 attending for weekly seminars. The overall figures for 2003 did not include the public lectures or Freilich attendances or exhibition attendances. Overall attendances each year at the HRC for combined conferences and seminars as well as public lectures would have averaged over 1000 and some years were well over that figure. We might therefore estimate a total of people reached of at least 50000–60000 and, with exhibitions added, well into the hundreds of thousands. Not bad for a research-only centre with two permanent academic staff, a third to come in 2004 and only a part-time Executive Officer for the very successful Freilich programme.

No Director of the HRC was ever just a Director of the HRC. Iain McCalman was also engaged as President of the Australian Academy of the Humanities with a number of major issues. And this was in addition to McCalman's other roles as Executive Member of the International Consortium of Humanities Centers and Institutes, now situated at Harvard; member of the International Advisory Committee for the Humanities Research Institute, University of California; President of the Australian Chapter of the Consortium of Humanities Centers and Institutes; Council member of the National Academies Forum; member of the Reference Committee of the Commonwealth Review of Higher Education, the consulting committee of the Commonwealth National Research Priorities, the Advisory Board of the Research Institute in the Humanities and Social Sciences, Sydney University, the Executive of the National Science Communication Committee and the National Symposium on Innovation, Melbourne. He had also delivered the British Academy, Centenary Conference address, June 2002; was a Fellow of the Royal Historical Society, of the Australian Academy of the Social Sciences and the Australian Academy of the Humanities; and had held many Visiting Research Fellowships in the United States and the United Kingdom, most recently at All Souls, Oxford. Then in 2003 he became one of only 24 Australian scholars of national and international eminence to receive the prestigious Federation Fellowship, a move by the Federal Government to persuade such eminent Australians to remain in the country. His project would be to explore the work of Philippe de Loutherbourg, an eighteenth century European artist, scientist, engineer and set-designer who pioneered revolutionary developments in the technique and culture of multimedia through the agency of 'spectacles.' It was to culminate in a book, a video film and a digital CD-ROM/DVD publication. De Loutherbourg would have been immensely gratified. So presumably would another idiosyncratic eighteenth century identity, Giuseppe Balsamo, self-styled Count Cagliostro and snake-oil merchant of renown, whose story McCalman told through the eyes of Cagliostro's contemporaries in *The Seven Ordeals of Count Cagliostro*, published by HarperCollins in 2003 and praised for its wit and elegance by among others Norman Davies, author of *Europe: a History*, and no mean practitioner of those arts himself. That publication was translated into a number of languages including French, German and Japanese.

McCalman's award of the Federation Fellowship meant of necessity the end of his term as Director of the HRC. However, it was to the

HRC's enormous benefit and a great enhancement of its intellectual base that Iain McCalman would be staying at the HRC as a Federation Fellow. Professor Adam Shoemaker was appointed as Director in August 2003 for six months, given his profound interest in all aspects of humanities scholarship at the University. A former Commonwealth Scholar who had completed his doctorate on Aboriginal Literature at ANU under Bob Brissenden in the early 1980s, Shoemaker returned to the University in 2001 after 15 years spent working in Toulouse, Antwerp, Ottawa and Brisbane in positions as varied as Deputy Director of the European Community Pavilion at World Expo 88 and Pro Vice-Chancellor at the Queensland University of Technology in 1999-2000. Shoemaker brought with him a total belief in, as he put it, 'the persuasive power of the Arts' and a strong commitment to enhancing the core role of the HRC as a progenitor of the humanities both within, and beyond, the academy.

During his six-month tenure he emphasised the need for communication and clarity in conveying the message of the HRC to the world via its publications, its website, its scholarship and its administrative structure. Shoemaker concentrated the Centre's external activities by securing backing for outreach courses on 'Re-enactment History' in Sydney and Melbourne, raised funds for the potential creation of a new HRC Postdoctoral Award and oversaw the establishment of an administrative alliance with the Faculty of Arts. Perhaps most important, the major conference, festival and film competition 'AD – The Art of the Documentary' occurred in late November 2003 during his tenure as Director. As he stated, 'Along with the landmark HRC conference and exhibition "Art and Human Rights" in August of the same year (so successfully convened by Caroline Turner) "AD" was one of the largest, most international and most diverse academic events of its type ever held at the ANU.' Its convener and Artistic Director, Dr Catherine Summerhayes, worked closely with the HRC to secure the participation of, *inter alia*, Alexander Sokurov, director of the acclaimed film *Russian Ark*, as well as scholars and film-makers from India, Canada, New Zealand, Bosnia-Herzegovina, the United States and France. As Shoemaker put it 'there are turning points which remind us that Universities can play a very important part in divining – and defining – future trends relating to artistic and intellectual practice. *The Art of the Documentary* was one such event.'

Considering the future of humanities research and the HRC, Professor Shoemaker noted that often observers dwell upon the difficulties faced by scholars and practitioners in the Creative Arts and Humanities. But, to cite a contrary example, it is worth reminding ourselves that a fascination with creative performance in society (both past and present) is as strong now as it has ever been, whether the performance is live, recorded digitally or computer-generated. I believe that this offers a tremendous opportunity for Humanities scholars to, once again, show just how important their insights can be: they analyse why and how we are fascinated by these phenomena. And they do so in a way which is – at its best – relevant, lucid and powerful. To my mind those last three words summarise the qualities of what staff, postgraduates and research visitors to the HRC achieve with their work every day.[19]

The successor to McCalman and Shoemaker, to take up appointment in February 2004, in one of those turns of fate which even a Victorian sensation novelist might have hesitated to employ, was to be none other than the HRC's first Director, recently retired as Director of the Centre for Research in the Arts, Social Sciences and Humanities, blessed with the felicitous acronym CRASSH at Cambridge and modelled on the HRC. It may be said that this decision by the Vice-Chancellor Ian Chubb to appoint Professor Donaldson was received with signal acclaim. And Donaldson would be returning to a Centre which more than fitted his description of such Centres as 'vital agencies of change for the universities, a principal avenue through which, even in times of great financial hardship, new people, new ideas, new ways of thinking are constantly introduced into the academy'.[20]

A glimpse of what was to come can perhaps be gained by looking at what Donaldson himself had been doing for the last ten years – continuing his own exemplary scholarship at Edinburgh and Cambridge and also founding a new centre at the latter university. Among the activities of CRASSH were four lectures in 2002 by the late Edward Said, who had been sadly prevented by the fatal illness of his mother from taking up an invitation to the HRC in 1987. 'Humanism and Knowledge' was the topic of Said's lectures, parts of which were televised by the BBC. His timely lesson was that liberal-minded western scholars had 'grown accustomed to lamenting the failure of humanism and the humanities', but that the issue was rather, as was reported on the Centre website, the narrowness with which, 'such scholars envisaged these terms'.

Many did not think beyond the particular academic disciplines or social and cultural transitions in which they themselves happened to have grown up, and their view of humanism and the humanities was often as a consequence élitist, defensive, partial and despondent. Said offered a more optimistic, open, and pluralistic view of a humanism that embraced forms of knowledge eastern and western, contemporary as well as social and political as well as literary.[21]

CRASSH itself was doing just that already under Donaldson's Directorship, offering national and international connections and wide-ranging research projects that also embraced the arts with theatre, music and visual arts as well as new media initiatives, and included as well, science's view of humanism. This of course was what Donaldson had been doing while Director of the HRC. Themes at CRASSH such as the 'Organisation of Knowledge' brought a broad range of scholars from many disciplines, including the sciences, and countries, as well as reaching out to those beyond the academy and into schools, bringing scholars in the universities, libraries and other cultural institutions together, contributing to the formation of government policy in areas such as the UK government report into creativity, reaching back in the past, heading and helping to build a European network of the humanities (CHCI) and above all extending the definitions and crossing barriers to knowledge caused by narrow disciplinary definitions. Donaldson proclaimed his goal when commenting during the first birthday celebrations of CRASSH on the report 'Imagination and Understanding' prepared by CRASSH management committee member Emma Rothschild for the UK Council of Science and Technology on the relationship of the arts and humanities to science and technology. Rothschild had spoken of the necessity to 'communicate in two languages', much as Sir Charles Snow had said in his Rede lecture *The Two Cultures*, some forty years before. We do not seem to have progressed much – possibly the reverse, in fact. But Donaldson was trying to do something about it. 'The central philosophy of the Rothschild report', he said, 'is in some ways comparable with that which led to the establishment of CRASSH. Both the report and the centre are driven by a strong wish to pursue intellectual enquiry across traditional disciplinary boundaries'.[22] In the 2001 annual report he had said:

> The massive acceleration of academic research over recent years, combined with the increasing pressures of

university life, have led ironically to a wider fragmentation of knowledge, and ever more intense specialization. Colleagues in neighbouring disciplines are not always fully aware of the nature of each others' work, or able fully to benefit from their expertise. It has therefore become increasingly urgent to think of ways of enlivening and reconfiguring knowledge both within and beyond the University; of enabling academics to learn about and build upon each others' ideas, and to share their knowledge and research interests more widely between institutions and within the global community . . . CRASSH has been created precisely to meet this challenge.

These included encouraging such interdisciplinary connections as collaboration with the Newton Institute of Mathematical Sciences.[23]

Professor Malcolm Gillies, Deputy Vice-Chancellor Education and former President of the Australian Academy of Humanities.

Back at the HRC, plans were already in train for 2004, 2005 and beyond through strategic planning undertaken over the previous two years, just as Donaldson would have wished. The themes will be 'Asia-Pacific' and 'Cultural Landscapes' respectively. The aim is just such a broad interdisciplinary approach which had always distinguished the HRC and the focus will be as diverse as Islamic gardens, British art and the contemporary megacities of China. A joint project on gardens is already in train between the HRC and CRASSH as well as the Huntington Library, California, The Yale Center for British Art, the Mellon Centre for British Art in London and the Getty. This collaboration with major international cultural institutions in North America and the UK has been initiated by Donaldson and McCalman. The art and cultural expertise of the Centre has been greatly enhanced with Grazia Gunn, a noted art expert and one of Australia's most respected curators, joining the HRC as a long-term Visiting Fellow in 2004 with a special interest in the gardens research project. HRC projects will relate to philosophy, literature, history, environmental studies, bioethics, new media – and the list is not finalised at the time of writing. Another emphasis will be on expanding the new teaching programmes in both higher degree research degrees and coursework higher degrees. The HRC is also developing programmes for schools (the latest a joint project with the Freilich Foundation where HRC Visiting Fellow Professor Mbulelo Mzamane, a poet, activist and friend of Nelson Mandela had visited schools in the ACT to speak with school children about tolerance and race issues) and has continued its Summer Schools for teachers as well as working towards teacher resources, especially in the area of history. The Centre will of course continue developing strategic initiatives to promote humanities scholarship and research nationally, while expanding national and international linkages, especially with museums, libraries and other cultural institutions. These partnerships will be broadened beyond the HRC's traditional bases in Europe and North America, with a special focus on our own region of the Asia-Pacific especially in 2004 when the theme is 'Asia-Pacific'. Research priorities for the next two years will emphasise interdisciplinary research under the broad theme of 'The Humanities in Society'. At the time of writing the HRC was engaged in over 10 major collaborative international and national research projects. These were, of course, in addition to the individual research of the staff and Fellows. The contributions of short and long term Fellows were as impressive as ever. All this has placed the Centre at the leading edge of humanities research in this country and a

Professor Ian Donaldson and Grazia Gunn in the HRC Director's Office, Old Canberra House, 2004.

partner in an international network of humanities discourse, which is just where it ought to be, according to the verdict of hundreds of eminent visitors over the past thirty years.

Professor Malcolm Gillies, Deputy Vice-Chancellor Education at ANU and a former President of the Australian Academy of Humanities whose appointment as Deputy Vice-Chancellor has greatly enhanced humanities studies at ANU, has defined the significance of the humanities and humanities research in this way

> Why are the humanities important? Because they are about people, their values and their beliefs. We are rapidly realizing in the twenty-first century that people – as individuals and in groups – matter every bit as much as things. The current state of the world suggests that without deep understanding of particular cultures, heritages, languages, and arts, we misdirect our efforts in politics and business, in science and technology. Great inventions are not adopted because they are not well adapted to the needs and wants of people. Moreover, those creative ideas fostered by the humanities and arts are

now finally being recognized as of immense importance to the future development of society. Technology now provides exciting new vehicles for the greater sharing and propagation of these humanistic ideas.[24]

A good description of the work of the HRC as a centre for humanities research emerged from a work-in-progress seminar delivered by Dr Jonathan White, a Visiting Fellow from the University of Essex, in November 2003. White described the nineteenth-century experimental collaboration of the foremost English scientist of his day, Sir Humphry Davy, with scholars in the Neapolitan Museum of Antiquities, amongst them Monsignor Rosini, keeper of the collection of ancient scrolls. Because of Davy's scientific skills, in particular his advances in the developing field of chemistry, he had come to Naples to help in opening some of the crumbling and infinitely precious papyrus scrolls containing works of ancient classical writers discovered in the ruins of Herculaneum. Davy's activities in the museum at Naples, and in particular his relations with Monsignor Rosini, were not without tensions. In the opening of his new book on Italian culture, White uses details of the chemical experiments, disciplinary sensitivities and human problems in cross-cultural communication provided by this story as a 'trope for our own attempts at cultural history'. But the concept of a chemist and a classical scholar from two very different countries brought together in an attempt to extend knowledge is a fruitful concept also for the story of the HRC. The truth is that in every discipline we need to strive for what one member of the audience at White's seminar called a real dialogue across scholarship, and what the nineteenth century Neapolitan Rosini referred to as 'the literary republic'.[25] However difficult a literary republic of scholars may be it is a vital necessity of human endeavours. To contribute to the rich dialogue of a 'literary republic' of scholars of all disciplines, and bring knowledge systems together in such a way as to provide a focal point for humanities discourse in Australia, has perhaps been the greatest achievement of the HRC.

The challenge is now greater than ever. It has perhaps never been better described than in the words of Deryck Schreuder, written in 1994:

> Humanity cannot live by the spreadsheets of financial advance alone – any more than modern society can rest its character and capacity in a narrow view of technological growth. This extraordinary decade of the 1990s has already

witnessed the collapse of a Super Power, a great empire state that could dominate half the world and reach the moon yet fail to meet the fundamental aspirations for civil rights and material well being for its citizens. The human prospect necessarily includes a quest for human dignity and human security. By that great historical and global perspective, the humanities are far from being a luxury for a prosperous great power – or even a middle size power of small population, living in a great island continent. The subjects of critical enquiry in the disciplines which compose the humanities give a fundamental character and coherence to the functioning of intelligent and compassionate human societies. . . for all their so-called irrelevance and lack of utility, their potential to be viewed as merely a decorative form of high culture, the humanities actually provide the very well-springs of our open society and culture. The alternative, of a world which undervalues the contribution of the critical research and writings in the humanities, is a kind of ideological clotting of the arteries – with the potential of the ultimate collapse for that culture and society.[26]

The events of the decade to which Schreuder referred had of course seemed in general to be positively liberating, at least at the time. The events of the succeeding decades had been quite the reverse. And the doctrines of economic rationalism he had condemned had become more entrenched than ever. The future could hardly be said to be entirely rose-coloured. But the only thing we know about the future, as the great British military historian Sir Michael Howard told one of the authors in 1989, is that it will be different from the present, and in the way in which we least expect. The Berlin Wall fell shortly after. And the HRC is better prepared than ever at the time of writing to greet the future, whatever that future might be.

Notes

1. McCalman, 'Director's Report', *Annual Report 2001*, p. 1.
2. Benjamin Penny, communication with the authors 21 Nov. 2003.
3. National Europe Centre website: http://www.anu.edu.au/NEC/
4. CCR Annual Reports; HRC internal financial reports for the University 1995-2003 (unpublished)
5. HRC, *Annual Report 2001*.
6. Centre for Cross Cultural Research website: http://www.anu.edu.au/culture/ (staff profiles and Annual Reports).
7. Adam Shoemaker, *HRC Bulletin*, Feb. 2002 (not paginated).
8. As reported by Convener and Dean of Arts, Professor Adam Shoemaker, in his submission for the second year review of National Institutes, Oct. 2003.
9. Adam Shoemaker, communication with the authors, 5 Dec. 2003.
10. Professor Bruce Bennett communication with the authors, 30 Mar. 2004.
11. Professor Ian Chubb, speech notes supplied to authors from Vice-Chancellor's office.
12. McCalman, 'Reconfiguring the humanities', A Public Lecture by Professor Iain McCalman at the National Library of Australia, Thursday, 12 Sept. 2002.
13. 'Cash first, Dr Nelson', *The Sydney Morning Herald*, 24 Feb. 2003.
14. McCalman, 'Tall tales and true: the selling of historic Endeavour', *The Australian*, 1 Oct. 2003.
15. Paul Pickering, communication with the authors, 24 Nov. 2003.
16. Brian Kennedy, Letter to the Vice-Chancellor Professor Ian Chubb, 26 Aug. 2003.
17. Hilary Charlesworth, email to Professor Adam Shoemaker, 21 Aug. 2003.
18. Conference statistics as supplied by HRC Programmes Manager Leena Messina.
19. Adam Shoemaker, communication with the authors, 5 Dec. 2003.
20. Donaldson, Address to Symposium in the *Centre on Working outside the Academy*, Apr. 1990.
21. CRASSH annual report 2002: http://www.crassh.cam.ac.uk/centre/annualreport2002.html (consulted 18 November 2003).

[22] Director's Introduction CRASSH, 2002 Annual Report, op. cit (consulted 20/11/03)
[23] Director's Introduction, CRASSH 2001 Annual Report, op. cit (consulted 18/11/03)
[24] Malcolm Gillies, communication with the authors, 30 Mar. 2004.
[25] Jonathan White, *Lineages in Italian Cultural History*, forthcoming, and communication with the authors, 21 Nov. 2003.
[26] Schreuder, '"National Needs" and the Humanities', *Creative Nation*, pp. ix-xvi.

Appendix A

Humanities Research Centre Annual Themes

1977: Literary Translation
1978: Medieval Art and Culture
1979: Drama
1980: Romanticism and Revivals
1981: Australia and the European Imagination
1982: Insight and Interpretation
1983: The Renaissance
1984: Landscape and the Arts
1985: Hellenism: Rediscovering the Past
1986: Feminism and the Humanities
1987: Europe and the Orient

1988: Use of the Past
1989: Film and the Humanities
1990: Biography and Autobiography
1991: Histories
1992: Europe
1993: Sexualities and Culture
1994: Freedom, Liberty and the Individual in Western and Non-Western Societies
1995: Africa
1996: Science and Culture
1997: Identities
1998: Home and Away: Journeys, Migrations and Diasporas
1999: Religion, Society and Values
2000: Law and the Humanities
2001: Enlightenment
2002: Latin America
2003: Culture, Environment and Human Rights
2004: Asia-Pacific
2005: Cultural Landscapes

Appendix B
Humanities Research Centre Visitors

Visiting Fellows and their Projects 1974–1990

Professor C.K. Abraham	Department of French and Italian, University of California, Davis	July-September 1981 Norman Satirists
Professor L.L. Albertsen	Department of German Philology, University of Aarhus	February-May 1977 German Poetry since Schiller
Professor J.J. Auchmuty	Formerly Vice-Chancellor, University of Newcastle, NSW	July 1975-June 1976 The American War of Independence
Professor B. Bailyn	Department of History, Harvard University	June-July 1984 The Peopling of America
Dr Deidre Bair	New York	August-October 1990 Biography: Essays in Theory, Methodology and Criticism
Mr J.B. Bamborough	Principal, Linacre College, Oxford	January-May 1979 Burton's *Anatomy of Melancholy*

Dr S. Bann	Modern Cultural Studies, University of Kent	July-September 1984 Garden Landscapes
Professor J.C. Barker	Department of History, Trent University	March-August 1988 Tocqueville and Australian Historiography
Professor Zygmunt Bauman	Department of Sociology, University of Leeds	July-September 1982 Objectively-grounded Interpretation
Mrs P.J. Bawcutt	Department of English, University of Liverpool	July-September 1983 William Dunbar
Professor John Bender	Department of Comparative Literature, Stanford University	July-September 1990 Impersonal Narration
Professor J.A.W. Bennett	Professor of Medieval and Renaissance English, Magdalene College, University of Cambridge	March-April 1976 Gibbon's English Reading; *Piers Plowman*
Professor Francis Berry	Department of English, Royal Holloway College, University of London	May-August 1979 Pagan Mythologies and English Poets
Ms Virginia Blain	School of English, Macquarie University	May-July 1986 Feminist Companion to English Literature
Professor Morton Bloomfield	English Department, Harvard University	June-August 1978 Medieval and Renaissance Tragedy
Professor J.V. Bony	Department of History of Art, University of California, Berkeley	June-September 1978 Revitalisation of Gothic Architecture
Professor James Boon	Department of Anthropology, Cornell University	July-August 1987 Anthropology, Literature and Bali
Mr D. Bostock	Tutorial Fellow in Philosophy, Merton College, University of Oxford	September-November 1975 Problems in Philosophy of Mathematics
Dr A.E. Boyd	Department of Music, University of Hong Kong	May-August 1987 The *gamelan* in the music of Claude Debussy
Dr Graham Bradshaw	Department of English, University of St Andrews	June-September 1986 Shakespeare's *Hamlet*
Dr R.F. Brissenden	English Department, ANU	May-August 1976 Convener, Fourth David Nichol Smith Seminar; edn of *Joseph Andrews*
Dr D.J. Bromfield	Centre for Fine Arts, University of Western Australia	June-September 1987 Influence of Far Eastern Art on Western Art in the Late Nineteenth Century
Professor Norman Bryson	Department of Art History, University of Rochester	October-December 1990 Gender in Jacques-Louis David

Mr Peter Burke	Faculty of History, Emmanuel College, University of Cambridge	July-August 1983 Renaissance History
Dr Margaret Burrell	Department of French, University of Canterbury	February-April 1978 French Medieval Romance
Dr Michael Butler	Department of German, University of Birmingham	July-September 1979 Twentieth-Century German Literature
Professor A.D.E. Cameron	Department of Classics, Columbia University	May-July 1985 The Foundation of Constantinople
Dr J.K. Campbell	Fellow, St Antony's College, Oxford	March-May 1985 History of Modern Greece
Professor Roger Cardinal	Faculty of Humanities, University of Kent	April-June 1988 Natural Signs
Mr D.J. Carter	School of Humanities, Deakin University	December 1986-February 1987 Convener, Literary Journals; Australian Literary Studies
Professor M.T. Cartwright	Department of French, McGill University	April-June 1988 Art, Literature and Medicine in the Eighteenth Century
Dr J.P. Casey	Fellow in English, Gonville and Caius College, University of Cambridge	September-December 1979 The Cardinal Virtues
Professor Ross Chambers	Department of Romance Languages, University of Michigan	May-August 1982 Nineteenth-Century Literary Narrative; Baudelaire
Professor Chung Chong-Wa	Department of English, Korea University	January-April 1978 D.H. Lawrence
Dr Lorna J. Clark	Independent Scholar, Montreal	April-September 1990 The Life of Sarah Harriet Burney
Dr J.E.M. Clarke	Department of Russian, University of Melbourne	January-June 1981 Grammar of A.A. Barsov
Professor John Clive	Department of History, Harvard University	June-July 1980 Nineteenth-Century European Historiography
Dr Lorraine Code	Department of Philosophy, Queen's University, Ontario	May-August 1986 Ideals for Women Working
Professor Richard Coe	Department of French Studies, University of Warwick	May-September 1976 Autobiography of Childhood and Adolescence
Mr Paul Connerton	University of Cambridge	December 1981-September 1982 Social Formation of Memory
Professor Maurice Cranston	Department of Political Science, University of California, San Diego	June-September 1990 Biography of Rousseau
Dr Patricia Crawford	Department of History, University of Western Australia	May-July 1986 Women in Seventeenth-Century England

Dr D.A. Cressy	History Department, California State University	May-July 1988 Celebration and Commemoration
Professor J.M. Crook	Department of History, Bedford College, University of London	May-June 1985 Classical Tradition in British Imperial Architecture
Dr Ann Curthoys	School of Humanities and Social Sciences, NSW Institute of Technology	January-March 1986 Aboriginal/European Relations
Dr G.E. Davie	Department of Philosophy, University of Edinburgh	March-December 1977 Scottish Influence on Australian Education
Professor G.A. Davies	Department of Spanish, University of Leeds	July-September 1984 Spanish Court in the early Seventeenth Century
Mr Peter Davies	Formerly of the Jacaranda Press	March 1975-February 1976 Historical Dictionary of Australian English
Professor R.G.A. de Bray	Department of Slavonic Languages, ANU	January-December 1978 Old Church Slavonic
Dr Susan Dermody	Faculty of Humanities, University of Technology, Sydney	August-October 1989 Experimental Feature Film
Dr Leslie Devereaux	Department of Anthropology, Faculty of Arts, ANU	January-September 1986; July-December 1989 Co-convener Film and the Humanities
Professor L.A. Dittmer	Department of Music, University of Ottawa	April-June 1978 Motets of Adam de la Halle
Dr L.A.C. Dobrez	Department of English, ANU	January-June 1982 Modern European Writing and Existential Thought
Dr J.E. Docker	Sydney	January-February 1984 Australian Fantasy Literature of Exploration
Dr Jonathan Dollimore	School of English and American Studies, University of Sussex	January-March 1988 Sexuality, Transgression and Sub-Cultures
Professor T.S. Dorsch	Department of English, University of Durham	October 1976-March 1977 English Antiquaries
Dr Andrzej Drawicz	Slavic Institute, University of Cologne	January-September 1979 Contemporary Russian Literature
Mr Peter Dronke	Lecturer in Medieval Latin, University of Cambridge	June-September 1978 Medieval Latin and Vernacular Literature
Mrs Ursula Dronke	Vigfusson Reader in Old Norse, University of Oxford	June-September 1978 Ancient Scandinavian Literature and Mythology
Professor M. Dufrenne (jointly with Philosophy, Arts, ANU)	University of Paris-Nanterre	September-December 1978 Aesthetics

Professor B.F. Dukore	Department of Drama and Theatre, University of Hawaii	May-July 1979 Ibsen, Shaw and Brecht
Professor Paul Eakin	Department of English, Indiana University	July-September 1990 Autobiography as a Referential Art
Professor Leon Edel	Department of English, University of Hawaii	June-August 1976 Henry James
Professor E.L. Eisenstein	History Department, University of Michigan	January-March 1988 French Publicists in Politics, 1780-1850
Em. Professor R.W.V. Elliott	Master, University House, ANU	January-December 1987 Runes
Professor Richard Evans	School of European History, University of East Anglia	April-June 1986 History of Feminism
Dr Margaretha Fahlgren	Cathedral School, Uppsala	September-December 1990 Women's Autobiographies in Sweden
Professor C.F. Fantazzi	Department of Classical and Modern Languages, University of Windsor	March-May 1983 Renaissance Latin Love Poetry in Italy
Professor J. Fletcher (with Arts Faculty, ANU)	Department of Comparative Literature, University of East Anglia	January-April 1988 Popular Fiction
Dr Valerie Flint	Department of History, University of Auckland	December 1977-September 1978 Honorius Augustodunensis
Professor J. Flower	Department of French, University of Exeter	October 1976-February 1977 Literature and Politics in France since World War I
Professor Reginald Foakes	Department of English, University of California, Los Angeles	September-December 1990 Shakespeare's Tragedies in the Modern World
Professor C.W. Fornara	Department of History, Brown University	March-May 1983 Historiography of Ammianus Marcellinus
Professor A.D.S. Fowler	Department of English Literature, University of Edinburgh	May-September 1980 Theoretical Aspects of Genre
Dr Peter France	School of European Studies, University of Sussex	July-September 1977 Translation of Rousseau's *Rêveries du Promeneur Solitaire*
Professor J.D. Frodsham	School of Human Communication, Murdoch University	January-June 1977 Convener, Translation Conference
Dr A.J. Frost	Department of History, La Trobe University	January-December 1984 Perception of the Australian Landscape
Professor D. Gallop (with Arts Faculty, ANU)	Department of Philosophy, Trent University, Ontario	May-July 1985 Dreaming in Ancient Thought

Professor J.R. Garagnon	Department of French, Monash University	April-July 1981 Seventeenth and Eighteenth-Century French Literature
Dr P.D.A. Garnsey	Fellow in History, Jesus College, University of Cambridge	October-December 1976 Roman Social and Economic History
Professor K. Garrad	Discipline of Spanish, Flinders University	February-May 1975 Edn of Bishop Rosendo Salvado's New Norcia Diaries, 1875, 1876
Professor C.J. Geertz	School of Social Sciences, The Institute of Advanced Study, Princeton	June-August 1987 Anthropological Studies of Morocco and Indonesia
Dr C.A. Gerstle	Japan Centre, ANU	March-September 1987 Tragedy in Japanese Drama
Professor J. Goldberg	Department of English, Temple University	July-August 1983 Court Masques and Spenser, Jonson, Shakespeare, Donne
Professor Eric Gould	Department of English, University of Denver	January-March 1974 Australian Poetry since 1890
Mr J.J. Graneek	Formerly Librarian, ANU	March-September 1976 Jewish Proselytes and Apostates
Professor D.H. Green	Professor of Modern Languages, University of Cambridge	June-September 1978 Medieval German Literature
Mrs Dorothy Green	Formerly English Department, ANU	December 1976-April 1977 Revision of H.M. Green's *History of Australian Literature*
Dr Heather Gregory	History Department, University of New England	July-September 1985 Family in Renaissance Florence
Dr Clive Griffin	Tutor in Spanish, Trinity College, University of Oxford	January-April 1986 The Book in Europe
Professor R. Grimsley	Department of French, University of Bristol	July-September 1980 Enlightenment Studies
Mr Sasha Grishin	Fine Art, ANU	March 1977-February 1978 Byzantine Frescoes
Dr Elizabeth Gross	Department of General Philosophy, University of Sydney	April-June 1986 Feminine Desire
Dr Harriet Guest	Department of English, University College, London	July-September 1990 William Hodges
Dr Sneja Gunew	School of Humanities, Deakin University	May-July 1986 Migrant Writing in Australia
Professor K.S. Guthke	Department of German, Harvard University	July-August 1984 Biography of B. Traven
Dr H.G. Hall	Department of French, University of Warwick	February-April 1984 French Comedy (Seventeenth and Eighteenth-Century)

Professor A.C. Hamilton	Department of English, Queen's University, Ontario	May-July 1985 Spenser Encyclopedia, Elizabethan Romance
Mr P.R. Hardie	Lecturer in Classics, Magdalene College, University of Cambridge	July-September 1988 Virgil and the Latin Epic Tradition
Professor J.P. Hardy	Department of English, ANU	January-December 1976 Dr Johnson
Dr Bernard Harrison	Department of Philosophy, University of Sussex	September-November 1976 Moral Philosophy
Dr R.R.K. Hartmann	Language Centre, Exeter University	January-June 1977 Translation
Professor Ihab Hassan	Department of English, University of Wisconsin, Milwaukee	June-August 1990 Cross-Cultural Autobiography
Assoc. Professor A.J. Hay	Institute of Fine Arts, New York University	June-August 1987 The Chinese Universe in Chinese Art
Professor Peter Herbst	Department of Philosophy, The Faculties, ANU	July-December 1981; September 1985-September 1986 Planning of 1982 Conferences; Critical Enquiry
Professor R.D. Herrman	Department of Philosophy, University of Tennessee	June-September 1974 Existentialism; Seventeenth-Century Metaphysics
Professor M.F. Herzfeld	Department of Anthropology, Indiana University	July-September 1985 Historical Allusion in the Self-Presentation of Greeks Today
Professor P.L.R. Higonnet	Department of History, Harvard University	June-August 1981 Politics in Eighteenth-Century France and America
Dr Christopher Hill	Oxford (Visiting Professor, The Open University)	January-March 1981 Seventeenth-Century English History
Dr Roger Hillman	Modern European Languages, ANU	January-July 1989 Narrative in Literature and Film; Co-convener, Film and the Humanities
Professor E.D. Hirsch	Department of English, University of Virginia	May-August 1982 The Historicality of Meaning
Dr Ursula Hoff	London	August-October 1984 Symbolism in Australian Landscape Painting
Professor J.M. Holquist	Slavic Department, Indiana University	December 1975-July 1976 Dostoevsky; Russian Literature and Science
Dr J. Anne Hone	School of Teacher Education, Canberra College of Advanced Education	February-July 1981 Late Nineteenth-Century School Curricula in Australian Colonies

Dr Mihály Hoppál	Ethnographical Institute, Budapest	September-December 1989 Visual Anthropology
Dr R.J. Howat	Department of Music, University of Western Australia	May-August 1987 Debussy and Oriental Art and Philosophy
Dr Cicely Howell	Canberra	March-May 1984 Inheritance Strategies, AD 400-1700
Dr Michael Hunter	Department of History, Birkbeck College, University of London	July-September 1982 Atheism in Early Modern England
Dr I.R. Indyk	Sydney	December 1981- March 1982 The Concept of Authority in Eighteenth-Century English Literature
Dr F.C. Inglis	School of Education, University of Bristol	March-May 1984 Political Meanings of English Landscape
Dr Michael Jackson	Department of Anthropology, Massey University	January-August 1982 Literature and Moral Concern
Mr Dan Jacobson	Department of English, University College, London	June-August 1981 Writers on Romanticism and Nationalism
Professor M.L. Jacobus	Department of English, Cornell University	January-June 1985 Wordsworth, Feminist Literary Criticism
Mrs Elizabeth Jeffreys	Adult Education, University of Sydney	April-November 1978 The Troy Legend in France and Byzantium
Mr R.H.A. Jenkyns	Classics, Lady Margaret Hall, University of Oxford	April-August 1985 Virgil: Classical Tradition
Ms H.I. Jessup	Freelance Architectural Historian, Washington DC	June-August 1987 Dutch Architects in Indonesia
Professor H.D. Jocelyn	Department of Latin, University of Manchester	July-September 1979 Roman Drama
Dr S. Beynon John	School of European Studies, University of Sussex	July-October 1979 Nineteenth and Twentieth- Century French Drama
Professor P.H. Jones	Department of Philosophy, University of Edinburgh	July-September 1984 David Hume
Dr David Jopling	Department of Psychology, Emory University	July-December 1990 Self-Knowledge and Self-Determination
Dr Rüdiger Joppien	Department of Fine Arts, University of Cologne	August-December 1975; November 1981-January 1982 Artists on Maritime Voyages, 1760-1860; Applied Arts in Australia

Dr R.D. Jordan	Department of English, University of Melbourne	January-March 1981 Seventeenth-Century English Literature
Dr F.P.R. Just	British School at Athens	April-August 1985 Greek Nationalism
Dr Ann Kaplan	Humanities Institute, State University of New York, Stony Brook	September-December 1989 Cross-cultural Film Analysis
Mr Russell Keat	Department of Philosophy, University of Lancaster	February-July 1982 Concepts of Meaning and Interpretation in Psychoanalysis
Dr Douglas Kelly	Classics Department, ANU	August-November 1988 The History of Warfare in Ancient Greece
Professor F. Kermode	King's College, University of Cambridge	October-November 1988 History and Value
Mr Gary Kildea	Documentary Film-Maker, Canberra	April-September 1989 Ethnographic Film
Em. Professor H.C. Knutson	Department of French, University of British Columbia	September-November 1988 Molière in a European Context
Professor Manji Kobayashi	Department of English, Kobe University	September 1976-May 1977 Modern Australian Poetry; Translations into Japanese
Dr P.F. Kornicki	Fellow, Robinson College, University of Cambridge	June-September 1987 Publishing and the Use of Information in Nineteenth-Century Japan
Professor Hans Kuhn	Department of Modern European Languages, Germanic Section, ANU	March-June 1978 Convener, 1980 Conferences
Professor Franz Kuna	Department of English and American Studies, Universität Klagenfurt	July-October 1989 Theories of Context
Professor Victor Lange	Department of German, Princeton University	August-November 1977 German Literature
Professor J.R. Lawler	Department of Romance Languages, University of Chicago June-August 1981	A.R. Chisholm; Baudelaire
Ms Sylvia Lawson	Independent Scholar, Sydney	March-July 1989 The Sydney Opera House
Professor André Lefevere	Department of English Literature, University of Antwerp	May-November 1977 Literary Translation
Professor H. Lehmann	Historisches Seminar, University of Kiel	March-July 1980 Émigré Lutherans
Professor A.H.T. Levi	Department of French, University of St Andrews	June-September 1985 Hellenism in France in the Seventeenth and Eighteenth Centuries

Ms K. Lilley	Junior Research Fellow in English, St Hilda's College, University of Oxford	July-September 1988 The Australian Elegy
Professor Lawrence Lipking	Department of English, Northwestern University	June-September 1986 Abandoned Women and Poetic Tradition
Dr Peter Loizos	London School of Economics	July-September 1989 Ethnographic Filmmaking
Dr Emily Lyle	School of Scottish Studies, University of Edinburgh	October 1976-April 1977 Scottish Oral Literature in Australia
Mr C.J. Lyndon Gee	Composer and Conductor	May-September 1975 Contemporary Music: Berio and Bussotti
Professor G.F. Lytle	Department of History, University of Texas at Austin	May-August 1983 Patronage in the Renaissance
Assoc. Prof. P. McCarthy	Department of French, Haverford University	May-September 1982 Samuel Beckett
Mr David MacDougall	Australian Institute of Aboriginal Studies, Canberra	July-December 1989 Representation of Social Experience
Dr Judith McKenzie	Junior Research Fellow in Classical Archaeology, St Hugh's College, University of Oxford	April-June 1990 The Architecture of Alexandria
Dr Alwynne Mackie	Department of Philosophy, La Trobe University	July 1978-June 1979 Expressionism in Modern Art
Dr I.W.F. MacLean	Lecturer in French, University of Oxford	October-December 1983 Interpretation in the Renaissance
Dr Roy MacLeod	Department of History, University of Sydney	Three months in 1990 The Art of Scientific Biography
Mr H. McQueen	Canberra	June-August 1984 The Cityscape in Australian Literature
Dr P. Magdalino	Department of Medieval History, University of St Andrews	March-June 1985 Image of Athens in Byzantine Literature
Professor W.P. Malm	School of Music, University of Michigan	May-August 1987 Shamisen Concert Music in the Nineteenth Century
Professor George Marcus	Department of Anthropology, Rice University	May-July 1989 Culture and Wealth
Professor P.J. Marshall	Department of History, King's College, University of London	July-August 1987 The Indian Writings and Speeches of Edmund Burke
Mr P.J.T. Martin	English Department, Monash University	February-April 1980 The Poetry of Inward Experience

Dr Audrey Meaney	School of English, Macquarie University	May-September 1978 Witchcraft in Anglo-Saxon England
Professor Anne Mellor	Department of English, University of California, Los Angeles	June-September 1990 The Bluestockings: English Women of Letters, 1780-1830
Professor Ronald Mellor	Department of History, University of California, Los Angeles	June-September 1990 Oriental Religions in the Roman West
Dr John Meyer	Perth	January-December 1976 History of the Piano Concerto
Professor B.E. Moeran	Department of Anthropology and Sociology, SOAS, University of London	July-September 1987 Folk Craft Poetry, 1850-1950, in Japan and Europe
Professor Sidney Monas	Department of Slavic Languages, University of Texas at Austin	May-September 1977 The Myth of St Petersburg
Professor E.S. Morgan	Faculty of History, Yale University	September-December 1987 Popular Sovereignty in England and America
Professor J.E. Morpurgo	Department of English, University of Leeds	April-August 1975 The Paperback Movement and Sir Allen Lane
Ms Meaghan Morris	Sydney	March-May 1986 Women's Travel Journals
Ms S.M. Morris	London	July-October 1984 Australian and New Zealand Watercolours
Professor A.P.D. Mourelatos	Department of Philosophy, University of Texas at Austin	August-December 1978 Plato and Pre-Socratic Philosophy
Dr D.C. Muecke	Department of English, Monash University	February-July 1979 Shakespeare's Irony
Professor Saul Novack	Department of Music, Queens College, City University of New York	July 1975-January 1976 Chromaticism in Triadic Tonality
Mr K.M. O'Neill	King's College, University of Cambridge	January-March 1980 André Gide and Jacques Rivière
Professor S. Orgel	Department of English, Johns Hopkins University	July-August 1983 Inigo Jones, Ben Jonson
Professor Anne Paolucci	Department of English and Comparative Literature, St John's University, New York	February-May 1979 Hegel's Theory of Comedy
Professor Brian Parker	Department of English, University of Toronto	June-August 1988 A Critical Edition of *Coriolanus*
Professor R. Parker	Department of English, Cornell University	January-June 1985 Wordsworth

Assoc. Professor A.T.L. Parkin	Department of English, University of British Columbia	June-August 1987 Japanese Influence on Playwrights in Western and Eastern Europe
Dr David Patterson	Oxford Centre for Post-Graduate Hebrew Studies	July-August 1980 Modern Hebrew Literature, Modern Jewish History
Dr M.C. Phillips	Department of English Literature, University of Edinburgh	August-September 1980 Pope and Blake
Professor Sarah Pomeroy	Department of Classics, Hunter College, CUNY	June-July 1986 Xenophon's *Oeconomicus*
Dr B.W.F. Powell	Oriental Institute, University of Oxford	May-August 1987 A Study of the *Shinkabuki* Playwright, Mayama Seika
Professor S.S. Prawer	Professor of German, University of Oxford	March-May 1980 The Jews in Germany, Heine
Dr W.R. Prest	Department of History, University of Adelaide	September 1980-February 1981 The Professions in early Modern England
Professor Cecil Price	Department of English, University of Swansea	August 1975-February 1976 Drama and Society in the Eighteenth Century
Professor N.D. Quarry	School of Architecture, NSW Institute of Technology	May-August 1987 Modern Architecture of Europe and Japan
Mr Peter Quartermaine	Department of English, University of Exeter	July-September 1978 Visual Arts in Australia
Professor K.F. Quinn	Department of Classics, University of Toronto	June-July 1981 Literature as a Social Phenomenon
Professor P. Rafroidi	Centre for Irish Studies, University of Lille	October 1980-April 1981 Irish Literature in English
Dr Peter Read	Department of History, Research School of Social Sciences, ANU	April-September 1990 A Biography of Charles Perkins
Mr Jonathan Rée	Department of Philosophy, Middlesex Polytechnic, London	December 1980-April 1981 Organisation of Knowledge
Ms Sian Reynolds	School of European Studies, University of Sussex	July-September 1977 Jean Allemane; Emmanuel Le Roy Ladourie
Dr D.W.R. Ridgeway	Department of Archaeology, University of Edinburgh	July-September 1985 The First Western Greeks and their Impact on Italy
Professor J.O. Robinson-Valéry	Institut des Textes et Manuscrits Modernes, CNRS, Paris	July-October 1987 Europe in its Relationship to the Orient as seen by Valéry, 1895-1945
Dr Lyndal Roper	Junior Research Fellow, Merton College, University of Oxford	July-September 1986 History of Sexuality

Professor R.M. Rorty	Department of Philosophy, Princeton University	May-September 1982 Heidegger against the Pragmatists
Dr D.B. Rose	Australian Institute of Aboriginal Studies, Canberra	March-August 1988 An Ethnographic Encounter with Australian Aborigines
Professor Marilyn Rose	Translation Centre, SUNY, Binghamton	January-July 1977 Literary Translation
Dr M.J. Rosenthal	History of Art, University of Warwick	June-August 1984 British Landscape Painting
Mr Robert Rosenthal	Special Collections, Regenstein Library, University of Chicago	July-September 1976 Australian Libraries and the Role of the HRC
Dr D.T. Runia	Huygens Research Fellow, Netherlands Organisation for Pure Research, Amsterdam	August-December 1987 Philo and the Beginnings of Christian Philosophy
Mr Alan Ryan	Tutorial Fellow in Politics, New College, University of Oxford	August 1974-January 1975 Property in Political Thought: Locke, Hegel, Mill, Marx
Professor A.J. Sambrook	English Department, University of Southampton	January-April 1988 Biography of James Thomson
Professor Trevor Saunders	Department of Classics, University of Newcastle upon Tyne	April-July 1986 Ancient Greek Penology
Dr Tilo Schabert	Institute of Political Science, University of Munich	August-October 1974 Philosophical Foundations of the Modern Age
Dr Robert Sellick	Department of English, University of Adelaide	June-December 1981 Biography of Ludwig Leichhardt
Professor Robert Shackleton	Professor of French, University of Oxford	July-September 1980 The Early French Enlightenment
Dr E.S. Shaffer	Department of English and Comparative Literature, University of East Anglia	April-July 1982 Literary and Biblical Criticism
Professor Roger Sharrock	Department of English, King's College, University of London	January-September 1977 Romanticism and Autobiography
Dr Kevin Sharpe	Department of History, University of Southampton	December 1989-June 1990 Charles I
Dr Susan Sheridan	School of Humanities, Deakin University	March-September 1986 Convener, Feminism and Humanities Year; Christina Stead
Professor G.M. Sifakis	Department of Classics, University of Crete	July-October 1985 Old Attic Comedy
Professor D. Simpson	English Department, University of Colorado at Boulder	June-August 1988 Romantic Poetry and Classical Epic

Professor Quentin Skinner	Professor of Political Science, Christ's College, University of Cambridge	April 1989 Renaissance Political Thought
Dr S. Smiles	Department of Art, Exeter College of Art and Design	July-September 1984 George Rowe, A.B. Johns
Mr Robert Smith	Department of Fine Arts, Flinders University	February 1975-February 1976 Giotto; Biography of Laurie Thomas
Professor Daniel Snell	Department of History, University of Oklahoma	May-August 1990 History of the Ancient Near East
Professor Gayatri Spivak	Department of English, Emory University	July-August 1986 Feminism in the Third World
Dr Margaret Stoljar	Modern European Languages, ANU	February-June 1988 European Literature in Colonial Australia
Professor L. Stone	Department of History, Princeton University	September-October 1983 Divorce and Society in Eighteenth-Century England
Dr D.M. Sullivan	Fellow, St Catherine's College, University of Oxford	June-August 1987 Interaction in Art between East and West since the Sixteenth Century
Mr Stewart Sutherland	Department of Philosophy, University of Stirling	July-December 1974 Dostoevsky
Professor P.L.A. Sweeney	Department of Indonesian and Malay, University of California, Berkeley	May-August 1987 Poet and Audience: the Malay World and Europe
Mr A. Tatlow	Department of Comparative Literature, University of Hong Kong	July-September 1987 Brecht's Response to East Asian Culture
Dr M.L.M. Thiersch	School of Drama, University of New South Wales	June-December 1981 Biography of Ludwig Leichhardt
Mr Paul Thom	Department of Philosophy, The Faculties, ANU	July-September 1983 Rhetorical Categories in Musical Thought in the Renaissance
Mr K.V. Thomas	Reader in Modern History, University of Oxford	July-September 1983 Early Modern English History
Ms Helen Topliss	Melbourne	September 1980-February 1981; May-October 1984 Tom Roberts Convener, Landscape Conferences
Professor Leo Treitler	Department of Music, State University of New York at Stony Brook	June-August 1978; May-September 1981 Musical Literacy in the Middle Ages

Ms Anna Tröger	Institute of Sociology, University of Hanover	July-October 1986 Schutz and Merleau-Ponty
Dr A. von Schönborn	Department of Philosophy, University of Missouri	May-August 1980 Karl Leonard Reinhold
Professor S. Vryonis	Department of History, University of California, Los Angeles	August-September 1985 Nature and Diffusion of Byzantine Culture
Professor A. Walicki	Institute of Philosophy and Sociology, Polish Academy of Sciences	July-September 1980 Polish Romantic Nationalism
Professor J.M. Wallace	English Department, University of Chicago	September-November 1988 The Senecan Context of *Coriolanus*
Professor G.F. Waller	Department of English, Wilfred Laurier University, Ontario	May-August 1979 English Drama and the Court, 1580-1640
Mr Neville Weston	Department of Art and Design, Padgate College of Education	April-August 1975 European Influence in Contemporary Australian Art
Dr R.S. White	Department of English, University of Newcastle upon Tyne	July-December 1979 Keats on Shakespeare
Dr P.J. Widdowson	School of Humanities, London Polytechnic	April-July 1984 Thomas Hardy in History
Professor Max Wilcox	Department of Biblical Studies, University of North Wales	January-April 1988 Jesus in First-Century Jewish Society
Dr John Wilders	Tutorial Fellow in English, Worcester College, University of Oxford	December 1975- September 1976 Shakespeare's History Plays
Mr Paul Willemen	British Film Institute, London	August-October 1989 Third Cinema Theories
Mr John Willett	London	May-July 1979 German Theatre, 1918-1933
Professor C.M. Williams	History Department, The Faculties, ANU	February-April, October-December 1979 Henry Marten
Professor Gordon Williams	Thatcher Professor of Latin, Yale University	May-August 1981 Tragedies of Seneca
Dr Margaret Williams	School of Drama, University of New South Wales	July-September 1981 Australian Drama in the Nineteenth Century
Dr P.B. Wilson	Faculty of English, University of Cambridge	April-July 1985 English Tragedy and Hellenism
Mr Iain Wright	Faculty of English, University of Cambridge	March-October 1982 Myth, Primitivism, and Modern Writing

Dr F. Zelger	Director, Oskar Reinhart Foundation, Winterthur	May-June 1980 History as a Subject of Art
Professor Zhu Hong	Chinese Academy of Social Sciences, Beijing	April-June 1988 Nineteenth- and Twentieth-Century British Fiction

Conference Visitors 1984–1990

Herr H.I. Arnold	Göttingen	Literary Journals May 1987
Professor F.M. Barnard	Department of Political Science, University of Western Ontario	Romantic Nationalism May 1980
Professor T.D. Barnes	Department of Classics, University of Toronto	Use of the Past Seminar May 1988
Dr J. Barrell	Faculty of English, University of Cambridge	Landscape and the Arts I July 1984
Professor Judith Becker	School of Music, University of Michigan	The Occident and the Orient August 1986
Professor Jan Bialostocki	Museum Narodowe, Warsaw	Romantic Nationalism and Myths and Heroes May-June 1980
Dr R. Braidotti	Columbia University Programs in Paris	Feminist Enquiry as a Transdisciplinary Enterprise August 1986
Professor Julianne Burton	Department of Literature, University of California, Santa Cruz	Coming to Terms with the Photographic Image July 1989
Dr A. Callen	History of Art, University of Warwick	Feminist Enquiry as a Transdisciplinary Enterprise August 1986
Professor A.M. Cameron	Department of History, King's College, London	Use of the Past Seminar May 1988
Mr Peter Conrad	Student in English, Christ Church, Oxford	Self and Text September 1990
Dr D.J. Constantine	Faculty of German, University of Oxford	Hellenism in Europe June 1985
Dr Mireille Corbier	CNRS, Paris	Roman Family II, July 1988
Dr R. Clogg	Department of Byzantine and Modern Greek, King's College, University of London	Eastern Europe, July 1980 Hellenism and Neohellenism, 1985
Professor F. D'Andria	Department of the Study of Antiquity, University of Lecce	Greek Colonists July 1985
Professor N.Z. Davis	Department of History, Princeton University	Renaissance Performances August 1983

Professor J.J. Duggan	Department of Comparative Literature, University of California, Berkeley	Transmission in Oral and Written Traditions August 1981
Professor A. Ellenius	Department of Art History, University of Uppsala	Myths and Heroes June 1980
Professor Martin Esslin	Department of Drama, Stanford University	Modern European Drama July 1979
Professor L.D. Ettlinger	Department of the History of Art, University of California	South Wind July 1983
Dr Ruth Finnegan	Open University, UK	Transmission in Oral and Written Traditions August 1981
Professor Denton Fox	Department of English, University of Toronto	Waning of the Middle Ages August 1978
Professor Northrop Frye	Massey College, University of Toronto	Northrop Frye Seminar June 1986
Dr J.S. Gage	Lecturer in the History of Art, University of Oxford	Landscape and the Arts 1 July 1984
Professor J.F. Gebhard	Institut für Politische Wissenschaft, University of Erlangen-Nürnberg	Romantic Nationalism May 1980
Professor R. Goldthwaite	Department of History, Johns Hopkins University	Patronage Conference May 1983
Professor Jack Goody	Faculty of Social Anthropology, University of Cambridge	Transmission in Oral and Written Traditions August 1981
Professor Phyllis Grosskurth	University of Toronto	Self and Text September 1990
Professor Bjarni Gudnason	University of Iceland	Old Norse Workshop June 1978
Professor Robert Halsband	Department of English, University of Illinois	Fourth David Nichol Smith Seminar August 1976
Mr Ian Hamilton	London	Literary Journals May 1987
Professor Keith Hopkins	Department of Sociology, Brunei University	Roman Family I: July 1981 Roman Family II: July 1988
Professor A. A. Jardine	Harvard University	Feminism and the Humanities July 1986
Professor Barbara Jelavich	Department of History, Indiana University	Eastern Europe July 1980
Professor Charles Jelavich	Department of History, Indiana University	Eastern Europe July 1980
Professor J.W. Johnson	Department of English, University of Rochester	Australia and the European Imagination May 1981
Ms C.I. Kaplan	American Studies, University of Sussex	Feminist Criticism and Cultural Production May 1986

Professor E.L. Keeley	Creative Writing, Princeton University	Hellenism and Neohellenism August 1985
Professor Alvin Kernan	Graduate School, Princeton University	Shakespeare and Jonson May 1979
Ms A.F. Kuhn	Institute of Education, University of London	Feminist Criticism and Cultural Production May 1986
Professor Lars Lönnroth	Aalborg Universitetscentre, Denmark	Old Norse Workshop May 1979
Professor F.S.L. Lyons	Trinity College, University of Dublin	Irish Nationalism November 1980
Professor John MacQueen	School of Scottish Studies, University of Edinburgh	Early Middle Ages April 1978
Professor H.M. Maier	Southeast Asia Program, Cornell University	Europe and the Exotic July 1987
Professor G.G. Migone	Torino	Literary Journals May 1987
Professor Karl Miller	Department of English, University College, London	Literary Journals May 1987
Professor W.J.T. Mitchell	Department of English, University of Chicago	Literary Journals May 1987
Dr Partha Mitter	School of African and Asian Studies, University of Sussex	Europe and the Orient July 1987
Professor Masao Miyoshi	Department of English, University of California, Berkeley	The Occident and the Orient August 1987
Professor Peter Munz	Department of History, Victoria University of Wellington	Early Middle Ages April 1978
Professor Bill Nichols	Cinema Department, San Francisco State University	Coming to Terms with the Photographic Image July 1989
Professor T. Nipperdey	Institut für Neuere Geschichte, University of Munich	Romantic Nationalism May 1980
Professor D.A. Pearsall	Department of English, University of York	Waning of the Middle Ages August 1978
Professor Jorge Preloran	Department of Theatre, Film and TV, University of California, Los Angeles	Film and Representations of Culture September 1989
Dr Marc Piault	CNRS, Paris	Film and Representation of Culture September 1989
Professor O. Pritsak	Department of Linguistics, Harvard University	Eastern Europe July 1980
Professor Heinz Rupp	Deutsche Seminar, University of Basel	Early Middle Ages April 1978
Professor Richard Saller	Department of History, University of Chicago	Roman Family II July 1988
Professor Gunter Schilder	Department of Geography, State University of Utrecht	Australia and the European Imagination May 1981

Professor J.W. Scott	The Institute for Advanced Study, Princeton	Feminism and the Humanities July 1986
Professor Ihor Sevcenko	Department of Byzantine History and Literatures, Harvard University	Byzantine Conference May 1978
Professor John Shearman	Courtauld Institute, London	Mannerism June 1977
Professor J.E. Stevens	Professor of English, University of Cambridge	South Wind July 1983
Professor C.R. Stimpson	Institute for Research on Women, Rutgers University	Feminist Enquiry as a Transdisciplinary Enterprise August 1986
Dr. Gaylyn Studlar	Theatre and Film Studies, Emory University	Film and Representations of Culture September 1989
Dr Susan Treggiari	Department of Classics, Stanford University	Roman Family II July 1988
Dr Jeremy Treglown	Editor *TLS*, London	Literary Journals May 1987
Professor F.M. Turner	Department of History, Yale University	Hellenism in Europe June 1985
Professor K. Vondung	Institut für Politische Wissenschaft, University of Erlangen-Nürnberg	Romantic Nationalism May 1980
Dr Vera von Falkenhausen	Department of Byzantine History, University of Pisa	Hellenism and Byzantium May 1985
Dr A. von Schönborn	Department of Philosophy, University of Missouri	Interpreting and Understanding July 1982
Professor A. Wallace-Hadrill	University of Reading	Roman Family II July 1988
Dr Helen Wallis	British Library	Australia and the European Imagination May 1981
Professor David Waterhouse	Department of East Asian Studies, University of Toronto	The Occident and the Orient August 1986
Dr R. Weissman	Department of History, University of Maryland	Patronage Conference May 1983
Professor Glyn Williams	Department of History, Queen Mary College, University of London	Australia and the European Imagination May 1981
Hon. C.M. Woodhouse	Department of Greek, King's College, London	Hellenism and Neohellenism August 1985
Professor D.E. Worster	Department of American Studies, University of Hawaii	Landscape and the Arts II August 1984
Professor J. Wrede	Department of Swedish Literature, University of Helsinki	Myths and Heroes June 1980

Summer Fellows, Visiting Scholars, and Short-Term Visitors

Ms Martha Ansara Creative Arts Fellow	Independent Filmmaker, Sydney	July-September 1989 Always Was, Always Will Be, Video Tape and book – The Old Swan Brewery Dispute
Dr N.J. Austin	Classical Studies, Massey University	January-February 1983 The Family of Constantine
Dr T.W. Bestor	Department of Philosophy, Massey University	January-February 1984 Plato's Theory of Language
Mr David Blackburn	British Artist	August-September 1977 Lecturing, Exhibiting, Working in Pastels
Dr David Boyd	Department of English, University of Newcastle	July-September 1989 Characterization in American Film
Mr P.J. Burns	Department of History, James Cook University	April-May 1983 Dutch Colonial Administration
Dr Alan Clark	Department of French, University of Canterbury	January-February 1990 Mitterrand: Ideas, Expression, Action
Dr R.P. Corballis	Department of English, University of Canterbury	January-February 1980 Tom Stoppard
Dr C. Cordner	Melbourne	February-March 1984 Aesthetics
Dr Hugh Craig	English Department, University of Newcastle	December 1987-February 1988 Elizabethan Art Theory
Ms Barbara Creed	Cinema Studies, La Trobe University	July-September 1989 Horror and the Monstrous Feminine
Dr W. Dean	English Department, University of Otago	January-February 1986 George Chapman
Dr Richard Freadman	Department of English, University of Western Australia	January-February 1988 Critical Essays on Contemporary Literary Theory
Dr J. Gray	English Department, James Cook University	January-March 1981 The Language of *Pearl*
Professor D. Hamer	Department of History, Victoria University of Wellington	December 1986-February 1987 New Towns in the New World
Dr Jocelyn Harris	English Department, University of Otago	November 1975-February 1976 *Sir Charles Grandison*
Professor A.J. Hassall	Department of English, James Cook University	February-June 1988 Classic Australian Fiction

Ms Pam Heckenberg	School of Drama, University of NSW	December 1982-February 1983 Nineteenth-Century Australian Drama
Dr Peter Hempenstall	Department of History, University of Newcastle	January-March 1984 Biography of E.H. Bergmann
Ms M. Holloway	Department of Visual Arts, Monash University	January-February 1986 Australian Art
Dr Cicely Howell	Canberra	November 1983-February 1984 Inheritance Strategies, AD 400-1700
Mrs Amirah Inglis	Canberra	January-March 1986 Spanish Civil War
Professor John Jensen	Department of History, University of Waikato	November 1979-January 1980 Modern Nationalism
Mr Don'o Kim	Sydney	May-June 1987 A Chamber Opera Libretto
Dr W.A. Krebs	English Department, ANU	January-February 1985 Australian Dictionary (Collins)
Professor Heath Lees	School of Music, University of Auckland	December 1987-March 1988 Music in Modernism
Professor J.A. Leith	Department of History, Queen's University, Kingston, Ontario	September 1974-July 1975 Art and Music as Propaganda in the French Revolution
Mrs Doris Lessing	London	March 1985 Word Festival, 1985
Dr Susan Magarey	Research Centre for Women's Studies, University of Adelaide	May-August 1986 Revisiting the 1890s
Dr C.G. Mann	Department of Modern Languages, James Cook University	September-December 1989 Transtextuality in the works of Marguerite Duras
Professor Earl Miner	Department of English, Princeton University	September 1977 Translation
Dr R. Morse	Department of English, University of Leeds	October 1982-March 1983 Rhetorical Convention in the Renaissance
Dr Satendra Nandan	Formerly University of the South Pacific	December 1987-May 1988 Patrick White and V.S. Naipaul
Miss Brenda Niall	Department of English, Monash University	October-December 1983 October-November 1987 Biography of Martin Boyd
Professor Peter Norrish	Department of Romance Languages, Victoria University of Wellington	November 1981-January 1982 Modern French Drama
Dr Denise O'Brien	Department of Anthropology, Temple University	October 1983-April 1984 Fiction and Ethnography

Professor Patrick O'Farrell	School of History, University of New South Wales	February 1989 Irish History
Dr J.M. Penhallurick	School of Liberal Studies, Canberra College of Advanced Education	January-March 1983 Systems of Time in Modern English
Dr E. Perkins	English Department, James Cook University	October-December 1985 Australian Literature
Dr Roy Perrett	Department of Philosophy, Massey University	September-October 1990 Philosophical Autobiography
Mr W.F. Richardson	Department of Classics, University of Auckland	March-May 1976 Anatomical Terminology in Greek and Latin
Dr P.L. Rose	Department of History, James Cook University	January-February 1980 Wagner's Social and Artistic Thought
Mr J. Rowland	Canberra	January-March 1984 Translations of Voznesensky
Dr Hazel Rowley	School of Humanities, Deakin University	January-February 1990 Biography of Christina Stead
Dr P.A. Rule	Department of History, La Trobe University	July-December 1987 Early Eighteenth-Century Jesuit Figures in China
Mr Jörg Schmeisser	Hamburg	July-September 1975 Lecturing, Exhibiting Etching
Professor G. Seddon	Department of Architecture and Planning, University of Melbourne	March-April 1985 Australian Conservation History
Dr A. Shboul	Department of Semitic Studies, University of Sydney	January-February 1979 Non-Islamic Monuments in Arabic Literature
Dr B. Sherry	Department of English, University of Sydney	January-February 1983 Literature and the Visual Arts
Dr C.O. Sowerwine	Department of History, University of Melbourne	February-April 1986 Modern French History
Ms Jennifer Strauss	English Department, Monash University	February-July 1988 Images of the Artist in Australian Poetry
Dr J.E.P. Thomson	Department of English, Victoria University of Wellington	March-May 1988 Late Nineteenth-Century Theatre in New Zealand
Dr C.B. Thornton-Smith	Department of French, University of Melbourne	March-June 1987 French Perceptions of Colonial Australia
Dr J.G. Tulip	Department of English, University of Sydney	October-December 1985 David Campbell
Dr Nancy Underhill	Department of Fine Arts, University of Queensland	September-December 1985 October-November 1986 Sydney Ure Smith

Dr Brenda Walker	Department of English, University of Western Australia	January-February 1986 Samuel Beckett
Dr J.A. Walter	School of Humanities, Griffith University	July-October 1987 Themes in Australian Culture
Professor Paul Weaver	Department of Classics, University of Tasmania	December 1982-February 1983 Roman Personal Nomenclature
Dr J.E.G. Whitehorne	Department of Classics, University of Queensland	December 1975-January 1976 Greek Literature
Dr N. Zurbrugg	School of Humanities, Griffith University	December 1982-January 1982 Beckett and Proust

Visiting Fellows and Other Visitors, 1991-2004

Note: Conference Visitors are listed separately below, but it is not possible to list all conference visitors and visiting lecturers as records are incomplete and there are many names that are not listed who came to the HRC in this decade

Name	Institution	Date and Topic
Dr Aletta Biersack	Anthropology University of Oregon	1991
Dr Terry Bilhartz	History, Sam Houston State University	May to July 1991 Historical Profession in the United States
Professor Richard Bosworth	History, University of Western Australia	July to October 1991 Explaining Auschwitz & Hiroshima: Historians and the Second World War
Professor Peter Brown	History, Princeton University	April, 1991 Body and Society
Dr Peter J. Cochrane	History, University of Sydney	January to April 1991 Gender Relations in Nationalist Ideology
Dr Tony Cousins (Visiting Scholar)	English, Macquarie University	September, 1991 Fictions of Love and Power in Shakespeare's Poems
Professor Ann Curthoys	History, Faculty of Arts, University of Technology, Sydney	1991
Dr Susan Dermody	Humanities and Social Sciences University of Technology, Sydney	1991 Documentary, Technology and the Unconscious
Dr Mary Edmunds	Australian Institute of Aboriginal and Torres Strait Islander Studies	June to September 1991 Changing Habits: Anthropology History and Spanish Nuns
Professor John Ellis	Germanic Literature University of California, Santa Cruz	1991 Historical Analysis of the Criticism, Theory & Study of Literature in Germany
Mr Miles Fairburn (Visiting Scholar)	History, Victoria University of Wellington	June to August 1991 The Social World of W.J Cox: A Study of A Casual Labourer and Deprivation in New Zealand 1880-1925
Dr Paul A. Gillen (Visiting Scholar)	Humanities, University of Technology, Sydney	June to July 1991 Cultural & Historical Philosophy of Jack Lindsay

Mr Christopher L. Healy	History University of Melbourne	July to September 1991 Reading Popular Historical Consciousness
Professor Dale Kent	History University of California, Riverside	June to September 1991 The Vocabulary of Power in Early Medicean Florence
Dr Peter Kuch	Humanities Avondale College, NSW	June to July 1991 Yeats and AE
Dr John Lechte	School of Behavioural Sciences Macquarie University	1991
Dr Stuart F. Macintyre	History University of Melbourne	1991 Historical Consciousness and Historical Writing in 19th century Australia
Dr Jill Matthews (Visiting Scholar)	Women's Studies Program The Australian National University	1991
Dr Drusilla Modjeska	Freelance Scholar NSW	1991 Art in the Twenties
Dr Russell Poole (Visiting Scholar)	English Department Massey University	September to October 1991 Skaldic Poetry as a Form of Historical Discourse
Professor Arthur Quinn	Rhetoric University of California, Berkeley	May to September 1991 The Antinomies of Pure History
Dr Mark Rivière (Visiting Scholar)	James Cook University	1991
Dr Leonie Rutherford (Visiting Scholar)	English & Communication Studies, University of New England	1991
Mr Julian Thomas	Research School of Social Sciences, The Australian National University	February to May 1991 National Histories and the Audio-Visual Past
Dr Robert Tristram (Visiting Scholar)	Sociology & Social Work Victoria University of Wellington	June to October 1991 Ten Fallacies in Modern Historiography
Mr Fengzhen Wang	Critical Theory Institute of Foreign Literature Chinese Academy of Social Sciences	April to July 1991 Twentieth-Century Western Critical Theory and its Reception in China
Professor Menhui Wen	Foreign Literature Chinese Academy of Social Sciences	January to March 1991 Late Nineteenth Century and Early Twentieth Century British Fiction
Dr Dianne O. Bennett (Visiting Scholar)	Anthropology Victoria University of Wellington	July to November 1992 Notions of Europe and Perceptions of Self and Community in Greece

Mr David Carter (visiting Scholar)	Humanities Griffith University	February to March 1992 The Literary and Political Careers of Judah Waten
A/Professor Katerina Clark	Department of Comparative Literature, Yale University	February to July 1992 Interrelation between the new culture of Revolutionary Russia in the 1920s and avant-garde culture of Contemporary Europe
Dr Bryan Coleborne (Visiting Scholar)	Monash University College	August to October 1992 Contemporary Irish Fiction and Cultural Politics
Dr Susan Dermody	Humanities and Social Sciences University of Technology, Sydney	1992 Documentary, Technology and the Unconscious
Dr Paul Eggert	English ADFA, University College of New South Wales	September to December 1992 D.H. Lawrence and Italy
Professor Jonas Frykman	European Ethnology University of Lund	May to August 1992 Cultural Analysis of Identity Formation in Historical Perspective in Europe
Dr Harry Garlick (Visiting Scholar)	English University of Queensland	1992-1993 Literature
Professor Judith Mara Gutman	Committee on Liberal Studies Graduate Faculty, New School for Social Research, New York	1992 Image and Word in relationship to Social Change in Europe
Dr Adrian N. Jones	Department of History La Trobe University	1992 European Revolutions, 1789-1989
Dr Harold W. Love (Visiting Scholar)	Commerce University of Otago	1992 Epistemology and Professional Discourses
Professor Paul Michael Lützeler	German, Comparative Literature, European Studies Washington University, St. Louis	May to July 1992 Essays on Europe as a Literary Genre
Dr Margaret Maynard (Visiting Scholar)	Department of Art History University of Queensland	1992 Dress as Cultural Practise in Nineteenth Century Australia
Professor Thomas McFarland	Princeton University	February to October 1992 An edition of the Opus Maximum of Samuel Taylor Coleridge
Dr Patrick O'Meara	Department of Russian Trinity College, Dublin	July to September 1992 The Personality Cult in Contemporary Soviet Historiography
A/Professor Roslyn Pesman	History University of Sydney	July to September 1992 Representations of the Trip to Europe in the writing of Australian women

Dr Leonid V. Polyakov	Philosophy Academy of Sciences of the USSR	May to August 1992 The Problem of Europe in Russian Religious, Philosophical and Political Thought in XIX and XX Centuries
Professor Alain-Marc Rieu	Philosophy University of Strasbourg	July to October 1991 The Question of Culture in Contemporary Europe
Dr Margaret Stoljar	Modern European Languages The Australian National University	January to December 1992 European Literature in Colonial Australia
Dr Julian Thomas (ARC Fellow)	University of Melbourne	1992 National Histories and the Audio-Visual Past
Professor Andrzej Walicki	Department of History University of Notre Dame	August to November 1992
Dr Peter West (Visiting Scholar)	School of Education University of Western Sydney	1992 How Boys Became Men in Penrith, NSW
Dr Janet M. Wilson (Visiting Scholar)	English University of Otago	1992-1993 Literary Patronage in the Reign of Mary Tudor 1553-7
Professor Kurt Wolff	Sociology Brandis University	June to August 1992 Loma, Experience, Inquiry, Bearings
Mrs Gladys Yang	Foreign Languages Press, Beijing	1992
Professor Xianyi Yang	Foreign Languages Bureau, Beijing	1992
Professor Henry Abelove	English Literature Wesleyan University	June to August 1993 The Making of the Modern Heterosexual
Dr Dianne Chisholm	English University of Alberta	June to August 1993 Avant-garde Sexualities
A/Professor Tony D. Cousins (Visiting Scholar)	School of English Macquarie University	September to October 1993 Shakespeare's Sonnets and Narrative Poems
Dr Desley Deacon (Visiting Scholar)	American Studies University of Texas at Austin	January to June 1993 The Genealogy of Morals
A/Professor John D'Emilio	History University of North Carolina	May to August 1993 Twenty Years of Fighting
Dr Gary Dowsett	School of Behavioural Sciences Macquarie University	July to September 1993 Homosexualities, Gay Communities and Class
A/Professor Lisa Duggan	Department of American Civilization, Brown University	June to August 1993 Sapphic Slashers
Professor David Halperin	Literature Massachusetts Institute of Technology	January to April 1993 Queering the Canon

Dr Anne-Marie Hilsdon (Cass) (Visiting Scholar)	School of Social Science Queensland University of Technology	August to December 1993 Sex and the Military
Dr Annamarie Jagose (Visiting Scholar)	English University of Melbourne	October to December 1993 Sexual 'Inversions'
Dr Vicki Kirby	Visual Arts University of California at San Diego	June to September 1993 Corporeographies
Dr Martha A. Macintyre (Visiting Scholar)	Sociology La Trobe University	April to May 1993 Mariantismo and Machismo
Dr Alastair MacLachlan (Visiting Scholar)	History University of Sydney	August 1993 to February 1994 History Exploded
Dr Brian Massumi	Comparative Literature and Communications McGill University	1993 Masochism and Popular Culture
A/Professor Dorothea Olkowski	Department of Philosophy University of Colorado	July to August 1993 Violence and Pornography in the Regimes of Desire
A/Professor Cindy Patton	Rhetoric and Communication Temple University	May to August 1993 Resistance Without 'The Subject'
Professor Barry Rose (Visiting Scholar)	Tasmania	November to December 1993
Ms Gayle Rubin	San Francisco	1993 Leatherman
Professor Carole Vance	Sociomedical Sciences Columbia University	1993 1. Contested Images 2. Frigidity, Feminity and the Gendered Body
Professor Martha Vicinus	English Language & Literature University of Michigan	1993 Women who Dressed as Men, 1660-1950
Professor Paul Weaver	Classics University of Tasmania	1993-1994 Familial Structures in Roman Imperial Society
Mr Charles Zika (Visiting Scholar)	Department of History University of Melbourne	1993 Visual Images of Witchcraft and the Construction of Female Sexuality in Early Modern Europe
Dr Ina Bertrand (Visiting Scholar)	School of Education La Trobe University	1994 Australian Television News
Professor Jonathan Bordo (Sabbatical Fellow)	Cultural Studies Program Trent University	1993-1994 The Monument Without a Witness
Dr Howard Brasted (Visiting Scholar)	Department of History University of New England	1994 Jinnah, the Movement for Pakistan and Muslim Identity, 1935-48

A/Professor Barbara Caine	History Department
University of Sydney	1994
Can a Woman Be Free?
A/Professor Dipesh Chakrabarty	Social Theory
University of Melbourne	1994
The Problem of 'Freedom' in British India
Dr Timothy Clark	English and Linguistics
University of Durham	1994
The Literary Theory of Maurice Blanchot
Qing Dai	Nieman Foundation
Harvard University	1994
Freedom, the Persistent Search and Irrevocable Loss – Stories of the Leftist Opposition Within the CCP
Dr Suzanne Dixon	Department of Classics
University of Queensland	1994
Freedom and the Family
Dr Sabina Flanagan	History
University of Adelaide	1994
St Ursula and the 11,000 Virgins
Mr J. A. Grieve
(Sabbatical Fellowship)	Faculty of Arts
The Australian National University	1994-1995
Dr Susan James	Faculty of Philosophy
Girton College,
University of Cambridge	1994
The Passive Body and the Active Mind
Mr Peter Lamarque	Department of Philosophy
University of Stirling	1994
Aesthetics and the Literary Work
Professor Joan Landes	School of Social Science
Hampshire College	1994
Liberty's Body
A/Professor Mabel Lee	School of Asian Studies
University of Sydney	1994
The Individual and the Meaning of Personal Freedom in 20th Century China
Dr Ian Mabbett	Department of History
Monash University	1994
Buddhism in its Social and Political Setting
Professor John McLaren	Humanities Department
Victoria University of Technology	1994
Literature as Politics
Professor Michael Moses	English Department
Duke University	1994
Big Daddy
Dr Pamela Nunn
(Visiting Scholar)	School of Fine Arts
University of Canterbury,
New Zealand	1994
Armed and Dangerous
Professor Felicity Nussbaum	Department of English
Syracuse University	1994
Narratives of Maternity, Sexuality and Empire in the Enlightenment

Professor Orlando Patterson	Sociology Harvard University	1994 A Historical Sociology of Freedom
Dr Paul Patton	Department of General Philosophy University of Sydney	1994 Freedom, Power and Subjectivity
A/Professor Peggy Phelan	Department of Performance Studies Tisch School of the Arts	1994 Race, Sex and Censorship
Professor Anne Phillips	Department of Politics and Government London Guildhall University	1994 Freedom, Individuality and Difference
A/Professor Ross Poole	School of History, Philosophy & Politics Macquarie University	1994 Nationalism, Identity and Morality
Professor Dennis Porter	Department of French and Italian, University of Massachusetts	1994 Rousseau's Legacy
Professor Wilfrid Prest	Department of History University of Adelaide	1994 Albion Ascendant
Professor Stephen Prickett	Department of English University of Glasgow	1994 The Origins of Narrative
Professor James Scott	Council on Southeast Asia Studies, Yale University	1994 The State and People Who Move Around
Professor Quentin Skinner	Christ's College University of Cambridge	1994 Three Traditions of Liberty
Professor Niall Slater	Department of Classics Emory University	1994 Politics
A/Professor Peter Stupples (Visiting Scholar)	Art History/Russian and Slavonic University of Otago	1994 Abstract Art, Freedom and the Self
Professor Ken Taylor (Sabbatical Fellow)	Faculty of Environmental Design University of Canberra	1994 Cultural Landscapes
Dr Sue Thomas (Visiting Scholar)	English Department La Trobe University	1994 The Iconography of British Women's Relationship to the State
Dr Dan Urman	Department of History Ben-Gurion University of the Negev	1994 Syria-Israel Relations in Antiquity
E/Professor Paul Weaver	Classics University of Tasmania	1994 Familial Structures in Roman Imperial Society
Professor Jeffrey Weeks	Department of Economics and Social Sciences University of the West of England	1994 Sexual Values in the Age of AIDS
Professor Peter Wilson (Visiting Scholar)	Anthropology University of Otago, New Zealand	June-July 1994 Freedom, Difference and the Avoidance of Premature Extinction

Professor A.B. Woodside	History Department University of British Columbia	1994 Freedom and Despotism in Late Traditional Vietnam and China
Dr George Abungu	Coastal Archaeology National Museums of Kenya Fort Jesus	1995 The Swahili and the Overseas World
Dr Pal Ahluwalia (Visiting Scholar)	Politics University of Adelaide	September-December 1995 Into, out of or inventing Africa
Professor Bassey W Andah	Archaeology and Anthropology University of Ibadan	1995 1. African Development in Cultural Perspective; African Anthropology, Nigeria's Indigenous Technology 2. Emergence and Development of Urban Forms and Traditions of Settlement in the Forest and Savanna Zones of West Africa
A/Professor Janet Beizer	French Language & Literature University of Virginia	1995 Metamorphoses of the Vampire
Professor Bruce J. Berman	Political Studies Queen's University, Kingston	1995 The Door of Custom
Professor David Bindman	History of Art University College, London	1995 The Image of the African in Eighteenth-Century British Art
Dr Ian Britain	History University of Melbourne	1995 Australian Expatriates Since World War II and Questions of National Identity. Public School Mythology in England and Australia
Dr Peter Brown	Department of Modern European Languages The Australian National University	1995-1996 Identities and Convergences in the Pacific
Dr Joanna Casey (Visiting Scholar)	Anthropology Erindale College, University of Toronto	1995 The Use of Indigenous Wild Resources in the Agricultural Economy of Northern Ghana, West Africa
Professor Dipesh Chakrabarty	Ashworth Centre for Social Theory University of Melbourne	1995 The Problem of 'Freedom' in British India
Dr Jennifer Clark (Visiting Scholar)	History University of New England	1995 The 60s Phenomenon

Dr Julian Cobbing	History Rhodes University	1995 Epistemological Issues in Contextualising the Rise of Zulu Kingdom c. 1805-25
Professor Graham Connah	Archaeology and Palaeoanthropology University of New England	1995 Africa: Precolonial Achievement
Professor Catherine Coquery-Vidrovitch	University of Paris 7	1995 Colonization, Urbanization and Women in Sub-Saharan Africa
Dr David Dorward	History La Trobe University	1995 Out of Africa
Dr Saul Dubow	History School of African & Asian Studies, University of Sussex	1995 A History of Social Thought in Modern South Africa
Professor Norman Etherington (Visiting Scholar)	History University of Western Australia	June-July 1994 Reshaping conventional narrativity in South African Historiography
Professor Toyin Falola	Department of History University of Texas at Austin	1995 1. Religion and Violence in Contemporary Nigeria; 2. Alternative History
Professor Gareth Griffiths (Visiting Scholar)	English University of Western Australia	July-August 1995 A History of African Literatures in English (East and West)
Dr Judith Johnston (Visiting Scholar)	English University of Sydney	January-April 1995 Louisa Anne Meredith
Professor Antony Hopkins	Pembroke College, Cambridge	1995 1. Britain and the Conquest of Africa; 2. Imitators and Innovators: African Merchants in Lagos; 3. British Imperialism
Mr Nigel Lendon (Visiting Scholar)	School of Arts The Australian National University	January-December 1997 Wangarrtja
Dr John Lonsdale	Trinity College Cambridge	1995 The Door of Custom
Dr Thomas McCaskie	West African Studies University of Birmingham	1995 Landscape into History
Dr Jock McCulloch (Visiting Scholar)	Social Enquiry Deakin University	May-August 1995 Black Peril, White Virtue
Dr Kogila Moodley	Social and Education Studies University of British Columbia	1995 Federalism and Multi-culturalism as a means to nation-building in South Africa

Dr David Moore (Visiting Scholar)	Political Science Flinders University	1995 Generating Ideology
Dr Henry Wangutusi Mutoro	Department of History University of Nairobi	1995 Coast–Interior Relations
Ms Elizabeth Reid	United Nations Development Program	1995 The HIV Epidemic in Africa
Ms Alinah Kelo Segobye	History & Archaeology University of Botswana	1995 People, Landscapes and Resources in East-Central Botswana
Professor James Walvin	History Provost of Alcuin College, University of York	1995 Images of Africa
Ms Jocelyn Wogan-Browne	English University of Liverpool	1995 Authorized Virgins
Dr Simon Burrows (Sabbatical Fellow)	History Department University of Waikato	1996 The Political Culture of the Periphery
Ms Adelaide Baird (Conference Visitor)	Queensland	1996
Professor Marilyn Butler	Exeter College, Oxford	1996 1. Companion to Romanticism 2. The Xth David Nichol Smith Seminar
Dr Bronwen Douglas	History La Trobe University	1996 Linnaeus to Darwin
Mr Gavin Edwards	Department of English University of Sydney	1996 Narrative Order 1740-1830
Professor Clive Emsley (Visiting Lecturer)	Department of History The Open University	1996
Dr Patricia Fara	Darwin College Cambridge University	1996 The New Men of Natural Philosophy
Dr Martin Fitzpatrick	Department of History University of Wales	1996 Joseph Priestley and Rational Dissent
A/Professor Ann Galbally (Sabbatical Fellow)	Department of Fine Arts, Art History and Cinema Studies University of Melbourne	1996 Public Patronage of the Arts in Melbourne 1930-1956
Professor Peter Gay	Joint Department of History Colombia University	1996
Dr Nick Haslam	Department of Psychology New School for Social Research	1996 Boundaries and Essences
Dr Judith Hawley	Royal Holloway College, London	1996 The Circle of Arts and Sciences

A/Professor Marianna Jaimes-Guerrero	San Francisco State University	1996 The Indigenous Dialiectics of Science vs Culture
Professor Evelyn Fox-Keller	Massachusetts Institute of Technology	1996 Women's Studies
Dr Margot Lyon (Sabbatical Fellow)	Anthropology School of Humanities The Australian National University	1996 Emotion: Bridging Somatic and Social Works
Professor Jerome McGann	Department of English University of Virginia	1996 The Xth David Nichol Smith Seminar
Dr James Moore	History of Science and Technology Open University	1996 God, Sex and War
Dr Howard Morphy	Linacre College, Oxford	1996 The Concept of Form in the Arts and Natural Sciences
Professor David Okpako	Department of Pharmacology and Therapeutics University of Ibadan	1996 Pharmacology and the Culture of Healing in Indigenous African Medicine
Dr Mark Philp	Oriel College, Oxford	1996 Political Careers and the Pursuit of Knowledge
Dr Dorothy Porter	Birkbeck College, University of London	1996 Natural Science and Social Sciences
Professor Claude Rawson	Department of English Yale University	1996 The Xth David Nichol Smith Seminar
Dr Nicholas Reid (Sabbatical Fellow)	English Department University of Otago	1996 Twentieth Century Anglo-American Epistemologies and Theories of Mind
Dr Marie Mulvey Roberts	University of the West of England	1996 Women Versus Science
Dr Michael Rosenthal	History of Art University of Warwick	1996 Home and Away
Professor Anne Salmond	Maori Department University of Auckland	1996 Thinking From Between
Dr Simon Schaffer	History and Philosophy University of Cambridge	1996 Calculation, Field Trials and Enlightenment Values of Science
Professor Stephen Shapin	Department of Sociology University of California, San Diego	1996 The Body of Knowledge
A/Professor John Schuster (Sabbatical Fellow)	University of Wollongong	1996 Process and Continuity in the History of Science

Professor Robert Webb	Department of History University of Maryland	1996 Origins and Diffusion of the Philosophical Necessarianism of David Hartley (1705-1757)
A/Professor Laurie Whitt	Philosophy/Humanities Michigan Technological University	1996 Science, Power and Native People
Dr Sarah Williams	University of Otago	1996 Culture as Intellectual Property
Dr Jan Wilson	Department of History University of Otago	1995-1996 Colonialism and the Human Sciences in Nineteenth Century Britain and Australia
A/Professor Richard Yeo (Visiting Scholar)	Humanities Griffith University – Nathan Campus	1996 Encyclopaedias and Scientific Culture since the Seventeenth Century
A/Professor Jane Bennett	Department of Politics Goucher College	1997 Ethics, Aesthetics and Cyborg Identities
Dr Alice Bullard	School of History, Technology Georgia Institute of Technology	1997 Primitivism and Penal Colonization
Dr Margaret Burns (Visiting Scholar)	Department of Archaeology and Anthropology Faculty of Arts, The Australian National University	1997 Cultural Identity in New Caledonia
Dr Annabel Cooper (Visiting Scholar)	Womens Studies Program University of Otago	December 1996-February 1997 The changing significance of 'child sexual abuse' in New Zealand, 1950s-1980s
Mr Michael Davis		1997 European Constructions of Indigenous Authority
Professor Jane Fajans	Department of Anthropology Cornell University	1997 Autonomy and Relatedness
Dr Elaine Fantham	Department of Classics Princeton University	1997 The Roman World of Cicero's *de Oratore*
Professor Sidney Harring	School of Law City University of New York	1997 The Role of Law in Structuring Aboriginal Identity in Relation to the State
Professor Peter M. Hill (Sabbatical Fellow)	Slavonic Studies University of Hamburg	1997 The Macedonians in Australia 1987-1997

Dr Roger Hillman (Sabbatical Fellow)	Department of Modern European Languages The Australian National University	1997 Classical Music as Cultural Marker in European Cinema
Dr Duncan Ivison	Department of Politics University of York	1997 Co-convener of 'Indigenous Rights, Political Theory and the Reshaping of Australian Institutions'
Dr Derek Layder	Department of Sociology University of Leicester	1997 Social Life in Modernity
Professor Vera Mackie (Sabbatical Fellow)	History/Women's Studies University of Melbourne	1997 Citizenship and Identities in Contemporary Japan
Professor Kenneth Maddock (Visiting Scholar)	Anthropology Macquarie University	July-October 1997
Professor Vincent Megaw (Visiting Scholar)	Archaeology Flinders University of South Australia	July-September 1997
Professor Fergus Millar	Brasenose College, Oxford University	1997 The Cultural History of the Near Eastern Provinces of the Roman Empire
Dr Gino Moliterno (Sabbatical Fellow)	Department of Modern European Languages The Australian National University	1997 The Routledge Encyclopedia of Contemporary Italian Culture
Dr Radhika Mohanram (Visiting Scholar)	Women and Gender Studies University of Waikato	January-February 1997 (Antipodean) Feminist Aesthetics
Professor Garth Nettheim	Faculty of Law University of New South Wales	1997 Outstanding Issues: Law and the Resolution of Indigenous Peoples' Just Claims on Australia
Dr Michael O'Hanlon	Department of Ethnography The Museum of Mankind, London	1997 Constituting 'Melanesian Art'
Mr Aubrey Parke (Visiting Scholar)	Archaeology & Anthropology The Australian National University	January-March 1997
Dr Paul Patton	Department of General Philosophy, University of Sydney	1997 Co-convener of 'Indigenous Rights, Political Theory and the Reshaping of Australian Institutions'
Dr Roy Perrett	Philosophy Department Massey University	1997 Indigenous Rights, Political Theory and the Reshaping of Australian Institutions

A/Professor Douglas Porpora	Department of Psychology, Sociology & Anthropology Drexel University	1997 Moral Emotions
Dr Glenda Sluga (Visiting Scholar)	Department of History University of Sydney	1997 A History of Self and National Self-Determination
Professor Darko Suvin	Department of English McGill University	1997 On Creativity, Agency and Emotions in Brecht
Dr Lee Taylor (Visiting Scholar)	NSW	1997
Dr Udo Thiel	Department of Philosophy Faculty of Arts The Australian National University	1997 Self-Consciousness and Personal Identity in Eighteenth-Century Philosophy
Dr Helen Topliss (Visiting Scholar)	ACT	1997
Professor Terence Turner	Department of Anthropology University of Chicago	1997 Affect, Bodiliness and Myth Among the Kayapo of Brazil
Professor Margaret Wilson	School of Law University of Waikato	1997 The Effect of MMP on the Citizenship Rights of Maori
Dr John Wunder	Department of History University of Nebraska-Lincoln	1997 Legal History of the Chinese in the United States during the Nineteenth Century
Dr Judith Barbour	Department of English University of Sydney	1998 Alibis of Vineland
Dr Bill Bell	Department of English Literature Edinburgh University	1998 Scatterlings of Empire
Professor Bruce Bennett (Visiting Scholar)	Languages, Literature & Communication ADFA, University College of New South Wales	1998 1. Literary and Historical Study of Australian Writing Since the Eighteenth Century 2. Australian/Asian Literary Links Since 1945, with Emphasis on Romanticism
Professor Trevor Bryce (Visiting Scholar)	Christchurch, New Zealand	1998 Population Movement and Political and Cultural Interactions in the Late Bronze and Early Iron Ages
Dr Malcolm Campbell (Visiting Scholar)	Department of History University of Auckland	1998 The Irish in the United States and Australia

Professor Dipesh Chakrabarty	Ashworth Centre for Social Theory, University of Melbourne	1998 The Problem of 'Freedom' in British India
Dr Deirdre Coleman	Department of English University of Sydney	1998 Cultural History and Politics of Romanticism
Dr John Docker	Humanities Research Centre The Australian National University	1998 Sephardi and Ashkenazi Identities in Australia
Dr Paul Duro (Sabbatical Fellow)	Department of Art History and Visual Studies The Australian National University	1998-1999 The Influence of Nature and the antique on 19th Century French Painting
Professor David Fitzpatrick	Department of Modern History Trinity College, Dublin	1998 Migration and Fraternity
Dr Kate Flint	Faculty of English Oxford University	1998 America and the Victorian Cultural Imagination
Professor Peter Hansen	Department of Humanities & Arts, Worcester Polytechnic Institute	1998 British Mountaineering 1786-1953
Professor Jonathan Lamb	Department of English Princeton University	1998 The Unpreserved Self in the South Seas
Dr Andrew Moore (Visiting Scholar)	Department of Humanities Faculty of Arts & Social Sciences University of Western Sydney, Macarthur Campus	1998 Campelltown's Irish Rebels of 1798
Dr Meaghan Morris	Humanities University of Technology, Sydney	1998 Irishness and Migration in the work of Ernestine Hill
Dr David Murray (Sabbatical Fellow)	Department of Anthropology University of Adelaide	1998 Mapping Mardi Gras
Dr Iorwerth Prothero	Department of History University of Manchester	1998 Comparative Study of the French Deported to Noumea and British-Irish Convicts Transported in the 1850s
Dr Penelope Russell (Visiting Scholar)	History University of Sydney	1998
Professor James Walvin (Visiting Fellow)	Department of History University of York	1998 African Diaspora
Dr Maureen Warner-Lewis	Department of Literatures in English University of the West Indies	1998 The Monteaths of Kep
Dr Eileen Yeo (Visiting Scholar)	School of Cultural & Community Studies University of Sussex	1998 Meanings of Motherhood in Europe and America, 1750 to the Present
Dr Louise Antony	Department of Philosophy University of North Carolina at Chapel Hill	1999 Feminism as Humanism

Dr Roland Boer	Biblical Studies (Hebrew) United Theological College, Sydney	1999 Calvin Comes to Blacktown
A/Professor Stephen Bokenkamp	Department of East Asian Languages & Cultures Indiana University	1999 Archaelogical Evidence for the Spread of Lingbao Daoism
Dr Colin Campbell	Department of Sociology University of York	1999 The Easternisation of the West
Dr Annie Coombes	History of Art and Cultural Studies, Birkbeck College, University of London	1999 The Colonial Encounter in Australia, South Africa, and Canada
Dr Kenneth Dean	Department of East Asian Studies, McGill University	1999 Taoist Ritual
Professor Robert Holton	Department of Sociology Flinders University of South Australia	1999 Convenor of HRC Conference, Max Weber, Religion and Social Action
Dr Sandra Holton	History Department University of Adelaide	1999 Convenor of HRC Conference, Max Weber, Religion and Social Action
Dr Christa Knellwolf	School of English, Communications and Philosophy Cardiff University	1999-2002 Literary Engagements with Science in the Early Modern Period
Professor Sturt Manning	Department of Archaeology University of Reading	1999 Field Projects in Cyprus and the Aegean
Dr Cindy McCreery	School of History University of New South Wales	1999 Living with the Sea
Dr Philip Mead (Sabbatical Fellow)	School of English, European Languages & Literature University of Tasmania	1999 Shakespearean Institutions in Australia
Dr Jon Mee	Department of English University College, Oxford	1999 The Poetics and Politics of Enthusiasm
Dr John O'Carroll (Sabbatical Fellow)	Faculty of Social Inquiry University of Western Sydney, Hawkesbury	1999 Dismembering the Book
Dr Clare O'Farrell	School of Cultural and Policy Studies Queensland University of Technology	1999 Michel Foucault as a Cultural Icon
Professor Gianfranco Poggi	Political and Social Theory European University Institute	1999 Have the Classics Lost their Bearing?
Professor Richard M. Rorty	Department of Comparative Literature Stanford University	1999

Dr Paul A. Rule (Visiting Scholar)	Religious Studies Program La Trobe University	1999 Selective Annotated Bibliography of Writings on Chinese History, Thought and Institutions in Western Languages
Dr Margaret Steven	History RSSS, The Australian National University	1998-1999 Life and Time Study of Alexander Berry (1781 to 1873), Scottish Sargent, Merchant and Prominent New South Wales Colonist
Dr John Tasioulas	Philosophy Corpus Christi College, Oxford University	1999 Cosmopolitan Ethics
Clara Tuite	English Melbourne University	November-December 1999 The Wild Man from Borneo
Professor Barbara Andaya	Asian Studies School of Hawaiian, Asian and Pacific Studies, University of Hawaii at Manoa	2000 Law, Gender and Intertextuality in Early Modern Southeast Asia
Dr Roger Benjamin	Humanities Research Centre The Australian National University	2000 "Andalusia in the Time of the Moors"
Professor Christine Chinkin	Department of Law London School of Economics	2000 Dispute Resolution of Compliance in International Law
Professor William Connolly	Department of Political Science Johns Hopkins University	2000 Brain Waves, Cultural Practice and Legal Norms
A/Professor Jim Davidson (Visiting Lecturer)	Asian and International Studies Victoria University of Technology	2000 Burying and Memorialising the Body of Truth
Dr Kieran Dolin	Department of English University of Western Australia	2000 'The Best We Can Do'
Professor Barbara Donagan	Huntington Library	2000 Law, War and Society
Dr John Gage	Architecture and History of Art University of Cambridge	2000 Colour and Landscape in Aboriginal Australia
Dr Ann Genovese	Justice Research Centre, Sydney	2000 The Limits of Narrative?
Dr Barry Godfrey	Criminology Keele University	2000 The Prosecution of Inter-personal Violence in England and Australian Cities, 1880-1930
Professor Jean Howard (Visiting Lecturer)	Department of English & Comparative History Columbia University	2000 The Geographies of Early Modern Drama

Professor E. Ann Kaplan	Department of English and Comparative Literature State University of New York at Stony Brook	2000 Trauma, Cinema, Witnessing
Dr Christa Knellwolf	School of English, Communications and Philosophy Cardiff University	2000 Literary Engagements with Science in the Early Modern Period
Dr Rosalinde Kearsley	Ancient History Documentary Research Centre Department of Ancient History Macquarie University	2000 Law and Social Reality in the Roman Empire
Dr Kevin Knox	Division of Humanities and Social Sciences California Institute of Technology	2000 Advocates of Natural Philosophy
Professor Alison Mackinnon	History and Gender Studies Institute of Social Research University of South Australia	2000 Fracturing Modernity
Professor Brian McKnight	Department of East Asian Studies University of Arizona	2000 The Place of Law in Traditional China
Professor John McLaren	Faculty of Law University of Victoria, British Columbia	2000 Contested Understanding of the Rule of Law in British Colonies
Professor Patricia Parker (Visiting Lecturer)	English & Comparative Literature Stanford University	2000 Mulberries, Moors and More
Dr Deborah Rose	Anthropology Research School of Social Sciences Australian National University	2000 Trial by Native Title
Professor John Sutherland (Visiting Lecturer)	Modern English Literature University College, London	2000 Biography and Stephen Spender
Dr Peter Sutton		2000 Regional Variations in Australian Indigenous Land and Marine Tenure Systems
Mr Adam Tomkins	School of Law King's College London	2000 Separating Power
Dr Bryan Ward-Perkins	Trinity College, Oxford	2000 The Fall of Rome and the End of Classical Civilisation
Dr Don Watson		2000 Paul Keating and the Keating Years
Dr Leslie Witz (Visiting Lecturer)	History Department University of Western Cape, Cape Town	2000

Dr Nancy Wright	Department of English University of Newcastle	2000 Ideas of Property Law in the Legislation and Literature of Colonial New South Wales
Professor Donna Andrew	Department of History University of Guelph	2001 Gambling in Enlightenment Britain
Professor Edward Andrew	Department of Political Science University of Toronto	2001 Patrons of Enlightenment
Dr Roger Benjamin	Humanities Research Centre The Australian National University	2001-2002 1. French Art History 2. Art History and Visual Culture 3. 'La France musulmane'
Dr Hilary Carey	Department of History University of Newcastle	2001 Australian Millennium
Dr Alexandra Cook	Department of Political Philosophy Victoria University of Wellington	2001 Jean-Jacques Rousseau and Botany
Dr John Docker	Humanities Research Centre The Australian National University	2001-2004 Sheer Folly and Derangement
Dr Erika Esau (Sabbatical Fellow)	School of Humanities The Australian National University	2001 Images of the Pacific Rim
E/Professor David Fieldhouse	Imperial and Naval History Jesus College Cambridge University	2001 Iraq
Dr Martin Fitzpatrick	Department of History and Welsh History University of Wales	2001 The Enlightenment World
Dr Christopher Forth	School of Humanities The Australian National University	2001-2002 Conquering Virility
Dr John Gage	Department of Architecture and History of Art Cambridge University	2001
Dr Amareswar Galla	Executive Director, Australian Forum for Cultural Diversity University of Canberra	2001-2004 Cultural Heritage
Professor Aaron Garrett	Department of Philosophy Boston University	2001 Enlightenment Minds, Mores, and Animals
Professor John Gascoigne	Department of History University of New South Wales	2001 The Pacific and the European Mind 1763-1840
M. Pierre Georgel (Visiting Lecturer)	Musée de l'Orangerie, Paris	2001 La Collection Paul Guillaume

A/Professor Jane Goodall (Sabbatical Fellow)	College of the Arts, Education and Social Sciences University of Western Sydney; Bankstown Campus	2001 Out of Natural Order
Dr Simon Haines (Sabbatical Fellow)	School of Humanities The Australian National University	2001- 2002 1. Rousseau and Romanticism 2. Wordsworth to Wittgenstein
Dr Andrew Hassam (Visiting Lecturer)	Australian Studies University of Wales	2001 1. The Illicit Heritage of Englishness 2. British/Australian History
Professor Ihab Hassan (Visiting Lecturer)	University of Wisconsin-Milwaukee	2001 From Postmodernism to Postmodernity
Professor Ian Hunter (Visiting Lecturer)	Griffith University	2001 Claiming Enlightenment
Professor Peter Hunter (Visiting Lecturer)		2001 Transforming Public Policy after Apartheid
Ms Joanna Innes	Department of Modern History Somerville College, University of Oxford	2001 Rethinking the Age of Reform
Dr Christa Knellwolf	Humanities Research Centre The Australian National University	2001 Early Modern Science and Exploration
Dr David Lemmings	Department of History University of Newcastle	2001 From Consent to Command
Dr Alastair MacLachlan	Humanities Research Centre The Australian National University	2001- 2004 The Politics of Eighteenth Century English History
Professor Ian Maclean	Department of History All Souls College, Oxford University	2001 Explaining the Preternatural in Late Renaissance Natural Philosophy
Dr S. Timothy Maloney (Visiting Lecturer)	Music Division University of Ottawa	2001 Marshall McLuhan, Northrop Frye and Glenn Gould
Dr Carleen Mandolfo	Department of Religious Studies St Mary's College of California	2001 Psalm 88 and the Holocaust
Dr Brian Massumi	Department of Communication University of Montreal	2001 Visuality and Ways of Theorizing Vision (Philosophy)
Dr Janet McCalman (Visiting Lecturer)	University of Melbourne	2001 The Morals of Biology
Professor Randall McGowen	Department of History University of Oregon	2001 Money and the Enlightenment

Dr Jon Mee	Department of English University College, Oxford	2001 The Open Theatre of the World
Dr Nicholas Mirzoeff	Department of Art and Comparative Literature State University of New York at Stony Brook	2001 Enlightening Signs
Professor Mbulelo Mzamane (Visiting Lecturer)	Vice Chancellor University of Fort Hare, South Africa	2001 Human Righting the Legacy of Apartheid in South Africa
Professor Serge Rivière	Department of Languages and Cultural Studies University of Limerick	2001 Lasting Impact of Enlightenment Values on French Travelers to the Pacific and Australia (1800-1830)
Professor Nicholas Rogers	Department of History Centre for Twentieth Century Studies, University of York	2001 Representing the Hero in Georgian Britain
Dr Nigel Rothfels	Center for Twentieth Century Studies, University of Wisconsin–Milwaukee	2001 An Enlightened Elephant
Dr Gabriele Schwab	Department of English and Comparative Literature Critical Theory Institute University of California – Irvine	2001 Savages and Cannibals
Professor Candace Slater	Department of Spanish and Portuguese Doreen B. Townsend Center University of California, Berkeley	2001 Entangled Edens
Dr Paul Turnbull (Visiting Lecturer)	South Seas Project James Cook University	2001 Working with Historical Complexity in the Networked Environment
Dr Maiken Umbach	Department of Modern European History University of Manchester	2001 Visual Texts
Dr Kapila Vatsyayan (Visiting Lecturer)	India International Centre	2001 Folk Arts of India and Australian Aboriginal Art
Professor Andrew Vincent	Department of Political Theory University of Wales, Cardiff	2001 1. Nationalism and Contemporary Political Theory 2. Political Theory at the close of the Century
Professor Kathleen Wilson	Department of History State University of New York at Stony Brook	2001 Breasts, Sodomy and the Lash
Dr Hilda Araujo	Director of Centre of Research and Technology for Andean Countries, Peru	2002 Pictography, Art and Social Symbolism in Sarhua, Peru

Dr Glen Barclay	Humanities Research Centre The Australian National University	2002-2004 International Relations in the Middle East
Professor Bruce Bennett (Adjunct Professor)	School of Languages, Literature & Communication ADFA, University College of New South Wales	2002 Australian Literary and Cultural History
Dr David Blaazer (Sabbatical Fellow)	School of History ADFA, University College	2002 Sterling! Money, Markets and British Identities since 1797
Dr Tim Bonyhady	The Centre for Cross-Cultural Research The Australian National University	2002-2004
Professor Christine Chinkin	Department of Law London School of Economics	2002 Human Rights
Professor Humberto Dilla	Latin American Faculty of Social Studies	2002 Local Development and Participatory Democracy
Dr John Docker	Humanities Research Centre The Australian National University	2002 Sheer Folly and Derangement
Professor John Earls	Departmento de Ciencias Sociales, Universidad Catholica del Peru	2002 Waris, Wankas and Inkas
Dr Miriam Estrada	Office of the High Commissioner for Human Rights	2002 Implementation of National Human Rights Plans
E/Professor David Fieldhouse	Imperial and Naval History Jesus College Cambridge University	2002 Imperial and Naval History
Professor Stephen Frith (Sabbatical Fellow)	University of Canberra	2002 Rhetoric and Architecture
Professor Amareswar Galla	RSPAS The Australian National University	2002 Cultural Heritage
Dr Debjani Ganguly	English School of Humanities The Australian National University	2002 Caste and Dalit Cultural History
Dr Valentine Gatrell	Gonville & Caius College, Cambridge University	2002 Laughter and its Enemies
Professor Alan Gross (Sabbatical Fellow)	Department of Rhetoric University of Minnesota-Twin Cities	2002 When Nations Remember
Dr Howard Hanley	National Institute of Standards & Technology, USA	2002 de Loutherbourg, Milton, Turner

Dr Andrew Hassam	Australian Studies University of Wales	2002 1. The Illicit Heritage of Englishness 2. British/Australian History
Dr Maria Hernandez-Llosas	National Council of Scientific and Technical Research of Argentina	2002 National Identity, Multiculturalism and Heritage Management between Argentina and Australia
Dr Minoru Hokari	Keio University	2002 Historical and Contemporary relationship between Japanese and Indigenous Australians
Professor Peter Jones	Formerly University of Edinburgh, UK	2002 Enlightenment World
Dr Roseanne Kennedy (Sabbatical Fellow)	Faculty of Arts The Australian National University	2002 The Cultural Politics of Trauma and Memory
Dr Christa Knellwolf	School of English, Communications and Philosophy, Cardiff University	2002 Literary Engagements with Science in the Early Modern Period
Dr Alastair MacLachlan	Humanities Research Centre The Australian National University	2002 The Politics of Eighteenth Century English History
Dr Isabelle Merle	Centre de Recherche et de Documentation sur l'Océanie Université de Provence	2002 The First Fleet
A/Professor Donna Merwick	The Australian National University	2002 Seventeenth Century New York and American History
Dr Marsha Meskimmon	School of Art and Design Loughborough University	2002 Memory, History and Corporeal Aesthetics in the Work of Doris Salcedo, Amalia Mesa-Bains and Cecilia Vicuna
Ms Margo Neale (Sabbatical Fellow)	Program Director, Gallery of First Australians National Museum of Australia	2002 Indigenous Studies
Dr Brigida Pastor	Department of Hispanic Studies University of Glasgow	2002 The Evolving and Representation of Male and Female Roles in Cuba and Spanish Cinema
Dr David Pear	Humanities Research Centre The Australian National University	2002-2004 Percy Grainger
Professor Claude Rawson (Visiting Lecturer)	Department of English Yale University	2002

Professor Kathryn Robinson	Head Division of Anthropology Research School of Pacific and Asian Studies, The Australian National University	2002 Indonesian Women
Dr Ruben Stehberg	Archaeology Museo Nacional de Historia Natural, Santiago	2002 The Conservation and Re-Value of Archaeological Sites in Chile
Dr Anthony Street	School of Divinity Cambridge University	2002 Avicenna and the Sirazi Questions
Mr Jaime Tamayo	Prado de las Azucenas Guadalajara Jalisco, Mexico	2002 Revolution and Nationalism in Jalisco, Mexico. The left in the West of Mexico
Professor Helen Tiffin	School of English University of Queensland	2002 Writing the Garden in the Caribbean
Dr Marcus Wood	Department of English & American Studies Sussex University	2002 Slavery and the English Imagination
Dr Angela Woollacott	History Department Case Western Reserve University	2002 Gender and the Politics of Empire
Professor Jack Barbalet	Department of Sociology University of Leicester	2003 Weber's Protestant Ethic and the Spirit of Capitalism
Dr Glen Barclay	Humanities Research Centre The Australian National University	2003 International Relations in the Middle East
Professor Tim Bonyhady	The Centre for Cross-Cultural Research, The Australian National University	2003
Dr Melinda Cooper	Department of Sociology Macquarie University	2003 Policing Life
Professor David de Laura (Visiting Lecturer)	University of Pennsylvania	2003 Arnoldism in the Antipodes
Dr John Docker	Humanities Research Centre The Australian National University	2003 Sheer Folly and Derangement
E/Professor David Fieldhouse (Sabbatical Fellow)	Imperial and Naval History Jesus College Cambridge University	2003 Iraq as a British Dependency 1918-1932
Professor Norbert Finzsch	Department for Anglo- American History University of Cologne	2003 English Biological Warfare during French and Indian War, Pontiac's Rebellion and the Colonialization of Australia
Dr John Gage	Architecture and History of Art University of Cambridge	2003 Colour in Art

Professor Amareswar Galla	RSPAS The Australian National University	2003 Cultural Heritage
Professor Katherine Gibson (Sabbatical Fellow)	RSPAS The Australian National University	2003 Cooperativism and Communal Subjects – enterprise culture, economic landscapes and human rights for the 21st century
A/Professor Jane Goodall	College of the Arts, Education and Social Sciences University of Western Sydney; Bankstown Campus	2003 Presumption and the Vital Spark
Professor Julie Graham	Department of Geosciences University of Massachusetts	2003 Cooperativism and Communal Subjects – enterprise culture, economic landscapes and human rights for the 21st century
Dr Howard Hanley	National Institute of Standards & Technology, USA	2003 de Loutherbourg, Milton, Turner
Dr Andrew Hassam	Australian Studies University of Wales	2003 1. The Illicit Heritage of Englishness 2. British/Australian History
Professor Ihab Hassan	English and Comparative Literature, University of Wisconsin-Milwaukee	2003 Antipodean Encounters
Dr Minoru Hokari	Keio University	2003 Historical and Contemporary relationship between Japanese and Indigenous Australians
Professor John Keane	Centre for the Study of Democracy University of Westminster	2003 Global Civil Society
Dr Michael Kindler (Sabbatical Fellow)	Tomakomai Komazawa University	2003 Australian Literature and the Rights of Indigenous People
Professor Lily Kong	Department of Geography National University of Singapore	2003 Geographies of the Sacred
Professor Jonathan Lamb	Department of English Princeton University	2003 The Things Things Say
Dr Alastair MacLachlan	Humanities Research Centre The Australian National University	2003 The Politics of Eighteenth Century English History
Dr Brian Massumi	Department of Communication University of Montreal	2003 Visuality and Ways of Theorizing Vision (Philosophy)

Dr Charles Merewether	Getty Research Institute	2003 The Specter of Being Human
A/Professor Donna Merwick	The Australian National University	2003 Seventeenth Century New York and American History
Dr Mbulelo Mzamane	South Africa	2003 Human Righting the Legacy of Apartheid in South Africa
Dr John O'Leary (Sabbatical Fellow)	Victoria University of Wellington	2003 Native Rites and Native Rights
Dr David Pear	Humanities Research Centre The Australian National University	2003 Percy Grainger
Professor Peter Putnis (Sabbatical Fellow)	Communication & Education University of Canberra	2003 Against the Enlightenment: the Localization of Progress
Dr Catherine Rigby (Sabbatical Fellow)	School of Literary, Visual and Performance Studies Monash University	2003 Recasting the Limestone Plains
Professor Kathryn Robinson	Head Division of Anthropology Research School of Pacific and Asian Studies, The Australian National University	2003 Indonesian Women
Professor Kay Schaffer	Department of Social Inquiry Adelaide University	2003 Life Narratives and Human Rights within a Global Context
Professor Sidonie Smith	Women's Studies Program University of Michigan, Ann Arbor	2003 Life Narratives and Human Rights within a Global Context
Dr Nigel Spivey	Emmanuel College University of Cambridge	2003 Art Deep Time. Hand-prints from Arnhem Land
Professor Barbara Stafford	Department of Art History and the College University of Chicago	2003 Neoronal Aesthetics
Dr Anthony Street	School of Divinity Cambridge University	2003 Avicenna and the Sirazi Questions
Ms Catherine Summerhayes (Sabbatical Fellow)	School of Humanities The Australian National University	2003 Preparation of Monographs
Professor Ken Taylor (Sabbatical Fellow)	Division of Science and Design University of Canberra	2003-2004 John Sulman, Town Planner
Dr Petra Ten-Doesschate Chu	Department of Art and Music Seton Hall University	2003 Landscape Paintings of French painter Gustave Courbet (1819-1877)

Dr Jonathan White	Department of Literature University of Essex	2003 Lineages of Italian Culture
Dr Glen Barclay	Humanities Research Centre The Australian National University	2004 International Relations in the Middle East
Professor Tim Bonyhady	The Centre for Cross-Cultural Research The Australian National University	2004
Dr Michael Carter (Sabbatical Fellow)	Department of Art History and Theory University of Sydney	2004 Naked Humans?
Dr Stephen Chan	Department of Cultural Studies Lingnan University	2004 Mapping the Global Popular
A/Professor Barbara Creed	School of Fine Arts, Classical Studies and Archaeology University of Melbourne	2004 The Darwinian Screen
Dr Tony Day	Carolina Asia Center University of North Carolina, Chapel Hill	2004 Literature, identity, and freedom in postcolonial Indonesia
Dr John Docker	Humanities Research Centre The Australian National University	2004 Sheer Folly and Derangement
Professor Clive Emsley	Department of History The Open University	2004 Crime, control and the European nation state c.1750-1950
Professor Amareswar Galla	RSPAS The Australian National University	2004 Cultural Heritage
Professor Bill Gammage	Humanities Research Centre The Australian National University	2004 Australian History, Specifically Aboriginal Land Management; the History of New Guinea
Dr Leela Gandhi	School of English La Trobe University	2004 Affective Communities
Dr Jeanette Hoorn	School of Fine Arts, Classical Studies and Archaeology University of Melbourne	2004 The Darwinian Screen
Dr Caroline Hughes (Sabbatical Fellow)	School of Politics University of Nottingham	2004 The Politics of Community in Post-Intervention Societies
Dr Po-Keung Hui	Cultural Studies Lingnan University	2004 The Making of a Communal Economic Subject – A Comparative Study on the Community Currency Projects in Hong Kong and Australia

Dr Koichi Iwabuchi	International Studies Division International Christian University	2004 Reimagining the "national" through intersections between the "transnational" and the "multicultural" in Japan
Professor Neville Kirk	Department of History and Economic History Manchester Metropolitan University	2004 Nation, Empire, Class and Race in the History of Relations between Britain and Australia, 1901 to the present
Mr Kiyoshi Kojima (Sabbatical Fellow)	Iwanami Shoten Publishers	2004 Formation of knowledge of Asia in Japan after World War II
Professor Lily Kong	Department of Geography National University of Singapore	2004 Geographies of the Sacred
Professor Marilyn Lake	History Program La Trobe University	2004 On Being a White Man, Australia, c.1900
Professor Vera Mackie	Centre for Research and Graduate Studies, Humanities Division Curtin University of Technology	2004 Globalisation and the Body
Dr Alastair MacLachlan	Humanities Research Centre The Australian National University	2004 The Politics of Eighteenth Century English History
A/Professor Donna Merwick	The Australian National University	2004 Seventeenth Century New York and American History
Ms Marian Pastor Roces	TAO Management Inc. The Philippines	2004 Contemporary Art Museums and the Ambitions of Cities in the Asia Pacific
Dr David Pear	Humanities Research Centre The Australian National University	2004 Percy Grainger
Professor Kathryn Robinson	Head Division of Anthropology Research School of Pacific and Asian Studies, The Australian National University	2004 Indonesian Women
Professor Anjali Roy	Department of Humanities and Social Sciences Indian Institute of Technology	2004 Globalizing Post-Colonialism
Professor David Saunders	Faculty of Arts Griffith University	2004 Historicising Juridification
Professor Jon Sigurdson	European Institute of Japanese Studies Stockholm School of Economics	2004 Culture and Technological Change in China's Political Posters

Dr Judith Snodgrass	Centre for Cultural Research, Asian History and Cultural Studies University of Western Sydney	2004 Buddhism in Australia
Dr Anthony Street	School of Divinity Cambridge University	2004 Avicenna and the Sirazi Questions
Professor Ken Taylor (Sabbatical Fellow)	Division of Science and Design University of Canberra	2004 John Sulman, Town Planner
Professor Helen Tiffin	Post-Colonial Studies Queen's University	2004 The Wild Man from Borneo
Dr Danielle Tranquille	Department of French University of Mauritius	2004 Representation of the Indian Ocean in travelogues. A Reading of 18th and 19th Century Travelogues
Professor Pnina Werbner	School of Social Relations Keele University	2004 A comparison of Contemporary Sufi Cults in South Asia and Indonesia
Professor David Worrall	Department of English Literature St. Mary's College	2004 William Thomas Moncrieff and Post-Colonial Drama, 1816-32
Professor Shunya Yoshimi	Institute of Socio-Information and Communication Studies University of Tokyo	2004 "Americanization" and the Politics of Cultural Studies in the Asia-Pacific Region

Conference Visitors 1991–2004

Name	Institution	Dates & Conference Attended
Professor Shao Dazhen	Art History Central Academy of Fine Arts, Beijing	March 1991 Modernism and Post-Modernism in Asian Art
Professor Femme Gaastra	Rijksuniversiteit Te Leiden The Netherlands	June 1991 Materials to Representation
Dr Gillian Beer	Girton College Cambridge	July 1991 Heritage and Memory (Sydney)
Professor David Lowenthal	University College, London	July 1991 Heritage and Memory (Sydney)
Professor Roy Mottahedeh	Islamic History Harvard University	July 1991 Heritage and Memory (Sydney)
Professor Peter Novick	History University of Chicago	July 1991 Heritage and Memory (Sydney)
Professor Gauri Viswanathan	English and Comparative Literature, Columbia University	July 1991 Heritage and Memory (Sydney)
Professor Marshall Sahlins	University of Chicago	October 1991 Histories in Cultural Systems (Melbourne)
Mr David Bomford	National Gallery London	May 1992 The Articulate Surface:
Professor Jean Barrea	Social Sciences Collège Jacques, Belgium	June 1992 The European Moment?
Professor Martyn P. Thompson	Political Sciences Tulane University, USA	June 1992 The European Moment?
Professor Anna Rutherford	English University of Aarhus, Denmark	July 1992 Europe: Representations of Change
Dr Sidra Stich	Berkeley, USA	March 1993 Lips of Coral
Professor Jane Gallop	Modern Studies Program University of Wisconsin, Milwaukee	June 1993 Jane Gallop: Named Seminar
Professor Thomas W Laqueur	History University of California, Berkeley	July 1993 Regimes of Sexuality
Ms Pat Brassington	Artist Tasmanian Art School	July 1993 Breath of Balsam
Dr Barbara Creed	Cinema Studies La Trobe University	July 1993 Breath of Balsam

Professor Trinh T. Minh-Ha	Women's Studies University of California, Berkeley	August 1993 Forces of Desire
Dr Maurice Marks Goldsmith	Philosophy Victoria University of Wellington	June 1994 Ideas of Liberty
Dr Thanet Aphornsuvan	History Thannasat University	July 1994 Asian Paths to the Idea of Freedom
Em/Professor Josef Silverstein	Political Sciences The State University of New Jersey	July 1994 Asian Paths to the Idea of Freedom
Dr Jean Andréa	France	August 1994 Roman Family III
Dr Jane Gardener	Classics University of Reading	August 1994 Roman Family III
Dr Elizabeth Baigent	New Dictionary of National Biography, Oxford University Press	February 1995 National Biographies and National Identity
Professor Colin Matthew	Editor, New Dictionary of National Biography	February 1995 National Biographies and National Identity
Professor George Brooks	History Indiana University	June 1995 Africa: Precolonial Achievement
Dr David Collett	Project Manager Tasmanian Aboriginal Land Council	June 1995 Africa: Precolonial Achievement
Dr Kevin MacDonald	Institute of Archaeology University College, London	June 1995 Africa: Precolonial Achievement
Professor Martin Chanock	Legal Studies La Trobe University	July 1995 Out of Africa: Texts for Understanding the African Past
Professor Heribert Adam	Sociology and Anthropology Simon Fraser University	September 1995 What is Happening in Africa Today?
A/Professor Peter Alexander	English University of NSW	September 1995 What is Happening in Africa Today?
Mr John Omer-Cooper	History University of Otago	February 1995 What is Happening in Africa Today?
Dr Christopher Saunders	History University of Cape Town	February 1995 What is Happening in Africa Today?
Ms Felicity Baker	London	July 1996 The Xth David Nichol Smith Seminar

Professor Robert Markley	English West Virginia University	July 1996 The Xth David Nichol Smith Seminar
Professor Deirdre McCloskey	Economics Erasmus University of Rotterdam/University of Iowa	July 1996 The Xth David Nichol Smith Seminar
Dr Bridget Orr	English Princeton University	July 1996 The Xth David Nichol Smith Seminar
Professor Marcia Pointon	History of Art University of Manchester	July 1996 The Xth David Nichol Smith Seminar
Professor Brean S. Hammond	English University of Wales	July 1996 The Xth David Nichol Smith Seminar
Dr Fiona Robertson	Department of English Studies University of Durham	July 1996 The Xth David Nichol Smith Seminar
Dr Alan Saunders	Science Unit ABC	July 1996 The Xth David Nichol Smith Seminar
Dr Jocelyn Hackforth-Jones	Art History Richmond College	August 1996 Re-imagining the Pacific
Professor Joan Kerr	University of NSW	August 1996 Re-imagining the Pacific
Dr Sylvia Kleinert	Archaeology and Anthropology The Australian National University	August 1996 Re-imagining the Pacific
Professor Jonathan Lamb	Princeton University	August 1996 Re-imagining the Pacific
Dr Diane Losche	College of Fine Arts University of NSW	August 1996 Re-imagining the Pacific
Professor Fred Myers	New York University	August 1996 Re-imagining the Pacific
Ms Margo Neale	Queensland Art Gallery	August 1996 Re-imagining the Pacific
Mr John Pule	Artist, New Zealand	August 1996 Re-imagining the Pacific
Em/Professor Bernard Smith	University of Melbourne	August 1996 Re-imagining the Pacific
Professor Terry Smith	University of Sydney	August 1996 Re-imagining the Pacific
Ms Judy Watson	Artist	August 1996 Re-imagining the Pacific
Dr Ragbir Bhathal	University of Western Sydney	August 1996 Science and Other Knowledge Traditions

Dr Michael Bravo	History & Philosophy University of Cambridge	August 1996 Science and Other Knowledge Traditions
Dr Michael Davis	Heritage & Culture ATSIC	August 1996 Science and Other Knowledge Traditions
Mr Michael Dodson	ATSIC Justice Commissioner	August 1996 Science and Other Knowledge Traditions
Professor Roy MacLeod	History University of Sydney	August 1996 Science and Other Knowledge Traditions
Ms Anita Herle	Archaeology and Anthropology Cambridge University Museum	August 1996 Science and Other Knowledge Traditions
Dr Thomas Heyd	Philosophy University of Victoria	August 1996 Science and Other Knowledge Traditions
Dr Jeanette Hope	NSW	August 1996 Science and Other Knowledge Traditions
Dr Sylvia Kleinert	Archaeology and Anthropology The Australian National University	August 1996 Science and Other Knowledge Traditions
Dr Maureen Perkins	History University of Western Australia	August 1996 Science and Other Knowledge Traditions
Mr Stephen Schneirer	Gunjii Jindibah Centre Southern Cross University	August 1996 Science and Other Knowledge Traditions
Mr Tracker Tilmouth	Director Central Land Council, Alice Spring	August 1996 Science and Other Knowledge Traditions
Dr Peter Lineham	Massey University	September 1996 Enlightenment, Religion and Science in the Long Eighteenth Century
Professor Knud Haakonssen	Boston University	September 1996 Enlightenment, Religion and Science in the Long Eighteenth Century
Dr Elisabeth Haakonssen	Boston University	September 1996 Enlightenment, Religion and Science in the Long Eighteenth Century
Dr Joanna Bourke	History Birkbeck College, University of London	September 1996 The Natural Sciences and the Social Sciences
Professor Evelleen Richards	Faculty of Arts University of Wollongong	September 1996 The Natural Sciences and the Social Sciences

Professor Sandra Herbert	History University of Maryland	September 1996 The Natural Sciences and the Social Sciences
Dr Jan Wilson	History University of Otago	September 1996 The Natural Sciences and the Social Sciences
Professor Bryan Turner	Faculty of Arts Deakin University	September 1996 The Natural Sciences and the Social Sciences
Dr Iwan Morus	Social Anthropology Queen's University	September 1996 The Natural Sciences and the Social Sciences
A/Professor John Schuster	Science and Technology Studies University of Wollongong	September 1996 The Natural Sciences and the Social Sciences
Professor Hamilton Cravens	Historical Studies Iowa State University	September 1996 The Natural Sciences and the Social Sciences
Dr Irmline Veit-Brause	Social Inquiry Deakin University	September 1996 The Natural Sciences and the Social Sciences
Professor Randall Collins	Sociology University of California, Riverside	July 1997 Emotion in Social Life and Social Theory
Professor Joseph H De Rivera	Psychology Clark University	July 1997 Emotion in Social Life and Social Theory
Professor Paul Ekman	Psychiatry University of California, San Francisco	July 1997 Emotion in Social Life and Social Theory
A/Professor Lee Harrington	Sociology and Anthropology Miami University	July 1997 Emotion in Social Life and Social Theory
Professor Theodore D. Kemper	Sociology St John's University	July 1997 Emotion in Social Life and Social Theory
Professor Jerome Neu	USA	July 1997 Emotion in Social Life and Social Theory
Professor Robert C Solomon	Philosophy University of Texas	July 1997 Emotion in Social Life and Social Theory
Dr Casper Wouters	Amsterdam The Netherlands	July 1997 Emotion in Social Life and Social Theory
A/Professor Jeremy Webber	Graduate Studies Program in Law, McGill University	August 1997 Indigenous Rights, Political Theory and the Reshaping of Institutions

A/Professor Laurie Whitt	Philosophy Michigan Technology University	August 1997 Indigenous Rights, Political Theory and the Reshaping of Institutions
Professor Iris Young	Graduate School of University of Pittsburgh Public Affairs	August 1997 Indigenous Rights, Political Theory and the Reshaping of Institutions
Dr Saul Dubow	School of African and Asian Studies University of Sussex	April 1998 Sir Keith Hancock Symposium
Professor Shula Marks	School of Oriental and African Studies, University of London	April 1998 Sir Keith Hancock Symposium
Dr David Richardson	Economics and Social History University of Hull	April 1998 Black Diasporas in the Western Hemisphere
Professor Edward Alpers	USA	April 1998 Black Diasporas in the Western Hemisphere
Dr Brian Moore	History University of West Indies	April 1998 Black Diasporas in the Western Hemisphere
Professor James Chandler	University of Chicago	April 1998 Re-Orienting Romanticism
A/Professor Gauri Viswanathan	English and Comparative Literature, Columbia University	April 1998 Re-Orienting Romanticism
Dr Joanna De Groot	History University of York	April 1998 Re-Orienting Romanticism
Professor Mary Jacobs	English, Cornell University	April 1998 Re-Orienting Romanticism
Professor Allan Pasco	French and Italian University of Kansas	April 1998 Re-Orienting Romanticism
Dr Chloe Chard	Independent Scholar, London	April 1998 Re-Orienting Romanticism
Mr Paul Arthur	English University of Western Australia	April 1998 Re-Orienting Romanticism
Professor Paul Lützeler	Humanities Washington University	August 1998 Adventures of Identity
Dr Alistair Thomson	Centre for Continuing Education, University of Sussex	September 1998 Scatterlings of Empire (Adelaide)
Dr Bill Jones	History and Archaeology University of Wales	September 1998 Scatterlings of Empire (Adelaide)
Dr Philip Payton	UK	September 1998 Scatterlings of Empire (Adelaide)
Dr Graham Huggan	English and American Literature and Language Harvard University	September 1998 Scatterlings of Empire (Adelaide)

Professor Robin Cohen	Sociology University of Warwick	September 1998 Scatterlings of Empire (Adelaide)
Professor Thomas Bartlett	Modern Irish History University College, Dublin	October 1998 Tenth Irish-Australian Conference (Melbourne)
Mr Luke Gibbons	School of Communication Dublin City University	October 1998 Tenth Irish-Australian Conference (Melbourne)
Professor John Deigh	Philosophy Northwestern University, USA	June 1999 Martha Nussbaum
Professor Martha Nussbaum	The Law School University of Chicago	June 1999 Martha Nussbaum
Professor Ronald De Sousa	Canada	June 1999 Martha Nussbaum
Professor Richard Freadman	English La Trobe University	June 1999 Martha Nussbaum
Dr Christopher Cordner	Philosophy University of Melbourne	June 1999 Martha Nussbaum
Dr Huw Price	Traditional & Modern Philosophy, University of Sydney	July 1999 Richard Rorty
Professor Jenny Lloyd	Philosophy University of NSW	July 1999 Richard Rorty
Dr Peter Nickerson	Religion Duke University	August 1999 The History of Daoism
Dr Gregory Bailey	Languages, Linguistics & Cultures, La Trobe University	September 1999 Max Weber, Religion and Social Action
Dr Ian Mabbett	History Monash University	September 1999 Max Weber, Religion and Social Action
Professor Bryan Turner	Faculty of Arts Deakin University	September 1999 Max Weber, Religion and Social Action
Professor James Walvin	History University of York	September 1999 Max Weber, Religion and Social Action
Professor Christiane Bender	Sociology University of Heidelberg	September 1999 Max Weber, Religion and Social Action
Professor Margaret Ferguson	English University of California, Davis	June 2000 Women and Property in Early Modern England
Professor Wilfrid Prest	History University of Adelaide	July 2000 Those Lasting Alliances of Habits
Professor Philip Girard	Dalhousie Law School Canada	July 2000 Those Lasting Alliances of Habits

Mr Alex Castles	South Australia	July 2000 Those Lasting Alliances of Habits
Mr Ruan O'Donnell	University of Limerick, Dublin	July 2000 Those Lasting Alliances of Habits
Professor Hilary Charlesworth	Centre for International and Public Law, The Australian National University	July 2000 Feminist Explorations of International Law Workshop (London School of Economics)
Ms Robin Banks	Coogee	December 2000 Constructing Law and Disability
Professor Terry Carney	Faculty of Law University of Sydney	December 2000 Constructing Law and Disability
Dr Jane Clapton	Human Services Griffith University	December 2000 Constructing Law and Disability
Ms Maurice Corcoran	DDA Standards Project	December 2000 Constructing Law and Disability
Dr Marian Corker	King's College London	December 2000 Constructing Law and Disability
The Honorable Elizabeth Evatt	NSW	December 2000 Constructing Law and Disability
Mr Phillip French	People with Disability NSW	December 2000 Constructing Law and Disability
A/Professor David Green	Social Work La Trobe University	December 2000 Constructing Law and Disability
Mr Graeme Innes	Human Rights and Equal Opportunity Commission	December 2000 Constructing Law and Disability
Ms Kelley Johnson	La Trobe University	December 2000 Constructing Law and Disability
Dr Melinda Jones	Law University of NSW	December 2000 Constructing Law and Disability
Dr Rosemary Kayess	Social Policy University of NSW	December 2000 Constructing Law and Disability
Mr Bruce Maguire	Brailleways	December 2000 Constructing Law and Disability
Ms Lee Ann Marks	Law and Legal Studies La Trobe University	December 2000 Constructing Law and Disability

Dr Christiana Newell	School of Medicine University of Tasmania	December 2000 Constructing Law and Disability
Dr Marcia Rioux	Robert Centre York University, Canada	December 2000 Constructing Law and Disability
Ms Sue Tait	Intellectual Disability Review Panel, DHS, Melbourne	December 2000 Constructing Law and Disability
Professor Peter Hulme	Literature University of Essex	February 2001 4th Biennial Conference of the Australian Association for Caribbean Studies
Mr Alexander Cook	History Cambridge University	March 2001 The XIth David Nichol Smith Conference
Dr Joanna De Groot	History University of York	March 2001 The XIth David Nichol Smith Conference
Dr John Greene	French University of Louisville	March 2001 The XIth David Nichol Smith Conference
Dr Harriet Guest	Centre for Eighteenth Century Studies, University of York	March 2001 The XIth David Nichol Smith Conference
Dr Susannah Helman	History University of Melbourne	March 2001 The XIth David Nichol Smith Conference
Dr Shino Amanda Konishi	History University of Sydney	March 2001 The XIth David Nichol Smith Conference
Professor Jonathan Lamb	English Princeton University	March 2001 The XIth David Nichol Smith Conference
Professor Robert Maccubbin	English College of William and Mary	March 2001 The XIth David Nichol Smith Conference
Professor Robert Markley	English West Virginia University	March 2001 The XIth David Nichol Smith Conference
Dr Bridget Orr	English Fordham University	March 2001 The XIth David Nichol Smith Conference
Dr Ali Peker	Architecture Middle East Technical University	March 2001 The XIth David Nichol Smith Conference
Professor Marta Petrusewicz	History City University of New York	March 2001 The XIth David Nichol Smith Conference
Dr Glynis Ridley	English Queen's University of Belfast	March 2001 The XIth David Nichol Smith Conference

Mr Paul Tankard	English Monash University	March 2001 The XIth David Nichol Smith Conference
Ms Philippa Tucker	History Victoria University of Wellington	March 2001 The XIth David Nichol Smith Conference
Dr Tamara Wagner	English Cambridge University	March 2001 The XIth David Nichol Smith Conference
Professor Katerina Clark	Comparative Literature Yale University	June 2001 Adventures of Dialogue
Dr Rajeev Patke	English Language and Literature, National University of Singapore	June 2001 Adventures of Dialogue
Professor Meaghan Morris	Cultural Studies Lingnan University	June 2001 Adventures of Dialogue
Professor Christine Chinkin	Law London School of Economics	July 2001 Art and Human Rights Workshop
Mr Dadang Christanto	Artist University of the Northern Territory	July 2001 Art and Human Rights Workshop
Professor Peter Bondanella	West European Studies Indiana University	September 2001 The Importance of Italy
Dr Christa Knellwolf	HRC The Australian National University	September 2001 The Libertine Enlightenment (University of Queensland)
Dr Jon Mee	University College Oxford University	September 2001 The Libertine Enlightenment (University of Queensland)
Professor Kathleen Wilson	History State University of New York	September 2001 The Libertine Enlightenment (University of Queensland)
Dr C.W. Brooks	History University of Durham	September 2001 Law and the Enlightenment
Professor Douglas Hay	History University of York	September 2001 Law and the Enlightenment
Ms Joanna Innes	Modern History Somerville College	September 2001 Law and the Enlightenment
Professor David Thomas Konig	History Washington University	September 2001 Law and the Enlightenment
Dr Michael Lobban	Law Queen Mary and Westfield College	September 2001 Law and the Enlightenment
Professor Randall McGowen	History University of Oregon	September 2001 Law and the Enlightenment
Professor John Barrell	English & Related Literature University of York	November 2001 Spies and Surveillance in the 18th Century

Dr Geoffrey Cubitt	History University of York	November 2001 Spies and Surveillance in the 18th Century
Professor Michael Durey	Social Inquiry Murdoch University	November 2001 Spies and Surveillance in the 18th Century
Dr Joanna De Groot	History University of York	November 2001 Spies and Surveillance in the 18th Century, and March 2001 The XIth David Nichol Smith Conference
Professor James A. Epstein	History Vanderbilt University	November 2001 Spies and Surveillance in the 18th Century
Dr Harriet Guest	Centre for Eighteenth Century Studies University of York	November 2001 Spies and Surveillance in the 18th Century
Dr Jane Rendall	Centre for Eighteenth Century Studies University of York	November 2001 Spies and Surveillance in the 18th Century
Dr Sanjay Seth	La Trobe University	November 2001 Postcolonialism and Beyond
Professor David Garrioch	Historical Studies Monash University	March 2002 The Enlightenment World Workshop
Professor Ian Hunter	Humanities Griffith University	March 2002 The Enlightenment World Workshop
Dr Peter McNeil	Art History and Theory University of NSW	March 2002 The Enlightenment World Workshop
Dr Ian Percival	NSW	March 2002 The Enlightenment World Workshop
Dr Richard Yeo	Humanities Griffith University	March 2002 The Enlightenment World Workshop
Mr Reginald Clifford	TV Azteca	March 2002 Telenovelas and Soap Opera
Mr Peter Dodds	Actor Neighbours	March 2002 Telenovelas and Soap Opera
Dr Trisha Dunleavy	Victoria University of Wellington	March 2002 Telenovelas and Soap Opera
Dr Jorge Gonzalez	La Universidad Ibero Americana	March 2002 Telenovelas and Soap Opera
Dr Daniel Mato	Universidad Central de Venezuela	March 2002 Telenovelas and Soap Opera
Mr Ricardo Cojuc	ITESM, Cuernavaca Mexico	March 2002 Telenovelas and Soap Opera

Dr John Sinclair	Communication, Language and Cultural Studies, Victoria University of Technology	March 2002 Telenovelas and Soap Opera
Professor Graeme Turner	Critical and Cultural Studies University of Queensland	March 2002 Telenovelas and Soap Opera
Ms Gillian Arnold	McElroy Television	March 2002 Telenovelas and Soap Opera
Mr Cuauhtémoc Blanco	Screen Writer, Televisia	March 2002 Telenovelas and Soap Opera
Dr Rosalind Pearson	ITSEM Cuernavaca, Mexico	March 2002 Telenovelas and Soap Opera
Ms Angélica Arágon	ITESM, Cuernavaca, Mexico	March 2002 Telenovelas and Soap Opera
Mr Miguel Najera	ITESM, Cuernavaca, Mexico	March 2002 Telenovelas and Soap Opera
Ms Antoinette Collazo	ITESM, Cuernavaca, Mexico	March 2002 Telenovelas and Soap Opera
Dr Rodolfo Raffino	Museo de La Plata	April 2002 Landscape and the Symbol in the Inka State
Dr Maria Constanza Ceruti	Universidad Catholica de Salta	April 2002 Landscape and the Symbol in the Inka State
Ms Sonia Guillen	Centro Mallqui, Peru,	April 2002 Landscape and the Symbol in the Inka State
Dr Julinho Zapata	Universidad Nacional de San Abad	April 2002 Landscape and the Symbol in the Inka State
Professor Mariusz Ziolkowski	Andrean Archaeological Mission Warsaw University	April 2002 Landscape and the Symbol in the Inka State
Dr Llilian Llanes	Havana Biennial Director	September 2002 Art and Human Rights in Latin America
Mr Euridice Charon	University of Newcastle	September 2002 Diaspora of the Latin America Imagination
Dr Alejandro Alvarez	University of Havana	September 2002 Diaspora of the Latin America Imagination
Dr Ralph Newmark	Latin American Studies La Trobe University	September 2002 Diaspora of the Latin America Imagination
Dr Brian Burdekin	United Nations	September 2002 Diaspora of the Latin America Imagination
Mr David Bradbury	Independent Film Maker	September 2002 Diaspora of the Latin America Imagination

Mr Lorenzo Meyer	Mexico	September 2002 National Narratives and Identities in a Global World (La Trobe University, Melbourne)
Dr Jaime Tamayo	Mexico	September 2002 National Narratives and Identities in a Global World (La Trobe University, Melbourne)
Ms Ann Thomas	NSW	October 2002 Locations of Spirituality
Dr Roland Boer	Monash University	October 2002 Locations of Spirituality
Mr Andrew Jones	Media and Cultural Studies Southern Cross University	October 2002 Locations of Spirituality
Dr Lyn McCredden	Literary and Communication Studies, Deakin University	October 2002 Locations of Spirituality
Ms Jinki Trevillian	QLD	October 2002 Locations of Spirituality
Dr V Bharathi	India	January 2003 Books and Empire (Sydney)
Professor James West	USA	January 2003 Books and Empire (Sydney)
Dr Trevor Howard Hill	English University of South Carolina	January 2003 Books and Empire (Sydney)
Dr Mary Jane Edwards	English Carleton University	January 2003 Books and Empire (Sydney)
Professor Peter Shillingsburgh	English University of North Texas	January 2003 Books and Empire (Sydney)
Dr Leonard R. Koos	French and Film Studies Mary Washington College	January 2003 Books and Empire (Sydney)
Dr Valerie Letcher	Education University of Natal, South Africa	January 2003 Books and Empire (Sydney)
Dr Louise Poland	Victoria	January 2003 Books and Empire (Sydney)
Dr Lydia Wevers	Stout Research Centre for New Zealand Studies Victoria University of Wellington	January 2003 Books and Empire (Sydney)
Dr Bill Bell	English Literature Edinburgh University	January 2003 Books and Empire (Sydney)
Ms Christine Riding	Tate Gallery, London	March 2003 The Edwardians
Professor Robert Markley	English West Virginia University	April 2003 Frankenstein's Science
Dr Anita Guerrini	History University of California, Santa Barbara	April 2003 Frankenstein's Science

Professor Paul Turnbull	History James Cook University	April 2003 Frankenstein's Science
Dr Mark Levene (Freilich Foundation sponsored Conference Visitor)	University of Southampton	July 2003 Genocide and Colonialism (Sydney)
Dr Wendy Lower (Freilich Foundation sponsored Conference Visitor)	United States Holocaust Memorial Museum Washington, DC	July 2003 Genocide and Colonialism (Sydney)
Dr Jurgen Zimmerer (Freilich Foundation sponsored Conference Visitor)	University of Coimbra, Portugal	July 2003 Genocide and Colonialism (Sydney)
Professor Ben Kiernan	History Yale University	July 2003 Genocide and Colonialism (Sydney)
Professor Norbert Finzsch	University of Cologne	July 2003 Genocide and Colonialism (Sydney)
Dr Isabelle Stengers	Philosophy Free University of Brussels	August 2003 Towards an Ecology of Practices (Sydney)
Dr Maria Fernandez	History of Art Cornell University	August 2003 Towards an Ecology of Practices
Dr Simon Penny	Electrical and Computer Engineering, University of California, Irvine	August 2003 Towards an Ecology of Practices
Mr Stephen Zagala	Centre for Cross-Cultural Research, The Australian National University	August 2003 Towards an Ecology of Practices
Dr Paul Bains	Philosophy Murdoch University	August 2003 Towards an Ecology of Practices
Professor Brian Massumi	Communication University of Montreal	August 2003 Towards an Ecology of Practices
Professor Sandra Buckley	West Asian Studies McGill University	August 2003 Towards an Ecology of Practices
Dr Pia Ednie-Brown	Architecture & Spatial Information Architecture Laboratory RMIT University	August 2003 Towards an Ecology of Practices
Mr Stelarc	Artist Ohio State University	August 2003 Towards an Ecology of Practices
Dr Stephen Muecke	Humanities University of Technology, Sydney	August 2003 Towards an Ecology of Practices
Dr Andrew Murphie	Media and Communications University of NSW	August 2003 Towards an Ecology of Practices

Mr Michael Goddard	University of Sydney	August 2003 Towards an Ecology of Practices
Professor Christine Chinkin	Law & Politics London School of Economics	August 2003 Art and Human Rights
Dr Miriam Estrada	Chief Prosecutor United Nations, East Timor	August 2003 Art and Human Rights
A/Professor Pat Hoffie	Queensland College of the Arts Griffith University	August 2003 Art and Human Rights
Professor Mbulelo Mzamane	Poet and Activist South Africa	August 2003 Art and Human Rights
Mr Dadang Christanto	Artist Indonesia	August 2003 Art and Human Rights
Professor Rangachari Narayanan	India	August 2003 Art and Human Rights
Mr Michel Tuffery	Artist New Zealand	August 2003 Art and Human Rights
Mr Jon Cattapan	Victorian College of the Arts	August 2003 Art and Human Rights
Dr Christiana Slade	Humanities Macquarie University	August 2003 Art and Human Rights
Dr Charles Green	Art History University of Melbourne	August 2003 Art and Human Rights
Dr Jonathon Mane-Wheoki	New Zealand	August 2003 Art and Human Rights
Ms Fiona Foley	Artist Australia	August 2003 Art and Human Rights
Dr Michael Mel	Artist Papua New Guinea	August 2003 Art and Human Rights
Ms Mella Jaarsma	Artist, Indonesia Canberra Contemporary Art Space	August 2003 Art and Human Rights
Mr Nindityo Adipurnomo	Artist, Indonesia Canberra Contemporary Art Space	August 2003 Art and Human Rights
Ms Nomsa Kupi-Manaka	Performing Artist South Africa	November 2003 South Africa Focus
Mr John Mateer	Writer Melbourne	November 2003 South Africa Focus
Professor Xiejun Chen	Director Shanghai Museum	February 2004 Transformations
Professor Corazon Alvina	Director National Museum of the Philippines	February 2004 Transformations
Professor Jyotindra Jain	Dean – School of Arts and Aesthetics Jawaharlal Nehru University, New Delhi	February 2004 Transformations

Ms Alison Carroll	Director Visual Arts Program Asialink	February 2004 Transformations
Dr Melani Budianta	Humanities University of Indonesia	April 2004 Cultures, Nations, Identities, and Migrations
Professor Kirin Narayan	Anthropology College of Letters and Science	April 2004 Cultures, Nations, Identities, and Migrations
Mr Dadang Christanto	Artist	April 2004 Cultures, Nations, Identities, and Migrations
Professor Richard Werbner	African Anthropology Manchester University	April 2004 Cultures, Nations, Identities, and Migrations
Professor Kenneth M George	Anthropology University of Wisconsin–Madison	April 2004 Cultures, Nations, Identities, and Migrations
Dr Koichi Iwabuchi	International Studies Division International Christian University	October 2004 Knowledge, Culture, Power
Mr Kiyoshi Kojima	Iwanami Shoten Publishers	October 2004 Knowledge, Culture, Power
Professor Shunya Yoshimi	Communication Studies University of Tokyo	October 2004 Knowledge, Culture, Power

Freilich Foundation Lecturers 1997–2003

1997	Phillip Adams	'Bigotry and the Bunyip'.
1998	Fr Frank Brennan	'The Wik Debate – A Legitimate Quest for Workability and Certainty or Just Downright Intolerance?'
1999	David Marr	'Bigotry in Australia Today: The Role of the Churches'.
2000	Les Murray	'Countermeasures'.
2001	Dr Evelyn Scott	'On the Evil of Tolerance and the Virtue of Intolerance'.
2002	Archbishop Peter Carnley	'Beyond Mere Tolerance: The Vocation of the Three Abrahamic Faiths in Creating the Conditions for World Peace'.
2003	Professor Ben Kiernan	'Genocide and Resistance in Cambodia and East Timor'.
1999	Professor Henry Reynolds	'Sovereignty, Indigenous Australia and Human Rights'.
2001	Professor John C. Turner	'Rethinking the Nature of Prejudice: From Psychological Distortion to Socially Structured Meaning'.
2003	Professor Donald Harman Akenson	'Intolerance: the E.Coli of the Human Mind'.
2000	Professor Marilyn Lake	'No Distinction of Any Kind: Modern Definitions of Human Rights,' in association with the 'Human Rights, Human Wrongs' conference.
2001	Sir Tipene O'Regan	'The Evolution of The Tribe: The Challenge for an Old Culture in a New Century,' in association with the Consortium of Humanities Centres and Institutes of Australia meeting.
2002	Dr Paul Connolly	'Growing Up in Bigotry: Northern Ireland,'
2002	Professor Mapule Ramashala	'Growing Up in Bigotry – South Africa', in association with the 'International Perspectives on Reconciliation' conference.

Appendix C

Humanities Research Centre Conferences

Humanities Research Centre

Title and Convener	Location and Date (Location is HRC unless otherwise noted)
The Impact of 17th and 18th Century Philosophy on Modern Thought; Professor Peter Herbst	August 1974
Seminar on Australian Biography	30 October 1974
Australia in the 1890s, Professor Manning Clark, Dr Geoffrey Serle and Professor Ian Donaldson	18-21 August 1975
Old Norse Workshop; Professor Hans Kuhn	10-13 May 1976
Shakespearean Comedy; Professor Ian Donaldson	14-16 May 1976
Phenomenology (in conjunction with the Philosophy Department, SGS, ANU); Dr Maurita Harney	12-14 June 1976
Parody; Professor Ian Donaldson and Dr Margaret Rose	2-4 July 1976

David Nichol Smith Memorial Seminar IV; (in conjunction with the National Library of Australia, the Australian Academy of the Humanities and the Australasian and Pacific Society for Eighteenth Century Studies); Dr Robert Brissenden	24-31 August 1976
Literary Translation; Professor J.D. Frodsham	9-15 May 1977
Mannerism and Manneristic Configurations; Professor Andrew McCredie	10-13 June 1977
Translation Seminar; Professor J.D. Frodsham	22-24 July 1977 2-4 September 1977
The Early Middle Ages; Mr L.J. Downer	22-25 April 1978
Byzantine Studies; Mrs Elizabeth Jeffreys and Dr M.A. Moffatt	17-19 May 1978
Medieval Music; Dr G.A. Anderson	9-12 June 1978
Old Norse Workshop; Professor Hans Kuhn	23-25 June 1978
The Waning of the Middle Ages (in conjunction with the Australian and New Zealand Association for Medieval and Renaissance Studies); Dr G.C. Kratzmann and Dr W.S. Ramson	7-11 August 1978
Tragedy; Dr Colin Mayrhofer	22-23 February 1979
Shakespeare and Jonson; Professor Ian Donaldson	14-18 May 1979
Modern European Drama; Professor Ian Donaldson	6-9 July 1979
Recent Australian Drama; Dr Marlis Thiersch and Dr Margaret Williams	27-28 August 1979
New Drama in English; Mr Roger Pulvers	29-31 August 1979
Romantic Nationalism in Western Europe; Professor Peter Herbst	11-15 May 1980
Myths and Heroes; Professor Hans Kuhn	13-16 June 1980
The Awakening of Eastern Europe; Professor Hans Kuhn and Dr A. Moffatt	7-11 July 1980
The Vth David Nichol Smith Memorial Seminar in Eighteenth Century Studies (in conjunction with the National Library of Australia); Professor J. Hardy	August 1980
Nationalism and Culture in Ireland; Professor O. Macdonagh and Mr W. F. Mandle, assisted by Mr P. Travers	4-7 November 1980
Christopher Hill Workshop; Professor Margaret Williams	13-16 February 1981
Australia and the European Imagination; Professor Ian Donaldson and Dr Alan Frost	5-10 May 1981
Workshop on Post-Graduate Research in the Humanities; Dr J.C. Eade	18-22 May 1981
The Family in the Ancient Roman World; Dr Beryl Rawson	4-6 July 1981
Speculative Fiction: The Australian Context; Mr C.R. Steele	18-19 July 1981
Transmission in Oral and Written Traditions; Mrs Elizabeth Jeffreys and Professor L. Treitler	24-28 August 1981

Understanding Texts; Text for what?; Dr L.A.C. Dobrez and Professor K. Ruthven	13-16 May 1982
Interpreting and Understanding; Professor Peter Herbst	5-8 July 1982
Creativity and the Idea of a Culture; Professor Peter Herbst	16-19 August 1982
Patronage, Art and Society in the Renaissance; Ms Pat Simons	The University of Melbourne; 16-19 May 1983
South Wind: Interactions in the Arts in Renaissance Europe; Dr Sasha Grishin and Dr W.S. Ramson	14-17 July 1983
Renaissance Celebrations and Performances; Mr W.G. Craven	24-27 August 1983
Editing Texts; Dr J.C. Eade	11-13 May 1984
Bernard Bailyn Seminar; Professor Paul Bourke	4-5 July 1984
Landscape and the Arts in Europe: 1700-1900; Ms Helen Topliss	12-15 July 1984
Australia and the New World 1800-1984; Ms Helen Topliss	27-30 August 1984
Byzantium and Hellenism; Mrs Elizabeth Jeffreys and Dr Ann Moffatt	10-13 May 1985
Hellenism in Europe since the Renaissance; Professor Graeme Clarke	7-10 June 1985
Ancient Hellenism: Greek Colonists and Native Populations; (in conjunction with the Frederick May Foundation for Italian Studies); Dr Jean-Paul Descoeudres and Associate Professor J.R. Green	The University of Sydney; 9-15 July 1985
Hellenism and Neohellenism: Problems of Identity; Mr J.B. Burke and Dr E. Gauntlett	The University of Melbourne; 25-30 August 1985
Feminist Criticism and Cultural Production; Dr Susan Sheridan	12-15 May 1986
Northrop Frye Conference	27-29 June 1986
Feminism and the Humanities: Enrichment, Expansion or Challenge?; Dr Susan Sheridan	10-13 July 1986
Feminist Enquiry as a Transdisciplinary Enterprise; (in conjunction with the Research Centre for Women's Studies) Dr Susan Magery	The University of Adelaide; 21-24 August 1986
The History of Books (in conjunction with the Centre for Bibliographical and Textual Studies, Monash University)	Monash University; 6-8 September 1986
Literary Journals; Dr David Carter	8-11 May 1987
Europe and the Exotic; Dr C.A. Gerstle and Dr A.C. Milner	9-12 July 1987
The Occident and the Orient; Dr C.A. Gerstle and Dr A.C. Milner	24-27 August 1987
Edmund Morgan Seminar; Professor Paul Bourke	28-29 October 1987
Timothy Barnes Seminar Roman History: Use of the Past; Professor Graeme Clarke	20-22 May 1988
Roman Family II: Marriage and Children; Professor Beryl Rawson	15-17 July 1988

Frank Kermode Seminar: History and Value; Professor K.K. Ruthven and Ms Marion Campbell	2-4 November 1988
Quentin Skinner Seminar: Political Discourse in Early Modern Europe; Professor Conal Condren	14-16 April 1989
Documentary Film Festival (in conjunction with the National Library of Australia); Professor Bill Nichols and Professor Julianne Burton	30 June-3 July 1989
Coming to terms with the Photographic Image; Dr Leslie Devereaux and Dr Roger Hillman	4-6 July 1989
Film and Representations of Culture (in conjunction with the National Library of Australia and the Goethe-Institut); Dr Leslie Devereaux and Dr Roger Hillman	25-28 September 1989
Civilisation Symposium (in conjunction with the National Gallery of Australia); Professor Graeme Clarke and Dr Sue-Anne Wallace	24-25 March 1990
Working outside the Academy: The Practicalities of Independent Scholarship; Sylvia Lawson	21 April 1990
Shaping Lives; Dr Peter Read	2-5 July 1990
Self and Text; Professor Ian Donaldson, Professor James Walter	28 September-1 October 1990
Modernism and Post-Modernism in Asian Art; (in conjunction with the Art History Department, ANU); Dr John Clark	22-25 March 1991
Peter Brown Seminar; Professor Graeme Clarke	5-7 April 1991
From Materials to Representations; Dr Campbell MacKnight	8-10 June 1991
Heritage and Memory; Professor Ann Curthoys	8-11 July 1991 (Sydney)
Histories in Cultural Systems; Professor Greg Dening	30 September-3 October 1991 (Melbourne)
The Articulate Surface: Dialogues on Paintings between Conservators, Curators and Art Historians (in conjunction with the National Gallery of Australia); Dr Jacqueline Macnaughtan and Dr Sue-Anne Wallace	1-3 May 1992
The European Moment? From Enlightenment to Romanticism; Dr Knud Haakonssen	6-7 June 1992
Europe: Representations of Change; Dr Margaret Stoljar	6-10 July 1992
The Changing Idea of an Australian University; (in conjunction with the Research School of Social Sciences, ANU, and Macquarie University; Professor Geoffrey Brennan and Professor Deryck Schreuder	16 September 1992
Intellectuals in Europe Today (in conjunction with the Centre for European Studies, Monash City Centre); Professor Brian Nelson	30 September-2 October 1992
The Idea of a Republic (one-day symposium, in conjunction with the Centre for Australian Studies, Australian Defence Force Academy); Dr David Headon and Dr James Warden	October 1992

Colonialism and Postcolonialism, The Humanities in a post-imperial world; Dr Nicholas Thomas and Dr Dipesh Chakrabarty	8-19 February 1993
Lips of Coral – Sex, Violence and Surrealism (in conjunction with the National Gallery of Australia); Dr Ted Gott and Dr Ken Wach	The National Gallery of Australia; 13-14 March 1993
The Dawn of History; Professor Stuart Macintyre and Dr Julian Thomas	17-18 April 1993
Jane Gallop Seminar; Dr Jill Matthews	11-13 June 1993
Regimes of Sexuality; Dr John Ballard	5-8 July 1993
Breath of Balsam: Reorienting Surrealism (in conjunction with the Museum of Contemporary Art, Sydney); Dr Sue-Anne Wallace	31 July-1 August 1993
Forces of Desire; Dr Jill Matthews	13-15 August 1993
Music and Musicians in Australian Culture 1930-1960; Dr Peter Read	25-29 September 1993
The 4Rs: wRiting, Repairing, Re-presenting, Re-creating the Text (in conjunction with the Australian Scholarly Editions Centre, Australian Defence Force Academy); Associate Professor Paul Eggert	8-10 April 1994
The Rhetoric of the Frame: Towards a Critical Theory of the Frame in Art; Dr Paul Duro	4 June 1994
Ideas of Liberty; Professor Barry Hindess	15-17 June 1994
Asian Paths to the Idea of Freedom; Professor A.J.S. Reid	4-6 July 1994
The Republican Conception of Freedom; Professor Conal Condren	5-6 August 1994
Roman Family III (in conjunction with the Classics Department, ANU); Professor Beryl Rawson and Professor Paul Weaver	12-14 August 1994
Commitments to Representation and Freedom (in conjunction with the National Gallery of Australia and the Museum of Contemporary Art, Sydney); Dr Sue-Anne Wallace	The Museum of Contemporary Art, Sydney; 16-17 September 1994
National Biographies and National Identity (in conjunction with the National Library of Australia and the Australian Dictionary of Biography, ANU); Professor John Ritchie and Mr Ian Templeman	1-3 February 1995
New Approaches to Film (in conjunction with the Department of Philosophy and the Film Studies Group, ANU; Dr Paul Thom	7-9 April 1995
Africa: Precolonial Achievement; Professor Graham Connah	10-12 June 1995
Out of Africa: Texts for Understanding the African Past; Dr David Dorward	3-6 July 1995
Programme Development through Research Workshop; (in conjunction with UNDP, HIV & Development Programme); Dr Elizabeth Reid	17-25 August 1995

New Directions in British History (in conjunction with the History Program, Research School of Social Sciences, ANU); Professor Paul Bourke and Professor Iain McCalman	16 September 1995
What is Happening in Africa Today? (in conjunction with the African Studies Association of Australasia and the Pacific); Professor Peter Alexander and Professor Deryck Schreuder	28-30 September 1995
The Making of a Public Intellectual: John Mulvaney, The Humanities and Public Policy (in conjunction with the Research School of Social Sciences, ANU, and the Sir Robert Menzies Centre for Australian Studies); Dr Tim Bonyhady and Dr Tom Griffiths	24-25 November 1995
Transcultural Exchanges: The Asia-Australia Art Connection; Professor Iain McCalman and Professor Anthony Milner	28 April 1996
Mad Cows and Modernity: The Crisis of Creutzfeldt-Jakob Disease; Professor Iain McCalman and Robin Wallace-Crabbe	25 May 1996
The Xth David Nichol Smith Seminar: Margins and Metropolis: Literature, Culture and Science, 1660-1830; Dr Ian Higgins and Dr Gillian Russell	2-5 July 1996
Re-imagining the Pacific: A Conference on Art History and Anthropology in honour of Bernard Smith (in conjunction with the National Library of Australia); Dr Diane Losche and Dr Nicholas Thomas	1-4 August 1996
Science and Other Knowledge Traditions (in conjunction with the Centre for Science in Society and James Cook University); Henrietta Fourmile, Dr David Turnbull and Dr Paul Turnbull	23-27 August 1996 (Cairns)
Enlightenment, Religion and Science in the Long Eighteenth Century (in conjunction with the Research School of Social Sciences, ANU); Professor Knud Haakonssen and Professor Iain McCalman	4-6 September 1996
The Natural Sciences and the Social Sciences; Professor Iain McCalman and Dr Dorothy Porter	6-9 September 1996
Questions of Time and History; Professor Dipesh Chakrabarty and Dr Benjamin Penny	16 October 1996
The Discovery of European Resources in Australian Libraries; (in conjunction with the Australian National University Library and the Gladys Krieble Foundation); Dr Colin Steele	15-17 November 1996
'Is "Racism" un-Australian?' The Revitalisation of Australian Discourses of Race and Pain (in conjunction with the Australian Institute of Aboriginal and Torres Strait Islander Studies)	21-22 February 1997
Emotion in Social Life and Social Theory; Dr Jack Barbalet and Dr Margo Lyon	9-11 July 1997
Indigenous Rights, Political Theory and the Reshaping of Institutions; Dr Duncan Ivison, Dr Paul Patton and Dr Will Sanders	8-10 August 1997
New Australian Images Through British Eyes; Dr Sasha Grishin	Drill Hall Gallery, ANU; 4 September 1997– 5 October 1997

The New Australian Racism? (in conjunction with the Research Centre in Intercommunal Studies, University of Western Sydney); Professor Dipesh Chakrabarty	13 October 1997
Fergus Millar Seminar: Identities in the Eastern Mediterranean in Antiquity; Professor Graeme Clarke	10-12 November 1997
Electronic Identities in East Asia: Media, Culture and Diasporas; Dr Morris Low, Professor Tessa Morris-Suzuki and Dr Benjamin Penny	21-22 February 1998
Sir Keith Hancock Symposium (in conjunction with the Research School of Social Sciences, ANU, and the Australian Academy of the Humanities); Professor Anthony Low	University House, ANU; 1-3 April 1998
Black Diasporas in the Western Hemisphere; Dr Barry Higman and Dr James Walvin	7-9 April 1998
Re-Orienting Romanticism; Dr Deirdre Coleman, Dr Peter Otto and Dr Clara Tuite	15-17 April 1998
Adventures of Identity: Constructing the Multicultural Subject; (in conjunction with the Goethe-Institut, Sydney, and the German Research Council); Dr John Docker and Dr Gerhard Fischer	The Goethe-Institut, Sydney; 30 July – 2 August 1998
Scatterlings of Empire: Anglo-celtic Migrations and Exchanges; (in conjunction with the University of Adelaide); Professor Wilfrid Prest and Graham Tulloch	Art Gallery of South Australia; 24-26 September 1998
Tenth Irish-Australian Conference: Ireland and Australia; (in conjunction with La Trobe University); Dr Philip Bull	La Trobe University; 28 September – 2 October 1998
Public Good: A conference for Patrick Troy; Dr Tim Bonyhady and Dr Mark Peel	11-12 December 1998
Martha Nussbaum: Named Seminar; Professor Robert Goodin and Dr David Parker	12-14 June 1999
The Humanities, Arts and Public Culture in Two Hemispheres: Annual Conference of the Consortium of Humanities Centres and Institutes; Professor John Frow and Professor Iain McCalman	Queensland Art Gallery; 5-7 July 1999
Richard Rorty: Named Seminar; Professor Graeme Clark	9-11 July 1999
The History of Daoism: in honour of Liu Ts'un-yan; Dr Benjamin Penny	6-8 August 1999
Max Weber, Religion and Social Action; Professor Robert Holton and Dr Sandra Holton	27-29 September 1999
Who's Centric Now? The Present State of Post-Colonial Englishes; (in conjunction with the Australian National Dictionary Centre, ANU, and Oxford University Press)	27-29 October 1999
Belonging; Dr Peter Read, Professor Henry Reynolds and Dr Deborah Rose	12-14 November 1999
Romancing the Tomes: Feminism, Law and Popular Culture; Professor Margaret Thornton	27-29 April 2000
Chinese Art: The Future (in conjunction with the National Gallery of Australia); Dr Caroline Turner	University House, ANU; 5 June 2000

Women and Property in Early Modern England: An Interdisciplinary Colloquium; Professor Margaret Ferguson and Dr Nancy Wright	30 June-1 July 2000
'Those Lasting Alliances of Habits' – Law, History and the Humanities in the Imperial World (in conjunction with the Faculty of Law, ANU); Dr Ian Holloway and Professor John McLaren	6-8 July 2000
Natural Law & Sovereignty in Early Modern Europe; (in conjunction with the Centre for Advanced Study in the Humanities, Griffith University); Professor Ian Hunter	Queensland Art Gallery; 7-9 July 2000
Feminist Explorations of International Law Workshop; (in conjunction with the London School of Economics); Professor Hilary Charlesworth and Professor Christine Chinkin	The London School of Economics; 28 July 2000
Lost in the Whitewash: Aboriginal-Chinese Encounters from Federation to Reconciliation; Dr Penny Edwards and Dr Shen Yuan-fang	1 December 2000
Constructing Law and Disability (in conjunction with the School of Law and Legal Studies, La Trobe University, and the Faculty of Law, University of New South Wales); Ms Melinda Jones and Ms Lee Ann Marks	4-5 December 2000
Landprints over Boundaries: Celebrating the Work of George Seddon; Professor Peter Beilharz and Dr Trevor Hogan	Sails Restaurant, Fremantle; 7-9 December 2000
Law in Chinese Culture; Professor Bill Jenner and Dr Benjamin Penny	9-10 December 2000
4th Biennial Conference of the Australian Association for Caribbean Studies; Dr Barry Higman, Dr Jacqueline Lo and Dr Marivic Wyndham	8-10 February 2001
The XIth David Nichol Smith Conference: The Exotic During the Long Eighteenth Century (1660-1830) (in conjunction with the National Library of Australia); Professor Iain McCalman and Dr Christa Knellwolf	The National Library of Australia; 26-28 March 2001
Indonesian Art; Dr Caroline Turner	4 April 2001
Adventures of Dialogue: Bakhtin and Benjamin; Dr John Docker and Dr Subhash Jaireth	21-22 June 2001
Art and Human Rights Workshop; Dr Caroline Turner and Ms Christine Clark	22-24 July 2001
The Libertine Enlightenment (in conjunction with the Faculty of Arts, University of Queensland); Professor Peter Cryle and Dr Lisa O'Connell	The University of Queensland; 21-22 September 2001
The Importance of Italy; Dr Gino Moliterno and Professor David Moss	21-22 September 2001
Law and the Enlightenment: The British Imperial State at Law, 1689-1832; Dr David Lemmings	26-28 September 2001
Foreign Bodies: Oceania and Racial Science 1750-1940; (in conjunction with the Research School of Pacific and Asian Studies, ANU); Dr Chris Ballard and Dr Bronwen Douglas	18-19 October 2001
Postcolonialism and Beyond; Professor Dipesh Chakrabarty and Dr Caroline Turner	15 November 2001

Spies and Surveillance in the 18th Century; Professor John Barrell and Professor Iain McCalman	28-29 November 2001
The Enlightenment World Workshop; Dr Christa Knellwolf and Professor Iain McCalman	1-2 March 2002
Telenovelas and Soap Opera: Negotiating Reality; Dr Christiana Slade	21-24 March 2002
Landscape and Symbol in the Inka State; Mr Ian Farrington	11-14 April 2002
The Dialectic Interpretation of Religious Phenomena; Professor Hans Mol	15-16 July 2002
New Feminist Histories of Gender and Colonialism; Dr Fiona Paisley and Professor Angela Woollacott	9 August 2002
Art and Human Rights in Latin America (Workshop); Dr Caroline Turner and Ms Christine Clark	2 September 2002
Diaspora of the Latin America Imagination; Dr Peter Read and Dr Marivic Wyndham	3-6 September 2002
National Narratives and Identities in a Global World: The Latin American Case (in conjunction with the Institute of Latin American Studies, La Trobe University); Dr Barry Carr and Dr Stephen Niblo	La Trobe University; 27-28 September 2002
New World, First Nations: Native Peoples of Mesoamerica and the Andes under Colonial Rule (in conjunction with the University of New South Wales); Dr David Cahill	The University of New South Wales; 2-4 October 2002
Locations of Spirituality: 'Experiences' and 'Writings' of the Sacred; Dr Minoru Hokari	26-27 October 2002
The Theory and Practice of Early Modern Autobiography; Dr Philippa Kelly	6-8 December 2002
23 Degrees South: The Archaeology and Environmental History of Southern Deserts (in conjunction with the National Museum of Australia); Dr Mike Smith	The National Museum of Australia; 15-18 January 2003
Books and Empire: Textual Production, Distribution and Consumption in Colonial and Post-Colonial Countries; Professor Paul Eggert and Professor Elizabeth Webby	The University of Sydney; 30 January–1 February 2003
Art Museums: Sites of Communication; Ms Susan Herbert and Ms Pamela McClelland Gray	14-15 March 2003
Frankenstein's Science: Theories of Human Nature from 1700 to 1839; Dr Jane Goodall and Dr Christa Knellwolf	22-24 April 2003
History Television Workshop: Professor Ian McCalman	11-12 May 2003
Forest, Desert and Sea (in conjunction with the School of Humanities and Indigenous Australian Studies, James Cook University); Professor Paul Turnbull	Townsville; 5-7 June 2003
Genocide and Colonialism (in conjunction with the Freilich Foundation); Dr Dirk Moses	Women's College, University of Sydney; 18-20 July 2003
Envisaging the Future: Digital Research and Scholarship in the Humanities; Dr Paul Turnbull	22-23 July 2003
Towards an Ecology of Practices; Dr Sandra Buckley, Dr Brian Massumi and Mr Stephen Zagala	2-3 August 2003

Art and Human Rights (in conjunction with the National Institute of the Arts, the National Institute of the Humanities, the Drill Hall Gallery and School of Art Gallery, ANU, and the National Gallery, National Museum and the Canberra Contemporary Art Space); Dr Caroline Turner, Professor Christine Chinkin, Ms Margo Neale and Ms Christine Clark	7-10 August 2003
State of Arts, Culture and Society in a Transforming South Africa; Professor Mbulelo Mzamane and Ms Christine Clark	24 November 2003
The Art of the Documentary (in conjunction with the National Institute of the Humanities); Dr Catherine Summerhayes	National Museum of Australia and Center Cinema, Canberra; 26-30 November 2000
Transformations: Asia-Pacific Museums in the Twenty-First Century (in conjunction with the National Museum of Australia and the Graduate Studies Program in Sustainable Heritage Development, Research School of Pacific and Asian Studies, ANU); Dr Amareswar Galla, Ms Margo Neale and Dr Caroline Turner	5-6 February 2004
Australian Art, Craft and New Media Now: Aesthetics, National and Politics (in conjunction with the National Gallery of Victoria and the Australian Centre for the Moving Image); Dr Charles Green	Melbourne; 25 February 2004
The Edwardians (in conjunction with the National Gallery of Australia); Dr Anna Gray and Ms Susan Herbert	The National Gallery of Australia; 12-13 March 2004
Cultures, Nations, Identities and Migrations; Dr Kathryn Robinson	15-16 April 2004
Urban Imaginaries (in conjunction with Lingnan University); Professor Meaghan Morris	Lingnan University, Hong Kong; 21-25 May 2004
David Nichol Smith Memorial conference *New Voyagings on Old Seas: Performances in Honour of Professor Greg Dening*; (in conjunction with the National Library of Australia and the Centre for Cross-Cultural Research); Professor Paul Turnbull and Associate Professor Paul Pickering	The National Library of Australia; 19-22 July 2004
Gandhi, Non-violence and Modernity; Dr John Docker and Dr Debjani Ganguly	2-3 September 2004
Lies, Conspiracy and Propaganda: A Europe-Asia Comparison; Dr Robert Cribb	26-27 September 2004
Trans-National History Conference; Professor Ann Curthoys and Professor Marilyn Lake	9-10 October 2004
Knowledge, Culture, Power: The Politics of Cultural Studies in the Asia-Pacific Region; Professor Tessa Morris Suzuki	23-24 October 2004

Freilich Foundation

Diasporic and Multicultural Approaches to South Asian Studies; Professor Dipesh Chakrabarty and Dr Kalpana Ram	7-8 August 1995
What Causes Bigotry?; Dr Benjamin Penny	12 May 2000
Cyberhate: Bigotry and Prejudice on the Internet (in conjunction with the Australia/Israel and Jewish Affairs Council); Mr Jeremy Jones and Dr Benjamin Penny	Australian Museum, Sydney; 5-6 November 2000
Human Rights, Human Wrongs: Government, Bigotry and Social Change in Australia, 1949-2000; Dr Benjamin Penny	10-12 November 2000
Bigotry and Religion in Australia, 1865-1950; Dr Benjamin Penny	7-9 December 2001
Flows of People – Waves of Bigotry (in conjunction with the Australian Centre for the Study of Jewish Civilisation); Professor Andrew Markus and Dr Benjamin Penny	Monash University, Melbourne, July 14 and National Maritime Museum, Sydney; 20 July 2002
International Perspectives on Reconciliation (in conjunction with Reconciliation Australia and the National Library of Australia); Dr Benjamin Penny	National Library of Australia; 21 September 2002
Our Fear of Strangers: Wogs, Refos and Illegals in the Public Imagination (in conjunction with the Hawke Research Institute, University of South Australia); Professor Alison Mackinnon and Dr Benjamin Penny	Art Gallery of South Australia; 6-7 December 2002
Genocide and Colonialism (in conjunction with the HRC); Dr Dirk Moses	Women's College, University of Sydney; July 2003

Appendix D
Humanities Research Centre Governance

Advisory Committee

Anderson, Professor G.A., 1978–1980

Borrie, Professor W.D., 1972–1974

Bourke, Professor P.F. (Director, RSSS), 1985–1995

Bryan, Mr Harrison, 1980–1983

Burke, Professor J.T. (President, Australian Academy of the Humanities), 1972–1975

Chandler, Dr G. (Director-General, National Library of Australia), 1975–1978

Clark, Professor Charles Manning Hope, 1972–1977

Clarke, Professor Graeme, 1980 (Director, 1990–1995)

Comin, Professor G.A.A., 1975

Connolly, Mr R., 1986

Covell, Professor R.D., 1981–1995

Crawford, Emeritus Professor R.M., 1972–1975

Culican, Mr W., 1975

Cushing, Dr R.G., 1987–1995

Daws, Professor G.A., 1978–1982

Devereaux, Dr L., 1987–1995

Dobrez, Dr L.A.C., 1982

Donaldson, Professor Ian, (Director, HRC), 1972–1990

Dr J.D. Ritchie, 1986

Eade, Dr J.C., 1982–1989

Elliott, Professor Ralph, 1972–1987 (Chairman, 1979–1987)

Field, Professor A., 1978–1979

Ford, Ms J., 1988–1995

Forge, Professor J.A.W., 1978–1985

Frodsham, Professor J.D., 1975–1977

Fry, Dr E.C., (Dean of the Faculty of Arts), 1972–1975

Grieve, Mr J.A., 1978

Herbst, Professor P., 1972–

Hillman, Dr R., 1986–1995

Horan, Mr R.J.C., 1973–1978

Horton, Mr W.M., 1987–1995

Johnson, Professor R. St. C. (Chairman, 1972–1978)

Jones, Dr R.M., 1986–1995

Kuhn, Professor H., 1972–1977

Lloyd, Dr G.M., 1985–1986

MacDonagh, Professor O., 1975–1984

McCaughey, Professor A.P., 1975–1979

McCredie, Dr, 1976–1977

McPhee, Mr J., 1986–1995

Molony, Professor John, 1978–1981

Passmore, Professor J.A., 1972–1977

Ramson, Dr W. (Dean of the Faculty of Arts), 1975–1981; (Chairman 1987)

Rawson, Professor Beryl, 1979–1985

Reid, Dr A.J.S., 1983–1985

Sawer, Professor G., 1973

Scales, Professor D.P., 1978–1980

Smith, Professor Bernard, 1972–1980

Spate, Professor O.H.K., 1972–1975

Thomas, Mr D., 1983–1985

Tucker, Professor G.S.L. Tucker, 1972–1974

Wang, Professor Gungwu, 1972–1982

Whitcombe, Dr Elizabeth, 1974–1975

Wilkes, Professor G.A., 1983–1985

Wurm, Professor S., 1989–1995

Youngson, Professor A.J., 1974–1979

Steering Committee

Adams, Dr David (Nominee of the Dean, Faculty of Arts), 1997

Ballard, Dr John, 1991–1994

Bonyhady, Dr Tim (Nominee of the Director of the Research School of Social Sciences), 1999

Bourke, Professor P.F. (Director, RSSS), 1989–1991

Brennan, Professor H.G. (Director, RSSS), 1991–1998

Campbell, Dr. R., (Dean of the Faculty of Arts), 1989–1994

Casey, Ms Dawn (Director, National Museum of Australia), 2001–

Clarke, Professor Graeme (Deputy Director, HRC), 1982

Curthoys, Professor Ann (Professor of History and Head of the

History Department, Faculty of Arts, ANU), 1995–1999

Cushing, Dr R.G. (Dean of the Faculty of Arts), 1987–1990

Daws, Professor G.A. (Pacific & S.E. Asian History, ANU), 1977–1983

Devereaux, Dr L., 1987–1990

Donaldson, Professor C.I.E. (Director, HRC), 1974–1990

Dorward, Dr David, 1993–1995

Eade, Dr. J.C., 1982–1989

Edwards, Dr Robert, AO, 2000–

Elliott, Professor R.W.V. (Master, University House, ANU), 1974–1987 (Chairman, 1979–1987), 1991–1992

Forge, Professor J.A.W. (Prehistory and Anthropology, ANU), 1981–1986

Fullerton, Ms Jan (Director, National Library of Australia), 2000–

Gray, Dr Anna (Representative of the Director of the National Gallery of Australia, Dr Brian Kennedy), 2000–

Grieve, Mr J.A. (Romance Languages, The Faculties, ANU), 1982–1988

Herbst, Professor P. (Philosophy, SGS, ANU), 1974–1984

Hillman, Dr R., 1986–1990

Hindess, Professor Barry (Professor of Political Science, Research School of Social Sciences, ANU), 1992–2000

Johnson, Professor R. St C. (Chairman), 1974–1979

Johnston, Professor G.K.W. (Deputy Director, HRC), 1976

Kuhn, Professor H. (Germanic Languages, ANU), 1974–1980

Kumar, Professor Ann (Faculty of Asian Studies, ANU), 1995–1997

Lloyd, Dr G. (Philosophy, The Faculties, ANU), 1985–1986

Matthews, Dr. J. (History, The Faculties, ANU), 1990–1994

McAllister, Professor Ian (Director, RSSS), 1997–1998

McCalman, Professor Iain, (Director, HRC), 1993– 2003, (Chairman, 1994–1995)

Milner, Professor Anthony (Dean, Faculty of Asian Studies), 1997–2000

Penny, Dr Benjamin (Project Officer, Academic), 1997–1998

Peterson, Dr N. (Acting Dean of the Faculty of Arts), 1991

Pettit, Professor P., 1990–1992

Ramson, Dr W.S. (Dean of the Faculty of Arts), 1978–1980; 1987

Rawson, Professor B.M. (Dean of the Faculty of Arts), 1981–1986, 1990

Reid, Professor A.J., 1992–1994

Ritchie, Dr J. (Acting Dean of the Faculty of Arts), 1986

Saha, Professor Larry (Dean, Faculty of Arts, ANU), 1994–1996

Sayers, Mr Andrew (Director, National Portrait Gallery), 2000– , (Chairman)

Scales, Professor D.P. (Romance Languages, ANU), 1977–1981

Schreuder, Professor Deryck (Associate Director, HRC), 1991–1993

Thomas, Professor Nicholas (Director, CCR), 1995–1999

Travers, Dr M. (Acting Dean of the Faculty of Arts), 1992

Turner, Dr Caroline (Deputy Director, HRC), 2000–

Turner, Professor Graeme, 2000–

Vaughan, Dr Gerard (Director, National Gallery of Victoria), 2000–

Williams, Professor David (School of Art, ANU), 2000–

Wright, Professor Iain (Head of the English Department, ANU), 1994–1995, (Chairman, 1995)

Appendix E

Humanities Research Centre Staff, 1974–2004

Note: In many cases, Annual Reports list administrative staff only by name, with no information on position. Annual Reports provide little or no information on administrative and secretarial staff for the years between 1978 and 1982.

Academic

Professor Ian Donaldson: Director, 1974–1990, 2004–

Mr R.J.C. Horan: Administrative Officer, 1974–1975; Research Secretary, 1975–1978

Professor Grahame Johnston: Bibliographer and Deputy Director, 1976

Mr C.L. Burmester: Part-time Bibliographical Adviser, 1977

Emeritus Professor Ralph Elliott: Acting Director, 1977–1978;

Honorary Librarian, 1998–

Dr J.C. Eade: Research Fellow, 1977–1982; Research Officer, 1982–1990

Mr James Grieve: Research Secretary, 1978–1981

Professor Graeme Clarke: Deputy Director, 1982–1990; Director, 1990–1995; Associate Director, 1995–1999

Dr Julian Thomas: ARC Postdoctoral Fellow, 1990–1992

Professor Deryck Schreuder: Associate Director, 1992–1993

Professor Iain McCalman: Associate Director, 1994–1995; Acting Director, 1994–1995; Director, 1995–2003; Federation Fellow, 2003-

Dr Clara Tuite: ARC Research Associate, 1995–1999

Dr Benjamin Penny: Project Officer, 1996–1999; Executive Officer, Freilich Foundation, 1999–

Dr John Docker: ARC Research Fellow, 1996–1998; Adjunct Senior Fellow, 1998–

Dr Helen Topliss: ARC Research Fellow, 1996–1997

Dr Libby Robin: ARC Postdoctoral Research Fellow, 1997–1998

Dr Brian Massumi: ARC QEII Fellow, 1998–2001

Mrs Betty Churcher: Adjunct Professor (joint HRC/CCR appointment), 1998–

Professor Bill Gammage: ARC Senior Research Fellow and Professor, 1998–2002; ARC QEII Senior Fellow, 2002–

Mr Alexander Cook: Research Assistant to Professor Iain McCalman, 1999–2001

Dr Caroline Turner: Deputy Director, 2000; – Acting Director for periods in 2000, 2001, 2002, March to August 2003

Dr Paul Pickering: ARC QEII Fellow, 2000–2004; – Acting Deputy Director for periods in 2000, 2001, 2002 and March to August 2003; Associate Professor and Director of Graduate Programmes, 2004

Dr Christa Knellwolf: Research Associate, 2000–2002

Ms Christine Clark: Research Assistant to Caroline Turner, 2001–2004

Professor Tim Bonyhady: Research Fellow (joint HRC/CCR appointment), 2001–

Ms Georgina Fitzpatrick: Research Assistant to Professor Iain

McCalman, 2003–

Professor Bruce Bennett: Adjunct Professor, 2003–

Professor Adam Shoemaker: Director, August 2003–January 2004

Administrative

Mrs Jennifer Kelly: Secretary, 1974–1976

Mrs Beverly Ricketts: Stenographer, 1975–1976

Mrs Marjorie Kestevan: Part-Time Typist, 1975–1976

Mrs Patricia Hutchison: Administrative staff member, 1976

Miss Mary Theo: Secretary, 1976–1988

Mrs J. Nandan: Typist, 1977

Mrs Elizabeth Smith: Administrative staff member, 1977

Mrs Julie Barton: Typist and Word-Processor Operator, 1977–1982

Mrs Dorothy Nicolls: Stenographer, 1978–1980

Mrs Jodi Parvey: Word-Processor Operator, 1982–1988, Centre Administrator: 1989–1997

Ms Krystyna Szokalski (Verhelst): Word-Processor Operator 1985–1986; Administrative staff member, 1986–1993

Mr William Verhelst: Word-Processor Operator, 1985–1986

Mrs Pearl Moyseyenko: Stenographer, 1986, Deputy Director's Secretary, 1986–1991

Miss Jennifer Grant: Administrative staff member, 1987

Ms Wendy Antoniak: Secretary, 1989–1991

Ms Janette Boucher: Administrative staff member, 1990

Ms Leena Messina: Administrative Assistant, 1991–1994; Secretary to Director and Conference Administrator, 1995–1997; Programs Officer, 1998–2001; Programs Manager, 2002–

Mrs Louise Bannister: Administrative staff member, 1991–1993

Ms Stephanie Stockdill: Administrative staff member, 1992–1997

Ms Lia Szokalski (Verhelst): Administrative staff member, 1992–1997

Ms Misty Cook: Publications Officer, 1995–1999

Ms Julie Gorrell: Executive and Liaison Officer (joint HRC/CCR appointment), 1997–2001

Ms Judy Buchanan: Administrative Assistant, 1997–

Ms Ann Palmer: Administrative Assistant, 1997–1998

Mr Garry Macgregor: IT Support Officer (joint appointment), 1999–2000

Ms Lindy Shultz: Publications Officer, 2000–2003

Ms Felicity Bowskill: Executive Officer, 2001

Ms Christine Clark: Projects Officer, 2003

Mr Glenn Schultz: IT Support (joint HRC/CCR/RSPAS/CAEPR/NEC appointment), 2001–

Mr Garrett Purtill: Executive Officer 2002–2003

Mr Owen Larkin: Executive Assistant to Professor Iain McCalman, 2002–2003

Ms Anna Foxcroft: IT Support (joint HRC/CCR/RSPAS/CAEPR/NEC appointment), 2003–

Ms Michelle McGinness: Executive Officer, 2003–

Appendix F
Humanities Research Centre Publications

1. HRC Monographs

Dobrez, Patricia (ed.) 1981, *Ways and Means: A Guide for Arts and Humanities Visitors to Australia*, HRC, Canberra

Jeffreys, E. & M. and Ann Moffatt (eds.) 1981, *Byzantine Papers*, HRC, Canberra

Donaldson, Ian (ed.) 1982, *Australia and the European Imagination*, HRC, Canberra

Eade, J.C. (ed.) 1983, *Directory of Research in the Humanities in Australia*, HRC, Canberra

Eade, J.C. (ed.) 1983, *Romantic Nationalism in Europe*, HRC, Canberra

(The papers presented in this Volume were compiled from a series of four conferences held by the HRC between May and November 1980.)

Eade, J.C. (ed.) 1984, *Editing Texts*, HRC, Canberra

(HRC Conference)

Eade, J.C. (ed.) 1984, *Projecting the Landscape*, HRC, Canberra

(Papers presented at the HRC during 1984)

Burke, John and Stathis Gauntlett (eds.) 1985, *NeoHellenism*, HRC, Canberra

Eade, J.C. (ed.) 1985, *Directory of Research in the Humanities in Australia and New Zealand*, HRC, Canberra

Donaldson, Ian, Peter Read, James Walker (eds.) 1992, *Shaping Lives – Reflections on Biography*, HRC, Canberra

(A selection of papers delivered at the HRC during 1990)

Gerstle, Drew and Anthony Milner (eds.) 1994, *Europe & The Orient*, HRC, Canberra

(HRC Conference)

Matthews, Jill Julius (ed.) 1994, *Jane Gallop Seminar Papers*, HRC, Canberra

(Proceedings of the Jane Gallop Seminar and Public Lecture 'The Teacher's Breasts' held in 1993 at the HRC)

Brown, Nicholas, Peter Campbell, Robyn Holmes, Peter Read, and Larry Sitsky (eds.) 1995, *One Hand on the Manuscript: Music in Australian Cultural History (1930-1960)*, HRC, Canberra

(Papers from conference 'Music and Musicians in Australian Cultural History 1930-1960', held at the HRC from 25-29 September 1993.)

Alexander, Peter F., Ruth Hutchinson and Deryck Schreuder (eds.) 1996, *Africa Today: A Multi-Disciplinary Snapshot of the Continent in 1995*, HRC, Canberra

(This Volume arose from the annual conference of the African Studies Association of Australasia and the Pacific. 'What is happening in Africa Today?', New College, University of New South Wales, Sydney, September 1995.)

McCalman, Iain, Jodi Parvey and Misty Cook (eds.) 1996, *National Biographies & National Identity: A Critical Approach to Theory and Editorial Practice*, HRC, Canberra

(Papers from conference 'National Biographies and National Identity: A Critical Approach to Theory and Editorial Practice', National

Library of Australia, February 1995.)

Wallace, Sue-Anne, Jacqueline Macnaughtan and Jodi Parvey (eds.) 1996, *The Articulate Surface: Dialogues on paintings between conservators, curators and art historians*, HRC, Canberra

(HRC Conference)

McCalman, Iain (ed.) with Benjamin Penny and Misty Cook 1998, *Mad Cows and Modernity: Cross-disciplinary reflections on the crisis of Creutzfeldt-Jakob disease*, HRC, Canberra

(Papers from conference 'Mad Cows and Modernity', jointly sponsored by National Academies Forum and HRC.)

Edwards, Penny and Shen Yuanfang (eds.) 2003, *Lost in the Whitewash: Aboriginal–Asian Encounters in Australia, 1901–2001*, HRC, Canberra

(CCR/HRC Conference)

Turner, Caroline and Nancy Sever (eds.) 2003, *Witnessing to Silence: Art and Human Rights*, HRC, Canberra

(Exhibition Catalogue)

2. HRC Journal: *Humanities Research* (joint with CCR)

Winter, 1997

Issue 1, 1998

Issue 2, 1998

Issue 3, 1998

Issue 1, 1999

Issue 2, 1999

Issue 1, 2000: 'Indigenous Knowledge'

Issue 1, 2001: 'Museums of the Future' (Part 1), online

Issue 1, 2002: 'Museums of the Future' (Part 2), online

Issue 1, 2003, 'Latin America', online

Issue 2, 2003, 'Monuments and Commemorations', online

3. Joint publication series with Macmillan

Butler, Michael 1985, *The Plays of Max Frisch*, Macmillan, London

Donaldson, Ian (ed.) 1983, *Transformations in Modern European Drama*, Macmillan, London

Donaldson, Ian (ed.) 1983, *Jonson and Shakespeare*, Macmillan, London

Flower, John 1983, *Literature and the Left in France*, Macmillan, London

MacDonagh, Oliver, W. Mandle and P. Travers (eds.) 1983, *Nationalism and Culture in Ireland*, Macmillan, London

Norrish, Peter 1988, *New Tragedy & Comedy in France, 1945-1970*, Macmillan, London

4. Joint publication series with Oxford University Press

Descoeudres, J. P. (ed.) 1991, *Greek Colonists and Native Populations*, OUP, Oxford

Kent, F.W., Patricia Simons and J.C. Eade (eds.) 1987, *Patronage, Art and Society in Renaissance Italy*, OUP, Oxford

McCalman, Iain, Jon Mee, Gillian Russell, Clara Tuite, Kate Fullagar (eds.) 1999, *An Oxford Companion to the Romantic Age: British Culture 1776-1832*, OUP, Oxford

Rawson, Beryl (ed.) 1991, *Marriage, Divorce, and Children in Ancient Rome*, OUP, Oxford

Weaver, Paul and Beryl Rawson (eds.) 1997, *The Roman Family in Italy: Status, Sentiment, Space*, OUP, Oxford

5. Papers from HRC Conferences with outside publishers

i. Books and Journal Special Editions

Donaldson, Ian, *All's Well that Ends Well: Shakespeare's Play of Endings*, first given at the HRC Conference on Shakespearian Comedy, May 1976, in *Essays in Criticism*, January 1977

Twelve Several Papers delivered at the Humanities Research Centre of the Australian National University the 13, 14, 15, & 16 February 1981 for the Christopher Hill Conference. HRC, 1981

Hardy, J.P. and J.C. Eade (eds.) 1983, *Studies in the Eighteenth Century V*, The Voltaire Foundation, Oxford

Sussex, Roland and J.C. Eade (eds.) 1984, *Culture and Nationalism in Nineteenth-Century Eastern Europe*, Slavica Publications, Columbus, Ohio

Donaldson, Ian and Tamsin (eds.) 1985, *Seeing the First Australians*, Allen & Unwin, Sydney

Rawson, Beryl (ed.) 1986, *The Family in Ancient Rome: New Perspectives*, Croom Helm, London

Sheridan, Susan (ed.) 1988, *Grafts: Feminist Cultural Criticism*, Verso Press, London

Clarke, G.W. (ed.) 1989, *Rediscovering Hellenism, The Hellenic Inheritance and the English Imagination*, Cambridge University Press, Cambridge

Clarke, G.W. (ed.) 1990, *Reading the Past in Late Antiquity*, Pergamon Press

Carter, David (ed.) 1991, *Writing Outside the Book*, Local Consumption Press, Sydney

Clarke, John (ed.) 1993, *Modernity in Asian Art*, Wild Peony Press, Sydney (*Modernism and Post-Modernism in Asian Art* – jointly held with the Art History Department, ANU, 22-25 March 1991).

Kelly, David and Anthony Reid (eds.) 1998, *Asian Freedoms: The idea of freedoms in East and Southeast Asia*, Cambridge University Press, Cambridge.

(Conference 'Ideas of Freedom in Asia', 1994)

Thomas, J. and S. MacIntyre (eds.) 1995, *The Discovery of Australian History, 1890-1939*, Melbourne University Press

Gerstle, C.A. and A.C. Milner (eds.) 1995, *Recovering the Exotic*, Harwood Academic Publishers

Devereaux, L. and R. Hillman (eds.) 1995, *Fields of Vision: Essays in Film Studies, Visual Anthropology, and Photography*, University of California Press

Caine, B. and R. Pringle (eds.) 1995, *Transitions: New Australian*

Feminisms, Alan and Unwin, Sydney

Duro, Paul (ed.) 1996, *The Rhetoric of the Frame: Essays on the Boundaries of the Artwork*, Cambridge University Press, Cambridge

Bonyhady, Tim and Tom Griffiths (eds.) 1996, *Prehistory to Politics: John Mulvaney, the Humanities and the Public Intellectual*, Melbourne University Press

Connah, Graham (ed.) 1997, *Transformations in Africa: Essays on Africa's later past*, Leicester University Press

Gray, Geoffrey and Christine Winter (eds.) 1997, *The Resurgence of Racism. Howard, Hanson and the Race Debate*, Monash University

Thornton, Margaret (ed.) 2002, *Romancing the Tomes: Popular Culture, Law and Feminism*, Cavendish Publishing, London

Cahill, David and Blanca Tovías (eds.), *New World, First Nations: Native Peoples of Mesoamerica and the Andes under Colonial Rule*, Sussex Academic Press (in preparation)

Wright, Nancy E., Margaret W. Ferguson and A.R. Buck (eds.) 2004, *Women, Property, and the Letters of the Law*, The University of Toronto Press

ii. Other Papers and Publications

Papers given at HRC Conference on *The Impact of Seventeenth and Eighteenth Century Philosophy on Modern Thought*, August 1974: Stewart R. Sutherland, *Hume on Morality and the Emotions*, *Philosophical Quarterly*, January 1976, pp. 14-23; Rolf-Dieter Herrmann, *Newton's Positivism and the A Priori Constitution of the World*, *International Philosophical Quarterly*, Vol. XV, No. 2, June 1975

J.P. Hardy's paper on Dr Johnson's *The Vanity of Human Wishes* and *Rasselas*, first given as Work-in-Progress Seminar, March 1976, in *Essays in Criticism*, October 1976

Papers given at Old Norse Workshop, May 1976, in *Parergon* (Bulletin of the Australian and New Zealand Association for Medieval and Renaissance Studies), No. 15, August 1976: John Simon, *Snorri Sturluson: His Life and Times*; Lars Lönnroth, *Ideology and Structure in* Heimskringla; Hans Kuhn, *Narrative Structures and Historicity in* Heimskringla; John Stanley Martin, *Some Aspects of Snorri Sturluson's View of Kingship*; Heinrich Stefanik, *Saga and Western*.

John Wilders' paper on *Love's Labour's Lost*, first given as Work-in-

Progress Seminar, September 1976, in *Essays in Criticism*, January 1977

Brissenden, R.F. and J.C. Eade (eds.) 1979, *Studies in the Eighteenth Century IV*, ANU Press

Parergon, No. 23 (April 1979), papers from the Medieval Conference.

Southern Review, XIII (1980), special number on Parody: papers from HRC conference, 1976

Miscellanea Musicologica, XI (1980), papers from the Mannerism Conference

Journal of European Studies, XI (1981), papers from the Translation Conference

Ruthven, K.K. (ed.) 1983, *Southern Review*, XVI, (March) (papers from the HRC Conference 'Understanding Texts: Texts for What?', May 1982)

Meridian, IV (May 1985), 2 papers from the Editing Texts Conference

AUMLA, No. 66 (November 1986) papers from the Northrop Frye Seminar

1995, *Voices*, The Quarterly Journal of the National Library of Australia, Spring, papers from the Dictionaries of National Biography Conference

2001, 'Introducing George Seddon' by Trevor Hogan published in *Thesis Eleven*, #65, May: 65-68 and reprinted in GASt Newsletter (Gesellschaft für Australienstudien e.V.) #15: 2001: 64-65

2001, George Seddon 'Perceiving the Pilbara: finding the key to the country' *Thesis Eleven*, #65, May: 69-92

2002, Papers by Ian Duffield, Cassandra Pybus, Hamish Maxwell-Stewart (with Peter Lines), Peter Hulme, Russell McDougall, Rosamund Dalziell and Sue Thomas in *Australian Cultural History*, No. 21, Russell McDougall (ed.) 'To the Islands: Australia and the Caribbean'

2002, 11th David Nichol Smith Conference, Papers published in special edition of *Eighteenth Century Life* entitled 'Exoticism and the Culture of Exploration'

Special Theme issue 'George Seddon: Landprints over Boundaries' *Thesis Eleven*, 74, August 2003, 3-112 featuring articles by Tom Griffiths, Peter

Beilharz, George Seddon, Trevor Hogan, Michael Crozier, David S. Trigger, Suzi Adams

Read, Peter and Marivic Wyndham 2003, 'The Diaspora of the Latin American Imagination', Special issue *Humanities Research*, Vol, X, No. 1, Latin America

Farrington, Ian (ed.), publication on Inka Conference (forthcoming)

Slade, Christiana (ed.), publication on Telenovelas Conference (forthcoming)

Libertine Enlightenment: Sex, Liberty, and Licence in the Eighteenth Century (London, Palgrave Macmillan) (forthcoming)

Turner, Caroline and Jennifer Webb, publication on Art and Human Rights Conference (forthcoming)

'Spies and Surveillance' (forthcoming)

6. Selected publications worked on at the Centre or Published as a Result of Fellowships

Abelove, Henry, Michèle Aina Barale and David M Halperin 1993, *The Lesbian and Gay Studies Reader*, Routledge, London

Abraham, Claude 1983, *Norman Satirists in the Age of Louis XIII*, Wolfgang Leiner (ed.), Papers on French Seventeenth Century Literature, 1983, Biblio 17/18, Tübingen, Paris-Seattle

Albertsen, Leif Ludwig 1978, *Lyrik der Synges*, Berlingske Forlag, Köbenhavn

Andrew, Edward 1993 (Winter), 'Out of Place: The Homeless Genevan's Refusal to Recognize his Dependence,' *iichiko* 77, pp. 58-73

Ansara, Martha 1989, *Always Was, Always Will Be: The Sacred Grounds of the Waugal, Kings Park, Perth*, ANU, Canberra

Bair, Deidre 1995, *Anaïs Nin: A Biography*, Bloomsbury, London

— 1990, *Simone de Beauvoir: A Biography*, Jonathan, Cape, London

Barclay, Glen 2002, 'Here We Go Again', in *The Diplomat*, Vol 1, No. 3, p. 16

— 2003, review of Joseph Braude, *The New Iraq*, in *The Age*, 21 April 2003

Bender, John 1987, *Imagining the penitentiary: Fiction and architecture of mind in eighteenth-century England*, University of Chicago Press, Chicago & London

Benjamin, Roger 2003, *Orientalist Aesthetics: Art, Colonialism, and French North Africa, 1880–1930*, University of California Press

Bennett, Bruce, Jeff Doyle, Satendra Nandan (eds.) and Loes Baker (assoc. ed.) 1996, *Crossing Cultures: Essays on Literature & Culture of the Asia-Pacific*, Skoob Books Ltd, London

Bennett, Professor J.A.W. 1976 (22 October), 'Gibbon and the Universities', *The Cambridge Review*, pp. 15-18

Berry, Francis 1982, '*Eyre Remembers*, an Extract' in *Aspects of Australian Culture*, J. Daalder and M. Fryer (eds.), Abel Tasman Press, Adelaide

Bondanella, Peter 2004, *Hollywood Italians: Dagos, Palookas, Romeos, Wise Guys, and Sopranos*, Continuum International

Bony, Jean 1981, 'Durham et la tradition saxoune', *Etudes d'art mediéval offertes à Louis Greecki*, pp. 79-85, Ophrys, Paris

— 1983, 'La Genèse de l'architecture gothique : Accident ou Nécessité?', *Revue de l'Art*, No. 58-59

Bordo, Jonathan 1961, 'The Witness in the Errings of Contemporary Art', in Paul Duro (ed.), *The Rhetoric of the Frame: Essays on the Boundaries of the Artwork*, Cambridge University Press, Cambridge

— 1994 (Spring), 'Terra Nullius Sublimed – The Wilderness Trope and the American Exception as Cultural Modernity', *Semiotic Review of Books*

Bosworth, Richard J.B. 1992, *Explaining Auschwitz and Hiroshima: Historians and the Second World War, 1945-1990*, Routledge, London

Boyd, David 1989, *Film and the Interpretive Process: A Study of Blow-Up, Rashomon, Citizen Kane, 8 1/2, Vertigo and Persona*, Peter Lang, New York

Britain, Ian 1997, *Once an Australian: Journeys with Barry Humphries, Clive James, Germaine Greer and Robert Hughes*, Oxford University Press, Oxford

Britain, Ian and Brenda Niall (eds.) 1997, *The Oxford Book of Australian Schooldays*, Oxford University Press, Oxford

Brooks, George E. 1993, *Landlord and Strangers: Ecology, Society, and Trade in Western Africa, 1000-1630*, Westview Press, Boulder, Colorado

Bull, Philip (with Frances Devlin-Glass and Helen Doyle) 2000, *Ireland and Australia, 1798-1998: Studies in Culture, Identity and Migration*, Crossing Press, Sydney

Caine, Barbara 1992, *Victorian Feminists*, Oxford University Press, Oxford

Carey, Hilary 2003, 'Australian Religious Culture from Federation to the New Pluralism', *Legacies of White Australia*, Laksiri Jaysuriya, David Walker and Jan Gothard (eds.), pp. 70-92, University of Western Australia Press, Perth

— 2003, 'What is the Folded Almanac? The Form and Function of a Key Manuscript Source for Astro-medical practice in Later Medieval England', *Social History of Medicine*, 16, 431-520

Carey, Hilary and David A. Roberts 2002, 'Smallpox and the Baiame Waganna of Wellington Valley, 1829-40: The Earliest Nativist Movement in Aboriginal Australia', *Ethnohistor*, 49.4, 821-69

Chong-wha, Chung 1981, 'The Leadership Novels of D.H. Lawrence: A New Approach', *Phoenix*, XXIII, pp. 25-42

— 1986, *The Anthology of Modern Korean Poetry*, East West Publications, London

Clark, Katerina 1995, *Petersburg, Crucible of Cultural Revolution*, Harvard University Press, Cambridge

Clark, Timothy 1997, *The Theory of Inspiration: Composition as a crisis of subjectivity in Romantic and post-Romantic writing*, Manchester University Press, Manchester

Clarke, J.E.M. 1981, 'From the History of Russian Linguistics: Karamzim's Analysis of the Pre-Literary State of the Slavonic Language', *Russian Linguistics*, 5, 235-43

Coe, Richard N. 1984, *When the Grass was Taller: Autobiography and the Experience of Childhood*, Yale University Press

Coleman, Deirdre (forthcoming) *Romantic colonization and British anti-slavery*, Cambridge University Press, Cambridge

Coombes, Annie E. 2000, 'Translating the past: Apartheid Monuments in Post-Apartheid South Africa', in Annie E. Coombes and Avtar Brah (eds.), *Hybridity and its Discontents*, pp. 173-197, Routledge, London

Coombes, Annie E. and Avtar Brah (eds.) 2000, *Hybridity and its Discontents: Politics, Science, Culture*, Routledge, London

Cooper, Annabel 1991, 'Mary Lee (1871-1939)', *The Book of New Zealand Women: Ko Kui Ma Te Kaupapa*, Charlotte Macdonald,

Merimeri Penfold and Bridget Williams (eds.), Bridget Williams Books, Wellington

Coquery-Vidrovitch, Catherine 1994, *Les Africaines: Histoire des femmes d'Afrique noire du xixe au xxe siècle*, Editions Desjorquères, Paris

Corballis, Richard 1984, *Stoppard: The Mystery and the Clockwork*, Amber Lane Press, Oxford

Cressy, David 1989, *Bonfires and Bells: National Memory and the Protestant Calendar in Elizabethan and Stuart England*, Weidenfeld and Nicolson, London

Crook, J. Mordaunt 1987, *The Dilemma of Style: Architectural Ideas from the Picturesque to the Post-Modern*, John Murray, London

Davie, George 1986, *The Crisis of the Democratic Intellect: The Problem of Generalism and Specialisation in Twentieth Century Scotland*, Polygon, Edinburgh

Deacon, Desley 1997, *Elsie Clews Parsons: Inventing Modern Life*, University of Chicago Press

Dean, William 1988 (March), 'The Date of *The Widow's Tears*: An Allusion to the Case of Post-Nati (Calvin's Case), 1608', *Notes & Queries*, pp. 59-60

Docker, John 1986, 'Antipodean Literature: A World Upside Down?', in *Overland*, pp. 103

— 1986 (October), 'In Defence of Melodrama: Towards a Libertarian Aesthetic', in *Australasian Drama Studies*, pp. 9

— 1988, 'In Defence of Popular TV: Carnivalesque v. Left Pessimism', *Continuum*, Vol. 1 No. 2, pp. 83-99

ten-Doesschate Chu, Petra 2003/04, 'Edify, Please, or Shock the Bourgeois: French Art during the time of Alfred Bruyas', essay in exhibition catalogue *French Paintings from the Musée Fabre, Montpellier*, National Gallery, Canberra

Dolin, Kieran 2002, 'The Case of Dr John Bodkin Adams; A "Notable" Trial and its Narratives', *REAL: Yearbook of Research in English and American Literature* 18, pp. 145-165

Dollimore, Jonathan 1989, *Radical Tragedy: Religion, Ideology and Power in the Drama of Shakespeare and his Contemporaries*, 2nd edn, Harvester Wheatsheaf, London

— 1990, 'Critical Developments: new historicism, cultural

materialism, feminism and gender analysis', *Shakespeare: Select Bibliographical Guides*, Stanley Wells (ed.) 2nd rev. edn, Oxford University Press, Oxford

— 1991, *Sexual Dissidence: Augustine to Wilde, Freud to Foucault*, Oxford University Press, Oxford

Dubow, Saul 1995, *Scientific Racism in Modern South Africa*, Cambridge University Press, Cambridge

Dufrenne, Mikel 1981, *L'inventaire des a priori*, C. Bourgois, Paris

Duggan, Lisa 1993 (Summer), 'The Trials of Alice Mitchell: sensationalism, sexology, and the Lesbian Subject in Turn-of-the-Century America', *Signs*, Vol. 18, No. 4

Dukore, Bernard F. 1981, *The Theatre of Peter Barnes*, Heinemann, London

—, (ed.) 1993, *George Bernard Shaw, The Drama Observed*, Pennsylvania State University Press, University Park

Duro, Paul 1997, *The Academy and the Limits of Painting in Seventeenth Century France*, Cambridge University Press, Cambridge

— 1998 (Autumn), 'Picturing Eden: Australian and American landscape painting', *Artonview*, 13, pp. 10-15

Eade, J.C. 1988, 'Looking for Directions: Elias Ashmole's Astrology in Action', *English Culture at the End of the Seventeenth Century*, Johns Hopkins University Press

— 1989, 'The Saturnian Date in Skelton's *Speculum Principis*', *Notes and Queries*, pp. 165

— 1989, *Southeast Asian Ephemeris: Solar and Planetary Positions, AD 638-2000*, Southeast Asia Program, Cornell University

Eakin, Paul John 1989, *Touching the World: Reference in Autobiography*, Princeton University Press, Princeton

Elliott, Ralph W.V. 1988, 'Hardy's One-Plane Dictionary', *The Thomas Hardy Journal*, Vol. 4, No. 3, pp. 29-47

— 1989, 'Literary Dialect in Chaucer, Hardy and Alan Garner', *Studies in English Literature*, The English Literary Society of Japan

— 1989, *Runes: An Introduction*, 2nd rev. edn, Manchester University Press, Manchester

— 1993, 'Runes and Restoration', *Images of Germany: Australian*

Insights, M. Thomas (ed.), Embassy of the Federal Republic of Germany, Canberra

— 1994, 'In Search of Râmen', *Encounters in Japan*, J. Duffy and G. Anson (eds.) Angus & Robertson, Sydney

— 1996, 'The Runic Script', *The World's Writing Systems*, Peter T. Daniels and William Bright (eds.), Oxford University Press, New York

Evans, Richard J. 1987, *Comrades and Sisters: Feminism, Socialism and Pacifism in Europe 1870-1945*, Wheatsheaf Books, Brighton

Falola, Toyin 1998, *Violence in Nigeria: The Crisis of Religious Politics and Secular Ideologies*, University of Rochester Press, Rochester

Flint, Valerie 1981, 'World History in the early twelfth-century: the *Imago Mundi* of Honorius Augustodunensis', *The Writing of History in the Middle Ages*, R.H.C. Davis (ed.) et al., Clarendon Press, Oxford, pp. 211-38

— 1982, 'Honorius Augustodunensis' Imago Mundi', *Archives d'histoire doctrinale et littéraire du moyen âge*, pp. 7-153

Innes, Joanna and A. Burns (eds.), 2003 'Introduction', *Rethinking the Age of Reform: Britain 1780-1830*, Cambridge University Press, Cambridge

Foakes, R.A. 1993, *Hamlet versus Lear: Cultural Politics and Shakespeare's Art*, Cambridge University Press, Cambridge

Fowler, Alastair 1982, *Kinds of Literature: An Introduction to the Theory of Genres and Modes*, Oxford University Press, Oxford

Frost, Alan 1987, *Arthur Phillip 1738-1814: His Voyaging*, Oxford University Press, Melbourne

Galla, Amar 2002, *Protection of Cultural Heritage in Southeast Asia: Workshop Proceedings, Hanoi, Vietnam, 9-13 April 2001*, International Council of Museums, Asia Pacific Organisation, Canberra and Paris

— 2002, 'Culture and Heritage in Development: Ha Long Ecomuseum, A Case Study from Vietnam', *Humanities Research*, Australian National University, Canberra

— 2002, *Technical Assistance of the DHR Stakeholder Workshop*, UNESCO and International Council of Museums, Darjeeling

Gallop, David 1988, 1990, *Aristotle on Sleep and Dreams: A Text and Translation with Introduction, Notes and Glossary*, University Press of

America, New York and London, Broadview Press, Peterborough, Ontario

Gascoigne, John 2002, *The Enlightenment and the Origins of European Australia* Cambridge University Press, Cambridge

Gaston-Hall, H. 1990, *Molière's* Le Bourgeois Gentilhomme: *Context and stagecraft*, University of Durham, Durham

Gerstle, C. Andrew (ed.) 1989, *18th century Japan: Culture and society*, Allen & Unwin, Sydney

Gerstle, C. Andrew (ed.) with Anthony Milner 1995, *Recovering the Orient: Artists, Scholars, Appropriations*, Harwood Academic Publishers, Switzerland

Gerstle, C. Andrew 1990, 'The concept of tragedy in Japanese drama', *Japan Review* Vol. 1, pp. 49-72

Gillen, Paul 1993, *Jack Lindsay: Faithful to the Earth*, Angus & Robertson, Sydney

Gillies, John 1994, *Shakespeare and the Geography of Difference*, Cambridge University Press, Cambridge

Goldberg, Jonathan 1986, *Voice Terminal Echo: Postmodernism and English Renaissance Texts*, Routledge & Kegan Paul, New York and London

Green, D. H. 1982, *The Art of Recognition in Wolfram's Parzival*, Cambridge University Press, Cambridge

Green, Dorothy 1984, (revision of H.M. Green), *History of Australian Literature*, 2 Vols, Angus & Robertson, Sydney

Grieve, James 1982, 'Intimations of Mortality: Another of the Meanings of Maupassant's "Pierre et Jean"', *Australian Journal of French Studies*, Vol. XIX No. 2, pp. 133-147

— 1982, *Marcel Proust, A Search for lost time: Swann's Way*, ANU, Canberra

— 1982, Review Essay 'On Translating Proust' *Journal of European Studies*, Vol. XII, pp. 55-67

Griffin, Clive 1993, *Mariano Azuela: 'Los de Abajo'*, Critical Guides to Spanish Texts, Grant & Cutler

— 1993, *The Crombergers of Seville*, Clarendon Press, Oxford

Grosz, Elizabeth 1989, *Sexual Subversions: Three French Feminists*, Allen

& Unwin, Sydney

Guthke, Karl S.B. 1987, *Traven: Biographie eines Rätsels*, M. Olten, Frankfurt-am-Main

— 1992, *B. Traven: The Life Behind the Legends*, Independent Publishers Group, Chicago

— 1993, *Die Entdeckung des Ich: Studien zur Literatur*, Francke Verlag, Tübingen

— 1993, *Trails in No-Man's Land: Essays in Cultural and Literary History*, Camden House, Columbia, South Carolina

Hamer, David 1990, *New towns in the New World: Images and perceptions of the nineteenth-century urban frontier*, Columbia University Press, New York

Hamilton, A. C. 1990, *Northrop Frye: Anatomy of his criticism*, University of Toronto Press, Toronto

Hardie, Philip 1993, *The Epic Successors of Virgil*, Cambridge University Press, Cambridge

Hardy J.P. and Alan Frost (eds.), 1989, *Studies from Terra Australis to Australia*, Highland Press, Canberra

Hassall, A.J. 1988, 'Quests', *The Penguin New Literary History of Australia*, L. Hergenhan (ed.), ch.24, Penguin Books Australia

Hassall, A.J. with J.F. Burrows 1988 (Summer), '*Anna Boleyn* and the Authenticity of Fielding's Feminine Narratives', *Eighteenth-Century Studies*, pp. 427-453

Hassan, Ihab 1986, *Out of Egypt: Scenes and arguments of an autobiography*, Southern Illinois University Press, Carbondale and Edwardsville

Hassan, Ihab 1990, *Selves at risk: Patterns of quest in contemporary American letters*, University of Wisconsin Press, Madison

Healy, Chris 1997, *From the Ruins of Colonialism: History as Social Memory*, Cambridge University Press, Cambridge

Hempenstall, Peter 1993, *The Meddlesome Priest: a life of Ernest Burgmann*, Allen & Unwin, Sydney

Herzfeld, Michael 1987, *Anthropology Through the Looking-Glass: Critical Ethnography in the Margins of Europe*, Cambridge University Press, Cambridge

Hill, Christopher 1984, *The Experience of Defeat: Milton and Some Contemporaries*, Faber and Faber, London

Hoff, Ursula 1986, *The Art of Arthur Boyd*, Andre Deutsch Ltd, London

Holquist, Michael with Katerina Clark 1984, *Mikhail Bakhtin*, Belknap Press, Cambridge, Mass. and London

Holton, Sandra 2003 (Spring), 'John Bright, Radical Politics, and the Ethos of Quakerism', *Albion*, Vol. 34, No. 4, pp. 584-605

Hong, Zhu 1992, *The Serenity of Whiteness. Stories By and About Women's Contemporary China*, translated by Zhu Hong, Ballantine Booth, New York

Hunter, Michael 1985, 'The Problem of "Atheism" in Early Modern England', *Transactions of the Royal Historical Society*, 5th ser., Vol. XXV, pp. 135-57

Indyk, Ivor and Elizabeth Webby (eds.) 1991, *Memory southerly*, No. 3, Angus & Robertson, Sydney

Inglis, Fred 1985, *The Management of Ignorance: A Political Theory of the Curriculum*, Basil Blackwell, Oxford

— 1990, *Media theory: An introduction*, Basil Blackwell, Oxford

Innes, Joanna 2003, 'Legislating for Three Kingdoms; How the Westminster Parliament legislated for England, Scotland and Ireland 1707-1830', *Parliaments, Nations and Identities in Britain 1660-1850*, J. Hoppit (ed.), Manchester University Press, Manchester

— 2003, 'Reform in English public life: the fortunes of a word', *Rethinking the Age of Reform: Britain 1780-1830*, Cambridge University Press, Cambridge

Innes, Joanna and A. Burns (eds.) 2003, *Rethinking the Age of Reform: Britain 1780-1830*, Cambridge University Press, Cambridge

Jacobson, D. 1982 (March), 'The Uselessness of Literature', *Quadrant*, pp. 61-4.

Jacobus, Mary 1986, *Reading Women: Essays in Feminist Criticism*, Columbia University Press, New York

Jacobus, Mary 1989, *Romanticism writing and sexual difference: essays on The Prelude*, Clarendon Press, Oxford

Jacobus, Mary 1999, *Psychoanalysis and the Scene of Reading*, Oxford

University Press, Oxford

James, Susan 1997, *Passion and Action: The Emotions in Seventeenth-Century Philosophy*, Clarendon Press, Oxford

Jenkyns, Richard 1998, *Virgil's Experience, Nature and History: Time, names and places*, Clarendon Press, Oxford

John, S.B.1981 (January), 'Irony, Satire and Judgment in Sartre's *L'enfance d'un chef'*, *Quinquirème*, No. 1, pp. 74-84

John, S.B.1981 (March), 'Insight and Madness in Sartre's *La Chambre'*, *Modern Languages*, Vol. LXII, No. 1, pp. 7-12

Jones, Peter (ed.) 1986, *A Hotbed of Genius: The Scottish Enlightenment 1730-1790*, Edinburgh University Press, Edinburgh

Joppien, Dr Rüdiger 1976 (October), *Three Drawings by William Hodges (1744-1797)*, *La Trobe Library Journal*, Vol. 5, No. 18, pp. 25-33

Joppien, Dr Rüdiger 1983 'Cataloguing the Drawings from Captain Cook's Voyage: A Task Completed', *Australian Journal of Art*, Vol. 3, pp. 59-78

Jordan, Richard D. 1989, *The quiet hero: Figures of temperance in Spenser, Donne, Milton and Joyce*, Catholic University of America Press, Washington D.C.

Kaplan, E. Ann 1987, *Rocking around the clock: Music television, postmodernism and consumer culture*, Methuen, New York and London

— 1989, 'Problematizing Cross-Cultural Analysis: The Case of Women in the Recent Chinese Cinema.', in *Wide Angle*, Vol. 2, No. 11, pp. 40-50. Reprinted in *Perspectives on Chinese Cinema*, Chris Berry (ed.) 1990, The British Film Institute, London. Translated into Chinese and reprinted 1991 in *Dangdai Dianying (Contemporary Film)*, No. 1, pp. 33-41

— 1991 (January), 'Melodrama/Subjectivity/Ideology: Western Melodrama Theories and Their Relevance to Recent Chinese Cinema,' in *East-West Film Journal*, Vol. 5, No. 1, pp. 6-27. Reprinted 1993 in *Melodrama and Asian Cinema*, Wimal Dissanayeke (ed.), Cambridge University Press, Cambridge, pp. 9-28

— 1997, 'Who's Reading What Signs and Why? Revisiting Cross-Cultural Research on Chinese Film, with focus on *Farewell My Concubine'*, in *Rethinking Chinese Cinema*, Sheldon Lu (ed.) 265-276, The University of Hawaii Press, Hawaii

— 2000, 'Aborigines, Film, and Moffatt's *Night Cries—a Rural Tragedy*: An Outsider's Perspective,' reprinted in *Picturing the 'Primitif': Images of Race in Daily Life*, Julie Marcus (ed.), LHR Press, Australia, pp. 61-73

— 2001, 'Trauma, Aging and Melodrama (with reference to Tracey Moffatt's *Night Cries*', in *Feminist Locations*, Marianne DeKoven (ed.), Rutgers University Press, New Brunswick, N.J., pp. 304-328

— 2002, 'Trauma, Cinema, Witnessing: Freud's *Moses* and Moffatt's *Night Cries*', in *Between the Psyche and the Social*, Kelly Oliver and Steve Edwin (eds.), Rowman and Littlefield, Lanham, MD, pp. 99-121

— 2003, 'Traumatic Contact- Zones and Embodied Translators', in *Trauma and Cinema: Cross-cultural Explorations*. E. Ann Kaplan and Ban Wang (eds.), University of Washington Press/ Hong Kong: Hong University Press, Seattle, pp. 46-63

Kearsley, Rosalinde 2001, *Greeks and Romans in imperial Asia: mixed language inscriptions and linguistic evidence for cultural interaction until the end of AD III*, Habelt, Bonn

Kermode, Frank 'The Limits of Theory', *Scripsi* Vol. 2 (April 1989), pp. 39-70

Kernan, Alvin B.1987, *Printing technology, letters and Samuel Johnson*, Princeton University Press, Princeton

Kiernan, Ben 2003, 'War, Genocide and Resistance in East Timor, 1975-1999: Comparative Reflections on Cambodia,' in *War and State Terrorism: The United States, Japan, and the Asia-Pacific in the Long Twentieth Century*, Mark Selden and Alvin Y. So (eds.), Rowman and Littlefield, Lanham, MD, pp. 199-233

Kornicki, Peter 1991, *Early Japanese Books in Cambridge University Library*, with N. Hayashi, Cambridge University Press, Cambridge

Kornicki, Peter 1992, 'Japan in the Australian Exhibitions', in *Shikaku no jukyuseiki*, T. Yokoyama (ed.), Kyoto

Kuna, Franz and Graeme Turner 1994, *Studying Australian Culture: An Introductory Reader*, Kovac, Hamburg

Lamarque, Peter 1996, *Fictional Points of View*, Cornell University Press, Ithaca

Lamarque, Peter and Stein Hangom Olsen 1994, *Truth, Fiction, and Literature: A Philosophical Perspective*, Clarendon Press, Oxford

Lange, Victor 1982, *The Classical Age of German Literature 1740-1815*, Holmes & Meier Publishers Inc, Edward Arnold, London

Lawson, Sylvia 1989, *The Outside Story: a feature length documentary*, Trinculo Productions Pty Ltd

Lipking, Lawrence 1988, *Abandoned Women and Poetic Tradition*, University of Chicago Press, Chicago

Lützeler, Paul Michael 1993, 'Von europäischer Republik, Joseph Görres' *Europa und die Revolution*', in *Aurora* Vol. 53, pp. 92-107

McFarland, Thomas 1992, *William Wordsworth: Intensity and Achievement*, Clarendon Press, Oxford

Macintyre, Stuart 1991, *A Colonial Liberalism: The Lost World of Three Victorian Visionaries*, Oxford University Press, Melbourne

Macintyre, Stuart (ed.) with Julian Thomas 1995, *The Discovery of Australian History 1890-1939*, Melbourne University Press, Carlton

Mackie, Alwynne 1989, *Art/Talk: Theory and Practice in Abstract Expressionism*, Columbia University Press, New York

MacLachlan, Alastair 1996, *The Rise and Fall of Revolutionary England: An Essay on the Fabrication of Seventeenth Century History*, Macmillan Press, London

Manning, S.W. 1999, *A Test of Time: the Volcano of Thera and the chronology and history of the Aegean and east Mediterranean in the mid-second millennium BC*, Oxbow Books, Oxford

Martin, P. 1982, 'A Flag for the Wind' in *Longman Cheshire Modern Poets*, Longman Cheshire, Melbourne

Maynard, Margaret 1994, *Fashioned from Penury: Dress as Cultural Practice in Colonial Australia*, Cambridge University Press, Cambridge

Mellor, Ronald 1993, *Tacitus*, Routledge, London

Meskimmon, Marsha 2003, *Women Making Art: History, Subjectivity, Aesthetics*, Routledge, London and NY

Meskimmon, Marsha 2003, 'Walking with Judy Watson: Painting, Politics and Intercorporeality' in *Unframed: The Practices and Politics of Women's Painting*, Rosemary Betterton (ed.), I.B. Tauris, London and New York

Moeran, Brian 1989, 'Of Chrysanthemums and Swords: Problems in Ethnographic Writing', *Criticism, Heresy and Interpretation*, No. 1, pp. 1-19

Morris, Meaghan 1988, 'Panorama: The Live, the Dead, and the Living' in *Island in the Stream: Myths of Place in Australian Culture*, Paul Foss (ed.), Pluto Press, Sydney

Morse, Ruth 1991, *Truth and Convention in the Middle Ages: Rhetoric, Representation, and Reality*, Cambridge University Press, Cambridge

Moses, Michael 1994 (Winter), 'Solitary Walkers: Rousseau and Coetzee's *Life and Times of Michael K*', in *South Atlantic Quarterly* Vol. 93, No. 1

Mourelatos, A.P. D. 1981, 'Astronomy & Kinematics in Plato's Project of Rationalist Explanation', in *Studies in the History and Philosophy of Science*, Vol. XII, No. 1 (1981), pp. 1-32

— 1981 (November), 'Pre-Socratic Origins of the Principle that There are no Origins from Nothing', in *The Journal of Philosophy*, Vol. 78, No. 11, pp. 649-65

Niall, Brenda 1989, *Martin Boyd: A Life*, Melbourne University Press, Melbourne

O'Brien, Denise (ed.) with Sharon W. Tiffany 1984, *Rethinking Women's Roles: Perspectives from the Pacific*, University of California Press, Berkeley

Parke, Aubrey 1988, 'Navatanitawake Ceremonial Mound, Bau, Fiji: Some results of 1970 investigations', in *Archaeol. Oceania*, Vol. 33, pp. 20-27

— 1995, 'The Qawa Incident in 1968 and Other Cases of 'Spirit Possession', in *The Journal of Pacific History*, Vol. 30, No. 2

Parker, David, Rosamund Dalziell and Iain Wright (eds.), *Shame and the Modern Self*, Australian Scholarly Publishing, Kew, Victoria

Parker, Reeve 1987 (Summer), 'Reading Wordsworth's Power: Narrative and Usurpation in *The Borders*, ELH, Vol. 54, No. 2, pp. 299-331

Parkin, Andrew (ed.) 1991, *W.B. Yeats's 'The Herne's Egg'*, Catholic University of America Press, Washington D.C.

— with Yu Kwang-Chung 1994, *Tolo Lights*, Shaw College, The Chinese University of Hong Kong, Shatin

Pastor, Brigida 2002, 'Femininity in Power, Masculinity in Crisis: The Cinema of Pedro Almodóvar', in *Letras Peninsulares*

Pear, David 2002, 'The Musical Rhythm of the Spoken Word', in *In a Nutshell*, University of Melbourne, Melbourne

— 2002, *Portrait of Percy Grainger*, University of Rochester Press, Rochester, NY, USA

— 2003, 'The Passions of Percy', in *Meanjin*, 62/2, 59-66

— 2004, 'Percy Grainger and 'The Commercial Slavery of Our Civilisation', in refereed papers of the *Blacking Symposium: Music-Culture-Society*

— 2004, 'Grainger's Top Ten', in *Newsletter Australian Music History Centre*, University of Melbourne, Melbourne, pp. 1-3

Pesman, Ros 1996, *Duty Free: Australian Women Abroad*, Oxford University Press, Melbourne

Phelan, Peggy 1997, *Mourning Sex: Performing Public Memories*, Routledge, London and New York

Phillips, Anne 1995, *The Politics of Presence*, Clarendon Press, Oxford

Phillips, Michael 1988, 'The Composition of Pope's *Imitation of Horace, Satire 11 i*', in *Alexander Pope: Essays for the Tercentenary*, Colin Nicholson (ed.), Aberdeen University Press, Aberdeen, pp. 171-93

Poggi, Gianfranco 2001, *Forms of Power*, Polity Press, Cambridge

— 2002, *Durkheim*, Oxford University Press, New York

Prawer, S.S. 1993, *Heine's Jewish Comedy: A Study of his Portraits of Jews and Judaism*, Oxford University Press, Oxford

Prest, Wilfred 1986, *The Rise of the Barristers*, Oxford University Press, Oxford

Prickett, Stephen 1996, *Origins of Narrative: The Romantic appropriation of the Bible*, Cambridge University Press, Cambridge

Qing, Dai 1994, *Yangtze! Yangtze!* Patricia Adams and John Thibodean (eds.), (English edition) Probe International, Earthscan Publications, London

Quinn, Arthur 1994, *A New World: An Epic of Colonial America from the Founding of Jamestown to the Fall of Quebec* Faber and Faber, Winchester, Massachusetts

Read, Peter 1990, 'Cheeky, insolent and anti-white: The split in the Federal Council for the Advancement of Aboriginal and Torres Strait Islanders-Easter 1970', in *The Australian Journal of Politics and History*,

Vol. 36, No. 1, pp. 73-83

Roper, Lyndal 1987, 'The Common Man, the Common Good, Common Women: the Gender and Meaning in the German Reformation Commune', in *Social History*, Vol. 12, pp. 1-21

— 1989, *The Holy Household: Women and Morals in Reformation Augsburg*, Clarendon Press, Oxford

Rose, Deborah Bird (ed.) with Tony Swain 1988, *Aboriginal Australians and Christian Missions*, Australian Association for the Study of Religions, Adelaide

— 'Jesus and the Dingo', loc. cit., pp. 361-75

Rose, M.G. (ed.) 1981, *Translation Spectrum*, State University of New York Press, Albany

Rowland, J.R. 1985, *The Sculptor of Candles: Poems by Andrei Voznesensky, Robert Rozhdestvensky, Novella Matveeva, Boris Slutsky, David Samoilov, Leonid Martynov*, The Leros Press, Canberra

Runia, David 1988, 'Philosophical Heresiography: Evidence in the Ephesian Inscriptions', *Zeitschrift für Papyrologie und Epigraphik*, Vol. 72, pp. 241-244

Ruthven, Ken K (ed.) 1992, *Beyond the Disciplines: The New Humanities*, The Australian Academy of the Humanities, Canberra

Sambrook, James 1991, *James Thomson, 1700-1748: A Life*, Clarendon Press, Oxford

Saunders, Trevor 1986, '"Gorgias" Psychology in the History of the Free-Will Problem', in *Gorgia e la Sofistica*, Siculorum Gymnasium, Torino

— 1991, *Plato's Penal Code: Tradition, Controversy, and Reform in Greek Penology*, Clarendon Press, Oxford

Schabert, Tilo 1989, *Boston politics: The creativity of power*, de Gruyter Studies on North America, Vol. 4, Walter de Gruyter Inc., Berlin

Seddon, George 1986 (September), 'A Snowy River Reader', *Meanjin*, pp. 309-45

Shaffer, Elinor 1988, *Erewhons of the Eye: Samuel Butler as Painter, Photographer and Art Critic*, Reaktion Books, London

Sharp, Kevin 1990, *Criticism and compliment: The politics of literature in the England of Charles I*, Cambridge University Press, Cambridge

Sheridan, Susan 1988, *Christina Stead*, Harvester-Wheatsheaf, New York

— (ed.) 1990, *Grafts: Feminist cultural criticism*, Verso, London

Sherry, Beverley 1991, *Australia's Historic Stained Glass*, Murray Child, Sydney

Simpson, David 1993, *Romanticism, Nationalism and the Revolt against Theory*, University of Chicago Press, Chicago

Smiles, Sam 1987 (Summer), 'Turner in Devon: Some Additional Information concerning his Visits in the 1810s', in *Turner Studies*, pp. 11-14

Smith, Robert, G. Robb and E. Smith (eds.) 1993, *Concise Dictionary of Australian Artists*, Melbourne University Press, Carlton

Snell, David 1997, *Life in the Near East 3100-322 BCE*, Yale University Press, New Haven

Strauss, J. 1990, *Stop laughing! I'm being serious: Three studies in seriousness and wit in contemporary Australian poetry*, Foundation for Australian Literary Studies, Townsville

Taylor, Ken 2003, 'Cultural Heritage Conservation and Tourism: Dilemma of the Chicken and the Egg', in *International Symposium and Workshop, Managing Heritage Environment in Asia, Jan 8-10*, pp. 13-20

— 2003, 'Cultural Heritage Management: The Role of Charters and Principles', in *The Journal of the Faculty of Architecture*, Vol. 19, pp. 170-183

— (with C. Tallents) 2003, 'Cultural Landscape Protection in Australia: Wingecarribee Shire Historic Landscape Study' in *International Journal of Heritage Status*, Vol. 2, No. 3, pp. 133-144

Thomas, Keith 1984, *The Perception of the Past in Early Modern England*, University of London, London

Thomson, John 1993, *The New Zealand Stage 1891-1900*, The Victoria University Press, Wellington

Thornton-Smith, Colin 1988 (September), 'S.T. Gill and Hubert de Castella', *Explorations*, No. 6, pp. 3-8

— 1989, 'The Eavesdropper as Narrator', in *Francois Mauriac: Visions and Reappraisals*, John E. Flowers and Bernard C. Swift (eds.), Berg Publishers, Gordonsville, Virginia

— (ed.) 1989, *Following the Runes: Writings for Ralph Elliott*, Centre for Research in the New Literatures in English, Adelaide

Topliss, Helen 1985, *Tom Roberts, 1856-1931: A Catalogue Raisonné*, 2 Vols,

Oxford University Press, Melbourne

Treitler, L. 1982, 'The Early History of Music Writing in the West', in *Journal of the American Musicological Society*, Vol. 35, pp. 237-79

Treitler, L. 1985, 'Reading and Singing: On the Genesis of Occidental Music-Writing', in *Early Music History*, Cambridge University Press, Cambridge Vol. IV, pp. 135ff

Umbach, Maiken 2002, 'Classicism, Enlightenment and the Other: Thoughts on Decoding Eighteenth-Century Visual Culture', in *Art History*, Vol. 25, No. 3

Underhill, Nancy D.H. 1991, *Making Australian Art 1916-49: Sydney Ure Smith, Patron and Publisher*, Oxford University Press, Melbourne

Urman, Dan and Paul V.M. Flesher 1995, *Ancient Synagogues: Historical Analysis and Archaeological Discovery*, 2 Vols, E.J. Brill, Leiden/New York

Vincent, Andrew 2002, *Nationalism and Particularity*, Cambridge University Press, Cambridge

Walicki, Andrzej 1982, *Philosophy and Romantic Nationalism: The Case of Poland*, Oxford University Press, Oxford

Walter, James (ed.) 1989, *Australian studies: A survey*, Oxford University Press, Melbourne

Walvin, James 1998, *An African's Life: The Life and Times of Olaudah Equiane, 1745-1797*, Cassell, London and New York

White, R.S. 1982, *Innocent Victims: Poetic Injustice in Shakespearean Tragedy*, published by the author, Newcastle Upon Tyne

— 1985, *Let Wonder seem Familiar: Endings in Shakespeare's Romance Vision*, Continuum International, London

— 1986, *Keats as a Reader of Shakespeare*, Continuum International, London

Widdowson, Peter 1984 (Winter), 'The Anti-History Men: Malcolm Bradbury and David Lodge', in *Critical Quarterly*, pp. 5-32

— 1986 (June), 'Hardy, 'Wessex', and the Making of a National

Culture', *Thomas Hardy Annual*, No. 4, pp. 45-69

Willett, John (ed.) 1990, *Bertolt Brecht letters*, translated by Ralph Manheim, Methuen, London

Williams, Gordon 1984, 'Roman Poets as Literary Historians: Some Aspects of Imitatio', in *Illinois Classical Studies*, Vol. VIII, No. 2, pp. 211-37

Williams, Margaret 1983, *Australia on the Popular Stage, 1829-1929: An Historical Entertainment in Six Acts*, Oxford University Press, Melbourne

Wogan-Browne, Jocelyn (translator) and Glyn S. Burgess (ed.) 1996, *Virgin Lives and Holy Deaths: Two Exemplary Biographies for Anglo-Norman Women*, Everyman, London

Woollacott, Angela (forthcoming), *Gender and Empire*, Palgrave Macmillan, London

Wright, Iain 1985, 'History, Hermeneutics, Deconstruction', in *Criticism and Critical Theory*, Jeremy Hawthorn (ed.), Edward Arnold, London, pp. 83-92

Ziegler, Philip (1990), *King Edward VIII: The official biography*, Collins, London

7. Staff Publications at The HRC

Tim Bonyhady

2000, 'An Australian Public Trust' in Stephen Dovers (ed.), *Environmental History and Policy: Still Settling Australia*, Oxford University Press, Melbourne, pp. 258-272

2000, with A. Sayers, Editor, *Heads of the People: A Portrait of Colonial Australia*, National Portrait Gallery, Canberra

2000, Editor, with M. Peel, *Urban Justice*, in a special edition of *Urban Policy and Research in Honour of Patrick Troy*, No. 18

2000, 'Governor Phillip's Legacy', in P. Troy (ed.), *Equity, Environment, Efficiency: Ethics and Economics in Urban Australia*, Melbourne University Press, Carlton, pp. 134-158

2000, 'Introduction' in T. Bonyhady and A. Sayers (eds.), *Heads of the People: A Portrait of Colonial Australia*, National Portrait Gallery,

Canberra, pp. 1-12

2000, 'Judith Wright tribute: Art and Activism', in *Ecopolitics: Thought and Action*, I, pp. 13-17

2000, 'Missing the Difference', *After the Garden*, Special edition of *The South Atlantic Quarterly*, Vol. 98, pp. 655-688

2000, 'Papunya Stories', in *Australian Humanities Review*: www.lib.latrobe.edu.au/AHR

2000, *The Colonial Earth*, Melbourne University Press, Carlton

2000, 'The First Aboriginal Memorial', in T. Bonyhady and A. Sayers (eds.), *Heads of the People: A Portrait of Colonial Australia*, National Portrait Gallery, Canberra, pp. 13-27

2000, with M. Levi and M. Peel, 'Introduction', in *Urban Justice*, in a special edition of *Urban Policy and Research in Honour of Patrick Troy*, Vol. 18

Betty Churcher

2002, Catalogue entries on Jon Molvig, Arthur Boyd, and Ian Fairweather for *Australian Art at the National Gallery*, Anne Gray (ed.), National Gallery of Australia, Canberra

2002, Catalogue essay 'The Sublime in Australian Art' for *The Sublime, Wesfarmers Collection*, Art Gallery of Western Australia

2003, Catalogue entry on Albert Tucker for *Artists in Action*, Nola Wilkins (ed.), Australian War Memorial, Canberra

Graeme Clarke

Letters of St. Cyprian, New York (Vol. 1 & 2, 1984, Vol. 3, 1986, Vol. 4, 1989)

1984, 'An illiterate Lector?', *Zeitschrift für Papyrologie und Epigraphik*, Vol. 57, pp. 103-104

1984-1985, 'Syriac Inscriptions from the Middle Euphrates' (with T. Muroaka), *Abr-Nahrain*, Vol. 23, pp. 73-89

1984-1985, 'A decorated Christian tomb-chamber near Joussef Pasha', *Abr-Nahrain*, Vol. 23, pp. 90-95

1984-1985, 'A funeral stele in the district of Membij: a preliminary report', *Abr-Nahrain*, Vol. 23, pp. 96-101

1985, 'Approaches to the 'Crisis' of the Third Century A.D.', in *Iris*,

1984, pp. 14-26, in *Classicum*, Vol. 26, No. 1, pp. 5-10

1984, 'W. Culican', in J. Zimmer (ed.), *The Archaeological Context: The Melbourne-Euphrates Expedition to Syria 1982-83: 1983-84*, Melbourne, and in A.G. Sagona (ed.) 1986, in *Opera Selecta: From Tyre to Tartessus*, Göteborg, pp. 27-34

1985, Review of Charles Thomas, *Christianity in Roman Britain to AD 500*, London, 1981, in *Ancient Society* Vol. 15, No. 1, pp. 55-57

1986, Review of T.D. Barnes, *Early Christianity and the Roman Empire*, London, 1984, in *Phoenix* Vol. 40, No. 2, pp. 247-8

1987 (with P. J. O'Connor), 'Inscriptions, Symbols and Graffiti near Joussef Pasha', in *Abr-Nahrain* Vol. 25, pp. 19-39 and Plates 1-10

1988, 'Funerary Inscriptions near Joussef Pasha, North Syria', *Abr-Nahrain* Vol. 26, pp. 19-29 and Plates 1-7

1989, 'A brief report on Jebel Khalid on the Euphrates: A Hellenistic settlement in North Syria', in *Primitiae*, Vol. 7, pp. 1-3

1989, Editor, *Rediscovering Hellenism, The Hellenic Inheritance and the English Imagination*, Cambridge University Press, Cambridge

1990, Editor, *Reading the Past in Late Antiquity*, Pergamon Press

1992, *Anchor Bible Dictionary*, Doubleday, s. vv *Cyprian* (Vol. 1, pp. 1226-1228), in *Religio Licita* Vol. 5, pp. 665-667

1992/3, 'Greek Graffiti from North Syria', *Mediterranean Archaeology*, Vol. 5, No. 6, pp. 6-9, plate 40

1993, with T. Hillard, 'A Limestone Altar from North Syria', *Mediterranean Archaeology*, pp. 1-5, plates 38-39

1994, 'Jebel Khalid on the Euphrates: The Acropolis Building', *Proceedings of the Second Macedonian Conference, Melbourne*, in *Mediterranean Archaeology* Vol. 7, pp. 69-75, plates 1-3

Lexikon für Theologie und Kirche, d. bb *Clinici*, Bd. 2, 1233-34, *Caecilius Cyprianus v. Karthago*, Bd. 2, 1364-1366, *Felicissimus v. Karthago*, Bd. 3, 1216

1995, With P. J. Connor and L.D. Mairs, 'Jebel Khalid: Report on 1993 Season', *Mediterranean Archaeology* Vol. 8

1995, 'Who cares about the Humanities?', a paper prepared for the Australian Academy of the Humanities' Jubilee Symposium (November 1995) in D.M. Schreuder (ed.), in *The Humanities and a*

Creative Nation, pp. 280-282

1996 'The Origins and Spread of Christianity', *Cambridge Ancient History* (revised edition), Vol. X, ch.15, Cambridge University Press, Cambridge

'Cultural Interaction in the Near East: The Evidence of Personal Names', in G. Bunnens (ed.), *Cultural Interaction in the Near East* (*Abr Nahrain* Supplement Series, Vol. 5)

1998, 'Two Mid-Third Century Bishops: Cyprian of Carthage and Dionysius of Alexandria: Congruences and Divergences', *Ancient History in a Modern University*, 2, pp. 317-28

1999, 'Identities in the Eastern Mediterranean in Antiquity', in *Mediterranean Archaeology*, 11:1-291

1999, 'Who built Shash Hamdan Tomb 1?', in *Mediterranean Archaeology*, 11:83-158

'Cyprian: His life and the chronology of his correspondence', in G.F. Diercks (ed.), in *Sancti Cypriani episcopi epistularium*, Turnholt, Vol. III D, pp. 679-709

1999, 'Jebel Khalid 1995', in *Chronique archaelogique en Syrie*, Vol. 2, pp. 47-53

1999, 'Jebel Khalid 1997', in *Chronique archaelogique en Syrie*, Vol. 2, pp. 251-253

John Docker

1994, *Postmodernism and Popular Culture: A Cultural History*, Cambridge University Press, Cambridge

1996, With Ann Curthoys, 'Is History Fiction?', *UTS Review*, Vol. 2, No. 1, pp. 12-37

1996, 'Debating Ethnicity and History: From Enzensberger to Darville/Demidenko, in Gerhard Fischer (ed.), *Debating Enzensberger: 'Great Migration' and Civil War*, Tübingen: Stauffenburg Verlag, pp. 213-224

1996, 'Postmodernism, Cultural History, and the Feminist Legend of the Nineties: Robbery Under Arms, the Novel, the Play', in Ken Stewart (ed.), *The 1890s*, University of Queensland Press, St Lucia, pp. 128-149, (reprinted by AustLit Gateway Internet Service 2001)

1996, 'A 'Hermaphroditic Position': Benjamin, Postmodernism and the Frenzy of Gender', in Gerhard Fischer (ed.), *'With the Sharpened Axe of Reason': Critical Approaches to Walter Benjamin*, Berg Publishers, Oxford, pp. 67-81

1996, '*The Satanic Verses* as a Post-Modern Novel', in Bruce Bennett, Jeff Doyle and Satendra Nandan (eds.), *Crossing Cultures: Essays on Literature and Culture in the Asia-Pacific*, SKOOB Books, London, pp. 149-153

1996, 'Comment on Centenary of Federation for Opinion Page', *The Australian*, 5 December

1997, 'Norman Lindsay, Kenneth Slessor, and the Artist-Aristocracy', in Philip Mead (ed.), *Kenneth Slessor – Critical Readings*, University of Queensland Press, St Lucia

1997, With Ann Curthoys, 'The Two Histories: Metaphor in English historiographical writing', in *Rethinking History*, Vol. 1, No. 3, pp. 259-273

1998, 'How Close should Writers and Critics Be?', *Australian Book Review*, July 2002, pp. 24-28, featured as the National Library Australian Essay

1998, 'Recasting Sally Morgan's *My Place*: The fictionality of identity and the phenomenology of the converso', *Humanities Research*, Vol. 1, pp. 3-22

1998, 'His Slave, My Tattoo: Romancing a lost world', in Debjani Ganguly and Kavita Nandan (eds.), *Unfinished Journeys: India file from Canberra*, CRNLE, Adelaide, pp. 181-200

1998, Review of Matthew Bernstein and Gaylyn Studlar (eds.) 1997, *Visions of the East: Orientalism in film*, Rutgers University Press, New Brunswick, *Media International Australia*, Vol. 87, pp. 153-54

1999, 'Reply to Philip Mendes', *AMESA Newsletter*, 10 November 1998, pp. 9, 12

1999, with Ann Curthoys, 'Time, Eternity, Truth and Death: History as allegory', in *Humanities Research*, Vol. 1, pp. 4-26

1999, 'Feminism, Modernism, and Orientalism', in Ann Curthoys and J. Schultz (eds.), *The Home in the 1920s, Journalism: Print, Politics and Popular Culture*, University of Queensland Press, St Lucia

1999, 'Review of Brian Kiernan', in *Studies in Australian Literary History, The Review of English Studies*, (New Series), Vol. 50, pp. 415-416

2000, 'The Image of Woman in A.D. Hope's Poetry', (*Australian Cultural Elites*), reprinted in David Brooks (ed.), *The Double Looking Glass: New and classic essays on the poetry of A.D. Hope*, University of Queensland Press, St. Lucia

2000 (with Gerhard Fischer), Editor, *Race, Colour, and Identity in Australia and New Zealand*, New South Wales University Press, Kensington

2000, 'Writing from Fragments', in Ann Curthoys and Ann McGrath (eds.), *Writing Histories: Imagination and Narration*, Monash Publications in History, Melbourne, pp. 28-39

2000 (with Gerhard Fischer), 'Adventures of Identity', in John Docker and Gerhard Fischer (eds.), *Race, Colour, and Identity in Australia and New Zealand*, New South Wales University Press, Kensington

2000, 'The Broken Years', in Ann Curthoys and Ann McGrath (eds.), *Writing Histories: Imagination and Narration*, Monash Publications in History, Melbourne, pp. 14-17

2000, 'The Rabaul Strike', in B.V. Lal and K. Fortune (eds.), *The Pacific: An Encyclopedia*, University of Hawaii Press, Honolulu, pp. 363-4

2000, 'Story of the Illins, a Russian-Aboriginal Family', Spectrum section, in *The Sydney Morning Herald*, 9 December 2000

2000, 'Religion: Who Doesn't Need It?', rolling column for *Australian Book Review*, October, p. 30

2000, 'Is Australian Reviewing Too Bland?', contribution to symposium, *Australian Book Review*, October, p. 28

2000, Review of Shirley Hazzard, 'Greene on Capri', in *Australian Book Review*, October, pp. 12, 14

2000, 'Where is Vietnam?', rolling column for *Australian Book Review*, Feb/March, p. 39

2000, Review of Robert Manne (ed.), 'The Australian Century: Political Struggle in the Building of a Nation', in *Australian Book Review*, Feb/March, pp. 7-8

2000, 'Autobiographies', *Australian Humanities Review*, June-August

2000, Review of Beatrice Hanssen, *Walter Benjamin's Other History: Of Stones, Animals, Human Beings and Angels*, for *Seminar: A Journal of Germanic Studies* (May), pp. 266-267

2001, 'In Praise of Polytheism', for 'A Vanishing Mediator? The

Absence/Presence of the Bible in Postcolonial Criticism', essays edited by Roland Boer for *Semeia*, 88, pp. 149-172.

1974, '"The Eternal Hermit": Christopher Brennan', ch.1 of John Docker, *Australian Cultural Elites* (reprinted by AustLit Gateway Internet Service, 2001)

2001, 'Arabesques of the Cosmopolitan and International: Lucien Henry, Baroque Allegory and Islamophilia', *Australian Humanities Review* e-journal, June.

2001, *1492: the Poetics of Diaspora*, Continuum, London and New York

2001 (with Gerhard Fischer), *Multicultural Identities: Theories, Perspectives, Models, Case Studies*, Stauffenburg Verlag, Tübingen

2001, 'Dystopia and Utopia: '1492 in Contemporary Literature', in John Docker and Gerhard Fischer (eds.), *Multicultural Identities: Theories, Perspectives,Models,Case Studies*, Stauffenburg Verlag, Tübingen

2001, Review of Claude Rawson, 'God, Gulliver, and Genocide: Barbarism and the European Imagination, 1492-1945 (2001)', *Journal of Genocide Research*, Vol. 5, No. 1, pp. 161-165.

2001, Co-editor (with Ann Curthoys), of a special section on 'Genocide? Australian Aboriginal History in International Perspective' in *Aboriginal History*, Vol. 25, (issue appeared in 2002)

2001, With Ann Curthoys, 'Genocide: Definitions, Questions, Settler-Colonies', the Introduction for 'Genocide? Australian Aboriginal History in International Perspective', in *Aboriginal History*, Vol. 25, pp. 1-15 (issue appeared in 2002)

2002, 'The Challenge of Polytheism: Moses, Spinoza, and Freud', in Jane Bennett and Michael J. Shapiro (eds.), *The Politics of Moralizing*, Routledge, New York and London, pp. 201-222

2002, 'Untimely Meditations: The Tampa and the World Trade Centre', *borderlands* e-journal, Vol. 1, No. 1. This essay was first published in slightly different form as 'Thirteen Untimely Meditations' in *Arena Magazine*, No. 55, Oct-Nov 2001, pp. 9-11

2002, revised entries for second edition of Horace Newcomb (ed.), *Encyclopedia of Television*, Fitzroy Dearborn Publishers, Chicago; *Prisoner* (with Ann Curthoys), *Hey Hey It's Saturday*, and *Seinfeld*

2002-2003, With Dr Subhash Jaireth, edited two special issues of *JNT: Journal of Narrative Theory*, of papers drawn from the

HRC international symposium *Adventures of Dialogue: Bakhtin and Benjamin*, 21-22 June 2001. Issues entitled 'Benjamin and Bakhtin: New Approaches, New Contexts', *JNT: Journal of Narrative Theory*, Vol. 32, No. 3, Fall 2002 (appeared early part of 2003), and 'Benjamin and Bakhtin – Vision and Visuality', *JNT: Journal of Narrative Theory*, Vol. 33, No. 1, Winter 2003.

2002/2003, '*Après la guerre*: dark thoughts, some whimsy', in *Arena Journal* 20, pp. 3-16.

2003, 'New History and the New Catastrophe', in *Arena Magazine* 66, August-September, pp. 32-36.

2003, 'The Enlightenment, Genocide, Postmodernity', in *Journal of Genocide Research*, Vol. 5, No. 3, pp. 339-360.

Ian Donaldson

1974, 'Shakespeare's Serious Indecency' (review/article of E.A.M. Colman, *The Dramatic Use of Bawdy in Shakespeare*), in *Essays in Criticism* Vol. XXIV, pp. 363-367

1974, *The World Upside-Down: Comedy from Jonson to Fielding*, The Clarendon Press, Oxford, second (paperback) edition, pp. 201

1975, 'The Satirists' London', in *Essays in Criticism*, Vol. XXV, pp. 101-22

1975, '"A Double Capacity": The Beggar's Opera' (from *The World Upside-Down*) in Yvonne Noble (ed.), *The Beggar's Opera: Twentieth-Century Interpretations*, Prentice-Hall, pp. 65-80

1975, 'Jonson's *Epigrams* CIII (To Mary Lady Wroth)', *The Explicator* 33

1975 (ed.), Ben Jonson, *Poems*, Oxford University Press: Oxford Paperbacks/Oxford Standard Authors, pp. 410

1977, 'Jonson and the Moralists', in *Two Renaissance Mythmakers*, ed. Alvin B. Kernan, English Institute Essays Johns Hopkins Press, Baltimore, pp. 146-64

1979 '"A Martyr's Resolution": Epicoene', reprinted in Robert W. Adams (ed.) *Ben Jonson's Plays and Masques*, W.W. Norton & Company, New York and London

1979, 'Language, Noise, and Nonsense: *The Alchemist*', reprinted in R.V. Holdsworth (ed.) '*Every Man in His Humour*' and '*The Alchemist*', London and Basingstoke

1980 '"The Legend of the Lost-and-Stolen Office": Parody in Dramatic Comedy', *Southern Review*, Vol. XIII (special number on Parody: papers from HRC conference, 1976)

1982, *The Rapes of Lucretia*, Clarendon Press, Oxford

1982, 'Fielding, Richardson, and the Ends of the Novel', *Essays in Criticism*, Vol. 32, pp. 26-47

1983, 'Pope and Feeling', *Studies in the Eighteenth Century*, V, J.P. Hardy and J.C. Eade (eds.), Voltaire Foundation, Oxford, pp. 33-50

1983, 'Tom Jones, XVII.iii and *Love for Love*', *Notes and Queries*, Vol. XXX, No. 1 (February), pp. 49-50

1983, 'Weavers, Gardeners, Gladiators, and the Lame: *Tristram Shandy*, viii. 5', *Notes and Queries*, Vol. XXX No. 1 (February), pp. 61-63

'Jonson and Anger', in *The Yearbook of English Studies*, Vol. 14, Satire Special Number, Essays in Memory of Robert C. Elliott, 1984, pp. 56-71

1985 (with Tamsin Donaldson), ed., *Seeing the First Australians*, Unwin Hyman, Sydney

1985, Editor, *Ben Jonson,* (Oxford Authors), Oxford University Press, Oxford and New York

1985, 'Editing a "Standard" Text: Ben Jonson', in J.C. Eade (ed.) *Editing Texts*, Humanities Research Centre, Canberra

1985, 'Centres and Circumferences: Australian Studies and the European Perspective', in Patricia McLaren-Turner (ed.), *Australian and New Zealand Studies,* British Library Publications, London

1985 'Fathers and Sons: Jonson, Dryden and *Mac Flecknoe*', in *Southern Review* (Adelaide), Vol. XVII, pp. 314-27

1986, 'Jonson's Magic Houses', *Essays and Studies*, pp. 39-61

1986, 'Falstaff's Buff Jerkin', in *Shakespeare Quarterly*, Vol. 37, pp. 100-101

1986, 'Drama from 1710-1780', in R.H. Lonsdale (ed.), in *Dryden to Johnson*, Vol. 4 of *The Sphere History of Literature in the English Language*, second edition revised, pp. 161-92, 397-400

1986, 'Samuel Johnson and the Art of Observation', in *English Literary History*, Vol. 53, No. 4, (Winter), pp. 779-99

1987, 'The Argument of "The Disabled Debauchee"', in *Modern Language Review* Vol. 82, pp. 30-34

1987-88, 'Ben Jonson and the Story of Charis', in *Sydney Studies in English*, Vol. 13, pp. 3-20

1987, 'Eucalyptic Visions' in symposium 'Through Foreign Eyes', in *The Cambridge Review* (December), pp. 152-3

1988, '"A Double Capacity": *The Beggar's Opera*' in Leopold Damrosch, Jr. (ed.), *Modern Essays on Eighteenth-Century Literature*, Oxford University Press, New York & Oxford, pp. 141-58 (reprinted from *The World Upside Down*, 1970)

1988, 'Concealing and Revealing: Pope's *Epistle to Dr Arbuthnot*', C.J. Rawson (ed.) assisted by Jenny Mezciems, in *Pope, Swift and their Circle*, special number of *The Yearbook of English Studies*, Vol. 18, pp. 181-99

1989, 'Research Without Books', in *The Age Monthly Review*, April

1989, 'The Arthur Boyd Australian Centre', in Camilla Bettoni and Joseph Lo Bianco (eds.) *Understanding Italy: Language, Culture, Commerce: An Australian Perspective*, Frederick May Foundation for Italian Studies, University of Sydney, pp. 226-231

1989, 'Defining and defending the humanities', in A.M. Gibbs (ed.) *The relevance of the humanities*, Australian Academy of the Humanities, pp. 18-36

1990, 'The future of research in the humanities', in *AUMLA*, Vol. 73, pp. 5-23

1991, Review of *Ben Jonson: A Life*, by David Riggs in *Essays in Criticism* Vol. XLI, pp. 253-61

1997, *Jonson's Magic Houses: Essays in Interpretations*, Clarendon Press, Oxford

J. C. Eade

1977, 'The Accuracy of Vincenzo Coronelli's Celestial Globe', in *Isis* Vol. LXVII, pp. 437-40

1979, 'Hogarth or Sidrophel – Which of them Blundered?', in *Notes & Queries*, n.s. Vol. XXVI, No. 1 (February), pp. 26-7

1979, 'Astronomical Reference in John Bellenden's 'Proheme of the Cosmographe'', *Scottish Literary Journal*, Vol. VI, No. 1 (May), pp.

69-71

1979, 'Lewis Theobald's Translation Rates: A Hard Bargain', *The Library*, 6th ser. I (June), pp. 168-70

1979, *Eighteenth-Century Studies in Australia since 1958*, Sydney University Press for the Australian Academy of the Humanities

1979, 'Don Alonzo "Gravelled": Astrology in *An Evening's Love*', in *Seventeenth Century News*, Vol. XXXVII, Nos.3-4 (Fall-Winter), 80-81

1979, 'The Ascendant and Angelica's Uncle', in *Notes and Queries*, n.s. Vol. XXVI , No. 6 (December), pp. 536-7

1979, 'Massinger and Stargaze: The Astrology of *The City Madam*', in *American Notes and Queries*, Vol. XVII, No. 10 (June), pp. 154-6

1979, (with Alison Hanham), 'Foxy Astrology in Henryson', in *Parergon*, No. 24 (August), pp. 25-9

1980, 'Shakespeare's *Macbeth*, I. ii. 205-8', in *The Explicator*, Vol. XXXVIII, No. 4 (Summer), pp. 32-3

1981, 'Astrological Analysis as an Editorial Tool: The Case of Fletcher's *The Bloody Brother*', in *Studies in Bibliography* Vol. XXXIV, pp. 198-204

1981, 'Marcantonio Michiel's Mercury Statue: Astronomical or Astrological?', in *Journal of the Warburg and Courtauld Institutes*, Vol. XLIV

1982, ''We ben to lewed or to slowe': Chaucer's Astronomy and Audience Participation', in *Studies in the Age of Chaucer*, pp. 53-85

1982, 'The Seventh Scarf: a note on *Murphy*', *Journal of Beckett Studies*, Vol. 7 (Spring 1982)

'Henslowe's Magic Decoded', in *Parergon*, No. 32 (April), pp. 39-44

1983 With J.P. Hardy, Editor, *Studies in the Eighteenth Century*, V, Voltaire Foundation, Oxford

1982, 'Astrological "Accident" in *Britannia Rediviva*', *Notes and Queries*, n.s. Vol. XXIX, No. 6, December), pp. 513-14

1983, 'Spenser's *Faerie Queene*, I.iii.16 (and) II.ii.46', in *The Explicator*, Vol. 41, No. 3 (Spring), pp. 11-14

1985, *The Forgotten Sky: A Guide to Astrology in English Literature*, Oxford University Press, Oxford

1985 (With Roland Sussex), Editor, *Culture and Nationalism in*

Nineteenth Century Eastern Europe, Slavica, Columbus, Ohio

1988, *Aristotle Anatomised: the 'Poetics' in England, 1674-1781*, Frankfurt

1987, 'Computer Dating for some Southeast Asian Inscriptions', Proceedings of the International Conference on Thai Studies Canberra, Vol. 3, No. 1, pp. 77-80

Ralph Elliott

1991, 'Coming back to Cynewulf', in *Old English Runes and their Continental Background*, ed. A. Bammesberger Carl Winter, Heidelberg, pp. 231-47

1998, 'Thomas Hardy, Epistolarian', in Charles P. C. Pettit (ed.), *Reading Thomas Hardy*, Macmillan Press, London

1998, 'Peter Meredith in Australia', in *Essays in Honour of Peter Meredith, Leeds Studies in English*, n.s. Vol. XXIX

1998, 'Runes in English Literature: From Cynewulf to Tolkien', in Klaus Düwel (ed.), *Runeninschriften als Quellen Interdisziplinärer Forschung* Walter de Gruyter, Berlin and New York

2000, five articles, totaling sixteen pages, in N. Page (ed.) *The Oxford Reader's Companion to Thomas Hardy*, Oxford University Press, Oxford

2000, 'Landscape and Geography', Derek Brewer and Jonathan Gibson (eds.), in *A Companion to the 'Gawain'-Poet*, ed. D.S. Brewer, Cambridge University Press, Cambridge

2000, 'Bread and Babies', in R. Morgan and R. Nemesvari (eds.), *Human Shows: Essays in Honour of Michael Millgate*, The Hardy Association Press, New Haven, pp. 7-20

38 book reviews in *The Canberra Times* during 2000, including works on Shakespeare, George Eliot, Henry Lawson, A.D. Hope, Australian Literature and Australian English.

Two full-length articles in *The Canberra Times* during 2000, one commemorating the 600th anniversary of the death of Chaucer and the other on the ANU's University House

2001, 'Collateral damage part of the softening-up process', a polemic against dishonest political language, in the *Canberra Times*, 10 November, pp. 8-9

Bill Gammage

1998, *The Sky Travellers: Journeys in New Guinea 1938-1939*, Melbourne University Press, Carlton, reprint

1998, 'Ned Kelly', in G. Davison, J. Hirst and S. Macintyre (eds.), *Oxford Companion to Australian History*, Oxford University Press, Melbourne

1998, 'John Black's "Anatomy of a Hanging: Malignant Homicidal Sorcery in the Upper Markham Valley"', in *Journal of Pacific History*, Vol. 33, No. 2, December, pp. 225-38

1998, 'The Scramble for Possession: Pastoral leasehold and agricultural freehold 1860-1900', in R Morton (ed.), *The Land and the People*, History Institute Victoria Inc.

1999, 'In Defence of Oral History', in *Word of Mouth* (Journal of Oral History Association of Australia), Vol. 37, pp. 21-24

2001, 'Mrs Aeneas Gunn', in M. Halligan (ed.), *Storykeepers*, Duffy & Snellgrove, pp. 125-131

2001, 'Thomas Derrick, VC, DCM' and 'William Kibby, VC', in J. Healy (ed.), *S.A.'s Greats*, Historical Society of South Australia, pp. 163; 165

2001, 'Closer Settlement' and 'Land', in W. Prest (ed.), *The Wakefield Companion to South Australian History*, Wakefield Press, pp. 111-112; pp. 300-303

J.A. Grieve

1979, 'The Anti-Christianity of Voltaire', in *Six Epicurean Lunches*, Canberra, pp. 1-9

1996, *Dictionary of Contemporary French Connectors*, Routledge, London and New York

Christa Knellwolf

2000, 'The Mechanic Powers of the Spirit: Medicine and the Mock-Heroic in Samuel Garth's 'The Dispensary'', in *Signatures*, University College of Chichester Vol. 1, pp. 88-106

2001, 'Olive Schreiner's 'Woman and Labour' and the Language of the Struggle for Women's Rights', in *Feminism, Aesthetics and Subjectivity*, University of Santiago de Compostela, pp. 155-178

2001, 'The History of Feminist Criticism', in *Cambridge History of Literary Criticism: Volume IX: Twentieth-Century Historical, Philosophical an Psychological Perspectives*, Cambridge University Press, Cambridge, UK

2001, 'Robert Hooke's Micrographia and the Aesthetics of Empiricism', in *Seventeenth Century*, Manchester University Press, Manchester

2002, Guest editor (with Robert Maccubbin) of a special issue, entitled *Exoticism and the Culture of Exploration*, of the refereed journal *Eighteenth-Century Life* Vol. 26, No. 3 (November)

2002, Guest editor of a special issue, entitled *Exoticism and the Representation of the Other*, of *Signatures* 5, in *Eighteenth-Century Life* Vol. 26, No. 3

2002, 'The Exotic Frontier of the Imperial Imagination', in *Eighteenth-Century Life* Vol. 26, No. 3

2002, 'Introduction' (with Iain McCalman), in *Eighteenth-Century Life* Vol. 26, No. 3

Iain McCalman

1993, 'The Infidel as prophet: William Reid and Blakean radicalism', in S. Clark and D. Worrall (eds.), *Historicizing Blake*, McMillan, London, pp. 24-42

1993, 'James Charles Bendrodt 1890-1950', *Australian Dictionary of Biography*, Melbourne University Press, Melbourne

1995, 'National Biographies and National Identity', in *Voices* (Special Issue), Spring, pp. 5 ff.

1995, 'New Jerusalems: Prophecy, Dissent and radical culture in Britain, 1786-1830', in K. Haakonssen (ed.), *Rational Enlightenment and Dissent*, Cambridge University Press, Cambridge, pp. 312-335

1996, 'Prophesying revolution: "Mad Lord George", Edmund Burke and Madame La Motte', in Malcolm Chase and Ian Dyke (eds.), *Living and Learning: Essays in Honour of J.F.C. Harrison*, Scolar Press, London, pp. 52-65

1995, 'The Future of the Humanities in the RSSS and the IAS', *HRC Bulletin*, No. 77, March, pp. 2-8

1995, 'The Humanities Research Centre "Africa Year"', in *ANU Reporter*, 14 June, p. 6

1995, 'New Dialogues of Science and Culture', in *ANU Reporter*, 1 November, p. 6

1998 (with Meaghan Morris), 'Public Culture', in *Knowing Ourselves and Others: The humanities in Australia into the twenty-first century, Australian Research Council Discipline Research Strategies*, National Board of Employment, Education and Training, 3, Commonwealth of Australia, Canberra, pp. 1-20

1998, 'Newgate in Revolution: Radical enthusiasm and romantic counterculture', in Ian Higgins and Gillian Russell (eds.) *Studies in the Eighteenth Century 10, Papers from the Tenth David Nichol Smith Memorial Seminar*, special issue of *Eighteenth Century Life*, Vol. 22, pp. 195-210

1999, With Jon Mee, Gillian Russell, Clara Tuite, Kate Fullagar, Editor, *An Oxford Companion to the Romantic Age: British Culture 1776-1832*, Oxford University Press, Oxford

1999, With John Brewer, 'Publishing', in Iain McCalman, Jon Mee, Gillian Russell, Clara Tuite, Kate Fullagar (eds.) *An Oxford Companion to the Romantic Age: British Culture 1776-1832*, Oxford University Press, Oxford

1999, With Maureen Perkins, 'Popular Culture', in Iain McCalman, Jon Mee, Gillian Russell, Clara Tuite, Kate Fullagar (eds.) *An Oxford Companion to the Romantic Age: British Culture 1776-1832*, Oxford University Press, Oxford

1999, 'Public Culture and the Humanities in Australia: A report', in *Public Culture*, Vol. 11 (Spring)

1999, 'Controlling the Riots: Dickens and Romantic Revolution', in *History*, Vol. 84, pp. 458-474

2001, 'Queen of the Gutter: The Lives and Fictions of Jeanne la Motte', in John Docker and Gerhard Fischer (eds.) *Adventures of Identity: European Multicultural Experiences and Perspectives*, Stauffenburg Verlag, Tübingen, pp. 111-27

2001, 'Spectacles of Knowledge: OMAI as Ethnographic Travelogue', in *Cook and Omai: The Cult of the South Seas* (Catalogue of exhibition), National Library of Australia with the Humanities Research Centre, pp. 9-15

2001, Co-editor (with Alexander Cook and Andrew Reeves), *Gold: Forgotten Histories and Lost Objects of Australia*, Cambridge University

Press, Cambridge

2001, 'Jeanne La Motte, Libertinism and the French Revolution' in John Docker and Gerhard Fischer (eds.) *Adventures of Identity: European Multicultural Experiences and Perspectives*, Stauffenburg Verlag, Tübingen, pp. 111-27

2001, With A. Reeves and A. Cook, Editor, *Gold: Forgotten Histories and Lost Objects of Australia*, Cambridge University Press, 344 Pages (Adjunct to National Museum of Australia's *Gold and Civilisation* Exhibition)

2001, Editor, *Cook and Omai: The Cult of the South Seas*, National Library of Australia with the Humanities Research Centre

2002, 'Global Perspectives' in *Manning Clark By Some of His Students*, Canberra, pp. 59-63

2002, 'Popular Constitutionalism and Revolution in England and Ireland' in Isser Woloch (ed.), *Revolution and the Meanings of Freedom in the Nineteenth Century*, Chicago, reprint, pp. 138-72

2003, *The Seven Ordeals of Count Cagliostro*, alternative title in USA, *The Last Alchemist*, Harper Collins, New York and Sydney; Random House, London

2003, General Editor, *The Enlightenment World*, Routledge, London and New York

2003, With Jon Mee, Editor, Charles Dickens, *Barnaby Rudge*, Oxford World Classics

2003, with Ann McGrath, Editor, *Proof & Truth: The Humanist as Expert*, Australian Academy of Humanities, Canberra

2003, 'Endeavouring reality', in *Meanjin*, Vol. 62, No. 4, pp. 33-9

2003, 'Javert's Hunt Comes to an End', Op-Ed article, in *New York Times*, 19 May

2003, 'Tall Tales and True. The Selling of Historical Endeavour', *Australian Higher Ed. Supplement*, 1 Oct., p. 32

2004, General Editor, *The Enlightenment World*, Martin Fitzpatrick, Peter Jones and Christa Knellwolf (co-eds.), Routledge, London

Brian Massumi

1996, 'To Kill is Not Enough: Gender as cruelty', *Continuum: Australian Journal of Media and Culture*, Vol. 11, No. 2, pp. 95-112

1996, 'New Jerusalems: Prophecy, Dissent and Radical Culture in England, 1786-1830', in Knud Haakonssen (ed.) *Enlightenment and Religion: Rational Dissent in Eighteenth Century Britain*, Cambridge University Press, Cambridge

1997, 'The Political Economy of Belonging and the Logic of Relation', in *Anybody*, MIT Press, Cambridge, Massachusetts, pp. 174-189

(Dated 1997, actually appeared in 1998), (guest ed.) 'Deleuze, Guattari and the Philosophy of Expression', special issue of *Canadian Review of Comparative Literature/Revue Canadienne de Littérature Comparée*, Vol. 24, No. 3, pp. 745-782

(Dated 1997, actually appeared in 1998), 'Deleuze, Guattari and the Philosophy of Expression, Involutionary afterword', in *Deleuze, Guattari and the Philosophy of Expression*, special issue of *Canadian Review of Comparative Literature/Revue Canadienne de Littérature Comparée*, Vol. 24, No. 3, pp. 745-82

1998, 'The Evolutionary Alchemy of Reason: Stelarc', in John Beckmann (ed.) *Virtual Dimension: Architecture, representation, and crash culture*, Princeton Architectural Press, New York, pp. 334-41

1998, 'Line Parable for the Virtual', in John Beckmann (ed.) *Virtual Dimension: Architecture, representation, and crash culture*, Princeton Architectural Press, New York, pp. 304-21

1998, 'The Brightness Confound', in Sarah Rodgers (ed.) *Body Mécanique: Artistic explorations of digital realms*, Wexner Centre for the Arts, Columbus, pp. 81-94

1998, 'Event Horizon', in Joke Brouwer (ed.) *The Art of the Accident* (Dutch Architecture Institute/V2_Organization, Rotterdam, pp. 154-68

1998, 'Architectures of the Unforeseen', *Newsline*, Columbia University School of Architecture, Planning and Preservation, New York, Fall, p. 6

1998, 'Remarks on Ritual: Local responses to Chinese nationalism in an age of global capitalism', in Kenneth Dean (ed.) *Lord of the Three in One: The spread of a cult in southeast China*, Princeton University Press, Princeton, pp. 288-89

1998, 'Gilles Deleuze', in Simon Critchley and William R. Schroeder (eds.) *Companion to Continental Philosophy*, Blackwell Press, Oxford

1998, 'Sensing the Virtual, Building the Insensible', in Stephen

Perrella (ed.) *Hypersurface Architecture*, special issue of *Architectural Design*, profile No. 133, Vol. 68, Nos.5/6, pp. 16-24

1998, 'Requiem for Our Prospective Dead: Toward a participatory critique of capitalist power', in *Polygraph*, special issue of *Legislating Culture*, Vol. 10, pp. 115-42 (reprint)

1998, 'Requiem for Our Prospective Dead: Toward a participatory critique of capitalist power', in Eleanor Kauffman and Kevin John Heller (eds.), *Deleuze and Guattari: New mappings in politics, philosophy and culture*, University of Minnesota Press, Minneapolis, pp. 40-63 (reprint).

1998, 'Einführung in die Angst', in Silvia Eiblmayr (ed.) and Clemens Carle-Haerle (trans.), *Zones of Disturbance/Zonen der Ver-störung*, Steirischer Herbst, Graz, pp. 48-97 (reprint: appeared too late for 1997 report)

1999, 'Strange Horizon: Buildings, biograms, and the body topologic', in *Architectural Design*, Vol. 69, pp. 12-19

2000, 'Espresar la conexión, arquitectura relacional/Expressing Connection: Relational Architecture' (bilingual: Spanish trans. Susie Ramsay), in Rafael Lozano Hemmer (ed.) *Vectorial Elevation: Relational Architecture No. 4*, , National Council for Culture and the Arts, Mexico City, pp. 183-208

2000, 'Painting: The Voice of the Grain (The Art of Bracha Lichtenberg Ettinger)', in Roos Pauwels (ed.) *Borderlines*, Palais des Beaux Arts/ Ludion, Brussels/Ghent

2000, 'Chaos in the 'Total Field, of Vision', in Elisabeth von Samsonow and Eric Alliez (eds.) *Hyperplastik: Kunst und Konzepte der Wahrnehmung in Zeiten der mental imagery*, Turia + Kant, Vienna, pp. 245-267

2000, 'Too-Blue: Color-Patch for an Expanded Empiricism', in *Cultural Studies*, Vol. 14, No. 2 (April), pp. 253-302

1999, 'Purple Phosphene', in *Angelaki* (UK), Vol. 4, No. 3 (December), pp. 219-221 (Note: actually appeared in 2000)

2000, 'Strange Horizon: Buildings, Biograms, and the Body Topologic' (complete text), in *Chaos/Control: Complexity: Proceedings from the Interdisciplinary Conference on Chaos Theory and the Human Sciences*, CD-ROM, University of Bielefeld, Bielefeld

2000, 'The Political Economy of Belonging and the Logic of Relation'

(Japanese Translation) in *Shiso* (Thought), No. 914 (August), pp. 8-30

2000, 'Requiem for Our Prospective Dead: Toward a Participatory Critique of Capitalist Power' (German Translation), in Olaf Arndt, *BBM: das Modell einer neuen Gesellschaftsordnung*, Internationalismus Verlag, Hannover, pp. 101-132

2000, 'The Autonomy of Affect' (Reprint), in William Rasch and Cary Wolfe (eds.) *Observing Complexity: Systems Theory and Postmodernism*, University of Minnesota Press, Minneapolis, pp. 273-297

Donna Merwick

1997, 'The Suicide of a Notary: Language. Personal Identity and Conquest in Colonial New York', in *Through a Glass Darkly: Reflections on Personal Identity in Early America*, North Carolina Press, Chapel Hill, pp. 122-156

1997, 'The Writing Man: The Shrinking World of the 'Note Republic' in Dutch Albany', in *de halve maen* Vol. 49, pp. 57-66

1999, *Death of a Notary: Conquest and Change in Colonial New York*, Cornell University Press, Ithaca, xi-xvi + 281 pages

1997, 'Crawford and Merle Curti: Their Friendship, Their Correspondence', in S. Macintyre and P. McPhee (eds.) *Max Crawford's School of History*, School of History, University of Melbourne, Melbourne, pp. 79-87

1997, 'Postmodernity and the Release of the Creative Imagination', in A. Curthoys and A. McGrath (eds.) *Writing Histories: Imagination and Narration*, (Monash Publications in History, Melbourne, pp. 18-27

2002, *Possession Albany, 1630-1710: The Dutch and English Experiences*, Cambridge University Press, vii-xii + 312 pages

Benjamin Penny

1996, appeared 1997, 'Buddhism and Daoism in the 180 Precepts Spoken by Lord Lao', *Taoist Resources*, Vol. 6, No. 2, pp. 1-16

1996, appeared 1997 (with B. Hendrischke), 'The 180 Precepts Spoken by Lord Lao: A translation and textual study', in *Taoist Resources*, Vol. 6, No. 2, pp. 17-29

1999, 'Meeting the Celestial Master', in *East Asian History*, Vol. 15, No. 16, pp. 53-65

1999, 'The Text and Authorship of Shenxian zhuan', in *Journal of*

Oriental Studies, Vol. XXXIV, No. 2, pp. 165-209

1999, Editor, *Humanities Research*, 1 and 2

2000, 'Immmortality and Transcendence', in L. Kohn (ed.), *Daoism Handbook*, Brill, Leiden, pp. 109-133

2001, 'The Internet and Research on Contemporary China: Falun Gong in Cyberspace', in *Chinese Studies Association of Australia Newsletter*, pp. 2-4.

2001, Review of Kohn, L, *God of the Dao: Lord Lao in History and Myth*, in *Journal of Chinese Religions*, No. 29, Fall

2001, Review of Addiss, S., *Old Taoist: The Life, Art, and Poetry of Kodojin* in *New Zealand Journal of Asian Studies*, Vol. 3, No. 1, pp. 147-149

2002, Editor, *Religion and Biography in China and Tibet*, Curzon Press, London

2002, 'Jiao Xian's Three Lives, ' in *Religion and Biography in China and Tibet*, Curzon Press, London

2002, 'Falun Gong, Prophesy and Apocalypse,' in *East Asian History*, 23 (June)

Paul Pickering

2000 (with Alex Tyrell), *The People's Bread: A History of the Anti-Corn Law League*, Leicester University Press, London

2000, '"Irish first": Daniel O'Connell, the Native Manufacture Campaign, and Economic Nationalism, 1840-44', in *Albion*, Vol. 32, No. 4, Winter, pp. 598-616

2001, '"And Your Petitioners &c": Chartist Petitioning in Popular Politics 1838-48', in *English Historical Review*, Vol. 116, No. 466, April, pp. 368-388

2001, 'The "Oak of English Liberty": Popular Constitutionalism in New South Wales, 1848-1856', in *Journal of Australian Colonial History*, Vol. 3, No. 1, April, pp. 1-27

2001, 'Conserving the People's History: Lessons from Manchester and Salford', in *Humanities Research*, Vol. VIII, No. 1, pp. 51-8

2001, '"The Finger of God": Gold and political culture in Colonial New South Wales', in I.D. McCalman et al. (ed.) *Gold: Forgotten Histories and Lost Objects of Australia*, Cambridge University Press,

Cambridge, pp. 21-43

2001, 'A Wider Field in a New Country: Chartism in Colonial Australia', in M. Sawer (ed.) *Elections, Full, Free & Fair*, Federation Press, pp. 28-44

2002 (with Owen Ashton), *Friends of the People: Uneasy Radicals in the Age of the Chartists*, Merlin Press, London

2002, 'Museums of the Future: Beyond East and West', in *Humanities Research*, Vol. IX, No. 1, pp. 1-3

Dec. 2001- Jan. 2002, Review of F. Crowley, *Big John Forrest 1847-1918, A Founding Father of the Commonwealth of Australia*, JAS – *Review of Books*, Issue 4

2002, Review of J. Hirst, *Australia's Democracy: A Short History*, *JAS- Review of Books*, Issue 10, November

2003, Editor (with Robyn Westcott) Special Issue of *Humanities Research* 'Monuments and Commemorations'

2003, '"Ripe for a Republic": British Radical Responses to the Eureka Stockade', *Australian Historical Studies*, No. 121, April, pp. 69-90

2003, 'The Hearts of the Millions: Chartism and Popular Monarchism in the 1840s', *History*, Vol. 88, No. 290, April, pp. 227-248

2003, 'Chartism and the Trade of Agitation in Early Victorian Britain', S. Roberts (ed.) *The People's Charter: Democratic Agitation in Early Victorian Britain*, Merlin Press, London, pp. 19-34

2003, 'R.J. Richardson', in K. Gildhart, N. Kirk & D. Howell (eds.) *Dictionary of Labour Biography*, Vol. XI, Palgrave Macmillan, Basingstoke, pp. 212-214

2003, 'James Scholefield', in K. Gildhart, N. Kirk & D. Howell (eds.) *Dictionary of Labour Biography*, Vol. XI, Palgrave Macmillan, Basingstoke, pp. 251-253

2003, 'James Wroe', in K. Gildhart, N. Kirk & D. Howell (eds.) *Dictionary of Labour Biography*, Vol. XI, Palgrave Macmillan, Basingstoke, pp. 292-293

2003, 'Conference Report: UK-Australian Labour History Conference, Manchester', *Labour History* (Australia), No. 85, November, pp. 227-8.

2003, Review: G. Moschonas, *In the Name of Social Democracy: The Great Transformation 1945 to the Present* and P. Norton (ed) *Parliaments and Citizens in Western Europe*, *Australian Journal of Political Science*,

Vol. 38, No. 3, pp. 577-578.

Libby Robin

1997, with Tom Griffiths (eds.), *Ecology and Empire: Environmental History of Settler Societies*, Keele University Press, Edinburgh

1997, 'Ecology: A science of empire?', in Tom Griffiths and Libby Robin (eds.) *Ecology and Empire: Environmental History of Settler Societies*, Keele University Press Edinburgh

1998, *Defending the Little Desert: The Rise of Ecological Consciousness in Australia*, Melbourne University Press, Carlton

1998 (ed. with Tom Griffiths), *Ecology and Empire: Environmental history of settler societies*, University of Washington Press, Seattle

1998, 'Ecology: A science of empire?', in Tom Griffiths and Libby Robin (eds.), *Ecology and Empire: Environmental history of settler societies*, University of Washington Press, Seattle

1998, 'Essay review of James Noble's Delicate and Noxious Scrub', in *Historical Records of Australian Science*, Vol. 12, No. 2, pp. 277-79

1998, 'Urbanizing the Bush: Environmental disputes and Australian national identity', in David Day (ed.) *Australian Identities*, Australian Scholarly Publishing, Melbourne, pp. 116-27

1998, 'Radical Ecology and Conservation Science: An Australian perspective', *Environment and History*, 4.2, pp. 191-208

'Review of Marjory Collard O'Dea, Ian Clunies Ross: A biography', in *Australian Historical Studies*, Vol. 3, pp. 392-93

1998, 'Natural History', in G. Davison, J Hirst and S. Macintyre (eds.) *Oxford Companion to Australian History*, Oxford University Press, Melbourne, pp. 250-51

1998, 'Field Naturalists' Clubs', in G. Davison, J Hirst and S. Macintyre (eds.) *Oxford Companion to Australian History*, Oxford University Press, Melbourne, pp. 461-62

1998, 'The Little Desert Case', in *Eureka Street*, October, pp. 28-31

1998, 'A Voice from the (suburban) Wilderness', in *Australian Humanities Review*, 30 September (Melbourne: La Trobe University Press), pp. 1-3, also on http://www.lib.latrobe.edu.au/AHR/archive/Issue-September-1998/robin.html

1998, 'A lone campaign for the Little Desert', in *Bogong*, Vol. 19, No.

3, September, pp. 15-18

1998, 'Ecology and its Empires', in *Australasian Science Incorporating Search*, Vol. 19, No. 5, pp. 21-22

1998, 'Feral Forests', in *Forest History Newsletter*, June

Short review of Ian Clunies Ross: A biography, in *Australian Book Review*, p. 60

Helen Topliss

1996, *Modernism and Feminism: Australian Women Artists 1900-1940*, Craftsman House/G+B Arts International, Roseville East, Australia

Clara Tuite

1995 (with Judith Barbour), 'William and Mary: Muse, Editor, Executrix in the Shelley Circle', in Maurice Blackman, Frances Muecke and Margaret Sankey (eds.), *The Textual Condition: Rhetoric and Editing*, Local Consumption Publications, Sydney

1999, with Iain McCalman, Jon Mee, Gillian Russell, Kate Fullagar, Editor, *An Oxford Companion to the Romantic Age: British Culture 1776-1832*, Oxford University Press, Oxford

Caroline Turner

2000, Editor, *Humanities Research*, (refereed, continuing)

2000, Editorial, *Humanities Research*, pp. 3-5

2000, With Morris Low, Editor, *Beyond the Future: Papers from the Conference of the Third Asia-Pacific Triennial of Contemporary Art*, Brisbane, 10-12 September 1999, Queensland Art Gallery

2000, 'Introduction', in Caroline Turner and Morris Low (eds.) *Beyond the Future: Papers from the Conference of the Third Asia-Pacific Triennial of Contemporary Art*, Brisbane, 10-12 September 1999, Queensland Art Gallery, pp. 9-12

2000, 'Gallery Welcome', in Caroline Turner and Morris Low (eds.), *Beyond the Future: Papers from the Conference of the Third Asia-Pacific Triennial of Contemporary Art*, Brisbane, 10-12 September 1999, Queensland Art Gallery, pp. 20-22

2000, 'Art Speaking for Humanity: The Asia-Pacific Triennial of Contemporary Art, *Art Journal* (New York), Vol. 59, No. 1, Spring, pp. 16-19

2000, Editor for East Asia and author of 'Asia Engagements: Tubes of Bamboo', pp. 18-21, and 'The Enigma of Japanese Art', pp. 38-41, in 'The Long Stare: Seeing Contemporary Asian Art Now', *Artlink*, Vol. 20, No. 2, July

2000, 'The Asia-Pacific Triennial of Contemporary Art – Bridge to Understanding', in *Aspac-Icom* (Bulletin of the Asia-Pacific Organisation, International Council of Museums), (Vols. 1 & 2, September, pp. 16-17

2001, 'Images of Mai', in *Cook and Omai: The Cult of the South Seas*, National Library of Australia (catalogue of the exhibition), Canberra, pp. 23-28

2001, 'Guo Jian', *Art AsiaPacific*, Issue 31 'China', pp. 95-96

2001, 'Editorial: Tomorrow's Museums' in *Humanities Research*, 'Museums of the Future/The Future of Museums', Vol. VIII, No. 1, pp. 1-3

2002, 'Linking Past and Future: Cultural Exchanges and Cross-Cultural Engagements in Four Asian Museums', in *Humanities Research*, 'Museums of the Future: The Future of Museums Part 2', Vol. IX, No. 1, pp. 13- 28.

2002, 'Imagined Workshop: the Second Fukuoka Triennale', 2002, in *International Institute for Asian Studies Newsletter*, No. 29, November, p. 46

2002, 'Affandi in Bali' for catalogue of touring exhibition, in *Crossing Boundaries; Bali: A Window to Twentieth Century Indonesian Art*, (Asia Society of Australia)

2002, Review 'Human Rights and Gender Politics: Asia-Pacific Perspectives', in *Asian Studies Review*, Vol. 26, No. 1, March

2003, With Nancy Sever, Editor, *Witnessing to Silence: Art and Human Rights*, (catalogue for exhibition *Art and Human Rights*), ANU Drill Hall Gallery and Humanities Research Centre, Australian National University, Canberra

2003, 'Artists and Human Rights: Witnessing to Silence', in Caroline Turner and Nancy Sever (eds.), *Witnessing to Silence: Art and Human Rights*, (catalogue for exhibition *Art and Human Rights*), ANU Drill Hall Gallery and Humanities Research Centre, Australian National University, Canberra, pp. 7-12

2003, 'Luc Tuymans: Premonition – the silence before the storm', in Caroline Turner and Nancy Sever (eds.) *Witnessing to Silence: Art and Human Rights*, (catalogue for exhibition *Art and Human Rights*), ANU Drill Hall Gallery and Humanities Research Centre, Australian National University, Canberra, pp. 45-49

2004, (with Glen St. John Barclay) *Humanities Research Centre: A History of the First 30 years of the HRC at The Australian National University*, Australian National University

8. Student Publications at The HRC

Michelle Antoinette

2002, 'Singapore opens up to the world. Site + Sight' in *Artlink*, Vol 22, No. 4, pp. 60-63, exhibition review

2002, 'Anthology of Art' contribution #22, at Jochen Gerz (ed.), in *The Anthology of Art: Art and Theory in Dialogue* website project, Braunschweig School of Art, http://www.anthology-of-art.net/inside/index.html

Robert Bell

2002, *Material Culture: aspects of contemporary Australian craft and design*, National Gallery of Australia, Canberra

2002, Entries in Anne Gray (ed.), *Australian Art in the National Gallery of Australia*, National Gallery of Australia, Canberra

2002, Introduction in Karen LaMonte, *Karen LaMonte*, New York, pp. 5

2002, (with Geoffrey Edwards) *'Transparent Things': expressions in glass*, electronic on-line catalogue, National Gallery of Australia, Canberra

2002, 'Crystal Clear: the architecture of the National Gallery of Australia' in *Artonview No. 23*, National Gallery of Australia, Canberra, pp. 12-17

2002, 'The Lady Vanishes', in *Artonview No. 23*, National Gallery of Australia, Canberra, pp. 23-24

2002, 'Material Culture: Aspects of Contemporary Australian Craft and Design in the World of Antiques and Art', in *Antiques and Art in Australia* 62nd Edition, Sydney pp. 152-153

2002, 'Material Culture', in *Craft Arts International* No. 55, Sydney pp. 81-83

2002, 'Nick Mount Scent Bottle' and 'Robert Baines La Columbella Tea and Coffee Set' in 'Acquisitions' in *The World of Antiques and Art* 63rd Edition, *Antiques and Art in Australia*, Sydney, pp. 201, 204

2002, 'Wood and design identity in Scandinavia' in *Designing Futures* conference papers Craftwest Centre for Contemporary Craft, Perth

2003, 'Decorative Arts and Design' in Pauline Green (ed.), *Building the Collection*, National Gallery of Australia, Canberra, pp. 249-259

2003, 'Crystal Clear: The architecture of the National Gallery of Australia' in Pauline Green (ed.) *Building the Collection*, National Gallery of Australia, Canberra, pp. 339-343

2003, 'Mid-twentieth century design at the National Gallery of Australia' in *The World of Antiques and Art* 65th edition, Antiques and Art in Australia, Sydney, pp. 187-189,

2003, 'A dialogue with Japan: Australian ceramics in the collection of the National Gallery of Australia' in *Arts of Asia*, Arts of Asia Publications Ltd, Hong Kong, Vol. 33, No. 6, pp. 47-53

2003, 'Like a Lizard Drinking: an Australian pottery idiom' in *Object*, Australian Centre for Craft and Design, Sydney, No. 41, pp. 45-48

2003, 'Dress 4 by Karen LaMonte' in 'Acquisitions' in *The World of Antiques and Art* 64th edition, Antiques and Art in Australia, Sydney, pp. 197-198

2003, 'Hard Edge: Geometry in design' in *Artonview*, National Gallery of Australia, No. 36, pp. 34-35

2003, 'Children's Gallery, National Gallery of Australia: 'Hard Edge: Geometry in design' in *Antiques in New South Wales*, JQ Pty Ltd, Sydney, p. 21

Bernice Murphy

2002, 'Local Bearings', essay in *A Constructed World*, (exhibition catalogue, English and Croatian, ed. and curator Branka Stipancic), Croatian Artists Association, Zagreb

2002, 'Centre Culturel Tjibaou: A museum and arts centre redefining New Caledonia's cultural future', *Humanities Research Centre*, Australian National University, Canberra, Vol .IX, No. 1, pp. 77-90

2002, 'Interdisciplinary Partnerships in the Redefinition of Culture and Museum' *Proceedings of the International Congress of the World Federation of Friends Museum*' WFFM, World Federation of Friends Museum, Sydney

2002, 'Museum of Contemporary Art, Sydney' in *Aboriginal Art Collections: Highlights from Australia's Public Museums and Galleries* edition, Susan Cochrane, Craftsman House, Sydney, pp. 46-52

2002, 'Constellations from Shanghai', *Shanghai Star*, (commissioned essay for exhibition of 3 artists from Shanghai, published in English and Mandarin), Casula Powerhouse, Sydney

2002, 'Clifford Possum Tjapaltjarri and Tim Leura Tjapaltjarri, Napperby Death Spirit Dreaming' in *Fieldwork*, (commissioned essays on the collection of marking opening of the new Australian galleries at Federation Square), National Gallery of Victoria, Melbourne

2003, 'James Doolin, 1932-2002', in *Art & Australia*, Fine Art Publishing, Sydney, Vol. 40, No. 3, pp. 402-403 (obituary article on American artist, died Los Angeles, 2003)

2003, 'Encircling the Muses: the multi-disciplinary heritage of university museums', in *Museologia* (bilingual texts, English and Portugese, Science Museum, University of Lisbon, Lisbon, No. 3, pp. 9-16

2003, 'Living practice, working theory, travelling light: Notes on René Boutin', catalogue essay for exhibition, in *René Boutin: Emergency Landing-Ground*, Artspace, Sydney (monographic installation of New Caledonian artist, exhibited Artspace, Sydney November 2003)

Angela Philip

2002, Exhibition Catalogue essay: *Lux Readings: Fiona Hooton*, Canberra Contemporary Art Space, Canberra

Acknowledgements

The authors are especially grateful to Professor Ian Donaldson, Professor Iain McCalman, Professor Graeme Clarke, Professor Ralph Elliott and Dr Paul Pickering, who all read the entire text and also to all those who agreed to be interviewed, including the above and especially Professor Anthony Low, Professor Deryck Schreuder, Professor Ann Curthoys, Professor Sasha Grishin, Professor Richard St Clair Johnson, Professor Anthony Milner, Dr John Docker, Dr Gino Moliterno, Dr Roger Hillman, Mr Colin Steele, Ms Leena Messina and Ms Jodi Parvey. Also we express our thanks to Professors Malcolm Gillies, Adam Shoemaker and Bruce Bennett for their most valuable quotes and to all the Fellows of the HRC whose reports, letters, photographs, literary gems and communications have made writing this history possible and given life and lustre to the story of this institution.

Preparation of appendices
Leena Messina and Harry Wise, with thanks to Judy Buchanan and Melinda Sung.

ANU E Press
The authors wish to thank all those at ANU E Press, including Vic Elliott, Colin Steele, Lorena Kanellopoulos, Bobby Graham, Brendan McKinley and Michael Birch.

Proof reading
Bobby Graham, Harry Wise, Melinda Sung, Penny Joy and Sally May.

Photography

Neal McCracken, Bob Cooper and Stuart Hay at ANU Photography; Damien Boyd at Coombs Photography; Ainslie Moore and Nick Wellbourne at ANU Marketing; and Heidi Smith; Jane Castles at the Australian Academy of Humanities; Mark Richmond at the University of Melbourne Archives; Celia Bridgewater and Katie Haynes at the Centre for Cross-Cultural Research; and Leena Messina, who took so many of the photographs reproduced in this book.

Photo credits

ANU Photography: pp. 3, 6, 10, 14, 31, 35, 36 (Bob Cooper), 38, 41, 78, 119 (Stuart Hay), 134, 141

Australian Academy of the Humanities: p. 27

Gabe Carpay: p. 62

D. Featherstone: p. 13

Julie Gorrell: p. 166

Melbourne University Archives: p. 2

Leena Messina: pp. 32, 144, 145, 146, 154, 177 (right), 184

Heidi Smith: pp. 193, 206 (bottom left) (details)

Lindy Shultz: pp. 227, 237

www.ingramcontent.com/pod-product-compliance
Lightning Source LLC
Chambersburg PA
CBHW040312240426
43666CB00030B/2920